Foundation Illustr

Vicki Loader
Barry Huggins

friendsof

DESIGNER TO DESIGNER™

Foundation Illustrator 10

© 2002 friends of ED

First published February 2002

Trademark Acknowledgements

friends of ED has endeavored to provide trademark information about all the companies and products mentioned in this book by the appropriate use of capitals. However, friends of ED cannot guarantee the accuracy of this information.

Published by friends of ED

30 Lincoln Road, Olton, Birmingham.
B27 6PA. UK.
Printed in USA

ISBN 1-903450-29-2

Foundation Illustrator 10

Credits

Authors	Vicki Loader, Barry Huggins
Concept Development	Jim Hannah
Technical Editors	Victoria Blackburn, Julie Closs, Libby Hayward
Graphic Editors	Deb Murray, Matthew Clark
Technical Reviewers	Peter Bone, Dan Caylor, Steve Cox, Denis E. Graham, Sunil Gupta, Brandon Houston, Mel Jehs, Scott A. Manning, David Martin, Michael Walston
Index	Fiona Murray
Cover Design	Katy Freer
Author Agent	Mel Jehs
Project Manager	Simon Brand
Proof Readers	Alice Myers, Catherine O'Flynn, James Robinson, Gavin Wray
Book Concept	Vicki Loader, Barry Huggins
Managing Editor	Chris Hindley

Gratitude to absent friends

About the Authors

Vicki Loader
www.vickiloader.com

Vicki's early years were spent in South Africa. Now she is resident in rural village England, a stone's throw from the heart of London, where she divides her days between freelance training (to private companies or through a select number of high-profile London-based training concerns), and writing instructional books with friends of ED.

A new business venture this year has been the formation of UK Trainers Direct (www.uktrainersdirect.co.uk) – an association of top-level trainers who market their services directly to private individuals and companies. In her limited spare time, she maintains a web site which functions as an ongoing training site by providing trainees with links to training resources.

Whenever possible she pushes the boundaries of creative software on a laptop computer, while sitting in the sun at a Mediterranean street café or on a tropical beach. During these difficult times, Cava, champagne cocktails, foreign movies, music, and tapas bars sit tantalisingly close by.

Barry Huggins
www.matrixtraining.com

Barry left behind his days in international Commerce and jumped enthusiastically onboard the Internet at a time when it was a vague notion in the public imagination. He saw the potential of the Internet as a golden opportunity to marry his passion for art, design and creativity with the new developing technologies. His computer generated design however soon brought him back to the international arena, creating designs for clients in Japan, the USA, Italy and Portugal.

Barry now has his own training and consultancy company in London – Matrix Training – where he specializes in graphics and multimedia applications for both the Internet and print publishing. On the increasingly rare occasions when he is not working, he indulges in his other passions of scuba diving in warm waters and playing saxophone. But as he readily admits, the distinction between work and play is becoming increasingly hazy and he wouldn't change that for the world.

Foundation Illustrator 10

▶▶▌

3   Creating Shapes   73

4   Working with Color   105

5   Drawing Paths   135

Introduction

What is Adobe Illustrator?

Long regarded as a leading illustration application, this latest release of Adobe Illustrator, with strong features for both print and web output, makes it an indispensable tool in any designer's arsenal. With Illustrator in your toolkit, you'll be able to draw and design logos, graphics, maps and more. You'll be able to add text and photographs as desired, and then re-purpose the artwork efficiently for both print and web output.

Constant revisions and additions to Illustrator, since it was first released as a Mac-only application in 1987, have allowed it to evolve into what it is today – a powerful application used for designing both print and web graphics. It can integrate with other design technologies, and it is adept at handling text and photographic images as well as allowing you to create your own vector graphics.

This latest version of Illustrator has lots of exciting and useful new features, including:

- Refinement of its web functionality, with the introduction of the **Symbol** creation tools and slicing tools, enhanced SWF and SVG export support, Metadata support and asset management functionality.

- Live distortion (including enveloping, **liquify** tools, warps).

- New graphic creation and modification tools.

- New selection tools and menu options.

- Support for scripting to automate repetitive production tasks.

- Tighter integration of the application with the other Adobe programs, allowing you to work effectively and more quickly between the applications.

If you are completely new to Illustrator, don't be intimidated by all these technical terms. For now, what you need to know is that you have is a production workhorse that will allow you to create, modify and integrate all the components needed for you to present a complete print and web solution to your client.

Who Should be Using Adobe Illustrator?

I guess it's just too simplistic an answer to just say 'you'! Yet, if you are involved in any aspect of illustration design, desktop publishing, web design, or animation, it is more than probable that Illustrator will help you to create your designs efficiently.

A consequence of the rapid development in the World Wide Web has been the growth of duality in the designer's responsibilities – designing for print and then having to re-purpose that same artwork for web circulation. In the past this often meant that graphics needed to be recreated from the ground up so that they were suitable for another medium, but with Adobe Illustrator you will find that this new demand made on designers has been completely catered for.

What Can You Create With Adobe Illustrator?

The large variety of materials that can be successfully produced in Illustrator could result in a very long list, so for the sake of brevity, I'll confine it to an overview. I'm sure that once you have completed this book, you'll think back to this list and wonder why various other uses were not included here.

- Logos and simple graphics for both print and web.

- Detailed and accurate floor-plans and architectural designs.

- Illustrations designed for inclusion in other publications.

- Fine art suitable for sale and distribution.

- Corporate materials including letterheads, business cards and other necessary stationery.

- Large format posters, combining text, graphic and photographic elements.

- Complete web designs.

- Graphics for inclusion in web animations, web pages, 3D packages and digital video.

- Brochures, pamphlets and other promotional materials.

How Will You Get Source Material into Illustrator?

Granted, a large portion of your artwork will be created from scratch within Illustrator, but there are a variety of input sources that may either provide that vital inspiration, or remain part of your final publication.

- Artwork can be drawn directly on the **Artboard** using either a mouse or a digital drawing tablet.

- Scanned line drawings are often used as the foundation of an illustration. There's many a novice Illustrator user who mistakenly thinks that what they see as final output was created totally from scratch without any external point of reference. This is not very often the case. We get an idea for a concept, rough out a thumbnail, scan it on the desktop scanner and then draw, refine and color up the final artwork using our traced image as our base.

- Images from both digital still cameras and scanned photographs can be imported, either for inclusion in the final artwork – or again, to be used as a point of reference.

- Digital images can be created or manipulated in Adobe Photoshop, or other programs such as Fireworks or Freehand, and imported directly into Illustrator.

- Stock clip art in appropriate formats can be utilized in Illustrator – which formats are suitable will be covered later.

- Text files from other text editors such as Simple Text, Notepad or Microsoft Word can be used.

- Converted photographs from Adobe Streamline can be imported.

Where Does Illustrator Fit into the Workflow?

Where Illustrator fits into the workflow is to a large extent dependent on what you are developing in the application.

- When the final output for your illustration is inclusion in a large text-heavy printed publication, you would not develop the entire publication in Illustrator. You would rather complete your illustration here and then export it in a format suitable to be imported into a page-layout application such as Adobe InDesign, QuarkXpress or Adobe Framemaker.

- If you were designing graphics to be used in an animation application such as Macromedia Flash, once again, you would design the graphics here and then export them in a SWF suitable for inclusion in Flash.

- Illustrator has all the functionality needed to produce posters, promotional materials or smaller brochures, and in this instance you could go direct to print from Illustrator.

- The choice is yours when it comes to web design – prepare and export graphics for inclusion in your web pages, or design, slice and export entire designs from within Illustrator.

The Aim of this Book

This book will teach you Illustrator from the very beginning, to a level at which you'll feel comfortable creating and manipulating a wide variety of artwork for print, for the Web, and for use with other applications (for example Adobe InDesign, Adobe Photoshop, and QuarkXpress). Accompanied by professional designers, and a few fictitious characters, you will take a journey through the essential tools and techniques that Illustrator has to offer, and learn a few designer secrets along the way. (The fictitious characters have no secrets that we know of – but then, if we knew them, they wouldn't be secrets, would they?)

Each chapter contains step-by-step practical exercises for you to work through, and then there's a real-world case study that runs in instalments from Chapters 3 to 16, but more on this a little later. As you progress, you'll notice that this book has a two-pronged approach – not only do we want to introduce you to this wonderful program, we also want to make sure you learn as much about what causes those little hiccups in production as possible, so that you can avoid these hitches in your own experience.

If you've used earlier versions of Illustrator and want to use this book to get up to speed with the new features, we think you'll be pleasantly surprised by our approach. You can choose to either work through the book, or dip into various chapters to get the low-down on tools and options such as the new symbol tools, the improved web production tools, the nifty Liquify tools and more.

Exercises and Case Study: Meet George and Lucy

As we mentioned previously in this introduction, there will be plenty of chance for you to practise your newly acquired skills, both in short practical exercises and with the development of our case study, so I guess it's time for you to meet and greet the clients: George Ribeiro and Lucy Reeves. These two characters were once urban warriors, dashing around New York, living for work and not working to live. Then one day it dawned on them that life was too short for all that nonsense, and they did what we would all like to do – sold all their trappings, packed up, and moved away from the grime and dirt of the city. Now based in Grenada, they have turned into gentle eco-warriors, and combined their love of open spaces, sunshine, and water with their daily work. They have started a new venture called Marine Quest, which is essentially a company offering short sail charters and dive holidays off the coast of Grenada.

As with any new venture, they have realized that they need to get an identity, a logo, and publicity materials, and of course, in this modern world, develop a website to get the news out to their potential clients. With all this in mind they have approached us and asked us to develop the materials for them, and this is where you come in. During the course of this book, you will constantly be developing new ideas and new materials for them to consider, using powerful Illustrator features to achieve this end. Of course, some ideas they will reject out of hand, others they will accept and then want changed – in fact they'll be just as demanding as any real world client you might meet. With this in mind, we will teach you some useful tricks and techniques to maximize your workflow whilst reducing the impact that their sudden whims will have on your time.

Oh, and one last thing, they have already an additional member of the family. A stray dog called Bardo who Lucy found hanging around the dive shack, and who George has reluctantly adopted. He'll feature in this development as well.

PCs and Macs

This book is for both PC and Mac users. We've stuck with each author's chosen system and also provided instructions for the alternative system.

Just as a quick reference, here are the main differences:

PC	Mac
Right-click	CTRL-click
CTRL	command
Alt	

What You'll Need to Know

No prior knowledge of Illustrator is required, but if you are familiar with older versions, want to refresh your knowledge, or get up to speed with all the new features in release 10, then you'll certainly find this book useful too.

You will need to be comfortable with either the Windows or Mac operating systems and know how to create folders, rename files, and so on. You will also need a basic knowledge of using the Internet.

Conventions

We've tried to keep this book as clear and easy to follow as possible, so we've only used a few layout styles:

- When you come across an important word or phrase, it will be in **bold type**.

- We'll use a different font to emphasize phrases that appear on the screen, code and filenames.

- Menu commands are written in the form Menu > Sub-menu > Sub-menu.

- Keyboard shortcuts appear like this: select the **Magic Wand** tool (w).

- When there's some information we think is really important, we'll highlight it like this:

> *This is very important stuff – don't skip it!*

Worked exercises are laid out like this:

Exercise Heading

1. Open the file start.psd

2. Do something.

3. Save your file as finish.psd

Files for Download

You will need to download the source files required to complete the exercises from our web site www.friendsofed.com, or you can use similar images of your own.

Support

If you have any questions about the book or about friends of ED, check out our web site www.friendsofed.com. There's a range of contact details there, or you can use feedback@friendsofed.com.

There's a host of other features on the site – interviews with top designers, samples from our other books, and a message board where you can post your questions, discussions and answers, or just take a back seat and look at what other designers are talking about. If you have any comments or problems, please write to us – we'd love to hear from you.

1 Getting Started in Illustrator

What We'll Cover in this Chapter:

- *Understanding your Artboard components*
- *The basic Illustrator interface*
- *Navigating your illustrations*
- *Saving illustrations*

By now, I'm sure you're just itching to get out there and experiment yourself. So, without further ado, let's dive right in.

I seldom make presumptions, but let me make this one – you have Adobe Illustrator open and proudly displaying on your desktop? If not, it would be a good idea to launch it now.

Understanding Your Artboard Components

Now let's move on to looking at the Artboard as it is created within an Illustrator document. If you have any sample files still open from the previous section, close them now, so that the only file you have open on your screen is that original file you created a little earlier.

Have a quick look at the screen, and what you should be seeing is a rectangle bounded by a solid black line, and possibly a couple of rectangles within that with dotted lines. Exactly what you see is dependent on the size of Artboard you created and the size and orientation of the paper in your printer. These shapes denote the different components of your drawing environment.

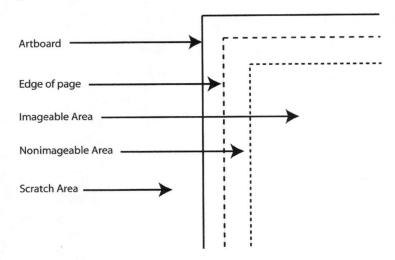

Artboard

The Artboard is depicted by the area bounded by the solid rectangle, and like your canvas in real life, the Artboard is where you place your material in an Illustrator document.

For the moment, we'll not be making any changes to the size of your Artboard, but you will see as your knowledge develops that there are instances in which you would like to make the Artboard bigger or smaller. An interesting point is that the maximum possible size of this Artboard is 5.76m square, great for that oversized art you may be creating.

Edge of Page

The larger rectangle with dotted lines shows the physical size of the paper that is presently in your selected printer.

Imageable Area

The imageable area, the innermost rectangle, corresponds to the area of the page on which your selected printer can print. I'm sure you are aware that many desktop printers cannot print right to the edge of the page, so if you are producing work that you want to print yourself, just make sure that all your artwork is placed inside this rectangle.

Nonimageable Area

The nonimageable area, the area between the two sets of dotted lines, simply means that although this area is part of the physical expanse of the page in your printer, any art placed here will not be printed. Just a big 'techie' word for a very simple concept – don't put anything in this area if you want it to be printed!

Scratch Area

If the Artboard is your canvas, then the Scratch area is your desk, your storage area. This is where you can keep parts of your artwork while you decide whether or not to use them. Because these objects are not within the imageable area of your page, they will not print.

Moving on from the Artboard and its components, we'll have a look at that plethora of palettes, tools, and menus.

The Basic Illustrator Interface

When you first look at the Illustrator interface, all those elements may be a little overwhelming. In this section, you'll be introduced to some of the basics and the logic of the interface. Don't worry, this is not going to be a blow-by-blow dismantling of every tool, palette, and command – rather it will be a cursory view just so that you start to feel at home. The detailed exploration will continue throughout the book, but we're building good solid foundations here.

Having a look at the interface, you'll notice a Menu bar that runs along the top of the screen. This is where you'll access various commands. To the left of the screen, there should be a tall palette, the Toolbox, and on the right hand screen, a number of tabbed palettes.

The Toolbox

This is full of the wonderful tools that you will be using to create the elements of your artwork, so getting familiar with how it works and the logic behind the arrangement of the tools is a good place to start. If you cannot see the toolbox, it may have been hidden from view. To redisplay it, go to the Window menu, and select Tools. To find it easily, note that the palettes have been listed alphabetically, so it's near the bottom of the first section of this menu.

As you look at the toolbox, you'll notice the horizontal dividing lines at various positions along the height of the toolbox. This is because, as far as possible, Adobe has placed the tools into logical groups according to their function. Understanding this logic from the outset will often help you decide which particular tool, or group of tools you need to use.

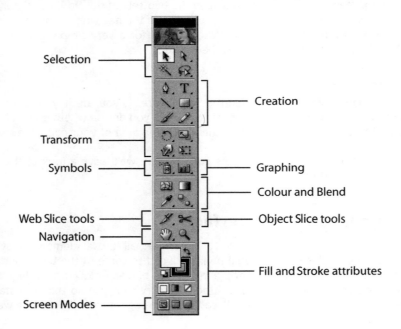

Selection — Creation — Transform — Symbols — Graphing — Colour and Blend — Web Slice tools — Object Slice tools — Navigation — Fill and Stroke attributes — Screen Modes

Okay, so maybe the logic doesn't follow through completely, but I guess even Adobe had problems when they were trying to arrange these tools. Nevertheless, there is a method evident here. If you want to select something, you need to use one of those tools in the top quadrant. If you are going to create something new, it's in the next section. If you want to transform this selected or newly created object, you'll use one of the tools in the third section.

At the risk of sounding like one of those awful infomercials on television, I just can't resist saying, "But wait, there's more!" You'll notice that some of the tool icons have a little arrowhead shape in the bottom right corner. This tells you that there are more tools hidden behind the one that is presently visible. To access the additional tools, hold your mouse down over the tool and they will display in what is called a flyout. Notice also, that there is a little tab at the right hand side of the flyout, called a tearoff. If you release the mouse whilst the cursor is over this, these tools will become separated from the main toolbox, and float in their own little palette on your screen.

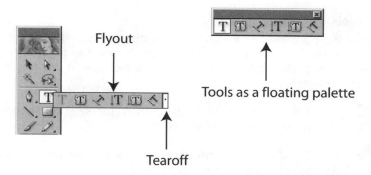

Flyout

Tools as a floating palette

Tearoff

Another feature of the toolbox is the tool tip that shows when you hover the cursor over a tool. This is useful because not only does it tell you what the tool is, thus giving an indication of its use, but it also tells you the shortcut for that particular tool, in brackets at the end of the name. If the tool tip does not display, you may need to enable this option. To switch tool tips on, display the General Preferences by choosing Edit > Preferences > General, and ensure that there is a tick next to Tool Tips as illustrated in the screenshot below.

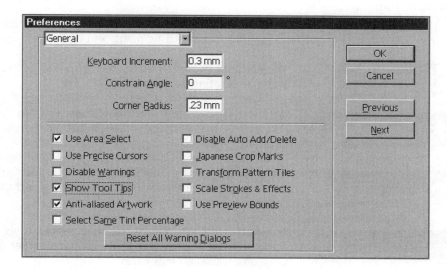

Don't worry about the rest of the boxes – these will be covered later.

Now let's have a quick look at the functions of each set of tools. If it all seems a little overwhelming at the moment, don't worry. The rest of the book will introduce the tools one at a time, and you will have a chance to get to grips with them then. You can select a tool to use by clicking on its icon, or by using keyboard shortcuts, which I have stated are in brackets after the tool name.

Selection Tools

One of the basic premises of working in Illustrator is 'select, then effect'. In other words, you need to select an element of your artwork before you try to change its fill, stroke (outline), or any other attributes. You would use the tools in this area of the toolbox to achieve this first step.

The **Selection** tool (V) is used for selecting either entire objects or entire groups of objects.

The **Direct Selection** (A) and **Group Selection** tools are used for selecting components of artwork.

Use the **Magic Wand** tool (Y) for selections based on color attributes.

Use the **Direct Select Lasso** tool (Q) and the Lasso tool to make freehand selections.

Creation Tools

This section of the toolbox contains all those tools that you will use for creating shapes, from the simplest primitive shape to complex artistic paths, and text.

The **Pen** tool (P) and its associated tools are used for creating and manipulating **Bezier** paths.

With the **Type** (T) and associated tools you can create text, text in a shape, and text on a path, both horizontally and vertically.

The **Line Segment** (\) tool is a new tool in version 10, used with the others on this palette for creating straight lines, arcs, spirals, and grids.

The **Rectangle** (M), **Ellipse** (L), and related tools will draw these primitive shapes, along with rounded corner rectangles, polygons, stars, and lens flares.

With the **Paintbrush** (B) tool you can paint artistic, calligraphic, and more art strokes using various options from the Brush palette and libraries.

For freehand strokes, use the **Pencil** tool (N), whilst the **Smooth** and **Erase** tools allow you to modify the paths you create.

Transform Tools

In a perfect world, every piece of artwork we created would be perfect when we first create it. But as we all know, it's not a perfect world, and Illustrator provides us with a number of tools that enable us to manipulate and transform our artwork until it meets our satisfaction. Remember that to use any of these tools, your artwork must be selected.

The tools on this palette allow you to **Rotate** (R), **Reflect** (O), and **Twist** your selected artwork.

Here you can **Scale** (S), **Shear**, and **Reshape** artwork.

New to Illustrator 10 are the six **Liquefy** tools, for transforming your art like putty.

The **Free Transform** (E) tool is a powerful tool that scales, rotates, distorts, or applies perspective to selected elements.

Symbolism Tools

Some of the tools that don't seem to fit into any neatly defined grouping are the new Symbolism tools, including the **Symbol Sprayer** (SHIFT+S). These are another new addition to the Illustrator 10 palette. With these tools, previously created symbols can be sprayed, scrunched, screened, and more!

Their importance lies in the way they allow you to easily create multiple occurrences of graphics while keeping an eye on that all important file size.

Graphing Tools

The options on the **Graph** tool palette are used for creating various styles of graphs, such as **Column Graphs** (J), in your illustrations. They are useful for communicating factual detail attractively.

Color and Blending Tools

While the tools in the transform section of the toolbox enable you to fine tune the shape and size of your graphics, the choices here allow you to concentrate on achieving the desired results with fancier Color fills and Blending options.

The **Gradient Mesh** tool (U) is particularly useful for applying subtle shading and color changes to objects, allowing you to create realistic painterly and 3D effects.

 With the **Gradient** tool (G) you fill objects with linear and radial gradient fills, where there is a gradual color transition from one color to another.

 The **Eyedropper** (I) and **Paintbucket** (K) tools are useful for sampling and applying both text and color attributes to objects, whilst the **Measure** tool is handy for measuring angles and distances.

 Create subtle shading, or morph shapes into each other with the **Blend** tool (W), and use the **Auto Trace** tool to trace simple bitmap shapes.

Slicing Tools

 Placed together on the toolbox are two sets of tools for slicing – the **Slice** tool (SHIFT+K) and **Slice Selection** tool on the left of the toolbox are for creating and selecting those all important web slices, whilst the **Scissor** (S) and **Knife** tools on the right of the toolbox are for cutting and slicing your graphics into new shapes.

Navigation Tools

As your artwork gets larger, or more intricate, you're going to need these tools to change your view of what is onscreen, and what will be printed.

 Use the **Hand** tool (H) to drag your document around the screen so that you can see parts that were not previously visible. The **Page** tool is handy for repositioning the imageable area on oversized artwork.

 The **Zoom** tool (Z) is for zooming in and out on the screen. However you will soon learn that there are more time-efficient ways of achieving the same results without switching to this tool.

Fill and Stroke Region

By making selections here, you will control whether it is the **Fill** or the **Stroke** (outline) that will be affected when you make a color change, and also whether the object will have a basic, gradient, or no fill, and similarly a basic stroke or no stroke. Remember that this section is only an overview of the toolbox, and you will learn the mechanics of the options in a later chapter.

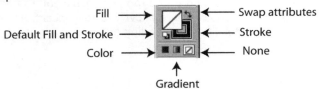

Fill — Swap attributes
Default Fill and Stroke — Stroke
Color — None
Gradient

Screen Modes

Often you may wish to view your artwork without the distractions of the menu bars and file names. Using the **Screen Mode** (F) buttons at the bottom of the toolbox, you can opt to view the screen in standard, full screen with a menu bar, or full screen without a menu bar.

That was a marathon session – hopefully you're still with me, and not worrying about how you are going to learn how to use all the options presented on the toolbox. Remember that as we work through the chapters and case study, the tools will be re-introduced and explored in detail.

The Floating Palettes

Take a peek at the Window menu. Notice the list of 24 standard palettes, and the additional library palettes! There's a lot of functionality and features built into these palettes, but don't worry, we're not going to look at each one here. Once again, they will be introduced in chapters where their features are relevant to the chapter contents. What we will do here is have a look at how to work with the palettes, view them, hide them, reorganize them, and access their context menus.

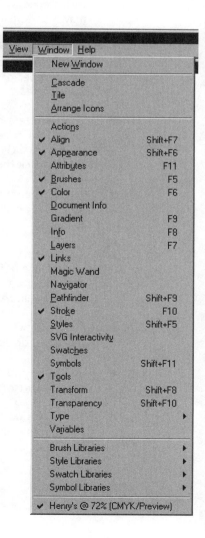

Going back to that concept of 24 plus palettes, could you imagine how crowded your screen would be if, for some obscure reason, you tried to open them all at once. To save valuable screen real estate, they have been grouped into presets, and we'll show you how to create your own grouped sets a little later. The screenshot below shows one of the standard groupings, where the Styles, Swatches, Brushes, and Symbols palettes have been grouped together.

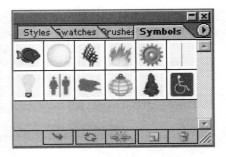

- To show a palette, go to the Window menu and select the palette you wish to display. Notice that some of the palettes have shortcuts and you may wish to learn a few of the ones that you use regularly.

- To close a palette, click on the **Close** icon on the palette. (Here is a platform difference: on a Mac, click the rectangular icon at the top left hand corner of the palette, on a PC, click the X icon at the top right of the palette.)

- To minimize a palette, in other words, show only the palettes title, click on the Minimize icon on the palette. (Another cross platform difference: on the Mac, click the rectangular icon on the top right of the palette, on the PC, click the Line icon to the left of the Close icon.)

- To toggle between Restore, Resize to Fit, and Minimize views of a palette, double-click on the palettes tab – the bit where the palettes name is displayed.

- To restore a palette, click that icon again – it will have changed appearance because the palette is minimized, and is accurately described as the Restore icon, but just remember it's in exactly in the same position as the Minimize icon on the palette.

- To interactively resize a palette, drag the bottom right hand corner of the palette in or out.

- To display the palette context menu, or further palette options, depress the little arrow icon near the top right hand corner of the palette.

- To move a palette across to a different position on the screen, click and drag on the very top bar of the palette, above the palette tab.

Palette Tab   Minimize   Close   Display options and menu

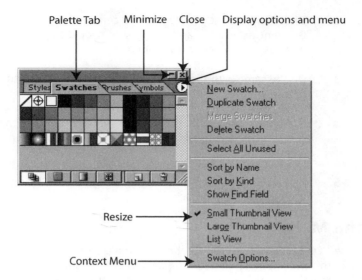

Resize

Context Menu

Sidebar – Hiding the Palettes

You'll find that throughout the text of this book, shortcuts will be introduced without drawing too much attention to them. However, here is one shortcut that you really need to know!

- To temporarily hide all open palettes and the toolbox, hit the TAB key once. To restore them, hit TAB again.

- To temporarily hide all the palettes, but keep the toolbox visible, hold down the SHIFT key and hit TAB once. To restore them, repeat the process.

This is a very useful shortcut for when the screen is looking a bit too cluttered. But you can imagine the panic if, by mistake, you hit the TAB key and all the palettes disappear along with your toolbox, and you had no idea why this has happened!

Creating Your Own Palette Groups

We mentioned earlier that you can create your own palette groupings to suit your own work style and preferences, so let's give that a try. Admit it, you've been sitting reading all this information, wishing that there was something practical that you could do.

1. Look at the row of palettes on the right hand side of your screen, and locate both the Gradient palette, and the Links palette.

2. Drag the Gradient palette into the center of the screen, by clicking on the Gradient palette tab and dragging. It should separate from the other two palettes with which it is grouped.

3. Do the same with the Links palette, but place it over the Gradient palette before you release the mouse.

4. If you were successful, the palettes should now move together as a group. Test this by clicking and dragging on the top bar of the palette, above the palette tab.

5. Restore the palettes to their original groupings by reversing the process and dragging them back.

Using the Menus

Now you've had a look at both the toolbox and the palettes, let's move on to the menus. Once again, this will not be an in-depth discussion of the commands on the menu. Instead, it is an introduction to the logic behind how the commands on the menus have been organized, so that you have a better idea of where commands are likely to be accessed.

Have a look at the File menu as we point out some of the features that are consistent across all the menus.

- Notice the horizontal dividing lines. As with the toolbox, Adobe have tried to group similar commands together and separate them from other commands by inserting a dividing line. Notice how all the various Save commands have been grouped together and how this is the same for the Print commands and other groupings.

- Every command has one letter in the command that has an underscore. This means that with the relevant menu displayed, you can simply type that underscored letter to access the command. For example in Open, typing the letter O would display the Open dialog box.

- On the right hand side of the menus, the shortcuts for the commands are displayed. Now, we're not expecting that you learn each and every shortcut – at this stage that would be silly. But if you find that you are constantly accessing a command from a menu, it would seem an ideal time to commit its shortcut to memory. Note that these shortcuts do not work if the menu is being displayed.

- Have another look at the File menu, and notice the three little dots (ellipsis) that follow some of the commands, for example Save for Web. The presence of an ellipsis is a sure indication that choosing that option will present you with another dialog box.

- Note the little arrows on the right of the menus next to some of the commands. This indicates that a submenu is available for this command, allowing you to make further choices.

- And finally, if an option on the menu is grayed out; it means that the option is not available to you at the present moment.

Underscored letters for easy command selection →

Keyboard shortcuts

Dividing lines which separate and group similar commands

Ellipsis indicating that selecting this option will present you with a further dialog box →

Arrow indicating submenu

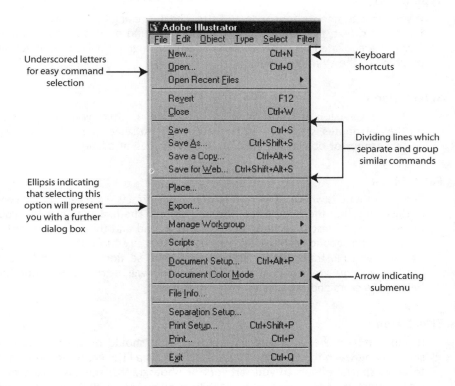

File Menu

This menu contains all the commands for dealing with your files as opposed to dealing with individual components of artwork. It is here where you access commands to open, close, save, export, and manage your files.

Edit Menu

The Edit menu contains the all-important Undo command, and various other commands for cutting, copying, and pasting elements. You can also edit your Preferences, your shortcuts, and your Document Color settings.

Object Menu

Whenever you have a graphic selected, and want to make changes to it; the Object menu is going to be your option. This includes options for transforming, blending, and distorting your objects, among other commands.

Type Menu

If you want to choose font style and size, check spelling, or perform a Find and Replace function on text, the option to do that will be found on this menu. Additional required features are located on either the Character or Paragraph palettes that you would display by going to the Window menu.

Select Menu

New to this version of Illustrator is the Select menu, where you can select objects based on their attributes, step through stacked objects to select the object you want; and save certain groups of objects as selection to be reloaded at a later stage.

Filter Menu

The Filter menu is where all the filters – the fancy effects – are kept. Notice when you look at this menu that there are three distinct sections. The first options allow you to re-apply or re-access the last used filter, but it is the second and third sections that need special mention. The second section, the first set of filters, are those that are used when you are working with Illustrator vector artwork. The third section, the second set of filters, are used when you are working with bitmaps. You will learn more about the difference between vectors and bitmaps in the next chapter.

Effect Menu

If you compare the Filter and Effect menus you should notice that there is a distinct similarity between the two, and you might find this a little confusing. They both allow you to apply special effects to your artwork or photographs. The essential difference is that whilst filters are permanent, using the Effect menu means that the special effect applied to your illustration can be undone or modified at a later stage, much like adjustment layers in Photoshop.

View Menu

The View menu includes features that allow you to zoom in and out of your illustration, and to change the way your artwork is displayed on the screen. You can also choose to display and use grids and guides from this menu.

Window Menu

If the View menu controls how your artwork is displayed, the Window menu controls what is floating above your artwork. It is where you access and display all those palettes, also known as floating windows – see the link?

Help Menu

This menu contains all the links to the Illustrator Help files, information about Illustrator and the active plug-ins, and links to a number of useful web pages.

The Status Bar

We've nearly finished our exploration of the interface, there's just one more component that deserves a mention here, the Status Bar, which is located down at the bottom left hand side of the screen.

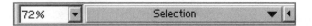

The field on the left hand side of the Status Bar provides options for zooming in and out of your illustration. You can either choose one of the preset magnifications by clicking on the arrow next to the zoom value, or you can type your own value by highlighting the present zoom percentage and typing a new value.

On the right of the Status Bar is an option for changing the information that is being displayed concerning your artwork. The default option is Current Tool, which is useful in that you always know which tool you have selected. To display the options available, click on the arrow and a fly-out menu appears.

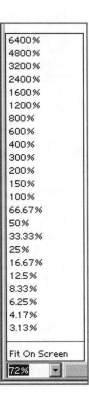

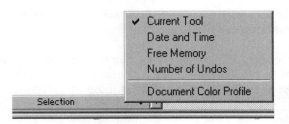

To end our little tour on a lighter note, hold down the ALT/OPTION key and click on the Status Bar Menu to display the additional options.

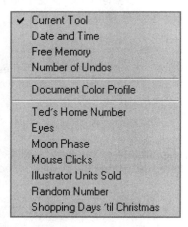

Choose the Eyes option and move your mouse around the screen, watching how the eyes follow your cursor. Most of these additional options are really just fun, but there is one I'd like to draw your attention to – Mouse Clicks. Throughout this book, you'll notice a very subtle, (and sometimes, not so subtle suggestion) that you learn shortcuts. One way of realizing just how often you click with the mouse in a work session is to note this value – you'll be surprised. Illustrator will continually count your mouse clicks until you exit the application, even if the option is not displayed on the Status Bar.

Navigating Your Illustrations

In this chapter you have been introduced to the Illustrator interface. Let's move on now, and show you ways that you can navigate around your illustrations, and control how they are displayed. This is important because as your artwork becomes larger or more complex, you'll often find the need to zoom in and out of the screen, view different parts of the work or change the way the artwork is displayed.

This will also give us an opportunity to start using some of the tools we've mentioned, access certain commands on the View menu, introduce some palettes, and, of course, you guessed it, start gently emphasizing the importance of those useful shortcuts.

It would be useful to have some art open for this little session, and as you have not yet created any of your own, I suggest we open that Tropical card.ai file again. As it was one of the files you recently opened, it may be listed on the sub-menu under File > Open Recent Documents. If not, open it as you did before.

View Menu

As we're concentrating on navigating around your images in this session, the commands on the View menu we'll highlight are those that deal with zooming in and out. Display the View Menu now, and locate the commands in the fourth section of the menu.

To ensure that you see the entire picture, choose View > Fit in Window (CTRL/CMD+0). Notice the zoom value displaying in the Status Bar. Now switch to view the illustration at 100% by choosing View > Actual Size (Cmd/Ctrl+1) and once again note that the value in the Status Bar has changed, displaying 100%.

Now zoom in on your illustration by choosing View > Zoom In (CTRL/CMD++) and zoom out by choosing View > Zoom Out (CTRL/CMD+-). If you're getting tired of always having to access the View menu to perform this simple task, you know there's an easier way – try the shortcuts that have been mentioned in this text, and displayed next to the commands on the View menu. You'll find it a lot faster and keep that mouse click total down!

Using Context Menus

Another way of zooming in and out of your illustration is achieved by using the Context menu, which will be displayed if you right-mouse click (PC) or CTRL+mouse click (Mac). The Context menu is an interactive menu that will change depending on what tool you have chosen and whether or not you have any artwork selected.

For the moment, because I'm assuming you have not selected any part of the illustration, your Context menu should look similar to the one displayed on the previous page. From this menu, choose either Zoom In or Zoom Out. Admit it, that's a little faster than always accessing the menu commands. And that's one of our aims in this book, to teach you the most effective and fastest way of achieving your desired results.

Using the Navigator Palette

You may remember that when we first looked at the palettes I said that we would only discuss them in detail when their functionality became relevant to what we were doing. That means we're now ready to have our first in-depth look at a palette – the Navigator palette.

If you've not changed the positioning of the palettes since you opened Illustrator that very first time, the Navigator palette should be located in the group of palettes at the top right hand corner of the screen. To bring it to the front of that palette grouping, click on the Navigator palette tab. Otherwise, choose Window > Navigator to display the palette.

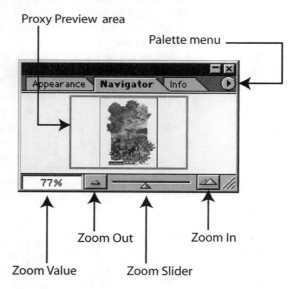

The Navigator palette is a handy method of zooming in and out of your illustration, and for dragging the visible part of your illustration around the screen, although I'll admit that once you become more familiar with shortcut methods of navigating, you will use this palette less.

To zoom out of the illustration, click on the small mountain icon on the left of the Zoom slider; to zoom in, click on the large mountain icon on the right. Notice that as you zoom in and out, the size of the red rectangle changes. This rectangle is showing you which part of the illustration is currently visible onscreen at the present level of magnification.

To illustrate this, zoom in to about 300%. You can do this by clicking on the large mountain icon, or by dragging the Zoom slider to the right, or by entering the exact value in the Zoom Value field. Notice how the rectangle no longer encompasses the entire illustration. To view a different part of your illustration, move your cursor over the Proxy Preview Area, and without clicking or dragging, notice how the cursor displays either as a pointing finger or as an open hand. With the cursor as a pointing finger (outside the red rectangle), click anywhere on the illustration in the Navigator palette, and that part of the illustration now displays on screen. With the cursor as an open hand (inside the red rectangle) click and drag to reposition the rectangle over the area you wish to view.

Using the Zoom and Hand Tools

Now let's look at the navigational tools on the toolbox, that enable you to control the level of magnification and the visible area of the artwork.

Zoom Tool

Select the **Zoom** tool (Z) from the toolbox. The cursor should change to a magnifying glass icon.

- To zoom in, click with the cursor on that area of the image you want to magnify. Notice the new zoom values will be reflected both in the **Status** bar and in the **Navigator** palette if it is still visible.

- To zoom out, hold down the ALT/OPTION key and click on the image. Again keep an eye on those changing magnification values.

- To zoom in on a particular area of the image, click and drag with the magnifying glass over an area.

- To quickly revert to 100% view, double-click on the **Zoom** tool icon on the toolbox.

Hand Tool

The **Hand** tool performs a similar function to dragging the red rectangle inside the **Navigator** palette, in that it allows you to reposition the artwork in the screen so that you can view a specific area.

Select the **Hand** tool (H) from the toolbox. The cursor should change to a hand icon. Click and drag on the screen to move the artwork around. Double-click on the **Hand** tool icon in the toolbox to fit the artwork in the window.

Sidebar: Navigation Shortcuts

We've just spent the last couple of pages introducing you to various ways in which you can navigate around your illustration, and here we are now, saying there's a more effective way – shortcuts. Instead of changing tools, accessing menu commands, or using the Navigator palette, nearly all of the above functions can be accessed with a few simple shortcuts. It just takes a little time to commit them all to memory, but in the long run they will save you so much time.

You've already seen some of them on the View menu:

- CTRL/CMD + 1 to view an illustration at Actual Size.

- CTRL/CMD + 0 to change the magnification level so that an entire illustration, no matter how big or small, is visible on screen.

- CTRL/CMD + + (plus sign) to zoom in.

- CTRL/CMD + - (minus sign) to zoom out.

Now add another three simple shortcuts and you can view any part of your illustration at any level of magnification without changing tools.

- To access the **Hand** tool whilst another tool is selected, simply hold down the SPACEBAR to temporarily switch to it. When you release the SPACEBAR, you're back with your original tool.

- Similarly to temporarily toggle to the **Zoom in** tool, hold down the CTRL/CMD and the SPACEBAR. You can either then click to zoom in, or click and drag to zoom in on a particular region.

- To temporarily access the **Zoom out** option, hold down CTRL + ALT + SPACEBAR/CMD + OPTION + SPACEBAR.

Screen Modes

Imagine this artwork on your screen at present is your own, your client has popped in to see how you are progressing, and you wish to show it to him in all its splendor, without the menu bars and title bars. It's time to switch screen modes.

At the bottom of your toolbox, there is a row of three icons representing different screen modes. To switch screen modes, either click on one of the icons, or type the letter F to cycle through the three modes. The left hand button is **Standard** screen display with the menu bar and file name title visible. With the middle button, the illustration goes **Fullscreen with Menu Bar**; and with the right hand option, **Full Screen**, there are no distractions – no menu bar, no file name, just the illustration.

Pushing those Navigation Shortcuts

Before we go on and learn some more skills, let's take a moment and practice all those navigation shortcuts we presented previously.

1. Clear your screen of all the palettes and the toolbar by hitting the TAB key.

2. Cycle through to **Full Screen** mode, by typing F twice.

3. Zoom in and out using CTRL/CMD++ and CTRL/CMD+-.

4. Use the SPACEBAR to access the **Hand** tool and drag the illustration around the screen.

5. Hold down CTRL/CMD + SPACEBAR and click and drag to zoom in on a particular region of the illustration.

6. Add OPTION/ALT to the combination, and click on the screen to zoom out.

7. Resize the illustration to Actual Size by pressing CTRL/CMD+1.

8. Fit the illustration in the window with CTRL/CMD+0.

9. Finally, to return to Standard screen mode (F) and re-display all the palettes and toolbox, click the TAB key.

Saving Illustrations

Our last section in this introductory chapter deals with the all-important concept of saving files. Granted, you have not yet created any artwork to save, but getting this skill under your belt at this early stage before you have anything of value that could be lost is a pretty good idea.

The four options for saving files are located on the File menu, as illustrated here. There are also options for exporting your Illustrator files in preparation for inclusion in other applications, but we'll not be looking at that feature until later in this book.

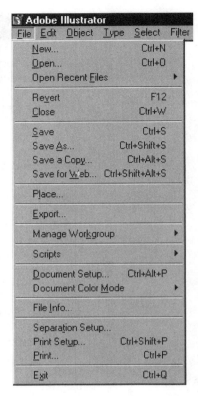

Saving a New File

The very first time you save a file, it does not matter whether you chose the Save (CTRL/CMD+S) or the Save As (CTRL/CMD), as the Save As dialog box will be displayed.

■ Choose File>Save or File>Save As. The Save As dialog box will be displayed.

- Navigate to where you wish to save your art. Take a few minutes to think about where to save it. So many times, we just save the file without thinking about where it is being saved, and then have to spend ages trying to find it on our hard drives. A little thought here that will save you time in the long run.

- Enter a sensible, descriptive name in the File name field.

- Select a file format from the Save as type drop-down menu. We'll not be going into any detail about the three options here. We're only at the starting gate in our Illustrator journey, so suffice to say that choosing the standard Illustrator (.ai) format will suit your needs at this stage. (Mac users: You will be given an option to append the file extension. With more and more studios incorporating the use of both Macs and PCs, choosing this option will make it easier for the PC to recognize your file and thus streamline your workflow, and avoid unnecessary delays.)

```
Adobe PDF (*.PDF)
Illustrator (*.AI)
Illustrator EPS (*.EPS)
SVG (*.SVG)
SVG Compressed (*.SVGZ)
```

- Click Save or press the ENTER/RETURN key, and a second dialog box will be displayed. For the moment, accept all the defaults as they are presented, ensuring that you are saving the file in an Illustrator 10 format.

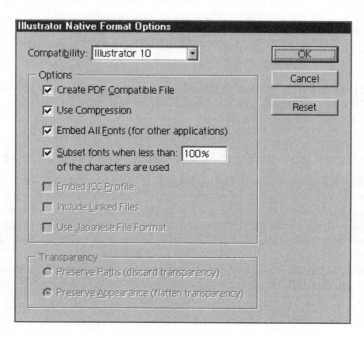

■ Click OK or the ENTER/RETURN key and your file will have been successfully saved with the name and location you specified.

Saving an Existing File

Once you have successfully saved a file for the first time, it has been saved with a specific name on your hard drive, but this is not the end of your work. You need to continually keep re-saving the illustration each time you make a significant change to it, as there is no Auto-Save function.

■ From the File menu, choose Save, or learn the shortcut CTRL/CMD+S. Your revised file will be saved over the previously saved file.

It's really a good idea to get used to doing this little routine often. It's easy to get so totally engrossed in what you are doing and forget to keep saving the file until something horrible happens like a power failure and you lose all that lovely work. Yes, I am speaking from experience!

Saving a File with a Different Name – Using the Save As Command

Occasionally you may decide that you wish to rename your file, or save it in another location. This is when you purposely choose the Save As command.

Choose Save As...(CMD/CTRL+SHIFT+S) from the File menu, and the Save as dialog box will be displayed.

■ Type a new name for the file, or navigate through to another folder to save your file.

■ Click Save or press the ENTER/RETURN key and your file will have been successfully saved with the new name or in the new location you chose.

It's important to note that the file name of your active file will have been changed, and the original file will have closed but will remain on your hard drive. This is different from the Save As a Copy command.

Saving a Copy of Your File – Using the Save a Copy Command

Whereas in the Save As command, you effectively changed the name or location of your active file and then worked on this newly named file, the Save a Copy command works quite differently. With this command, you continue to work on your original file, but you have saved a copy of that file to your hard drive. This copy is not an open or active file, and in order to access it, you would have to expressly open that file.

You might be asking what the purpose of this feature is, and when you might use it. Imagine you have got to a stage in your artwork where you are about to make a radical change to the contents, but in the back of your mind is a nagging thought, you're not quite sure if this is what you want to do. Saving a copy will place a closed, saved copy of your file on your hard drive, and you're free to continue working on the active file, safe in the knowledge that you have a back up copy stored.

- Choose File > Save a Copy. The Save a Copy dialog box will appear, and the word **copy** will be automatically inserted after the file name in the File name field. You can either choose to retain this name, or you may wish to rename the file with a descriptive name, which may make more sense to you at a later stage.

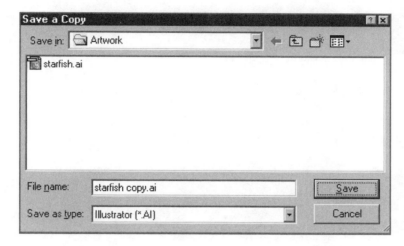

- Click Save or press the ENTER/RETURN key and a copy of your active file will be saved and closed with the original name with copy appended, or with a new descriptive name.

Preparing Your Images for Web Delivery – Using the Save for Web Command

The last save option that we will introduce here is the Save for Web command. We're not going to go into any detail on this option, because it is unlikely that at such an early stage you would wish to save an illustration for web delivery. Essentially, doing so will change the format from being a vector graphic into a bitmap graphic (more about the difference in the following chapter).

So, you're asking, why introduce the concept now? The reasoning behind this is that from the very beginning we want you to be aware that Illustrator is equally adept at creating images for both print and the Web. You don't need to have two separate applications to provide graphics for the different media – Illustrator provides all that functionality.

Summary

You've got to the end of the first chapter, and you have covered the basics of the Illustrator environment and interface. You've met the toolbox, the palettes, and the Artboard; you've learned how to create, open, and save files, and how to navigate an illustration, through menu options, the Navigator palette, and keyboard shortcuts.

You may be a little frustrated that you have not yet created any of your own original artwork, but I'm sure you understand that we need to get the basics firmly in place before you start on that exciting process.

Sail & Scuba

George Ribeiro
Marketing Director

Marine Quest Inc.
23 West Quay St. Georges Grenada W.I

2 Components of Illustrator Artwork

What We'll Cover in this Chapter:

- *The difference between bitmap and vector graphics.*

- *Viewing your artwork in different modes.*

- *Using Rulers, Grids and Guides for accurate placement of artwork.*

- *Understanding the different Selection Tools and when to use each one.*

- *Artwork components including Segments, Anchor points, Direction Points, and Handles.*

- *Grouping Artwork for convenience and efficiency, including locking and releasing artwork.*

- *Rearranging the stacking order of objects.*

- *An introduction to the concept of Layers, including the use of the Layers Palette.*

Bitmaps and Vectors

Although it probably isn't obvious at this stage, there are two very different kinds of computer graphics. You will come across these two different formats described in a variety of ways. Let's get off on the right foot and give you all the terms you are likely to encounter so there can be no confusion as to what kind of graphic you are working with.

The two graphics types are known as **Bitmaps** and **Vectors**. You may already have heard these terms. As computers and the Internet play an increasing role in our lives, more and more computer jargon has become absorbed into our everyday language. Understanding these terms correctly will save a lot of confusion and embarrassment later.

First, let's take a look at the other terms used to describe these types of graphics and the applications that produce them.

Bitmap Applications are also known as:

- Pixel based
- Raster
- Painting applications

Vector Applications are also known as:

- Object oriented applications
- Drawing applications

Now you can see what I mean by jargon. You don't need to memorize these, but it will come in handy at some time in the future when a printer or web design company starts hurling these words at you.

So, what are they? How do they differ and how do you know which one to use? Let me answer all those questions, and more. We're going to start by looking at **Bitmaps.**

Bitmap Graphics

Imagine you are looking at a completely blank, white computer screen. Now imagine placing an acetate sheet of graph paper over it. You have divided the screen up into a grid, or matrix. Effectively, this is how your computer will display bitmap images. Each small grid section within this matrix is called a **pixel** (short for **picture element**). Each pixel can be a different color and these different colored pixels will build up your picture, just like a mosaic.

At the most basic level, we have monochrome bitmaps. With monochrome bitmaps each pixel can be only one of two colors, black or white.

Take a look at the image below. This is a monochrome bitmap.

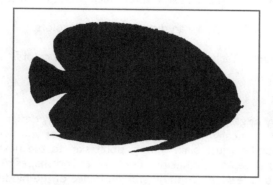

Here we see a section of the same image at a 750% zoom ratio. The **pixels** that make up the image can be seen along the edges as rectangular blocks.

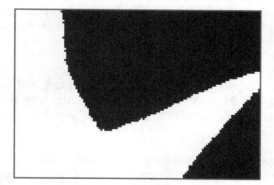

Bitmap graphics are much the same as a paintbrush and paper in the real world. Applying a brush stroke onto the paper colors an area of the paper in a similar way to "coloring in" a pixel in a bitmap application.

The days of monochrome bitmaps are long gone, thank goodness (although looking at some current multi-colored websites, perhaps we need to take a step back). The monochrome bitmap, known as a 1-bit image, is only capable of displaying two colors. By contrast, a 24-bit image or **true color image** can display up to 16.7 million colors – which means we can now produce images of photographic on computers.

I've highlighted two extremes in talking about 1-bit monochrome and 24-bit true color. Between these two extremes there are other color models, all described by the amount of colors they are capable of displaying, such as:

- **Grayscale** – Each pixel can display black, white or up to 254 shades of gray.

- **16 Color** – Each pixel can display one of 16 colors.

- **256 Colors** – Each pixel can display one of 256 colors.

Vector Graphics

This is the category of graphics that Illustrator was originally designed to deal with. Vector Graphics are mathematically defined objects. For those of you who are not numerically blessed or find numbers just plain boring, don't skip to the next chapter. Despite the dreaded math word, we are still talking about colors and shapes. All of the math is going on in the background leaving you in blissful ignorance of the hidden number crunching.

When you produce artwork in a vector application, you create shapes, lines, and colors. These elements are stored using a set of instructions. The code, the set of instructions that tells the computer what to display on the monitor, is hidden from view. All you see is the picture that these instructions generate. If you were to create a blue square and position it in the top right of the screen, the instructions would say something like:

```
SQUARE 75 75 B 600 100
```

This would tell the computer to create a 75x75 pixel square, and color it blue (B), with its center point 600 pixels from the left of the screen edge and 100 from the top of the screen edge. Remember you wouldn't see this code anywhere. All you would see is the blue square.

Every shape created is an independent object. We are no longer dealing in pixels. I stated earlier that a bitmap application is like painting with a brush on paper. If that is the case, then a vector application is analogous with cutting out paper shapes and positioning them on a master sheet of paper. The independent shapes never become part of the master sheet of paper beneath. Instead they remain independent, floating in several levels above the master sheet.

Take a look at the image below. This is a bitmap image.

This is the same image, generated in vector format.

The difference is quite apparent. The vector image loses the photographic realism. Each irregular, colored block is an independent object that goes towards building up the picture.

There's nothing new about vectors. The term has been used for many years. The next time you are watching an old war film and John Wayne is battling in the cockpit of his fighter plane and the voice over radio says "Bandits Vector 250", you'll know he's being told the enemy is on a heading of 250 degrees. That is the vector path he needs to take.

Now you know what a bitmap and a vector are and how they differ, but what are the pros and cons of each and which should you use and when?

The Benefits of a Bitmap

For photographs, bitmaps are clearly the better option. A 24-bit image will be able to store and display enough color information to recreate even the most complex scene with vivid color and subtle changes of tone.

Because we can zoom right in to one pixel, we can make undetectable changes to an image. If we were going to produce a glossy business brochure, we would engage a photographer to take publicity shots of the beach, and one of the diving boats heading out into turquoise waters. If by some professional oversight we later notice half a coconut floating on our otherwise perfect turquoise ocean, we simply zoom into the offending pixels and replace them with unblemished ones. This is a lot cheaper than getting the photographer back again.

If you are using images for the Web, only bitmap file formats are currently widely compatible. There are vector image formats that are usable on the Web, namely, Macromedia's Flash SWF (Shockwave Flash) format and Adobe's SVG (Scaleable Vector Graphics) format. However, both of these formats require a plug-in (a separate software utility) before they will work within a browser.

So what's the bad news?

The Disadvantages of Bitmaps

Bitmaps are generally large in file size. Color information must be stored for each pixel in an image. For a 24-bit image, this can create quite enormous file sizes. Storing these graphics somewhere is not such a major problem today with relatively cheap methods such as recordable CDs. A greater problem is working with the image on your computer. The more RAM your computer has, the faster it will allow you to edit and manipulate the image.

The really major problem is when you want to prepare images for the Web. Depending on your target web audience, users will employ a variety of methods to download your web graphics. These methods can be anything from a dial-up 14.4 kbps modem up to DSL and cable connections. If we were to compare Internet connections with train travel, the 14.4 kbps modem is equivalent to the old pioneering steam locomotives. The cable and DSL connections would be the Bullet train in Tokyo, which gets you to work ten minutes before you got out of bed. Obviously, the old modem user will be at a severe disadvantage if your images are large in file size.

There is a method to overcome the problem of large file sizes for the Web. It's called **compression**, and we'll be taking a look at it in chapter 16.

The other main disadvantage of bitmap graphics is one of **scalability**. Marine Quest will need a business logo. To be consistent and reinforce a strong brand image, it will be important that this logo appears wherever our business has a presence. Of course it means that the logo will need to be produced in different sizes. As an example, the logo will appear on our business cards. In this format the logo will be one inch square. On the brochure, which covers a larger area, the logo may be two inches square. On our business premises, on the boats, and at exhibitions, the logo may have to be anything up to six feet or more.

So can't we just increase the size of the bitmap logo? Technically, yes we can. It is possible to increase or decrease the dimensions. But professionally, it is something you would not wish to do, as quality will suffer. Remember how a bitmap graphic is created. Each pixel is given a color until the whole picture is built up. You can change the color of the pixel and you can delete the pixel, but if you try to select all the pixels that make up the artwork and tell them to be 300% larger, a process known as **interpolation** takes place. (Here we go, jargon.)

Interpolation describes the transformation between pixels. This is how artwork can be increased or decreased in size. In the case of increasing the size of artwork, pixels are added. This results typically in an "out of focus" effect. You can see all the individual color blocks, as they have simply been made larger. This undesirable effect is referred to as the image appearing **pixelated.** When artwork is decreased in dimensions, pixels are discarded, thereby losing information, which also renders a poorer quality finished image.

Bitmap images are known as **resolution dependent**. This means they are generated using a fixed number of pixels and therefore do not lend themselves well to scaling or printing at a higher resolution than they were intended for.

The Benefits of Vector Graphic Images

If scalability is a disadvantage in a bitmap graphic, it is an absolute boon for a vector graphic. This makes it unparalleled for logos, where multiple sizes will be needed. Because the artwork is stored as a set of instructions, it is a simple case of the application rewriting the instructions.

Instead of:

```
SQUARE 75 75
```

The instruction becomes:

```
SQUARE 300 300
```

The logo is scaled up 400%. There is no loss of quality as the artwork has been reproduced from scratch simply by the rewriting of the instruction set.

In addition to scalability, vectors are generally smaller in file size compared to bitmaps, a clear advantage when it comes to use on the Internet (assuming suitable plug-ins are installed on the users computer). The actual size of the vector depends on the complexity of the artwork. Each line or shape requires more instructions to describe it, so a highly complex vector could still grow to an undesirable file size.

Whereas bitmap images are known as **resolution dependent,** vector images are known as **resolution independent** as they can be scaled endlessly and printed on any printer at any resolution without loss of quality.

We know Illustrator is a vector application. We also know that if you want to produce graphics for the Web, the main supported image formats are all bitmap formats. Does that mean if you want to make beautiful buttons for your web site you must rush out and buy a bitmap application? Certainly not, everything you need is here in Illustrator. Illustrator can convert the vector artwork you produce into a bitmap. This procedure is known as **rasterization**. Despite the name, it's quite painless and simple to do. You may remember seeing this word mentioned earlier when I was listing the various ways in which bitmaps are described – raster, meaning a bitmap. All makes sense now doesn't it? Doesn't it…?

We are going to run through the process of rasterization in a later chapter, but at this stage it is important to gain an understanding of another term, which is closely connected with rasterization, anti-aliasing. Anti-aliasing will have a major impact on the way your converted graphic will look. To understand what anti-aliasing is and why it is necessary, we need to think about how a bitmap is created on the screen once again and compare that to a vector image equivalent.

In this following image I have zoomed in on a circle. The smooth edges confirm that this is a vector graphic.

This is a bitmap image of the same shape at the same magnification. Look carefully at the edge of the circle and you will be able to see the pixels in the bitmap, which gives the characteristic jagged edge or staircase effect.

So how do we go about creating smooth edges to our shapes in bitmap applications? Sadly, it's not possible to color in half a pixel. You either color the whole pixel or nothing at all. This is why you see the "staircase" effect when trying to create curves. **Anti-aliasing** provides the answer. The image below is a close up of the same bitmap image, but with anti-aliasing applied. Anti-aliasing adds extra pixels around the edges of the shape and uses transitional colored pixels to blend the shape into its background. It's another form of the **interpolation** discussed earlier. It's actually all an illusion. Our shape is just as jagged as it was originally, except the jagged edges are no longer visible when viewed at 100% due to the extra pixels and color transitions.

The image below shows the bitmap at 100%. This is how it will look on the Web or in print.

Now that small but critical technical point is out of the way, we can have a look at what happens when you rasterize a vector. The file Pixel_preview.ai contains a simple oval shaped web button graphic that will ultimately be rasterized so that we can add it to a web page. We now know that as soon as the vector artwork is rasterized, we will lose the beautiful smooth edges and see the jagged pixel edges of a bitmap. We also know this is not a problem because anti-aliasing will take care of the jagged edges by adding extra pixels in transitional colors so that the jagged edge is disguised. When the vector artwork is rasterized, the screen is divided up into an invisible grid of 1/72-inch increments. This invisible grid defines how the anti-aliased pixels will be placed. For this reason these anti-aliased pixels will have an impact on the final quality, position, and size of the converted graphic.

This is not something to be left to chance. Before rasterizing the artwork, it would be useful to see a preview of how Illustrator will deal with this and give us a chance to have some influence on the conversion. That is exactly what we can do by using a **pixel preview**. Let's try this out right now.

1. Open the file called `Pixel_preview.ai` from the download folder.

2. Go to View>Pixel Preview.

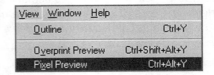

Zoom in to the graphic 800% and try moving the shape by very small amounts. You will notice it snaps to the invisible pixel grid. This can have the effect of making certain anti-aliased pixels disappear. This snapping action is automatically enabled as soon as you go into **pixel preview mode**. We are now going to switch off this snapping action. (You may find you cannot see the whole graphic at this zoom rate, as the palettes and toolbox hide it. This would be a good time to use that neat trick of hiding all the palettes and toolbox by pressing the TAB KEY. Press the same key to reveal them again.)

3. Go to View>Snap to Pixel. When there is no check next to this option, snapping is disabled.

4. Now try moving the shape by about half a pixel. You will find it no longer snaps to the invisible pixel grid and the anti-aliasing changes depending on where you finally position the shape. This results in the edges of the artwork being slightly more or less smooth.

We are talking about a very fine distinction here. A few more or less pixels of anti-aliasing around the graphic may seem like splitting hairs, but attention to detail such as this will help make you stand out from the crowd professionally.

You will get the chance to rasterize some artwork in later chapters, but for the moment, let's take a look at the other methods of viewing your artwork.

Viewing Artwork in Outline and Preview Mode

When you view artwork on the screen, by default you will be in **preview mode**. This means any fill colors, gradients, and patterns in your objects will be visible. The more complex your artwork, the longer it will take for your screen to update and display the art. This can slow down progress on even the fastest of computers. To overcome this, there is the option of viewing your artwork in **outline mode**.

To try these two modes, let's open up a fairly complex file.

- Within the Illustrator 10 application folder you will find a folder named samples. From this folder open the file called `Flower.ai`. The artwork shown below has been generated using an exciting and highly powerful tool called the Gradient Mesh. We'll be looking at this tool in depth in chapter 8, but for the moment we are going to use its results to view the artwork in outline mode.

- Unless you have changed any of the settings you will currently be in **preview mode**. Now go to View>Outline. You are now looking at the basic structure of the artwork without the color fills.

Although this is a complex piece of artwork, most medium-paced computers will be able to manipulate this flower without too much trouble, but imagine a group of these flowers and leaves as well as background scenery. This is when things will start to slow down on your computer and your productivity begins to suffer. This is also when the true benefits of the outline mode will become apparent. By displaying only the outlines, or skeleton of the artwork, your computer does not have to work as hard, so objects can be moved and edited faster.

There are other benefits of using outline mode that will reveal themselves as you begin to progress in Illustrator. One of the most useful is in being able to select "invisible objects". An example of an invisible object is a shape with no outlines or fill color. I know what you're thinking, "If it has no outline or fill, then surely it doesn't exist?" Well, in the real world you would be absolutely right. But, at the risk of sounding a little surreal, for an object to exist in Illustrator it doesn't have to be tangible.

So if you accept that premise, what's the point of an invisible object in the first place? One example is one of the most popular logo formats in the history of advertising and branding – running text around a circle. The text needs to be visible of course, but the original circle does not.

The image below shows the text in the default **preview mode**. The original circle is there, but is not visible, as it has no outline or fill color.

If you now decide you would like to apply a fill color to the invisible circle, you can either try playing the digital version of that well loved children's party game, "pin the tail on the donkey", and keep clicking with your mouse until you strike lucky and get the invisible outline, or go into **Outline mode** as shown below. (I know which method I'd choose.)

Eventually you will want to return to preview mode to view your work efforts. Go to View>Preview. You will now be returned to the default mode and all colors, fills, and patterns will be visible again.

> Here's a helpful little tip that might save you hours of time and money in calling technical help lines. As you begin to concentrate on the creativity aspect of your work and become more involved with advanced tools, it's very easy to forget that you may have gone into outline mode. If you are applying colors and the object to which you are applying them doesn't want to accept them, before you take your computer apart to find the "bug", just check to make sure you are in the right mode. It sounds too simple a mistake to make, but the simple ones are always the ones that will catch you out.

Rulers, Guides, Grids, and Positioning

If you were a designer or a magazine paste-up artist before the advent of computers, you would have had a large desk and an array of gadgets to help you keep your lines and other elements nice and straight, such as rulers, blue pencils, scalpels, French curves (honest), and scissors. Without these tools you would be guessing where to position things. In Illustrator, all these tools exist to simulate their real world counterparts. In fact, the Illustrator version of these tools is far superior, because no one can chew the end of your pencil and your ruler can't get buried under the invoices you're going to pay some day.

We're going to have a look at using the tools that will make your life easier as you design and lay out your print or web pages.

Rulers

Open the file called Layout.ai from the download folder. This file is set up as letter size format in portrait. The first thing we are going to do is display the rulers.

> **1.** Go to View>Show Rulers.

The rulers can also be shown or hidden by using the keyboard shortcut CTRL/CMD+R. They appear at the left and top of the screen. Take a look at the horizontal ruler at the top. This ruler's unit of measurement is points. Below, you will notice that the zero defines the left edge of the page.

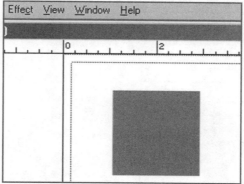

Now look at the vertical ruler on the left. The zero defines the bottom edge of the page. The point at which vertical zero and horizontal zero meet is known unsurprisingly as the **zero point**. So, the zero point for this page is the bottom left corner of the page. This means any objects placed on the page will be measured relative to the bottom left corner of the page. This default comes from the publishing industry where all measurements were taken from the bottom left corner and is also the basis for most graphs. Later you will get the chance to change the zero point and place it anywhere you wish. This flexibility will be particularly useful in the case of creating web pages, where measurements from the top left corner will be more useful.

If you could work only in point measurements you would be severely restricted, and so you have the option of setting up the ruler to display a variety of different units of measurement.

2. Go to Edit>Preferences>Units & Undo.

3. From the dialogue box that appears, select inches from the General drop-down box.

The default measurement is **points,** which is equal to 0.3528 millimeters.
The other options are:

- **Picas** (equal to 12 points or 4.2333 millimetres) – these are not commonly used today.

- **Millimeters**

- **Centimeters**

- **Pixels** – for use on the Web or any work designed for on screen use such as CDs and screen presentations.

Click OK after you have set inches.

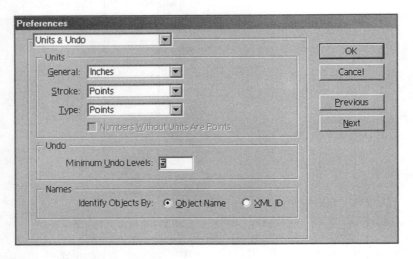

The rulers now display in inches.

4. Move the cursor slowly over the page. You will see a small dotted line on both the vertical and horizontal ruler that moves in unison with the movement of the cursor.

These dotted lines show you the current position of the cursor on the x and y-axis, x being the horizontal axis and y being the vertical. If you were to trying to position something on an exact x and y co-ordinate by looking at the rulers you have probably guessed that it would be very imprecise.

There is of course a much better way to assess an exact point on the screen. We are going to use the **Info Palette**.

Info palette

If you are still working with the default palette set you will see the Info tab in the top right of the screen. If you have closed it down, go to Window>Info. A check next to Info in the window menu means it is already open.

1. If you have not already done so, click the tab labeled Info. On the left of this palette you will see an x and y.

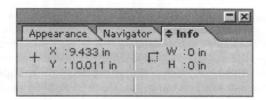

2. Move the cursor around the page as you did previously, but this time look at the x and y fields in the info palette. It's a little like driving without looking through the windshield, but don't worry, there's nothing to it.

3. Move the cursor down to the bottom left corner of the page. Depending on how close you are to the exact corner you will see the x and y reading is something like 0.000 in. You are now on the zero point.

4. Start to move the cursor vertically up the page. If there is no horizontal movement as you drag the mouse, you will only see the y numbers change in the Info palette. Now try dragging the cursor beyond the bottom edge of the page, so the cursor is no longer on the page at all. Rather than the y numbers dropping into a void, the readout now displays negative numbers.

5. Move the cursor horizontally on the page. Only the x numbers will change providing there is no vertical movement in the mouse. It is very difficult to do this, so it is a good exercise to assess whether you've had too much caffeine today.

You may be wondering what that red square in the top left of the page has to do with all this. We are going to find its exact x and y co-ordinate by using the info palette.

1. Using the **Selection** tool from the toolbox, click on the red square and then look at the Info palette.

The figures in the x and y fields are now displaying the co-ordinate for the top left corner of the square. Remember the zero point for this page is the bottom left of the page. So this co-ordinate is a reference relative to that point.

2. Now try moving the square to a different location on the page by clicking and dragging it. The x and y co-ordinates will change accordingly. You will find this function of enormous value as you start to work in earnest.

With the red square still selected, look at the Info palette again and you will see a "W" and "H" on the right of the palette. This displays the width and height of the selected object. The unit of measurement will be same as the setting you applied to the ruler via the Preferences earlier.

3. Now click on the yellow star. The info palette reads 2.5 in. For any irregular shape, the dimensions will describe a square or rectangle that encompasses the shape. This is called the **bounding box** and is depicted by a blue line. If you cannot see the bounding box it will have been disabled. To enable it again go to View>Show Bounding Box. If you see the words Hide Bounding Box, the bounding box is already enabled and will be visible when you select any object.

Guides

There is a rare breed among the human race, that small minority that can pick up a sheet of writing paper, take a calligraphic pen and write in beautiful, uniform, straight lines. For the rest of us who need some assistance in lining up objects, there are **guides**.

Of course, we don't need guides in order to write in straight lines in Illustrator. That happens automatically when we use the text tool, as you will see later. The use of guides in Illustrator is far more wide ranging. For example, if you were creating a business card or letterhead, you may want to line up the logo with a name or telephone number. In the case of a web page, you may want to line up a row of buttons in a navigation bar.

The great thing about guides is they make you feel very special because no one can see them but you. Let me clarify that statement. They are visible in Illustrator, but if you were to print the page you wouldn't see them. If you were producing a web page and viewed the page in a browser such as Microsoft Internet Explorer or Netscape Navigator you wouldn't see them either. They are the perfect unobtrusive designer's friend.

Let's get some practice with guides. The first thing to be aware of before using a guide is that you won't be able to create one unless the rulers are visible. Guides live behind each ruler so they must be visible first. If your rulers are not visible, you can enable them as before from the View Menu.

We will first create a horizontal guide.

1. Using the **Selection** tool, place the cursor on top of the ruler at the top of the page.

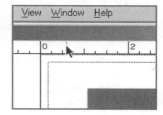

2. Now click and drag towards the middle of the page and you will see a blue guide appear.

Blue is the default color, but you can have other colors if you wish. You will get the opportunity to change colors and styles later. The reason for guides being blue goes back to pre-computer days when guides had to be drawn on the page in blue pencil. When the finished "camera ready" artwork was ready for processing, the blue color was not picked up on film and so the guides became invisible.

When you release the mouse button, your guide locks into place. If you want to move the guide to another location you will find you can't because Illustrator literally has locked it into place. So, before you can reposition the guide you will have to unlock it.

3. Go to View>Guides>Lock Guides. You will see a check against this option. By selecting the option, you remove the check, and disable the lock function. Now you can freely move the guide up or down.

4. Create a second guide by dragging again from the top ruler and position this anywhere on the page. Because the guides are unlocked, you can reposition this guide as you wish.

You may find you have trouble selecting a guide, as it is very thin. The best technique is to look for the feedback you get from the cursor. Click anywhere on the white part of the screen. This deselects any objects and guides that may have been selected. Hover the cursor over either guide without clicking. When you see a small black square appear near the black cursor arrow, as shown here, you are directly over the guide. Now you can click to select it.

When you select the guide, the cursor changes again to a different kind of arrowhead.

This new icon tells you the guide is now selected and can be moved.

Try dragging a couple of guides from the vertical ruler on the left in the same way.

Because the guides are non-printing and not visible in Web browsers you don't have to delete them before publishing your work. However, if you no longer need them, there are several ways to remove them. Try any of the following techniques.

- Select the guide and press the DELETE key on your keyboard.

- Select the guide and drag it back to the ruler from where it came.

- A fast way to remove multiple guides in one command is to go to View>Guides>Clear Guides.

Grids

As an alternative to guides you can use **Grids**. These are less flexible than guides but offer a global page method of lining up elements. The concept is similar to working on a sheet of graph paper. As with guides, grids are non-printing and not visible in Web browsers.

To enable grids:

1. Go to View>Show Grid. As with guides, the grid can be edited to different sizes, colors, and styles.

To change the look and size of the grid perform the following steps:

2. Go to Edit>Preferences>Guides and Grid. This opens the guides and grid dialog box.

3. In the bottom half of the dialog box labeled Grid, the following settings can be changed

    - Color – changes the grids color

    - Style – options are a singe line or a dotted line

    - Gridline Every – defines the amount of space between lines. The default is 1 inch.

    - Subdivisions – defines how each large grid section is subdivided into smaller grids. The default is 8.

- Grids in Back — check this box to place grids behind artwork, otherwise grids will be on top of the artwork.

To hide the grid go to View>Hide Grid.

Smart Guides

This exciting sounding heading is still good old guides but with an element of dynamism thrown in. You may have come across various "smart technologies" in your work or general reading and come to realize that some of them aren't so smart. But take my word for it, this implementation of the word "smart" is actually useful and works. We're going to create some smart guides in a later chapter but for the moment we're just going to see what information they offer.

1. Go to View>Smart Guides. This enables smart guides.

2. Using the **Selection** tool, place the cursor over any edge of the red square, but don't click. You will see the word "path" appear, along with a small blue x.

This tells you that the cursor is over a path or segment of the square. (Paths will be elaborated on later, but in this instance it refers to one edge of the square.)

3. Now place the cursor over any corner point of the square. The word "anchor" appears. This describes an anchor point and is the exact corner of the square.

4. Now place the cursor over the blue x in the center of the square and the word "center" appears, defining the true center of the square.

You can repeat this procedure on any of the objects on the page and even the edges of the page itself. In a later chapter we will use this information to dynamically create a guide for aligning new objects with existing objects. The main benefits of this tool over the standard guides are speed and the ability to create guides between objects at difficult angles.

Selecting Artwork

You are ahead of the game as far this section goes because you already selected an object when we looked at the Info palette. We are now going to look at the other selection tools and how they can help you to work more efficiently.

The role of the **Selection** tool is to select things. This is all it does. I'm not being derogatory about this humble tool but it does serve a very simple purpose. Let's try it out.

Selection Tool

1. Open the file called Selecting.ai from the download folder.

2. Click on the **Selection** tool in the toolbox. Now click on the orange square and you have a selected object. Now it is selected, you can reposition it and read its position co-ordinates and dimensions in the Info palette as you did earlier.

3. On the page you will see a square with a black outline. Selecting outline-only objects can be a little trickier. Because this square only has an outline, the middle is hollow. To select an outline object, place the cursor over the edge of the black outline and you will see a small black square appear next to the cursor. This is exactly the same as when you selected the guide earlier. Now you can click and you will have selected the square.

4. If you no longer want to keep the object selected, either select another object or click anywhere on a blank part of the screen.

5. There will be times when you want to select more than one object at a time. This could be to apply a uniform color or apply some other global transformation. Select the orange square. Now hold down the SHIFT key and click the yellow triangle. As long as the SHIFT key is pressed, you can continue to select objects all day or until the novelty wears off. Beware though. If while the SHIFT key is pressed you select an object, which has already been selected, that object will become deselected. This of course can work in your favor if you wish to deselect something that you didn't mean to select.

There is a faster way to select multiple objects but it depends on the placement of those objects on the page. The technique is known as "dragging a marquee" and is based on the notion of dragging an invisible rectangular area that encompasses the objects you wish to select.

Let's say you want to select both the orange square and the yellow triangle, but the SHIFT key is away being serviced.

Position the cursor somewhere to the upper left of the orange square, then click and drag diagonally towards the bottom right of the yellow triangle.

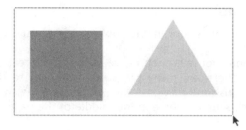

As long as the objects are touched or surrounded by the dotted marquee line that appeared as you dragged with the selection tool, they will become selected.

When would this technique not work? If you wanted to select the square, the triangle and the star in the top right of the page, but not the tree branch in the middle. The Selection tool can only create the marquee in a square or rectangular shape, so there would be no way of achieving this without also selecting the tree branch.

Does this mean if there are 37 different objects in different locations on the page and you want to select only 26 of them you will have to use the SHIFT key and make 26 selections?

Thankfully not, as we have a different selection tool known as the **Lasso** tool. The concept of a lasso is exactly the way this tool is used. You use it as if you were drawing a shape on the screen, enclosing all the objects you wish to select within your loop.

Lasso Tool

Try using the lasso tool now to select the star, triangle, and orange square.

1. Select the **Lasso** tool in the toolbox.

As you can see, there are two Lasso tools in this toolset. We want the black-headed arrow.

2. Start with the cursor above the upper left of the star and then drag so that you encompass the orange square and the triangle, but avoid the tree branch, as shown here.

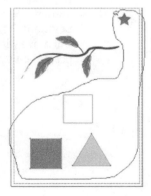

Direct Selection Tool

Next door to the selection tool in the toolbox is the **Direct Selection Tool**.

Whereas the selection tool selects an entire object, the direct selection tool selects only parts of an object. There are many times you will want to do this. One of the most common is to select just one side or corner of a square. As an example, we are going to manipulate the black square outline in the middle of the page.

1. Select the **Direct Selection** tool. Now click on any edge of the square with the black outline.

You will notice five white points appear called **anchor points**. We will be looking at anchor points in depth shortly. These anchor points define each corner and the center of the object. When an anchor point is white it is not selected.

2. Click the top right anchor point. The point goes blue, signifying it has been selected, unlike the other four points, which remain white and are, therefore, not selected. This is how the tool gets its name. The tool *directly* selects the clicked portion only. Now that you have selected one anchor point, you can drag it and the other points of the square remain unaffected.

When using this tool in combination with the shift key, it is possible to select multiple anchor points in the same way as when you selected multiple objects with the selection tool.

3. With the single anchor point still selected, keep the SHIFT key pressed and select two more anchor points on the square.

By dragging any one point, the other two selected points will move at the same time. Clicking the center anchor point selects all the points of the square simultaneously, which of course has the same effect as using the standard selection tool.

4. Click anywhere on a blank part of the screen to deselect the object. Now select any straight edge of the square. (You might have a misshapen square by now.) By clicking on any edge, you will automatically select the anchor point at either end of the edge. Any edge with an anchor point at either end is called a **Segment**. You can drag this segment and the two anchor points at either end will move with it, as shown in the diagram below. With this segment still selected, press the DELETE key on the keyboard and that segment only will be deleted.

I created an object with only an outline for this exercise because using the Direct Selection tool with outlines is easier than using it with a filled object. To demonstrate this, try clicking on the orange square with the direct selection tool. If you clicked anywhere on the main body of the square you will notice the five anchor points appear, but they will all be blue, which of course means they are all selected. By using the direct selection tool it is assumed you only want to select one or a range of anchor points, but not the whole shape. So when using this tool on a filled object, click on the very edge only. Once again look for feedback from the cursor. When you hover the cursor over the edge of the object you will see a small back square near the cursor that signifies you are in the correct location to click. When you see a small white square near the cursor it signifies you are directly over an anchor point or the center of the object.

Direct Select Lasso Tool

I have a sneaking suspicion that you have already worked out what this one is going to do. It's really a hybrid made up from the previous tools. Here's the scenario. You have a filled square and you want to select three corner anchor points only. You already know that you could use the direct selection tool and the SHIFT key to select all the points you want. But while you are carrying out this laborious process, life is passing you by and there's still so much you want to achieve. So the answer to your dreams is the aptly titled **Direct Select Lasso** tool.

1. This tool, as seen earlier, shares the same position as the lasso tool in the toolbox. So you will need to keep the mouse button pressed over the lasso tool until the fly-out appears and then select the **Direct Select Lasso** tool.

2. We are going to select the top left, top right, and bottom right anchor points of the orange square. Place your cursor somewhere above the top left corner of the top left anchor point and then drag your lasso encompassing the other two points. The diagram below demonstrates the route I took to make the selection. The added benefit of this tool is that it doesn't matter whether the object is a filled shape or just an outline, only the surrounded anchor points are selected.

3. Now that the anchor points are selected you can return to the **Direct Selection Tool** and edit the points as one entity.

Grouping objects

Open the file called Group.ai from the download folder.

Quite often when you need to create a piece of artwork, you will find it easier to build up the work from a number of individual components rather than using one large single piece of complex art. The matchstick man in this file is a good example of this situation.

Six objects make up the man. If you want to move the man somewhere else you will have to select all of the objects that make up the man first, using one of the techniques that you have learned. OK, it's not the end of the world, but what if you have a lot of matchstick men and you want to keep repositioning them? It would soon get tiresome.

The answer is to **group** multiple individual objects so they become one entity. By grouping objects, you combine them as if they were one object. This does not damage the artwork in any way, they are still independent objects, but grouped together for convenience and functionality. That's what we'll do now with the matchstick man.

1. Select all the objects that make up the man.

2. Go to Objects>Group. Now the man is one and can be moved as a single entity.

You might have noticed that the leg on the right is lower than the leg on the left. See what happens when I don't use guides! Because the objects have been grouped, we can no longer access individual shapes with the selection tool. Of course we could ungroup it. Let's do that now.

3. Make sure the man is selected and go to Objects>Ungroup. Now we are back where we started.

4. There must be a better way you may be thinking? There is. First group all the objects again. Now use the **Direct Selection** tool to select the leg on the right and you'll find you can select it as if it was completely independent. It hasn't affected the fact that your objects are a group. This is another great use of the **Direct Selection** tool.

Group Selection Tool

Now, let's look at a more complex group. Go back to the file called Selecting.ai.

In case you thought the tree branch was just a frilly bit of embellishment, we are going to use it to work with a group of groups. First of all, let me dissect how it was constructed.

Each leaf is composed of:

- The green base shape
- Three pale green highlights
- A dark green stem

These three components were then grouped.

The three leaf groups were then grouped.

Finally, the three leaf groups and the branch were grouped.

So, we have three groups in total:

- Group a – Leaf, highlights, and stem.

- Group b – Three leaves.

- Group c – Leaves and branch.

Accessing each group or component could be something of a trial. This is quite a commonplace scenario in complex artwork, but we have at our disposal the **Group Selection** tool. The name is a dead give away. Let's see how it works.

The **Group Selection** tool resides in the same toolbox location as the Direct Selection tool. It is differentiated by a plus sign in the top right corner.

1. With the **Group Selection** tool, click on one of the highlights on any of the leaves. This tool will drill down through as many levels of groups as it needs to in order to select the item on which you click. This highlight is now selected and can be edited as required.

2. Click the same place a second time. The next level group has now been selected, the entire leaf group.

3. Click the same place a third time. The other two leaves are selected that make up the next level group.

4. Click the same place a fourth time and the leaves and branch group are now selected.

Each consecutive click selects another group within the nested hierarchy of groups. If you were to deselect everything and then click on the brown branch once, you would only select that item. Click a second time and you would select the three grouped leaves also, so now you have everything selected.

This is a useful tool whose value outweighs its apparent simplicity when working with complex artwork.

It should be noted that when you have a group of groups, if you select any one group within the hierarchy and ungroup it, only that group is ungrouped, leaving the other groups intact.

Locking Artwork

One of the most infuriating things that can happen in a working day is setting up your page or web design, and then by accident moving an element and having to reposition it. It's very easy to overcome this by **Locking** the elements that you have finished with, to safeguard from accidental editing.

1. Select the tree branch artwork.

2. Go to Object>Lock>Selection. The entire tree branch group is now safe from editing. Just a helpful reminder here. You need to remember you have locked it, otherwise when you next try to select it and can't, it looks suspiciously like a devious strain of a virus.

3. To unlock the artwork, go to Object>Unlock All.

Artwork Components

We've already started to look at some of these components. We will now study them in a little more depth, which will help you to understand more about how objects are created and the kind of thinking pattern you will need to adopt when planning to draw certain shapes. In particular, we are going to look at:

■ Anchor Points

■ Path Segments

■ Direction Lines

■ Direction Points

Open the file called Art_components.ai from the download folder.

Anchor points are fundamental elements of every Illustrator object with the exception of text. Even the most basic object must consist of at least two anchor points. This example would describe a straight line. The line itself is the **Path Segment**. In the last exercise you manipulated a square and found this had four anchor points, one to define each corner, and four segments in between each pair of anchor points. The circle also consisted of four anchor points. So if both the square and circle were composed of four anchor points each, how is it decided that one is a square and one round? The answer is the type of anchor point. There are two different types:

- Smooth anchor points

- Corner anchor points

Take a look at the file that you just opened. On the right of the page I have created a semi-circle and a triangle. They both have three anchor points, but are completely different.

We are going to manipulate the individual anchor points, so the tool to use is? Of course, you knew all the time. The **Direct Selection** tool.

1. With the Direct Selection tool, click on one of the anchor points of the triangle. As you would expect, the anchor point changes to blue as it becomes selected and you can now move it, but nothing else happens. This is a **Corner point**. Typically you will see corner points on squares, triangles, rectangles, and straight lines, but not exclusively, as we will see shortly.

Now click on the edge of the semi-circle. You will see the three anchor points appear. Click on the topmost anchor point. This is a **Smooth point**, as the name suggests you will find smooth points on objects with rounded edges. There is also another component that makes up this smooth point. Emanating from the anchor point are two **Direction Lines**. Direction lines move like the handlebars on a bike. Clicking and dragging the **Direction Point** at the end of each line, as shown below, maneuvers the **Direction Lines**. Try dragging the point clockwise and then counter-clockwise. The direction lines move symmetrically.

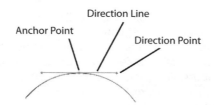

2. Now click on the edge of the heart shape. Remember it's important to click on the edge because this is a filled shape and not just an outline. What are we looking at? A rounded shape or a sharp cornered shape? Well, it was a sort of

trick question because it is both. It's a rounded shape but the bottom of the heart has a sharp point, as does the top middle of the heart.

3. Click on the topmost anchor point. You should now see the **Direction Lines** emanating from the anchor point. Even though this anchor point is within a rounded object, it is actually a corner point and the result is the "v" shape at the top of the heart.

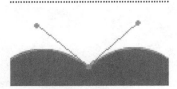

4. Click on one of the direction points and drag it clockwise. You will notice the other direction line does not move symmetrically as in the case of the smooth anchor point.

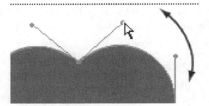

Drag Direction point clockwise

It is this combination of smooth points and corner points, direction lines and direction points that make up the myriad of objects that can be created with Illustrator. You will get the opportunity to work with all these components as well as making your own objects as we progress through the book.

Arranging the Stacking Order of Objects

Imagine a world where no two objects can collide. Cars, trains, fish, people all moving happily in different directions. If their paths do happen to intersect, instead of a collision-taking place, one passes in front and one passes behind. It would be as if each object existed in its own plane. No other object can infringe upon another's plane, so a collision becomes a physical impossibility. This utopian vision is exactly the way Illustrator works. Everything you create occupies its own unique plane and objects will happily pass in front or behind each other in perfect social harmony.

Let's get some experience of this principle.

Open the file called Stacking.ai from the download folder.

You can probably see the problem with this artwork. It's either a Picasso type abstract piece where fruit and vegetables are floating in space and time or I've got my stacking order completely wrong. That's one of the problems with this concept. If each object occupies its own plane or stacking level and several objects exist, then one of those objects will be right at the back of the stack and one at the front.

The stacking level order of an object is defined by the order in which it was created. Imagine you are going to draw three items of fruit, for example, an apple, an orange, and a pear. First you create the apple, then the orange, and, finally, the pear. The apple will now be at the back of the stack, the pear at the front, and the orange sandwiched between the two.

In the file you have open, the fruit bowl was created first, so this appears at the back of the stack and any attempt to display realism is in tatters. But this is easily remedied.

1. Select the fruit bowl.

2. Go to Object>Arrange>Bring to front.

Bring to front skips ahead of all other objects, irrespective of their stacking order and positions itself at the front of the stack.

The green tomato was created immediately before the red tomato, so the red tomato occupies the stack immediately in front of the green one. If you decide you want to position the green tomato in front of the red one and expose it to a bit more sun for ripening, you couldn't use the previous command, as that would place it in front of the bowl also. Instead, to move it one step at a time:

3. Select the green tomato and go to Object>Arrange>Bring Forward. Now the green tomato jumps forward one step only.

Take a look at the other options:

- Send to Back – this sends the object right to the back of the stack.

- Send Backward – just like Bring Forward, this will move the object one step at a time, but this time going back through the stack.

The order in which you create artwork really doesn't matter as you have complete flexibility in rearranging things later.

Introduction to the Layers Palette

Hopefully by now you are beginning to realize what a great idea the stacking order of objects is. It provides for endless flexibility and allows you to change the composition of your artwork at will.

What if I was to say it doesn't stop there, but there is an even more powerful way to order, restack, and compose artwork? Perhaps you are overcome by emotion and excitement at the prospect of this, and you have good reason to be. **Layers** add a whole new dimension to the structure of your artwork. Once again, I must refer back to those days of old when computers didn't exist.

As a graphic designer you would create the basic artwork on a sheet of art board. Let's say you are designing a record album cover. At the first creative meeting the client says "love the concept, but can you airbrush in the planet Jupiter in mid explosion". After three weeks of painstaking work you deliver the artwork of Jupiter exploding and the client says, "nice artwork, but we've changed our mind about Jupiter exploding, can we go back to the first idea". Not an uncommon scenario, but because you are a professional graphic designer you don't have to throw the artwork in the bin and start again. You have drawn the exploding Jupiter on a separate sheet of transparent acetate and laid it over the original art board. If the client wants a peaceful Jupiter, you just throw away the sheet of acetate. Following this principle you can add asteroids, aliens, sheep, anything at all, each drawn on its own sheet of acetate and, therefore, not affecting the work beneath.

What a great idea you're thinking. Why don't they use that idea in Illustrator? They do, it's called **Layers**. Everything you have leaned so far about the stacking order of objects is embodied in a layer. Each layer will have its own objects and they will reside on their own unique stacking level as we have already seen. Layers follow the same concept of each occupying their own unique plane, just like the sheets of acetate being stacked one upon the other.

Let's get some hands on experience of working with layers.

Open the file called Museum.ai from the Illustrator application sample art folder.

Don't be overwhelmed by the sheer weight of artwork in this file. We've moved on from squares and circles, but it's very easy to navigate around the artwork because multiple layers have been used. Each group of elements on this web page artwork have been arranged on their own layer.

Take a look at the **Layers Palette**. If you haven't changed the default layout of the palettes it should be towards the bottom right of the screen. If you have closed it, go to Window>Layers.

You can probably see only a few of the layers within the palette, so we are going to expand the palette revealing all the layers in this file.

Window	Help	
New Window		
Cascade		
Tile		
Arrange Icons		
Actions		
Align		Shift+F7
Appearance		Shift+F6
Attributes		F11
✔ Brushes		F5
✔ Color		F6
Document Info		
Gradient		F9
✔ Info		F8
✔ Layers		F7

1. Position the Layers palette in an area of the screen where you will have room to expand it, then position the cursor over the bottom right edge of the palette until a twin headed arrow appears. When this appears, drag down vertically and the palette will expand. Stretch it enough so you can see all the individual layers.

Each layer has a unique name to identify its contents. The layer at the top of the stack in the palette will display its artwork in front of everything else. It's helpful to think of those sheets of acetate again. The topmost sheet of acetate will display its artwork in front of everything else.

2. To the left of the layers palette, you will see rows of eye icons. These eyes will show or hide the artwork on that layer only. To hide the artwork on the topmost layer called NavBar, click the eye alongside that layer.

3. To make the artwork visible again, click the empty gray box where the eye appeared originally.

Selecting Artwork Within Layers

1. On the left of the page you will see a gray stone column piece of artwork. Select this column with the Selection tool and then look in the layers palette. Automatically, the layer called SubNav containing the image has become the active layer. When layers change to dark blue (assuming the default display color settings have not been changed) in the palette it signifies this is the current activated layer and any artwork created on this layer will reside here. The stone column artwork resides on the SubNav layer, which is why this layer suddenly became activated.

2. Now click on the word Home in the top left corner of the page. The layer called NavBar becomes activated, as this is where the "home" artwork resides.

Each layer has many individual objects within it. As you have seen, it is possible to simply select the artwork on the page and the corresponding layer will become activated automatically. However, you can also select individual objects from within the layer palette.

3. The NavBar layer contains a number of text buttons that run across the top of the screen. We are going to select some of these, but through the layer palette. In the layer palette, identify the NavBar layer. A gray arrowhead can be seen to the left of the layer name. Click this arrowhead and the layer expands to reveal **sub layers**. Each sub layer contains an individual object.

4. Click on the white circle in the sub layer called STORE. You will see the text object STORE becomes selected at the top of the page.

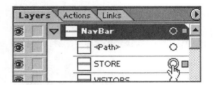

5. Now, click on the white circle in the sub layer called VISITORS. You will now see the text object VISITORS becomes selected at the top of the page. When you have finished editing within this layer, it would be a good idea to collapse the layer again so we can only see the main layers without the sub layers.

6. In the NavBar layer click the gray arrowhead, which is now pointing downward. This closes the sub layers.

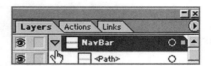

Changing the Stacking Order of Layers

Just as you can change the stacking order of objects within a layer, you can also change the stacking order of the entire layer. Let's say you want to place all the artwork on the Logo Bar layer behind the artwork on the Mask layer.

1. In the Layers palette, click and drag the layer called Logo Bar downward. As you drag, the cursor changes to a clenched fist and you will see a double black line appear below each layer as you pass it. When the double black line appears below the layer called Mask, release the mouse button.

The artwork on the page is no longer visible as it is hidden behind the artwork of the Mask layer.

None of this is permanent if you don't want it to be. To restack layers, just drag them up or down as required.

Outline and Preview Mode in Layers

We've looked at how to view artwork in preview and outline modes. However, when you have multiple layers it would be useful to be able to view just the current layer with all its colors intact and relegate all other layers that you are not working on to outline mode. This handy function is thankfully catered for. We are going to turn all layers except the Logo Bar layer into outline mode.

1.   Select the Logo Bar layer. It changes color.

2.   Click the black arrow button in the top right of the layer palette.

3.   Select Outline Others.

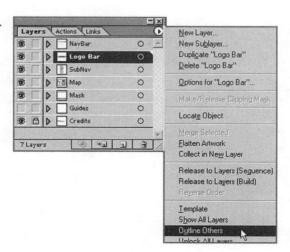

4. To revert to all layers in preview mode, click the same black arrow in the layers palette and select **Preview all layers**.

As you develop your skills in Illustrator you will find the functionality offered in layers becomes increasingly indispensable. In Chapter 12, you will get the opportunity to consolidate your current knowledge of layers and learn more about their role in artwork creation.

Summary

In this chapter we have looked at the important distinction between vector and bitmap graphics and how they relate to Illustrator. This distinction will always be a fundamental aspect of computer artwork and your knowledge will enable you to assess what kind of artwork you are looking at on screen without any doubt.

We have also examined the use of rulers, grids, guides, and the Info palette. These apparently basic tools are critical in setting the stage prior to creating your artwork.

You have also gained an overview of the different viewing modes, the various selection tools, their function and when each one should be used. Using these tools you can now select the different components that make up Illustrator artwork, and organize that artwork into groups and rearrange it on different levels.

You have also been introduced to the basic concept of layers and how you can select artwork within the Layers palette as well as hide, change the stacking order, and view artwork in outline mode.

This combination of basic skills that you have learned so far is a solid foundation for learning Illustrator. You should now have an understanding of some of the most fundamental tools and concepts in the program. In the next chapter we are going to begin producing some artwork of your own.

3 Creating Shapes

What We'll Cover in this Chapter:

- *Creating Basic shapes*

- *Rectangles, rounded rectangles and squares*

- *Ellipses and circles*

- *Irregular shapes: polygons, stars and spirals*

- *Straight lines and arc segments*

- *Grids: the Rectangular and Polar Grid tools*

At last that time has finally arrived. This is the chapter where you roll up your sleeves, get those hands dirty and start to draw. This is also the time that you finally get to meet George and Lucy, and start building that design for them.

We'll be introducing you to the various basic shape tools in Illustrator, then multi-sided polygons and stars, lines, arcs and spirals – and then finally we'll move onto creating rectangular and polar grids.

On Your Marks...

Just to make sure that there is no misunderstanding as we start to create these shapes what I'll suggest we do is all set our application to be using the same units of measurement. For the major part of this book, we'll be working in standard US letter paper size, with inches as our **General** unit of measurement, and points for both **Stroke** (outline) and **Type**, so let's get that done now.

What we will actually be doing is changing the Units Preferences for the entire application and for all documents that we create from this point on, and there is a special way to do this – we have to change the Preferences with no document open. This will create an application wide change in our set-up, otherwise if we changed the Preferences within a document, those changes would be relevant only to that document.

■   Launch Adobe Illustrator if it is not already running on your machine. If you have any documents open, close them so that all you are looking at is the Illustrator menu bar, toolbox and various palettes.

■   Choose Edit > Preferences > Units & Undo. Notice that as you look at the menu, the majority of the options are grayed out, and therefore unavailable to you at this moment.

■   Once you have chosen Units & Undo from the Preferences sub-menu, another dialog box, as illustrated below opposite, will appear. Set your General units to inches by choosing Inches from the drop-down menu, but leave the units for both the Stroke and Type at Points because this is how we generally measure the weight of outlines and the size of text in print. Of course, if you were designing a document for a web site you would be working in pixels, but now we are setting preferences for the entire application and not for the creation of a specific document.

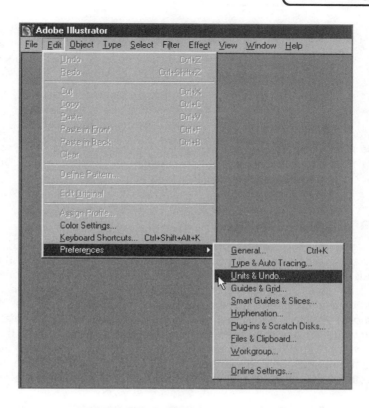

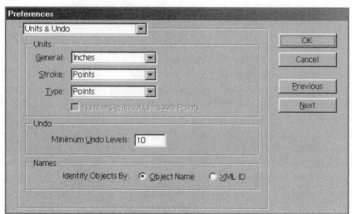

■ You'll also notice that there is a preference for the Undo Levels that you can set. While you might be tempted to push that limit up really high, remember that you are asking Illustrator to keep in memory more and more of the things you have done in the document and that could slow down your machine's performance. The default number of Undo levels is 5, but as I can assume fairly safely that because you are reading this book that you are a new-comer to Illustrator, let's just push that value up to 10. Once you feel more confident, you can always come back and change the value.

- Click OK, and we're ready to begin.

Before we start doodling, you should create a new document – File > New (CTRL/CMD+N). The Name, Size, Orientation, and Color Mode don't matter here, as we'll not be saving this document. It's only for you to practice your skills as we introduce new tools. But notice, your unit of measurements should be in inches.

Creating Basic Shapes

What I'll introduce you to now is the basic shape creation tools – the rectangles, rounded rectangles, and ellipses. Although simple in shape and in creation, these shapes form the basis of most complex logos, illustrations, and web designs that you see out there. Think of an instantly recognizable brand logo, look carefully at its outline shape, and then try and break it down into shape elements – circles, squares, and so on. You can do this with almost any object. With any luck, you should be able to see that many of those everyday forms are actually composed of these primitive shapes – in fact, that's how many of us draw even when we draw freehand with old-fashioned pencil and paper. Rough in those primitives, and then refine the outline shape afterwards. These shapes are, in many instances, your building blocks. Not convinced? Have a look at the example below:

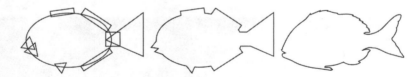

On the left you see a combination of rectangles, ellipses and triangles, which if you stretch your imagination just a little, should look vaguely like a tropical fish. In the second illustration, you see how the shapes have been molded into an outline using one of the functions you'll meet in Chapter 6. Finally in the right-hand illustration you should clearly see the outline of the fish after we have tweaked its shape, using path-editing skills that you will learn at the end of this chapter, and continue to develop throughout the rest of the book. And yes, you will be drawing this fish in a later chapter.

Creating Primitive Shapes

To display the flyout containing the primitive creation tools on your screen, firstly locate the **Rectangle** tool on the toolbox.

Click and hold your mouse down on the **Rectangle** tool until the tool flyout appears. You can choose to display the flyout palette as illustrated below by moving your mouse over the tearoff on the extreme right and then releasing the mouse, or you can choose to display the chosen tool on the toolbox by moving your mouse over it and, when it is highlighted, releasing the mouse.

The tools we are focusing on now are the primitive shapes on the left of the flyout - from left to right the **Rectangle** tool, the **Rounded Rectangle** tool, and the **Ellipse** tool. (You'll meet the other members of the flyout as and when we need their services.) These three tools all function in a very similar manner, so it makes sense to discuss them as a group.

There are two ways that you can create these basic shapes – one is dynamically, by clicking and dragging on the page, and the other is by specifying dimensions for your shape. Neither one is the more correct method, it really depends on what type of artwork you want to create.

Before we start creating, I suggest you press the letter D on the keyboard. This resets the colors to the standard white fill, black stroke. If you're not yet happy using all these shortcuts, click the little black and white square on the toolbox as illustrated below.

Default Fill and Stroke (D) ————

- To draw a primitive shape, simply select the relevant tool by clicking on it, and then click and drag diagonally on the Artboard. When the outline marquee that Illustrator draws as you drag the cursor is the desired size and shape, release the mouse, and there you have it – one shape. I suggest you try this out by selecting firstly the **Rectangle tool** (M) and drawing a shape, then the **Rounded Rectangle**, and then the **Ellipse**. You should be convinced by now that they work in a similar fashion.

Click with the
cursor here

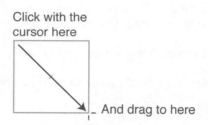

And drag to here

- To draw a shape by specifying measurements, select the tool and click, but don't drag, on the Artboard. As you release the mouse, a dialog box appears. Enter the desired measurements into the Width and Height fields, and click OK or press the RETURN/ENTER key. A small tip – if you want a shape with the same width and height measurement, just enter it into the Width field, and then click on the word Height. Illustrator will copy the precise values into the Height field for you. Try this with the rectangle tool, and you'll have drawn a square.

  If you want to draw an object with equal width and height measurements without specifying them beforehand, hold down the SHIFT key as you drag diagonally to create your shape – you must release the mouse button before you release the SHIFT key. Similarly, if you want to draw a shape from the center, hold down the ALT/OPTION key as you drag. As before, release the mouse button before you release the ALT/OPTION key.

"So, if I want to draw a symmetrical shape from the center..." Yes, you've got it – hold down both the SHIFT and the ALT/OPTION key.

Practice these techniques with rectangles and ellipses. The **Rounded Rectangle** tool works in a very similar way, but with one added complication – specifying the rectangle's roundness.

- Select the **Rounded Rectangle** tool, and click on the Artboard to display the Options dialog box. Note the new field at the bottom of the dialog box – Corner Radius. This is where you specify how rounded the corners will be. The greater the value, the more the corner will be rounded.

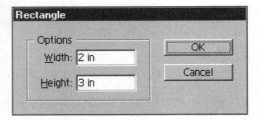

- And if you wish to control the corner radius as you dynamically draw your rounded rectangles, there are keyboard modifiers that you can use. Remember, these keys only work while you still have the mouse button depressed, you cannot use them to alter the corner radius after the shape has been created.

- Hold down the UP arrow to increase the corner radius.

- Hold down the DOWN arrow to decrease the corner radius.

- Press the L<small>EFT</small> arrow to create a shape with minimal corner radius – this normally results in a standard rectangle.

- Press the R<small>IGHT</small> arrow to modify the shape so that the corner radius is set at the maximum level.

Creating Polygons and Stars

You've mastered drawing the most basic of shapes now, so we'll move on from the four-sided type, to the multi-sided ones – stars and polygons. Remember, however, to bring all those skills you've just learnt with you, as the **Polygon** and **Star** tools function in a very similar way.

The **Polygon** tool and the **Star** tool look like these:

You're getting familiar with how these tools work, and I know you're already pre-empting me and thinking your way through how to draw polygons and stars, but just in case, let's mention those points again:

- To draw a shape dynamically, you click and drag until it is the required shape. Yet, there is a difference when compared to how the rectangles and ellipses were created. Note as you click and drag, that unlike the previous tools which drew from the edge of the shape, these tools start from the center and draw outwards as you drag.

- To set the exact measurements, you click on the Artboard, but do not drag, and the relevant Options dialog box is displayed.

Let's have a look at the Polygon dialog box:

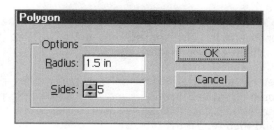

I heard that "aargh" as you saw the Radius field. Panic over – promise. This is no return to those math classes. **Radius** just means the measurement from the center of the polygon to each lines endpoint, and the Sides field indicates the number of sides in your polygon. But to be totally honest, it is seldom that you will approach your illustrations in such a clinical manner, and more often than not you will be drawing these shapes dynamically.

While we're on the subject of math, let's have a look at the **Star** tool Options dialog box.

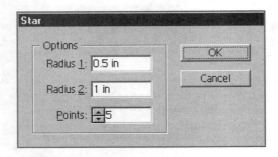

Double math? Not only do you have to contend with one radius, but they've now introduced a second! Again, don't get too worried about the high school connotations of these terms. Simply put, Radius 1 refers to the innermost points of the star, and Radius 2 refers to the outermost points of the star. Hopefully, the diagram below will allay those fears.

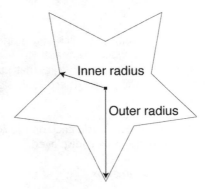

With all the tools discovered thus far, there's always been the use of the SHIFT key to constrain, either to a perfect circle or square, and ALT/OPTION to draw from the center, but from hereon in, things get a little more interesting.

As we mentioned earlier, the star and the polygon have characteristics in common, so we'll discuss their common ground together; and then add a little note on other features. I suggest that with each of the modifiers introduced below, you try them out firstly on the **Polygon** tool, and then repeat the process for the **Star** tool.

- With your Artwork file active, we're about to delete all the other doodles you may have created thus far. Apologies if there was a Picasso in the making. Choose Select > All (CTRL/CMD+A) and press the DELETE/BACKSPACE key to clear the screen.

- Select the **Polygon** tool, and start to drag – whatever you do, do not release the mouse button.

- Press the UP arrow repeatedly – do you see that you are adding sides to the polygon? In fact, you could keep on going until it looked like a circle. (Not that you'd want to.) And, yes, if you try this with the **Star** tool, you'll find it works in exactly the same manner.

- If you can increase the number of sides dynamically, you just know that there has to be a comparable way to decrease the number of sides. With either tool active, start to draw a shape and then press the DOWN arrow repeatedly, and you're reducing the number of sides. Keep going – remember the minimum number of sides a polygon or star may have is three – now you know how to create a triangle! Keep that mouse button down!

- Hold down the SHIFT key, and note how the base of the shape is aligned horizontally with the base of the page. You can let go of the mouse button now!

You may remember that the most obvious difference between the **Polygon** and **Star** tools when you looked at their Options dialog boxes was the fact that the **Star** tool has two radii. Therefore, logically, there must be a way to control that dynamically too.

- With the **Star** tool, click and drag with the mouse to create the initial shape. With the mouse button still down, press the CTRL/CMD key and drag with the mouse. Note how the inner radius has been pegged at the point at which you held down the CTRL/CMD key. The result is a spiky star. Release the CTRL/CMD key and note that the inner radius will increase as you drag, but the star is still spiky. Mouse button still down, there's one more option to discuss here.

- Hold down the ALT/OPTION key and notice the effect it has on the angle between the points – a bit of a bloated star! And let go of the mouse button now!

Case Study: Drawing Marine Signal Flags

With those simple skills under your belt, you're already in a position to start developing the materials for Marine Quest. Lucy and George have said that they want every piece of material to continue the marine theme, and what better way than to use these international marine flags on various components. I'm not sure if you're familiar with the flags, so here's a brief explanation.

These flags are international signals used by ships at sea. Used individually or in combination they have special meanings, and they can also be used to spell out short messages. Think of it as a double benefit, not only are you learning about Illustrator; but also you will pick up some marine knowledge along the way as well. This means that next time you pass a boat showing the following flags in combination, you don't just walk on by – they spell out PARTY!

What we will be doing in this exercise is drawing a number of the simple flags first. Then we'll return to our studies, learn a few more skills, and then draw a few more of the flags. So, let's do it.

1. Open the file `Flags.ai`.

2. Ensure that you have **Smart Guides** on by going to the View menu and checking that there is a tick next to Smart Guides.

3. Set your colors back to default fill and stroke, by pressing D, or clicking on the small white and black squares icon on the toolbox as we did before.

4. Display the Layers palette, and make sure that the Drawing Layer is visible (an eye is displayed in the first column) unlocked (there is no padlock in the second column) and active (click on the layer name to highlight it).

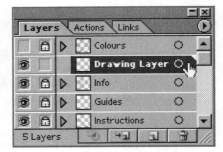

The Q Flag

To make your navigation of these 36 flags a little easier, I've created **Views** for you. This is a new skill for you, and we will explain how to generate your own later on in the book, but for the moment, just take advantage of the **Views** I've produced here.

Q Flag

1. At the very bottom of the View menu, you should notice a number of views, with the first being Q Flag. Choose this Q Flag option, and you will be zoomed in on that part of the illustration.

2. Select the **Rectangle** tool (M) from the toolbox, and position your cursor at the top left-hand corner of the guide you see on screen. To make sure that you are exactly in position, keep an eye out for the **Smart Guide** telling you that you are over an anchor point.

3. Click and drag in a diagonal direction as indicated by the arrow, until your cursor is over the bottom right hand corner anchor, and then release the mouse button. You've just created the first part of your design project – you've created the Q flag! You may be a little disappointed because we're not yet into coloring up our flags, but you can do that in the next chapter.

4. Save the file.

The H Flag

Let's go and do another one – the H Flag. The view has been created, so switch easily to it by choosing H Flag from the View menu. We'll create this flag slightly differently – just to stretch those skills a little – we'll specify measurements and use another handy shortcut to make both parts of the flag painlessly.

H Flag

1. Switch to the H Flag view, and ensure that you still have the **Rectangle** tool (M) selected.

2. Move your cursor over the top left-hand corner until the Smart Guides indicate that you are over an anchor, and then click, but do not drag, with the rectangle tool to display the Rectangle Options dialog box.

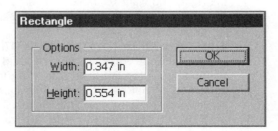

3. In the Width field, enter 0.347 in, and in the Height field, enter 0.554 in. If you have opted to work in another measurement system, don't worry.

By entering the "in" after the measurement, Illustrator knows that you are using inches, and will automatically convert that inch measurement to the exact same size in the system you are using.

4. Click OK or press RETURN/ENTER, and you should have one half of the H flag completed. Now for the lazy bit – instead of creating a second rectangle, we'll get Illustrator to do that for us!

5. Switch to the **Selection** tool (V) – the solid black arrow at the top left of the toolbox.

6. Ensure that your rectangle is still selected, and then press the RETURN/ENTER key. The Move dialog box should appear.

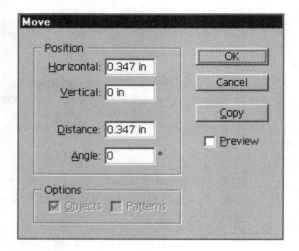

7. Enter the values as indicated in the screenshot above. The width of your original rectangle was 0.347 in. To create another one exactly aligned to the right, you want to move that same value, 0.347 inches, horizontally, and nothing vertically.

8. Illustrator will then move this copy 0.347in to the right by measuring the relative position of the top left-hand corner of the original, and positioning the top left-hand corner of the copy exactly 0.347in from that point. You do not have to enter the value in the Distance field, because Illustrator will listen to the Horizontal value you have just entered. If you want to put your mind at rest, you can enter the values, or just TAB through and Illustrator will copy those values into the Distance field.

9. Do not hit RETURN/ENTER or click on OK. You don't want to move the original rectangle, you want to move a copy – click on the Copy button.

And you should have two perfectly aligned rectangles, which create an H flag. If in error you did hit RETURN/ENTER, undo the action by going to Edit > Undo (CTRL/CMD+Z), and try again.

10.   Select both rectangles and group them by choosing Object > Group (CTRL/CMD+G). You'd hate for them to shift out of alignment by mistake, and by grouping them together you'll avoid that mishap.

11.   Save the file.

The I Flag

Before we resume our Illustrator voyage of discovery, we'll create one more flag – the I flag. This will give us a chance to use both the **Rectangle** and the **Ellipse** tool. Once again, the view has been created, so you can switch easily to that flag.

I Flag

1.   Select the **Rectangle** (M) tool from the toolbox, and position your cursor at the top left hand-corner (1) of the rectangular guide you see on screen. Remember that the **Smart Guides** will tell you when you are over an anchor point.

2.   Click and drag down to the bottom right-hand corner (2) to create your rectangular flag, releasing the mouse button when you are over the anchor point.

3.   Switch to the **Ellipse** tool (L). Move your cursor over the point at which the two straight guides intersect (3) at the center of the flag. Once again **Smart Guides** will aid you by flashing intersect when you are in the correct position.

4.   You are going to draw a perfect circle from the center, so have both hands ready for this, and steady yourself with your feet. Click and start to drag diagonally, but do not release the mouse. Hold down the SHIFT key, to draw a perfect circle, and also the ALT/OPTION key, to draw from the center. When your circle is the same size as the circular guide, release the mouse button and then the modifier keys.

5.   Save the file.

Optional Practice

For those of you lucky enough to have time on your side, there are some more flags that you can practice on now. For the rest of you, desperate to carry on, don't worry – there is a fairly complete flag file available for you to use in the other chapters.

Here are the flags you might like to try on your own, with a few hints and tips for their creation. In each instance, I have provided a view that you can access on the View menu, and guides that you can trace over.

L Flag   S Flag   W Flag

- **L Flag** – Create this flag simply by drawing four rectangles corresponding to the guides as shown. Remember to keep an eye out for those **Smart Guide** hints.

- **S Flag** – Two rectangles, one smaller than the other.

- **W Flag** – Three rectangles, each one smaller than the preceding one.

Drawing Lines

Enough practice, let's get back to those tools. If the previous section concentrated on the creation of simple shapes, it's time we stepped up a gear, and looked at the creation of lines. It's a sure stepping stone to those wonderful freehand drawings you'll be producing soon.

In this particular grouping of tools, we will explore the **Line Segment** tool, the **Arc** tool, and finally, the **Spiral** tool.

Using the Line Segment Tool

This is a new tool in Illustrator 10. Useful for drawing simple straight lines to highlight aspects of your illustrations, or to use as the basis of some funky logo design, the **Line Segment** tool functions in a way similar to how you may have begun to expect the Illustrator tools to react.

This is one of the beauties of the application. Skills learnt elsewhere can often be transferred to other tools, making the learning curve ever-steeper. So if you think about the other drawing tools you've met already in this chapter, you already know that there are two ways in which to use the tool, one by drawing dynamically on the page – the old click and drag story, and the other by entering precise measurements in a dialog box when you click on the page. Let's look at those options a little more closely.

■ Select the **Line Segment** tool and click on the Artboard to display the Line Segment Tool Options dialog box, and let's have a look at the options available to you.

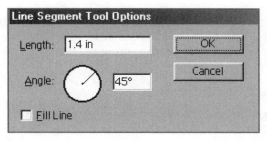

■ The Length option should be self-explanatory – it is describing the length of the line that you are about to draw.

■ The Angle field is nothing to worry about. Take the center of this star-like illustration as the point at which you would click on the Artboard with the Line Segment tool. If you wanted to draw a line that went from left to right, you would enter a value of 0 or 360 degrees, and moving counter-clockwise, you can see how the values change in the circular diagram below.

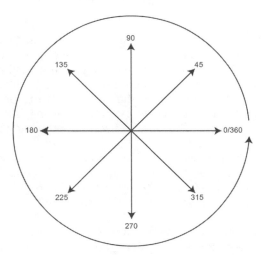

■ Incidentally, the values displayed in the dialog box will always be those of the last segment created. Restore the default values in the dialog box by pressing the ALT/OPTION key and noting how the Cancel button changes to Reset. Clicking on Reset restores the default values.

■ The final option, which says Fill Line does not exactly fill the line, but rather it uses the color that is presently the chosen Fill color as the line's color. This convoluted explanation may make more sense in the following chapter when you get on to discussing and applying color to your graphics, but for the moment we'll just accept the default colors you have chosen.

As I said earlier, the **Line Segment** tool can also be used to create lines dynamically, by clicking and dragging on the Artboard in the direction that you want the line to go, and dragging for as long as you want to make the line.

Using the Arc Segment Tool

The **Arc Segment** tool is another new feature added to the latest version of Illustrator. In previous versions if we wanted to create a simple arc, we more than likely would have created a circle, cut away most of the outline, then manipulated its shape, and finally, hoped to goodness that what we ended with was an arc similar to the shape we had initially envisaged. Have a look at the little fish below, and I'll explain what I mean.

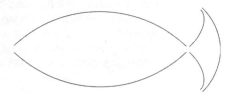

As a traditional artist, creating this shape on paper would have been relatively simple. No, I'd not have been able to just pick up a pencil and draw such perfect arcs; even my hand isn't that steady. Instead I would have relied on a trusted draughtsman's tool – the French curves. Trust me, it sounds a lot more exciting than it actually is. It's only a plastic stencil, but the various edges allowed for the perfect curve to be drawn with ease, each curve being used to make up a complete picture, all looking as if my perfectly stable hand had drawn it. Perhaps that's what Adobe had in mind when they introduced this tool.

Using any other of the myriad Illustrator drawing tools would never have given us those smooth fluent curves visible in the fish. With the arc, we can create these special shapes far more accurately and dynamically. With five very simple arcs, we are able to instinctively create this stylish fish graphic.

Let's first create an arc dynamically, and then we'll take a look at the Options dialog box a little later. Choose the **Arc Segment** tool, and click and drag on the Artboard to begin drawing that arc. Yes, it does feel kind of wild to start with, with a mind of its own. Don't worry, with a little practice, you'll soon have tamed this beast.

- Hold down the ALT/OPTION key as you drag with the **Arc Segment** tool, and notice how it extends from both sides of your point of origin. Similar to when you held down ALT/OPTION to draw those rectangles and ellipses from the center?

● Hold down the SHIFT key and drag. You may have expected the perfect arc, as you got a perfect circle and square earlier on – but then – how do we define the perfect arc? What is actually happening as you drag is that the arc is increasing in size, but is retaining its proportion as you drag. Still got that mouse down?

● Press the C key, for close, and notice how you now have a closed arc. Keep the mouse down, press C again, and it's now an open arc.

● Press F, for Flip, and press it again – one flipping arc.

One more – remember the stars, polygons, and rounded rectangles, and the role of the UP and DOWN arrows. Try them now, and notice how you can interactively increase or decrease the angle of the arc.

● Now you can let go of the mouse! What I suggest you do is have a practice, using the various keyboard modifiers, and see how they interact with the tool. Once you have played a little, you'll find that choosing these keyboard modifiers becomes second nature.

Now let's have a look at that Arc Segment dialog box.

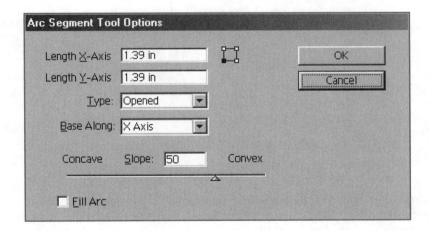

The first option to consider is the length of the arc on both the X- and Y-axis. If you can't remember your X from your Y, have a look at the graphic below. Notice in the illustration at the top, where the measurements for both the X and Y-axis are identical, the arc is equal in length along both the X (horizontal) and the Y (vertical) axis. Now look at the second arc, where the length of the X-axis is numerically twice as great as that of the Y, notice how the arc stays horizontal for twice as long before it starts to move vertically. And if you look at the second arc in the lower grouping, where the Y-axis length is twice that of the X-axis length, the vertical length of the arc is twice the horizontal length.

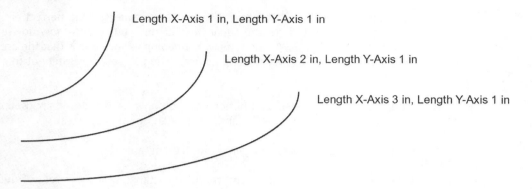

Length X-Axis 1 in, Length Y-Axis 1 in

Length X-Axis 2 in, Length Y-Axis 1 in

Length X-Axis 3 in, Length Y-Axis 1 in

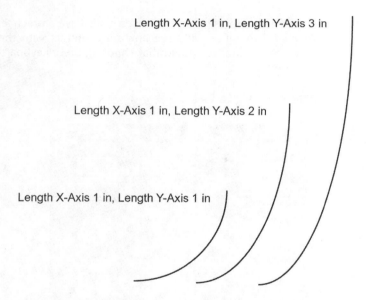

Length X-Axis 1 in, Length Y-Axis 3 in

Length X-Axis 1 in, Length Y-Axis 2 in

Length X-Axis 1 in, Length Y-Axis 1 in

Moving to the right of the Length X-axis and Length Y-axis fields you'll see an odd looking four-cornered box. This is known as the **Proxy**, which deals with the point of origin – in plain English, where the arc starts. You can change the point of origin by clicking and highlighting a different icon on the box. So, if you want to draw your arc, from the top right down, you would highlight the little box in that corner. Simple really.

Now that you know how big you want your arc to be, and where to start drawing, your next decision is whether to have a closed or open arc. You can choose this in the drop-down menu in the Type field. The difference between an open or closed arc is that when you choose the closed option, your arc will look more like a piece of pie, or a cheese wedge shape.

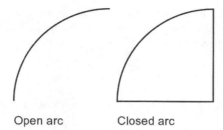

Open arc   Closed arc

A more difficult concept to grasp is the Base Along field. Have a look at the illustration below. Both arcs were drawn with the proxy – that little box thing – highlighted in the bottom left-hand corner. If you look at this, the base of an arc is determined as the end part of the arc, in this case where the arrowheads are. In the left-hand drawing, the base, the end, of the arc runs parallel to the X or horizontal axis, whereas in the right-hand arc, the base runs along the Y or the vertical, axis.

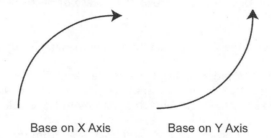

Base on X Axis   Base on Y Axis

Finally some terms that should be familiar – Concave and Convex – which describe the shape of the arc, whether it sinks in or bulges out. The Slope field determines how much the arc bulges, and you can control these by either typing in a value, or moving the slider bar underneath, and watching the value change.

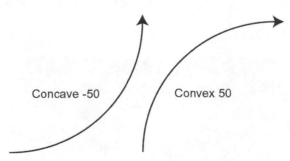

Concave -50   Convex 50

The last option on this dialog box, the Fill check box, determines whether or not you wish to have the area encompassed by the arc filled. All the above shapes are open shapes, you can see that they have no fill, and this is because that option has not been selected.

The more familiar you become with it and all its options, the clearer the picture will become. Go on – give that fish a go. You never know when it might come in handy as an illustration in your case study.

Creating Spirals

Now for a return to our nautical theme, with the introduction of the spiral tool.

Let's begin by clicking and dragging in an arc shape to start creating that spiral dynamically. And now as you drag across the page, I know you're saying to me, 'Yeah, I know, don't let go of the mouse.' That's right, because here come those modifier keys.

- SHIFT+drag to constrain the spiral to increments of 45 degrees.

- Press the UP and DOWN arrows to increase or decrease the number of winds in the spiral.

- Hold down the CTRL/CMD key to modify the amount of decay.

If you hold down Ctrl/Cmd and drag towards the center of the spiral, you are effectively increasing the amount of decay, and what happens is that the winds are closer together and the spiral looks less like a nautilus shell, and more like a coil.

Conversely, if you hold down Ctrl/Cmd and drag away from the center of the spiral, you are decreasing the amount of decay, and the winds are more loosely spread, and the nautilus shell shape reappears.

And of course you know by now that there will be a dialog box which will allow you to create a spiral by specifying its measurements. Go on display that dialog box, you know how to do it.

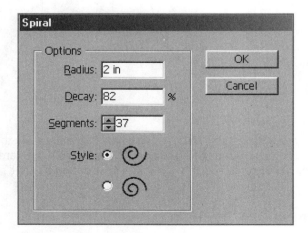

Let's create a perfect nautilus shell using the **Spiral** tool Options dialog box.

- The value that we enter in the Radius field is the distance from the center of the spiral to its outer point. We'll enter 2 for this value.

- Remember that Decay is the amount by which each wind decreases relative to the size of the wind outside of it. The higher the value, the more regular and closer the winds will be to each other, the lower the value, the shape looks more irregular and more closely resembles the nautilus shell as each internal wind is closer to the preceding wind. We'll enter 87 to help us create that nautilus shape with a decent amount of decay.

- A wind is another word for a revolution, and in the Illustrator spiral, each wind is made up of four segments – like four little joined arcs really. We don't want it to get too close in the center, so we'll choose 37.

- The final icons allow you to decide whether the spiral will wind anti-clockwise or clockwise from the center of the spiral. Click OK or press RETURN/ENTER and you should see a perfect nautilus shell. There is no need for you to save this simple graphic as we'll recreate it later, but could you imagine trying to draw that perfectly by hand?

If you have the time, try creating a number of different spirals by specifying the measurements. I'd suggest that you keep most of the measurements as they are for the moment, and change only the amount of decay each time, going up and down gently. It really helps your understanding of the decay concept if you give this a go.

Creating Grids

We have two grid drawing tools in Illustrator – the **Rectangular Grid** and **Polar Grid** tools – the two tools on the end of the flyout shown below.

All designers, be they web or print designers, know that at the base of that balanced design is the existence of that well thought-out grid. Granted we have a grid function in Illustrator that you have already met in the previous chapter. But that grid is pretty square, regular, and inflexible, what we have now is a grid we can control to give us just the right number of rectangular and horizontal divisions, and these divisions can be irregular. Round one to the **Grid** tool, but I'm not finished yet.

Sooner or later as your drawing skills develop, you're going to want to add that sense of realism to them, that perception of perspective, and although we will be showing you how to add perspective with the **Free Transform** tool in Chapter 6, using the grid as a basis for your perspective drawings is a very useful approach. Have a look at this example below, showing a basic grid, and how it would look after I had used the Free Transform tool to add some perspective and it might give you a clearer idea.

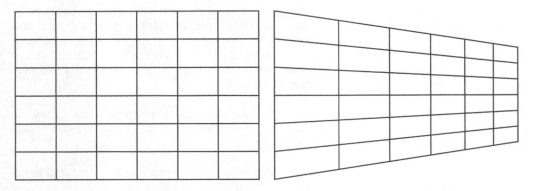

Basic Grid   Grid after using the Free Transform tool with Perspective

Maybe I've convinced you of the usefulness of the **Rectangular Grid**, but you're still looking at the **Polar Grid** a little strangely. Ever had to draw a diagram of a solar system? Or a scientific looking icon or logo? The **Polar Grid** tool is just the tool to make light work of that task.

Drawing Rectangular Grids

Imagine you are drawing the grid for a basic page-layout, possibly even for a brochure for your Marine Quest project. You have decided on an asymmetrical layout of five equally spaced columns and three equally spaced rows. Of course, you could carefully drag guides down from the ruler, watching your Info palette and Transform palette as you go; or you could use the **Rectangular Grid** tool to do it for you accurately and in seconds.

Drawing a Rectangular Grid

1. Create a new document by choosing File > New (CTRL/CMD+N). Choose **Letter** as your Artboard size, and **Landscape** as your Orientation. Once again do not worry about the other options, as you'll not be saving this document. Furthermore, after clicking OK, do not let the dotted lines through the page distract you, you know that they relate to the orientation of the paper in your printer; and as we'll not be printing this either, that information is of little concern to us.

2. Select the **Rectangular Grid** tool and click somewhere near the top left-hand corner of the page, we'll reposition the grid a little later. As you click on the stage, a dialog box will appear where you can tell Illustrator the details of the grid that you want.

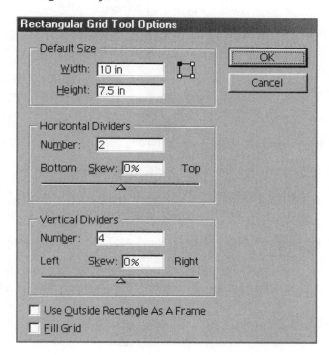

I'll explain what all the parameters in the dialog box are, relative to our particular grid:

- Our landscape letter page is 11 inches wide, but we want to have a 1/2 inch margin on the left and right hand side of the page, so we have set the width to 10 inches. Similarly, the height of the page is 8.5 inches, so we have subtracted an inch from that measurement as well.

- The grid must start from the point at which we clicked and expand to the right and down, so the top left corner of the Origin Point must be clicked.

- We want three rows, so you might be tempted to ask for three dividers – but no, always ask for one less divider than the total of rows or columns that you want – tricky one that. Don't forget it otherwise you might feel the tool is not listening to you! Similarly, we want five columns, so we need four vertical dividers.

■ We'll not enter a value for the Skew because we want the dividers to be equally spread on both the vertical and horizontal axis.

■ And finally because we do not want a separate **Frame** or a **Filled** grid, we'll leave those two options unchecked.

3. Once you release the mouse, on the page should be a perfect grid that can be used as the basis for a solid design grid.

4. Drag the grid into position roughly in the center of the page. You'll be learning more about Transforming and accurate positioning of objects in Chapter 6.

Let's go through those options again:

■ In Width and Height fields, enter the values for the size of your grid.

■ On the Origin Point icon, click at the point from where you wish the grid to start being drawn. This is relative to where you click on the page with the mouse.

■ For the Dividers, both Horizontal and Vertical, enter a value which is one less than the number of columns and rows that you want. Leave the Skew values at zero if you want regularly sized grids. If you want irregular grids, use the skew settings to help you set the offset or skew value of the dividers. Have a look at the example below:

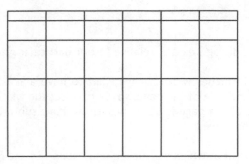
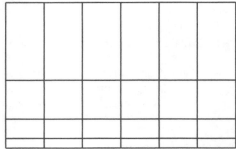

Horizontal Skew set at -100%   Horizontal Skew set at 100%

If we set a negative skew value for the Horizontal skew, the lines will be closer to each other at the top, with the distance between them doubling at each line, whereas if we set a positive value for Horizontal skew, the dividers are far from each other at the top, with the distance between them decreasing by half with each additional divider. Similarly, if we set a negative value for the vertical dividers, they will be closer to each other on the left, and with a positive value closer on the right, all the time with that space between dividers either halving or doubling in space.

■ Check Use Outside Rectangle As a Frame if you want a separate rectangular frame; and check Fill Grid if you want the grid to be filled with your current fill color.

You just know what's coming now – you've got used to this routine! I'm about to throw all those shortcut keyboard modifiers at you. Don't be concerned if you are feeling a little overwhelmed and wondering how you are ever going to remember them all, it will come with practice. I'm going to take a guess here, but I reckon you have the shortcuts for drawing a perfectly square grid on the tip of your tongue – yes, it is SHIFT, and to draw from the center, great – it's ALT/OPTION. Therefore you know that to draw a perfectly square grid from the center, you're going to hold down ALT/OPTION and SHIFT.

You do recall of course, how we used the UP and DOWN arrows when we were modifying the shape of our stars and polygon? We use them here again, with the addition of the LEFT and RIGHT arrows. As you are drawing that rectangle, use the UP arrow to increase the number of Horizontal dividers, and the DOWN to decrease them, and similarly, use the RIGHT arrow to increase the number of vertical dividers, and the LEFT arrow to decrease them.

Drawing Polar Grids

Now that you've met and mastered drawing rectangular grids, let's introduce you to those **Polar Grids**, and I bet you'll be thrilled because there really is very little new for you to learn here. I'll show you the dialog box, and you'll be nodding your head, saying come on, I know all that; I'll mention the keyboard modifiers, and you'll be challenging me to show you something new. Okay then – a quick whiz through that Polar Grid set-up, just so you can say, yes, I knew that!

First of all, let's have a look at that dialog box that will appear if we click on the page with the **Polar Grid** tool. You'll notice that there are only one or two differences from that shown when you used the **Rectangular Grid** tool, so we'll not labor the point too much!

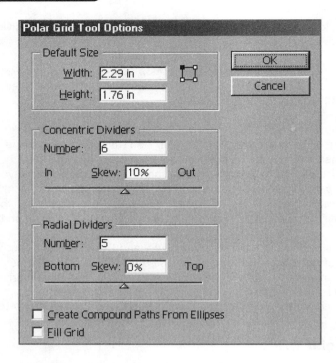

I'm assuming that the Width, Height, and Point of Origin options all make sense to you as they are identical to what you have just seen in the **Rectangular Grid** tool. But then we meet words like Concentric and Radial, and things get a little more complicated. It's that math class coming back again isn't it? We'll do it simply. You remember that the radius of a circle is the measurement from the center to the outside? Therefore the radial dividers are those that are going from the center to the outside, and the concentric dividers are the other ones!

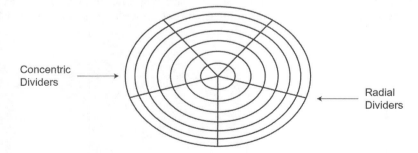

Concentric Dividers

Radial Dividers

What about these skew values? How do we work those out — especially if we're designing one of those solar system diagrams I mentioned earlier? Have a look at the diagram below. If we want the circles to be closer as they approach the center, enter a negative value, and conversely if they should be closer around the edge, then enter a positive value. Note again, that like the rectangular grid, that distance appears to be doubling or halving with each divider.

But have a look at what a skew does to those radial dividers! If we set a negative value, the dividers start at the bottom, rotating clockwise with the distance between them doubling each time and conversely, if we enter a positive value, they seem to be starting at the bottom and going anti-clockwise.

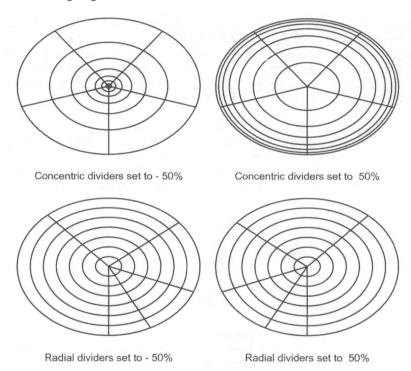

Concentric dividers set to - 50%   Concentric dividers set to 50%

Radial dividers set to - 50%   Radial dividers set to 50%

As with the **Rectangular Grid**, check Fill Grid if you want the grid to be filled with your current fill color. There is only one option that we'll not be explaining now, and that's the concept of a compound path! When we get to the chapter on **Complex Shapes**, we'll be spending quite a bit of time looking at compound paths so you might understand why I don't think I can explain it in one sentence here.

And to end off this section on basic shapes, I'll just remind you that SHIFT gives you a perfect circle, that ALT/OPTION will draw from the center, and that with the UP and DOWN arrows you can increase or decrease the number of circles. All done without releasing the mouse of course, but you knew that too!

Case Study: Drawing a Basic Compass

Before we move on to the exciting world of color, let's take a moment to practice some of our line segment skills by creating another component for our case study. In itself, the **Line Segment** tool is not exactly going to set the world afire, but its strength lies in the ability to specifically choose a line length and angle, which would have entailed a little more work in other versions.

We will use this tool to create a very basic compass, useful for our case study. Although, I can bet that George and Lucy, sticklers as they are for great design, will not be overly enthused by our design and we may have to rework it and embellish it in a later chapter, it's a good start to give them a notion of what's happening in our heads and to practice our accuracy skills. Artistic license and all that taken into account, we had better be fairly accurate in our depiction of the compass rose.

1. Create a new file by choosing File > New (CTRL/CMD+N). You sense some revision coming on, don't you? Make this file a standard letter sized page, set the orientation to portrait, choose inches as your unit of measurement and CMYK for your color mode, because essentially we are designing this graphic for print, although it may well be used on our web page as well.

2. Again, to ensure that we are all starting with the same Fill and Stroke colors, press the letter D on the keyboard to reset the colors to the standard white fill, black stroke.

3. Ensure that **Smart Guides** are on by checking that there is a tick next to Smart Guides on the View menu.

4. Select the **Line Segment** tool (\). With the **Line Segment** tool selected, click on the Artboard, preferably somewhere in the center. The tool options will be displayed.

5. In the Length field type in 2. If you followed the instructions above and are working in inches, it is not necessary to enter the 'in'; but if you chose to remain in a measurement system with which you are more familiar, then you must add those magic letters.

6. In the Angle field, type 0 and chose OK, or press the RETURN/ENTER key – and there you have it, one perfectly straight line drawn from left to right – or to be more nautically accurate, the line is pointing East!

7. To make things just a little more exciting, let's sneak in a filter to add some arrowheads to our compass rose. I know we don't look at Filters in

any depth till much later in the book, but just a little dip can't do us any harm, can it?

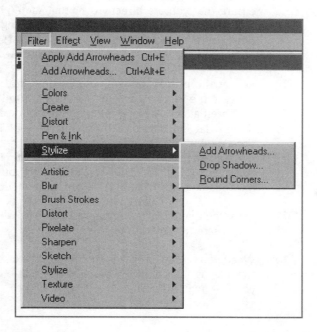

8. From the Filter menu, choose the option Stylize>Add Arrowheads. The following dialog box will appear, and because we're not really supposed to be in here, just chose the options as indicated in the dialog box below.

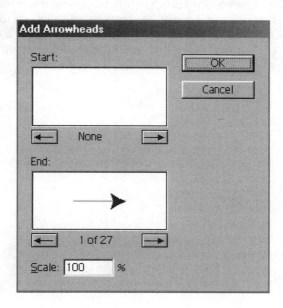

9. Move your cursor over that initial clicking point, the one at the left hand edge of the line, wait until you see the **Smart Guide** flash 'anchor' to ensure that you are directly over that same point, and click again. Keep the length the same, and type 45 in the Angle field. Another line, this time, we're on a heading of NE (North East). Don't forget to add that arrowhead again.

10. Repeat the process above, but this time in the Angle field, we need to increase the value by another 45 degrees. Do I detect another sigh about all these figures? Are you reaching for that desktop calculator? Stop, right there – let Illustrator do the math for you! The Angle field should be showing 45°. Click in after the value, don't erase it, and type '+45'. Press the Tab key, just to see Illustrator do the math. It should now be displaying 90 °. Click OK, or press Return/Enter, and you should now have another line, heading North. Another arrowhead needed.

11. I imagine that by now, you're pretty familiar with the process, so go ahead and create the rest of the rose

12. When your compass rose is completed, the last value being 270°+45, save the file as Compass.ai by choosing File > Save, then go and make yourself a cup of coffee. You deserve it!

Summary

Having looked at creating basic shapes and a whole fistful of shortcuts, I know you're just a little disappointed that somehow you are still locked in that old world of black and white movies! Interesting as they are, and how wonderful it is sometimes not to be distracted by color; we'll admit that a world always without color would be just that little bit – well, lacking in color. So, here we go! In the next chapter you'll be introduced to the wonderful world of color in computer graphics, including an in-depth study of the different color modes available to you within Illustrator.

4 Working with Color

What We'll Cover in this Chapter:

- *Understanding different Color Models including RGB, CMYK, HSB and Grayscale*

- *Color Gamuts*

- *Web Safe Colors*

- *Applying Color to Artwork, using:*
  - *Swatches Palette*
  - *Color Picker*
  - *Color Palette*
  - *Stroke Palette*
  - *Toolbox*

- *Gradients and Applying and Editing Gradients with the Gradient Tool*

▶

So, let's begin with a clean slate. For the moment, discard any thoughts about red and yellow making orange and similar legacies of school art class and keep an open mind as I take you into the diverse world of **color models**.

Color Models

In the world of computer generated art and graphics there are different color models. These are methods of describing color using mathematical models. The color model used for graphics on the web is different from the model used in graphics for print.

To demonstrate the difference, imagine you are looking at two versions of a travel brochure. One version is in the form of a web site. In this case, your monitor becomes the media or device on which you are viewing the graphics and text. The other version is a printed brochure and so paper is the medium upon which you are viewing. Now, turn off the lights in the room. The printed brochure becomes pretty useless without light. The website however is illuminated irrespective of whether a light is on or the sun is shining. This is because the monitor is transmitting its own colored light. Now, turn on the lights again. The printed brochure appears once more.

Now, there's nothing highly scientific about this fact on the face of it, but let's analyze exactly what is happening. The light source in the room is reflecting back from the paper revealing its colors. I shall go on to expand on how and why we see different colors, but this is the fundamental difference between the two color models. It's all a question of how light is manipulated by the different media, be it a monitor or paper.

We are going to explore the main color models you will come across, but let's start by the looking at the two primary models used in print and on the web:

- RGB

- CMYK

RGB Color Model

RGB stands for Red, Green, Blue. This is the color model used on the Web. It is also the model used for video and television. In fact, any time you are creating artwork that will not be printed, but rather viewed via a monitor, television, or some other type of screen, this is the model to use.

The RGB color model is known as an **Additive Color Model** because, in this model, adding all the colors of the spectrum together creates the color white. If you think back to physics class, you would have been told that white light is composed of all the different color wavelengths of visible light. This white light applies equally to the sun as it does to artificial light.

The earlier example of viewing the travel brochure on a web site via a monitor proves that no external light source is required to see the color produced by a monitor. The monitor itself produces the source of light. Within the monitor, three wavelengths of light (red, green, and blue) are used to simulate the colors in the real world. These three wavelengths, known as the **additive primaries**, are used at different intensities to achieve different colors. For instance, the red wavelength on its own will be seen as red. Green on its own is seen as green, and blue as blue. If the red and green are added together, the result will be yellow. What! I hear you say. Remember we're not dealing with conventional color mixing of pigment paint. You will get some hands on experience of mixing RGB color shortly and any doubts you may have will fade away.

Based on this brief journey into the secrets of RGB color, what do you imagine you would see if your monitor produced no red light, no green light, and no blue light? If you think it will produce black you would be absolutely right. The absence of all of the red, green, and blue light waves translates into black, which is the same as the absence of light, or no color. Now that's a bit more logical.

CMYK Color Model

If your artwork is to be printed in some form, RGB will be of little value. The color model used for print is **CMYK**: **C**yan, **M**agenta, **Y**ellow, and Blac**K**. K probably seems to be an unlikely choice for black but it is to avoid B being mistaken for Blue.

Let's contrast how this color model actually differs from the RGB model. Visualize a green leaf lying in the sun. We know that sunlight is white light that is composed of all colors. When light strikes the green leaf, the red and blue light is absorbed (subtracted) by the leaf, and the green light is reflected back, so our eyes perceive the color of the leaf as green.

In printed artwork, this principle works in exactly the same way. If you have a red logo printed on a sheet of paper, the red pigment in the paper absorbs the green and blue light, because there is no green or blue in red. The red light is reflected back by the pigment and our eyes perceive a red colored logo. If you think back to that printed travel brochure, every color your eyes perceive appears because some light is being absorbed, or subtracted, and some is reflected back. The reflected light is the color that appears.

I've been dropping in the word 'subtracted' because the CMYK model is called the **Subtractive Color Model**. Colors are created in this model by subtracting certain colors to make new ones. I've been talking about red, green, and blue, but let's see how cyan, magenta, and yellow work their way into this model.

The CMY colors are created by subtracting 100% of red or green or blue. The diagram below demonstrates this formula. This is exactly the same as what happened with the green leaf. If we look at the cyan tube in the diagram – we would see it as cyan in color. From the diagram, we can see that the red light wave emanating from the sun is absorbed by the cyan tube. Green and blue light waves, which make up cyan, are reflected back from the surface of the cyan tube, so we perceive the color as cyan. This same process occurs with the magenta and yellow tubes.

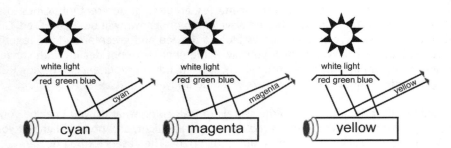

Now, where does black (K) fit into this? Cyan, magenta, and yellow form the basis for what is known as the **printed process colors**. Theoretically, all the colors of nature can be mixed by a combination of these three colors in print. The theory says mix C, M, and Y and you get black. In fact you get a sort of black. In reality you will get a muddy color. In print, truly rich blacks can only be achieved by using K (black). A typical mix to achieve a rich black would be something like:

Cyan 50%
Magenta 50%
Yellow 50%
Black 100%

I've rounded up the figures for ease, but any near combination produces a rich black.

You could happily continue your career in Illustrator with the knowledge of these two color models under your belt. You now know the difference between the two and when each should be used, but I'm going to introduce you to two more color models, which play an important part in computer graphics.

- HSB

- Grayscale

HSB

Hue/Saturation/Brightness (HSB) is based on the human eye's perception of color. **Hue** describes the pure color, for instance red, blue, and so on. Each color is depicted within a circle or color wheel and is positioned at a certain location relating to degrees.

Saturation describes the purity of the color with regard to the amount of gray in proportion to the hue. The measurement is based on a sliding percentage scale where 0% is gray or fully desaturated and 100% is the purest and clearest version of the hue / color or fully saturated.

Brightness refers to how light or dark the color is, where 0% is black and 100% is white. By setting a hue to 100% saturation and 100% brightness, you would achieve its most vibrant setting, but I wouldn't recommend you painting your house this color.

Grayscale

Many people might be forgiven for using the words "black and white" when they really mean grayscale. Humphrey Bogart never actually appeared in any black and white movies, but he did act in loads of grayscale ones. I know, it doesn't have the same romantic ring to it and we're not going to change the language of 100 years in order to be technically correct. But the distinction is a vital one if you are sending some artwork to print or producing a web graphic.

To understand true black and white, you will need to cast your mind back to Chapter 2 when I talked about a 1-bit bitmap image. In that mode you are not exactly overwhelmed with color choices. There are only two, black or white. The resulting picture appears as a solid, jagged-edged cut out.

Grayscale uses a total of 256 shades of gray. Not a lot you may think, considering we talk of millions of colors in a 24-bit image. But in fact 256 colors are all you need to achieve a photographic quality image. All the subtle tones of nature can be reproduced within this range of 256 shades. Look at the image to the right. This image uses a maximum of 256 shades, and all the shades of nature have been faithfully reproduced.

You may never need to refer to or use the HSB or Grayscale models again. The knowledge you now possess can only enhance your ability to make the important decisions about which color models to use and when. Hopefully you will now be in a position where you feel sufficiently informed, prior to starting out on any project, as to why you are using a certain color model.

Although we haven't looked at any color model examples in Illustrator in earnest yet, when we do shortly, you will find dramatic differences visually. To explain why you are seeing such dramatic difference we are going to look at **Color Gamuts**.

Color Gamuts

A color gamut describes a maximum range of colors that can be sensed, displayed, or printed by a given device or color model. Typical devices include monitors, printers, scanners, and, believe it or not, the human eye. Different color gamuts exist for each device or color model. The larger the gamut, the more colors it contains. In these days of high technology, boasting about power, speed, and performance of gadgetry, the human eye, that unsurpassed marvel of technology, enjoys the greatest color gamut. We can see many more colors than any monitor could hope to display. In turn, the monitor can display more colors than a printer can print.

The diagram is a depiction of how the various gamuts relate to each other. The shape is actually a 2D cut out of a 3D model. The outer "shark fin" shape describes the visible spectrum or, to put it another way, all the colors the human eye is capable of perceiving at 100% brightness.

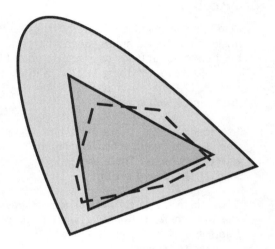

The triangle within this shape is the RGB gamut, or the colors that a monitor would be capable of displaying. The inner dotted line shape is the CMYK gamut, or the colors that would be printable on a printer.

Clearly the CMYK gamut is the smallest and, therefore, contains the fewest colors available for use. Now that you have some theory behind you, it's time to put this into practice and take a look at creating your own document and choosing the correct color model.

Applying Color to Objects

We are going to create a document for print and then get some experience of working with colors. So, if it isn't already open, launch Illustrator now and we can begin.

1. Go to File>New.

2. In the new document dialogue box, enter the details for a Letter-sized document with a CMYK Color Mode, and click OK. There are a number of ways to specify and apply color to objects in Illustrator. The method you choose will largely be down to personal choice, but we shall explore all the options.

3. Take a look at the fill and stroke box towards the bottom of the toolbox. The box labeled 'Fill' refers to the color to be used for the object's fill. The box

labeled 'Stroke' refers to the color to be used for the objects stroke or outline. Both the fill and stroke color can be preset so that any objects you create will be created with these predefined colors.

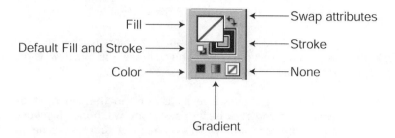

Fill → ← Swap attributes

Default Fill and Stroke → ← Stroke

Color → ← None

↓ Gradient

4. Using the **Selection** tool, double-click the fill box. This action will open the Color Picker. This offers you the easiest way to choose and apply color. In the middle of the color picker you will see a vertical bar containing the full spectrum of colors, starting with red at the top of the bar and going right through the color wheel to get back to red at the bottom of the bar. At either side of the vertical color bar you will see a pair of gray arrows. These arrows can be dragged up and down like a slider to achieve the desired range of colors. You can also click anywhere in the vertical color bar and that too will present the range of colors based on where you click.

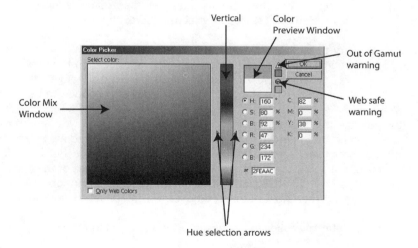

Vertical   Color
                Preview Window

Out of Gamut warning

Color Mix Window

Web safe warning

Hue selection arrows

5. Drag the hue selection arrows to the halfway point and the colors you are looking at should be around the blue/cyan range. The large square window on the left of the color picker displays the full range of shades within this particular color. The top left of the window is pure white, the top right of the window is the purest saturated hue and the bottom left and right reveal pure black.

Within this window you have a large range of colors to choose from. As you click within the window to choose your color you will see the preview window at the top right changing accordingly.

6. Choose a very pure hue by clicking in the top right of the color selection window. If you click high enough, you will notice a yellow triangle appear next to the preview window. This is an out of gamut warning. Remember we are in a CMYK document, which means we are producing artwork that will be printed as opposed to viewed on a screen. The color gamut for CMYK is smaller than the color gamut for RGB, so the warning is alerting you to the fact that the color you have chosen is out of the CMYK color gamut and will therefore not print as it appears here. Obviously we need to choose another color that is within the gamut.

7. Click the yellow warning triangle. Automatically, another color is selected which is the closest in color to your chosen one, but within the CMYK color gamut. By comparison, the revised color probably seems pretty drab next to your original selection, but this demonstrates well the greatly reduced range of colors that fall within the CMYK gamut compared to the RGB equivalent.

8. Try randomly clicking in the color window and note when the yellow warning triangle appears and disappears. This will help you to visualize which colors will fall outside the CMYK gamut. All of these out of range colors will be located in the top right of the color window. They also happen to be the most vibrant.

It is possible that you will have a predefined color mix that you intend to choose. In this case it would be futile clicking haphazardly in the color window. Entering numeric values offers a more precise way of choosing color. On the right of the color picker you will see a range of numeric boxes. These numeric boxes refer to three of the color models we have looked at so far, **HSB**, **RGB**, and **CMYK**. We are creating a print document, so we will apply some values to the CMYK numbered boxes, which are set to work in percentages.

9. Enter the following values into the C, M, Y and K boxes:

```
C 66
M 13
Y 75
K 2
```

In the small preview window you should be looking at a dark green color. If you have something else, just check you have entered the figures correctly. Click OK to close the color picker. You will see the color you selected appear in the fill color box.

If you are not happy with the color you chose and would like a darker shade, we can go back to the color picker and edit it.

10. Double-click the fill box to open the color picker again. When the color picker opens, type 20 into the K box, then click anywhere on the gray portion of the color picker. This will update your new setting. You will now see the small preview window split into two halves. The top half is the new color you have just created by typing "20" into the K box. The bottom half of the preview window shows you the color that is currently in the fill color box. This is the last color you selected. The purpose of this is to give you a reference point from where you can make slight adjustments to your color and make a constant direct comparison.

11. Click OK to close the color picker.

12. Close the file.

Using RGB Colors

We will now take a look at RGB color for the web and some other ways to choose and apply colors.

1. Create a new file, repeating the procedure as before, File>New.

2. Use the same settings as previously except for Color Mode. Set the mode to RGB Color.

3. Double-click the fill color box as before to open up the color picker again.

Choosing colors works in exactly the same way as with CMYK. This time we will look at the numeric values of the RGB model.

4. Enter the following values into the R, G and B boxes:

        R 255
        G 255
        B 255

Percentages are not used in the RGB model as with CMYK. Instead, a scale from 0 to 255 is used.

0 is the bottom of the scale and represents the lowest level of light and 255 the top of the scale and the highest amount of light.

The preview window will show you the color you have created, pure white.

Let's take a moment to recap, in case the white color you have just created has caught you out. You have mixed white by combining the highest amount of red light, the highest amount of green light, and the highest amount of blue light. Don't let the number 255 throw you. This is just the highest value of 256 possible shades. (255 + 0 = 256. 0 is a value in this case.) When we looked at the formulation of RGB color, we saw that all color light waves combined generated white. This is exactly what you have just done. You applied the highest amounts of red, green, and blue.

5. Now enter the following values into the R, G and B boxes and remember to click on the gray part of the color picker to update the settings.

```
R 255
G 0
B 0
```

This creates pure red.

6. Try adding new values to achieve pure green and pure blue. I've listed these below in case you get stuck.

```
Pure Green
R 0
G 255
B 0

Pure Blue
R 0
G 0
B 255
```

7. If you are feeling really confident you could attempt yellow.

```
Pure Yellow
R 255
G 255
B 0
```

Knowledge of the numerical values isn't actually essential as you can simply click on a color and there it is. Understanding how the value work is always preferable, and provides you with a more comprehensive awareness. The more you use color, the more these values will make sense. Over time, repetition will make them as familiar as ABC.

Keep the color picker open. We are going to look at another aspect of colors for the RGB model.

Web Safe Colors

I would bet that you are currently working on a color monitor and not a monochrome one. I would even bet that you are working on a monitor that is capable of displaying millions of colors. If so, it is your computer's graphics card that enables it to do so.

All computers sold in recent years are fitted with a graphics card capable of this feat. Even laptop computers of late have sufficient hardware to enable the display of millions of colors. I would feel pretty safe with my bet because the most recent research reveals that, as far as Internet usage is concerned, the majority of computers are indeed capable of millions of colors output. However, that means the minority are not seeing millions of colors. So what are they seeing? In many cases they will be seeing 256 colors. Talk about extremes. What will the impact be of you creating your web site graphics on your millions of colors monitor and the poor blighted soul attempting to view your web site on their 256-color monitor? In a word, **dithering**. I know what it sounds like. It doesn't mean this individual will be thrown into a state of indecision wondering what to do before having a complete breakdown. Dithering in this instance refers to how the 256-color monitor will display your graphics.

Let's break this down a little. The graphics card governs the ability of a 256-color display monitor. In this case the monitor is only capable of displaying 256 colors. If you create a graphic using your millions of colors computer, it is likely that many of those colors will not be able to be displayed on the 256 monitor. All is not lost though. The 256-color monitor will not give up hope and ignore the graphics. It will try to simulate the colors it cannot produce by using colors it can use and arranging them in a random manner. This process of "visual color mixing" is known as dithering and with the best will in the world and the greatest of intentions it looks pretty lousy. In the download folder open the file called `Dithering.ai` for a color example of dithering.

Out of this dire situation was born the **web safe color palette**. This uses a palette of 216 colors that will not dither. Of course it also means you are unlikely to get the actual color you need as you only have a choice of 216, compared with millions. But that is a decision based on the target audience of your website. It really comes down to choosing the lesser of two evils. Do you go for a color closer to your desired one and risk it dithering or pick a color that definitely won't dither and is very different to your first choice color. I wouldn't get too stressed over this point though. Analysis figures change every day so there's little point in quoting them here but if you check on the Internet or the computer press you will find the number of users these days with 256-color monitors is a tiny percentage globally. Your task will be to assess where in the world your market is and what their specific usage of 256-color monitors is.

For the sake of your growing all round knowledge and in the interests of dealing with all the extremes that you may encounter, we are going to assume we need to create colors using the web safe palette.

You should have the color picker open still, but if it isn't, double-click the fill box in the toolbox to open it.

1. In the bottom left corner of the color picker, click in the box labeled only web colors. Suddenly the limitations of the palette become apparent. The color picker now only offers you the 216 colors of the web safe palette. Try dragging the sliders at either side of the vertical bar and you will see the range of colors on offer in each case.

Interestingly, it doesn't matter which color you click on, if you look at the R, G, B numeric values you will find that they will display one of the following numbers:

```
0, 51, 102, 153, 204, 255.
```

2. Uncheck the Only Web Colors checkbox and select a color that isn't web safe. You will see a small cube appear next to the color preview window. Click this cube and your color will snap to the nearest web safe equivalent.

3. Choose a mid-blue color and click OK to close the color picker.

Exactly the same process is followed to create a color for the stroke as opposed to the fill. We are going to choose a stroke color now.

4. Double-click the **Stroke Color** box from within the toolbox.

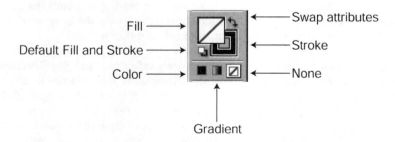

The stroke box jumps to the front and the color picker opens again.

5. The procedures are identical to when you were selecting fill colors.

6. Select a color of your choice and click OK to close the color picker.

We are going to move on from the color picker and look at other ways of choosing color.

The Color Palette

The **color palette** can be found on the right of the screen. If it has been closed, you will be able to open it by going to Window>Color.

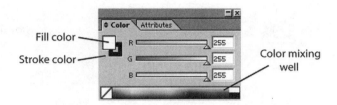

Fill color

Stroke color

Color mixing well

This provides you with a method of selecting and applying color direct from the screen. It can be a faster method, as you do not have to go into the color picker window. It also means you can see the color being applied to an object directly in front of you. This allows you to see your color choice in the context of the whole artwork.

The concepts however are exactly the same as when you used the color picker. Let's look at the components that make up the color palette. We first need to make sure that you can see the full palette.

1. Click the small black arrow button in the top right of the palette. From the pop-up menu that appears, the first line will display either Show Options or Hide Options. If Hide Options is the visible line, you are seeing the full palette and you can click anywhere on the screen to keep the setting as it is. If Show Options is the visible line, you only have half of the palette revealed and you can now select this option to reveal the rest of the palette.

2. The fill and stroke boxes can be seen on the left of the palette. Whichever of these boxes is at the front is the active box. So, if the fill box is at the front, you will be creating a fill color. Try clicking on each of the boxes in turn and you will see it jump to the front.

3. The color mixing well is a simple way to choose a color by clicking on it. This is similar to the color picker, except all the colors of the spectrum are contained in this one small mixing area. It can be difficult to select a precise color because of the size of the color well but there is no faster method. To the extreme right of the mixing well you will find a black and a white box. This is pure white and pure black.

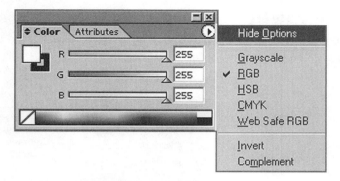

4. Pure white and more commonly pure black are colors you will probably use often, so let me introduce you to one of the most useful shortcuts in Illustrator. This shortcut allows you to set white as the fill color and black as the stroke color with one key press. To see the change take place, choose any colors for the fill and stroke color other than black or white. Now press D on the keyboard. Your previous fill and stroke colors have now been replaced by black and white. (D stands for Default, as in the default colors black and white.)

5. Finally, in this palette you can choose colors numerically by typing a number into the R, G, and B boxes or by dragging the sliders back and forth. We are going to create a fill color now using this method. Click the fill color box in the color palette to bring it to the front and therefore activate it. Type 230 into the R box, 0 in the G and B boxes, and press the ENTER key on the keyboard. Remember the range you have to play with in RGB, 0 up to 255. This value creates a dark red color. You will notice two other icons have appeared in the color palette. The **Web Color** warning icon and the **Out of Gamut** warning icon.

These warnings can be ignored if your intention is to create a color that does not need to be web safe and is not going to be printed. On this occasion, let's assume we are going to create a web safe color.

6. Click the **Web Safe** warning icon. The color jumps to the nearest web safe color, which in this case is 255.

7. This time type 229 into the R box instead of 230 as you did last time, then press the ENTER key. This is not a web safe color either, so click the web safe warning icon that has appeared. The color jumps to 204 this time, as this becomes the nearest web safe color to 229.

Even though we have created an RGB document, you may have been given a CMYK color value that you would like to include within the document. It is possible to change the settings in the color palette so that we can input and read a CMYK value.

8. Click on the black arrow button in the top right of the color palette again. The pop-up reveals all the color models you can work with. Select the CMYK option. The CMYK sliders and numerical input boxes now appear.

The Swatches Palette

The last method of using color we are going to look at is the **Swatches Palette**, which is shown below. This is analogous with a paint box palette in the real world. The swatches palette can be found on the right of the screen below the color palette. Once again if it is not there, it has been closed down. You can reveal it by going to Window>Swatches.

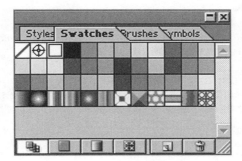

Illustrator provides you with a default palette offering a range of standard colors as well as other elements such as patterns and gradients (that we will look at later in the chapter). You can of course create and delete your own swatches and save entire palettes using just your choice of colors. We will also be doing this shortly. For the moment let's see how the swatches palette works. We are going to set up the fill box to receive a blue color.

1. Working in the toolbox at the left of your screen, click the fill color box to bring it to the front. This activates the fill box and allows you to edit the color. Click a blue swatch from within the swatches palette. If you look back at the fill box in the toolbox you will see that blue appears.

2. Click the stroke box in the toolbox to activate it. Now click a yellow color from within the swatch palette. You will see the yellow appear in the stroke box in the toolbox.

You have now used a range of methods for choosing color within the RGB and CMYK palettes. You are fully equipped and ready to actually apply some colors to objects on the page. In the following exercises you will build up your experience of creating by applying fill and stroke colors to a variety of pre-made objects.

Applying Color to Objects Using the Color Picker

From the download folder open the file called `Basic_color.ai`. This is an RGB document. The circle on the page has a red fill and a black stroke.

1. Using the **Selection** tool (V) click on the circle to select it. Take a look at the fill and color box in the toolbox. They now reflect the fill and stroke colors of the selected circle.

We are going to change the fill color of the circle to pale green using the color picker.

2. In the toolbox, click the fill color box to bring it to the front and enable it as the active box.

3. Double-click the same fill box and the color picker appears. If the Only Web Colors box is checked, click it to deselect it.

4. Choose a green color by selecting the green range of colors from the vertical mixing bar and then a pale shade of green from the large mixing window. Don't worry about the web safe or out of gamut warnings as this is an RGB document and we are not going to stick to web safe colors.

5. Click OK. The circle becomes updated with the color you chose.

6. Now we will change the stroke color. Make sure the circle is still selected on the page. In the toolbox, click the stroke color box to bring it to the front.

7. Double-click the stroke box to reveal the color picker. Choose a bright red and click OK.

Now we will use the **color palette** to change a color.

Applying Color to Objects Using the Color Palette

1. Make sure the circle is selected. Click the color fill box in the color palette. This brings the fill box to the front.

2. From within the Color palette, enter the following values in the R, G, and B boxes:

```
R 255
G 255
B 0
```

This creates yellow and fills the circle with that color.

3.   Now click the stroke box in the color palette. Use the sliders this time to create pure blue. Drag the B slider all the way to the right. Drag the R and G sliders all the way to the left.

4.   Finally we will use the **Swatches Palette** to give the circle an orange fill color. With the circle still selected, click the fill color box in the toolbox on the left to enable it. Click an orange swatch from the swatches palette.

All the methods you have just performed achieve the same result. It really is a case of personal preference in terms of which method you choose.

The one important factor about all these methods is that the object on the page must be selected before you can change its color. If you had five circles on the page and you wanted to apply a different color to each circle using colors from within the swatches palette, there is a faster method, dragging and dropping color from the swatches palette, which is what we will do next.

Dragging and Dropping Color

First make sure that the fill color box is at the front in the toolbox.

The five small circles are going to be changed to different colors from the swatches palette. The object you wish to drag a color onto must have an existing color to start with. These five circles all have a red fill. It is not necessary to select any of the circles beforehand, so click on a blank part of the screen to deselect anything that might be currently selected.

1.   In the swatches palette, click and drag a green color onto the first circle. Make sure you keep the mouse button pressed as you drag and release it as you place the cursor over the circle. You will see the circle change to the green color.

2.   Repeat the process dragging a different color from the swatches palette each time.

This is a real time-saver in this situation.

Applying a Value of None to the Stroke or Fill

What if you decide you don't want your circle to have a fill color or a stroke color? It doesn't mean you have to delete the circle and start again. You can simply apply to the stroke or fill a color of none. Which means of course it doesn't exist. We are going to do that now.

All of the methods you have used to apply color, the color picker, the color palette, and the swatches palette, allow you to apply a value of none to a fill or stroke. We will apply no color to the fill of our large circle.

Select the circle. In the toolbox click the fill color box to bring it to the front if it is not already there. Look at the three icons below the fill and stroke box as shown below. The icon on the right displays a red diagonal line. Click this icon to apply a color value of none to the fill of the circle. The fill box in the toolbox also displays the red line as confirmation.

If you look in the color palette and the swatches palette you will see the same icon. Clicking this icon in either of these palettes will have the same effect.

Remember, it is important that the fill box must be at the front of the toolbox or color palette if you want to affect the fill. The stroke box must be at the front if you want to affect the stroke.

Changing the Thickness of the Stroke

You are not limited to using the default stroke set by Illustrator. We are going to change the stroke's width on the circle.

The stroke palette appears on the right of the screen. If yours is closed down you can reveal it going to Window>Stroke.

1. Select the circle if you have not already done so. The stroke palette displays the current stroke thickness or **weight** of the selected circle. Use the drop-down box in the stroke palette to select a weight of 6 pt.

2. Alternatively you can use the up and down arrows in the stroke palette to increase or decrease the stroke weight by 1 point at a time. The numerical box will also allow you to type a number into the box.

You have now covered all the essential elements of creating and applying color to objects. I feel you are sufficiently armed to try applying these techniques to some actual artwork.

Case Study: Flags

From the download folder open the file called `Flags.ai`.

These Maritime flags are going to be used as design elements within our company's printed advertising brochure. For that reason this is a CMYK file. Each section of the flag has a color label template over it so you know which colors should be applied to which section of the flag. None of the flags have a current fill color, which means you won't be able to drag and drop a color. However, I am going to introduce a new sequence of tools in this section that will add to your productivity. Let's begin by applying color to flags A and B using the swatches palette. You will notice the swatches palette only contains the colors we need to use.

Before you begin you need to remember the following:

- Make sure the fill color box is at the front in the toolbox or the color palette.

- Select the section of the flag you wish to color. These flags do not currently have any fill color applied, which means that they are filled with fresh air and you won't be able to select it by clicking in the middle as there is nothing there to click on. You will only be able to select the section of the flag by clicking on the stroke of the object.

Apply the labeled colors to Flag A and B.

Now you have applied white, blue, and red. Take a look at Flag C. The colors in flag C are the same as you have used for flags A and B. So rather than make a trip back to the swatches palette each time, we will use a paired sequence of tools called the **Eyedropper** and **Paintbucket.** These tools work in unison with each other. It is a way of sampling or copying a fill or stroke color from one object and applying it to another object. The benefits are obvious so let's get some practice with this pair.

The Eyedropper tool

First we are going to use only the **Eyedropper**.

1. Select the blue section of flag C.

2. Select the **Eyedropper** tool, (I) from the toolbox, as shown below, and then click the blue section from flag A. The color is copied from flag A and applied to the selected section of flag C.

3. Select the white section of flag C with the **Selection** tool.

4. Select the **Eyedropper** tool from the toolbox and click the white section from flag A.

5. Use the same process to complete this flag.

This is still a little long winded in that you had to keep going to the selection tool each time. To cut down the process we will now bring into play the **Paintbucket** tool.

The Paintbucket Tool

The Paintbucket applies whatever the Eyedropper has picked up, so they work as a perfect pair. We are going to color flag D.

1. Using the **Eyedropper** tool click on the red of flag B to sample it.

2. The **Eyedropper** tool currently hides the **Paintbucket** tool as they share the same location in the toolbox. Keep the mouse button held down over the eyedropper tool and then select the paintbucket from the fly-out.

3. Take the **Paintbucket** icon to flag D and click on the edge of the stroke using the tip of the drip of the Paintbucket. It is important to click on the edge of the stroke as there is no fill color in this flag and so once again you would be clicking on fresh air and the object would not be recognized.

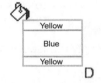

Well that's better, but still not as streamlined as it could be. What we really need is a keyboard shortcut to get us onto the fast track.

4. Make sure nothing is selected on the page. Select the **Eyedropper** from the toolbox and click the blue section of flag A to sample it.

5. Press and hold the ALT key on the keyboard and the Paintbucket appears. The Paintbucket will be the active tool as long as the ALT key is pressed. Now click the stroke around the blue section of flag D to color it.

If you are having trouble clicking on the edge of the stroke, try zooming in closer to make life easier.

You have now been introduced to all the techniques necessary to make completing the other flags a far less laborious task than it may have been otherwise. Work through the other flags and try using all the methods you have been shown so you build your familiarity with them.

When you have finished, you will want to view your efforts without the color labels. All the labels are on one layer called Colors. Click the eye in the layers palette next to this layer as you did in Chapter 2 to hide them.

You have been working on a customized swatch palette in this section. That is to say, you didn't use the Illustrator default palette but a set of colors that I created and saved as a unique palette. In the next section we are going to look at the finer points of the swatches palette and creating your own customized sets.

Organizing Your Colors

Create a new blank RGB document using all the default sizes.

Let's start by looking in depth at the swatches palette. The default swatches palette contains a variety of different elements: fills, gradients, and patterns. There aren't many different examples in this palette but already it's starting to look busy. It would make a lot of sense if we hid any element we are not currently using. The row of icons at the bottom of the palette allows you to do this.

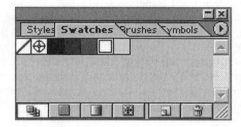

The first icon in the palette is depressed by default. This displays all swatches in the palette irrespective of what they are. Let's assume we are only using solid colors. We can make the swatches palette easier to work with by hiding everything else.

1. Click the second icon from the left in the swatches palette. Now only the solid colors are visible. Don't worry, you haven't deleted anything else, only temporarily hidden them from view.

2. Click the first icon again and all the swatches are visible.

3. Click the third icon from the left in the swatches palette. Now only the gradients are visible.

4. Click the fourth icon from the left to reveal only the pattern swatches.

5. Click the first icon again to reveal all.

In all cases, hover the cursor over each icon and a label will appear identifying the function of each icon.

Next we are going to change the way swatches are displayed.

1. Click the black arrow button in the top right corner of the swatches palette. The pop-up menu that appears allows you to carry out a variety of functions within the palette. Select Large Thumbnail View. This is a useful option for seeing colors or other swatches with more clarity. Obviously they take up more space in the palette and will not be as fast to access.

2. From the same menu select List View. A small swatch appears again with a descriptive line. This is more useful when using particular color palettes, such as Pantone, which we will be seeing shortly.

3. Return to the default view again from the pop-up menu, Small Thumbnail View.

Adding, Duplicating, Deleting, and Editing Swatches

If we were about to create our business logo for our web site and had decided on four colors that were going to be used, we could make a note of the formula for the color and scribble it on a piece of paper to refer to each time. But this is the 21st Century and there is a far better way. We will make our own custom palette of colors that we can use again and again without risk of using the wrong color by mistake. The first thing we need to do is clear all the clutter from the existing swatches palette, leaving us with a clean palette ready to fill with our own color set. During these exercises you will also learn how to add, delete, duplicate, and edit swatches.

Deleting Swatches

1. Make sure the entire palette is visible. You need to see right down to the last swatch in the palette. If this is not visible, place the cursor over the bottom right corner of the palette and drag down to expand it.

We need to keep white, black, and gray in the palette. The gray swatch is the fifth from the left in the top row. We are going to keep everything to the left of this gray swatch.

2. Click the sixth swatch in the palette (Light Gray) then hold down the SHIFT key and click the very last pattern swatch in the palette. All the swatches between the first and last are now selected.

3. Click the waste bin in the bottom right corner of the swatches palette and a box appears asking if you want to delete the swatch selection. Click Yes. This action

deletes the swatch from this document only. Any new documents you create will still display the default swatches. By saving a document you will automatically save the current set of colors within the swatches palette.

Now you are left with black, white, and gray. Next we are going to create just the new colors that we will use for the logo. There are a variety of ways of doing this and we will run through a range of them.

Adding Swatches

1. In the Swatches palette click the black arrow button in the top right corner and from the pop-up menu select New Swatch.

2. In the dialogue box that appears type Deep Aqua in the Swatch Name box. Make sure RGB is the selected color mode from the drop-down box. Enter the numbers in the RGB boxes as shown below and click OK.

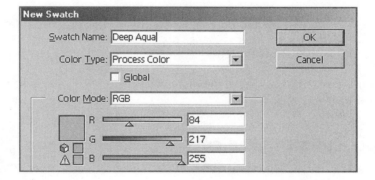

Take a look in the swatches palette and you have your very first customized swatch. We will now create a second swatch, but this time using the color palette, just as you did earlier.

3. In the Color palette, mix a blue fill color with the values:

```
R  29
G  0
B  233
```

This is not a part of our Swatches palette until you tell it to be so.

4. Click and drag from the fill color box in the color palette to the Swatches palette. When you release the mouse button the blue color will be a part of this swatch.

Now we will use the color picker.

5. Double-click the fill box in the toolbox to open the color picker and create an orange color with the following values:

    R 225
    G 215
    B 95

6. Now drag the orange color from the fill color box to the Swatches palette, and that completes our set of custom colors.

There's every chance that you may change your mind about one of the colors. Rather than delete and start again, we are going to edit the color. The deep aqua you created needs to be a little lighter so that is the one we will edit.

7. Double-click the deep aqua swatch in the swatches palette and the Swatch Options box opens. Change the G value to 232 and click OK. The swatch is now updated in the palette.

The more artwork you create, the more you will find this process a far more professional and streamlined way to work.

Introduction to Gradients

A gradient is two or more colors that blend into each other. This creates a subtle continuous tone of color similar to what we see in real life as light falls on an object.

Open the file called Gradients.ai from the download folder. This file contains two objects. The circle is filled with a **Radial Gradient** and the rectangle, a **Linear Gradient.**

Radial Gradients

The first thing you may notice is that the circle looks more like a sphere than a flat circle. We are going to edit the gradient and customize it.

1. Select the circle.

2. If the Gradient Palette is not visible on the left of the screen, open it by going to Window>Gradient. Click the black arrow button in the top right of the palette and select Show Options. If the words Hide Options appear, the palette

is already showing all options and you can click on a blank part of the screen to close the pop-up menu.

The Gradient Palette is now showing the type of gradient, for example Radial, and a sliding scale with white at the left and black at the right. We are going to change the gradient colors from black and white to yellow and red. Make sure the Swatches palette is visible as we are going to be selecting colors from it.

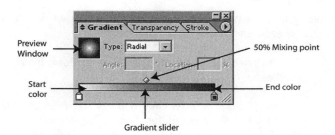

4. This time we will use another technique to apply a red color to the black end of the gradient. Click and drag from a red color in the swatches palette onto the black box at the right end of the slider in the gradient palette.

3. In the gradient palette, click the white square at the left of the sliding scale. It is this square that defines the white color. Press the ALT key and click a yellow color from the swatches tab. Yellow will replace the white.

4. This time we will use another technique to apply a red color to the black end of the gradient. Click and drag from a red color in the swatches palette onto the black box at the right end of the slider in the gradient palette.

5. The colors are at extreme ends. Next we will reposition the colors on the sliding scale.Click the yellow box in the gradient palette and drag it to the right about halfway along the slider. As you drag, notice the number in the location box changing. The location position goes from 0% at the left to 100% at the right. This completely changes the effect of the gradient, increasing the yellow and reducing the red.

6. Drag the yellow box back to the extreme left.

7. A more subtle effect can be achieved by using the diamond shape icon at the top of the color-mixing bar, as shown in the above figure. This icon represents the halfway point between two colors. Drag the diamond shape icon to the left. You will notice the number in the location box change again. This time it displays the position of the original midway point as a percentage on the slider. Dragging towards a color diminishes its size and increases the size of the color at the other end. Set the location at a point you feel happy with.

8. We are now going to save this gradient into the swatches palette. This will then be a permanent part of this document assuming you save the document. From within the gradient palette click and drag from the preview window and into the Swatches palette. You can release the mouse button anywhere in the Swatches palette. If you want to change the location of the swatch in the palette you can just drag it into the desired location.

Linear Gradients

The linear gradient works in the same way. This time we will create a three color gradient with black at each end and white in the middle.

1. Select the rectangle on the page. This object is filled with a white to black linear gradient.

2. In the gradient palette, click midway between the black and white boxes just beneath the Gradient Slider. This action creates a third color box. Look above the Gradient Slider and you will now see two diamond-shape icons, one between each pair of colors.

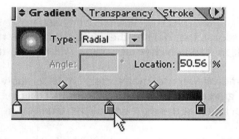

3. Apply a white color to this new color box.

4. Apply a black color to the white box at the far left of the gradient.

You should now have a three color gradient with black at both ends and white in the middle. This is a popular gradient for creating metallic effects.

Once you have created the gradient and saved it in the swatches palette you can apply it to an object to create very different effects. We are now going to look at how you can use these same gradients to "mould" your shape and create a 3D effect shape.

The Gradient Tool

Open the file called Gradient_tool.ai from the download folder. This file contains the same radial gradient that you just created. We are going to re-apply it using the **Gradient** tool to simulate different areas of light and shadow. The Gradient tool is an interactive way of applying a gradient to an object. Simply by clicking and dragging on or near a selected object or objects, you can instantly transform the effect.

1. Select the circle in the top left of the page.

2. Click on the **Gradient** tool in the toolbox.

3. The letters A and B joined by an arrow have been placed as a guide to show where to start dragging and where to stop. Click and drag from position A to position B. Your object will now look more spherical, depicting an object that has light falling on it from the top left.

   Try dragging in different directions. The formula follows a simple principle:

   - A long drag will create a gradient with a subtle continuous tone of colors.

   - A short drag will create a gradient with a sudden change of colors.

4. A single gradient can be applied to multiple objects as if they were one entity. We will use the artwork of the tall black building on the left of the page to illustrate this. The white rectangles depict the windows in the building. Behind the building, the gradient depicts the setting sun. The idea is to select all the white windows and apply the same gradient as in the background so it looks as if we are looking through real windows in the building. Select one of the white windows, and then holding down the SHIFT key, select all the others.

5. Click on the gradient sunset swatch in the swatches palette. You can see the problem. Instead of creating the illusion of looking through multiple windows, we see multiple independent gradients and the effect is lost. This is what we need to fix. Make sure all the windows are still selected.

6. Select the **Gradient Tool** and drag from position A to Position B. Voila! Windows.

Summary

In this chapter you have been introduced to the theory and working application of color within Illustrator. We have looked at the fundamental scientific theory of color and how it relates to color generated on a computer monitor. You now know the differences between common color models, including RGB, CMYK, HSB, and Grayscale, and which is appropriate to use depending on whether your work is destined for print or will be displayed on a screen.

You learned about Color Gamuts and the limitations imposed by each of the different gamuts in terms of the amount of usable colors. You are now able to create, delete, and edit colors within the color swatches palette and apply these colors to a variety of objects.

Finally, you have also learned about gradients and how they can be used to add a new dimension to your vector artwork. You have created, edited, and added gradients to the swatches palette. You also know how to use the Gradient Tool to interactively apply gradients to objects on the page.

During this chapter you have been applying colors to pre-made objects. In the next chapter you will continue creating your own objects using various advanced drawing tools, including one of the most versatile tools in any computer program – the pen tool and its associated editing tools. Add to this one of the exciting new additions to Illustrator 10, in the form of Symbols, and you are on your way to possessing a powerful grasp of tools and techniques at your disposal.

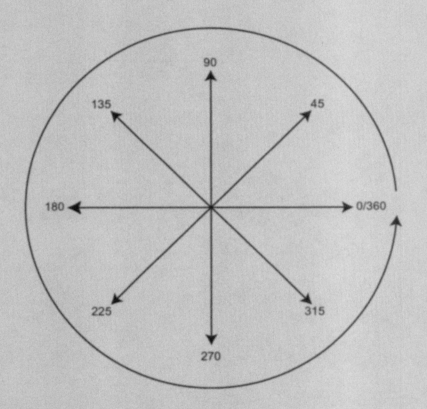

5 Drawing Paths

What We'll Cover in this Chapter:

- Drawing and editing freeform paths

- Working with paths and path components

- Creating Bezier paths with the Pen tool

- Manipulating and reshaping paths

Drawing Freehand Paths

Imagine that you're sitting at an old-fashioned drawing board. In front of you, there is a big, white, open expanse of paper just waiting to be filled with wonderful drawings. To the left of the board are all your stencils for drawing regular shapes, and on the right, your pencil box filled with your favorite pencils and graphic pens.

This is where we are right now in your journey through the Illustrator drawing tools. You've played with all the 'stencils', found them to be very useful for creating shapes and even the foundations of bigger and better artworks, but you're just itching to let fly creatively, to draw long, flourishing strokes with those pencils and pens.

Your Illustrator counterparts of those much loved tools are the **Pencil**, used to draw freehand lines, and the **Pen**, used for creating both irregular straight-edged shapes and smooth sleek curves, and of course, a combination of both. If you're like me, you're as excited about using these tools as you were that very first day you discovered pencils and crayons, and how fantastically they could be used to add that extra interest to any flat surface in the home!

Before we launch in though, we may need to do just a little revision. You remember in Chapter 2, where you discovered the components of Illustrator artwork – those anchor points, direction handles, and direction points? In your previous artwork, you had no control over where Illustrator placed those anchor points, or what type of anchor points were being created. You issued an instruction either by specifying measurements or clicking and dragging to create the shape, and Illustrator automatically did the math for you, plotting both the position and type of anchor points, but now you will begin to take control.

Using the Pencil Tool

One of the criticisms that many people level against computer-generated art is that its lines are too smooth, too perfect, it lacks that hand-drawn organic feeling. The **Pencil** tool is going to give you a chance to express all your creativity in a sketched manner.

Select the **Pencil** tool and draw on the page. As you drag with the mouse, you'll notice that Illustrator shows what you are drawing by showing a dotted line on the page. When you release the mouse, your object will be stroked and filled, using whatever colors are set in the toolbox.

Drawing a Heart

Before we look at the particular options for the pencil tool, let's just have a little practice and get those creative juices going. This is a milestone – you're drawing your own freeform object in Illustrator. Granted, you're tracing over a perfectly shaped heart, but remember we did tell you that most of us still rough out our designs on paper and then scan them in, so that we can draw and refine them in Illustrator. So, this is not cheating, I've just saved you the hassle of having to get the scanner out.

1. Open up the file called `Heart.ai`.

2. Zoom in on the shape until you feel comfortable working with it.

3. Select the **Pencil** tool (N).

4. Click and drag with the **Pencil** tool to trace the heart shape. As this is your first attempt, and you're more than likely using a clunky mouse to draw, do not worry if you cannot complete the shape in one movement. However, to keep the line as one continuous line, you must make sure that the original line is still selected when you continue drawing, and always make sure that you begin the next segment of the line directly over the last anchor point of the existing line, if an x appears next to the pencil a new path is being started, so go back and reselect the path to continue it.)

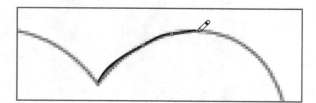

5.   As you approach the beginning of the line, hold down the ALT/OPTION key
      – notice the little circle below the cursor. Release the mouse button and
      then the modifier key. You have effectively created a closed shape.

6.   Don't close the file, and don't worry if the shape is a little shaky. We'll
      correct that in a moment.

If there was a real world equivalent of this pencil, it would have to be called the Magic Pencil.
In the real world, to correct your shape, you'd redraw over the areas, and then with an eraser
you'd gently try to remove the unwanted lines. The **Pencil** tool will do both for you.

Editing the Heart

With the heart shape still selected, we'll magically correct the shape by drawing over it.

1.   Ensure that the heart shape you have drawn is still selected. If it isn't,
      switch to the **Selection** tool (V), click on the heart, and then switch back
      to the **Pencil** tool (N).

2.   Position your mouse over a part of the heart that is correct, and then
      redraw the shape ensuring that as you do so, you finish with your mouse
      over an existing part of the line.

3.   Release the mouse and Illustrator will have redrawn the line for you.

You may have noticed that as you drew, Illustrator put down anchor points for you along
the length of the line. It did this by judging the shape of the line that you were drawing
and the settings for the **Pencil** tool. This means you have control – you can determine how
the **Pencil** tool will react when you use it. Let's have a look at those settings now. To access
this dialog box, you need to double-click on the **Pencil** tool in the toolbox.

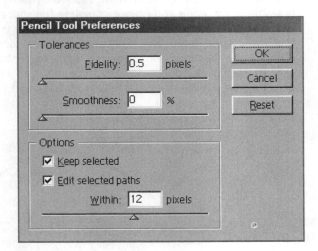

The first two settings, Fidelity and Smoothness, regulate how Illustrator interprets your mouse movements as you draw your shape.

- Fidelity controls how closely the path that Illustrator draws for you reflects the movement of the mouse. The lower the value, the more closely Illustrator will interpret the movement of the mouse. This will result in a more accurate reflection of the path you drew, but it will possibly be a little lumpy, with many points and therefore a more complex path.

  The higher the value, the less controlling you are being, giving Illustrator freedom to interpret your path. This may result in a less accurate reflection of the path you drew, but it will be smoother, and, with fewer anchor points, less complex. In the illustration here, the lumpy heart shape on the left hand side was drawn with Fidelity set to 0.5 pixels, which meant that Illustrator faithfully produced for me, every lump, bulge and wobble of the mouse as I dragged to create the shape. On the right-hand side, a beautifully smooth shape, produced with a high value of 20 pixels.

- Smoothness also affects how Illustrator interprets the shape or the smoothness of the path that it draws for you. The higher you set this value, the smoother the path it will draw, whereas the lower the value, the more faithfully Illustrator will reproduce all those twists, turns, and stutters. In the graphic here, the left-hand side was set to a low Smoothness value, with the right set to a high value.

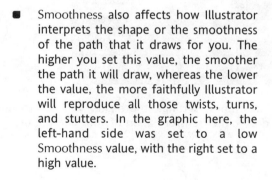

- The Keep selected option determines whether or not the path remains selected after you have released the mouse button. It is handy to keep this checked if you find that you battle to draw a complete line in one movement and need to constantly add to the end of the existing path you have drawn.

- In the exercise above, you were able to edit your heart shape by drawing over it because the option Edit selected paths was checked. This value gives how close the mouse must be to the selected line before Illustrator realizes that you want to actually edit it.

Using the Smooth Tool

Okay, you've drawn the line, the settings weren't quite what you wanted, and the path is all lumpy. What are your options? Delete it and start again? No, that's too much like hard work. Time to call in the trusty **Smooth** tool to sort out those problems:

There are a few rules for using the **Smooth** tool. Firstly, make sure that the line that you want to smooth is selected, otherwise Illustrator has no idea which line you wish to edit. Then, drag the **Smooth** tool over the portion of the line you wish to reshape.

Similar to the **Pencil** tool, the **Smooth** tool has options to control how radically Illustrator decides to smooth out your lumps and bumps. Remember that to access a tools preference dialog box, you double-click on the tool in the toolbox.

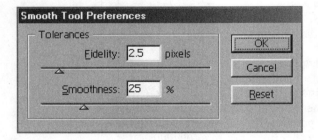

With both the Fidelity and the Smoothness settings, the higher you opt to make the settings, the smoother and more drastic the transformation of your line will be:

Using the Erase Tool

You just knew there had to be one of these floating around, didn't you? If you can draw with a pencil, there has to be some way that you can erase parts of a line.

As ever, the first thing you must do before attempting to erase a part is to select it first with the **Selection** tool (V). Then, place the eraser part of the tool over the path you wish to edit, and drag it over the path to erase parts of it. Just a word of warning – occasionally when you perform multiple erases on the same path, some parts will become disconnected, and therefore no longer selected. You will have to reselect those particular paths before you can continue to edit them. It's a pain in the neck, but that's what we've got.

Case Study: Drawing a Star Fish

In this exercise, we will draw a fairly basic starfish shape. Yes, I know, we could have just created a five-pointed star and been done with it, but one of the beauties of Mother Nature is that she creates each object with its own natural, organic, irregular characteristics and that is the aspect we want to copy here.

1. Open the file called `Pencil.ai`. You have been provided with a starfish shape to trace over, but if you're feeling confident and creative, feel free to ignore the shape and draw your own starfish.

2. Double-click the **Pencil** tool in the toolbox to display the tool preferences, and click on the Reset button to set the tool back to its default settings.

3. Zoom in using the Navigator so that the starfish pretty much fills the visible area in your screen. Remember, if the Navigator palette is not visible, you can display it by going to Window > Navigator.

4. Start to trace the starfish by clicking and dragging around its shape with the **Pencil** tool. Do not worry if the mouse slips and you make an awful mistake, we can always edit that later.

5. Continue to drag until you have nearly completed the shape. Hold down the ALT/OPTION key and release the mouse button when you have returned to the starting point.

6. If you cannot draw the shape in one movement, bear in mind that you can continue to add onto a line as long as it is still selected and you click and drag from the highlighted point at the end of the line.

7. Ensure that the path is still selected, and refine it by dragging with the **Pencil** tool over parts of the shape to redraw them.

8. If you still feel that it could do with a little more finesse, don't forget that you can use the **Smooth** tool to iron out some of those wrinkles.

9. Save and close the file.

Creating and Manipulating Bezier Curves

A word of warning here – there are many designers out there using Illustrator who still shy away from the **Pen** tool and working with those Bezier curves. Silly really. Okay, I admit that when you first start using it, you may find it non-intuitive, clunky, and peculiar. My advice to you is to not give up, but to persevere with it, and soon you'll wonder how you ever managed without it.

We'll start off with some relatively simple shapes, and then move through both creating and editing **Bezier** curves, so that by the end of the chapter we'll have you drawing seahorses.

Drawing Straight Edged Shapes with the Pen Tool

The easiest way to explain to you how the **Pen** tool draws straight lines is to take you back to days of old, when you played join the dots to reveal a hidden drawing. It's going to be very much like that, except this time, you're placing the dots, and Illustrator is joining them up for you! It's all to do with that vector activity going on in the background. By placing dots, more correctly known as anchor points, you are telling Illustrator the co-ordinates, length, and angle of each line. As you click on the Artboard with the **Pen** tool, Illustrator will naturally draw straight lines for you; and if you want to constrain the angle of that line to increments of 45 degrees, hold down the SHIFT key as you click to place the constrained line's anchor point.

Drawing a Yacht

To make it clearer, let's cut to the chase and draw a yacht straight away. Granted, it's not going to be the most sophisticated of yachts, but it will illustrate our point quite clearly.

1. Open the file Yacht.ai. Okay, I admit it, it doesn't look like a yacht at all, but in a few minutes it will, mark my words. To the right of the letters you can see a completed yacht, just to give you an idea of what it is you can expect to see:

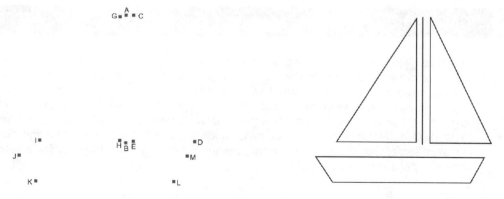

2. Select the **Pen** tool (P).

3. The first object we will draw will be the yacht's mast – a straight line drawn from A to B. Click and release the mouse button on the square below the letter A. The mast has to be perfectly straight, so to confine the line to increments of 45 degrees, SHIFT+click on the square labeled B.

4. Now for the foresail. But be careful. You may recall how we compared drawing straight lines with the Pen tool to playing join the dots. If you click on Point C now, you will extend the line from Point B through to Point C, which is not what we want. You need to deselect the initial line. One way would be to switch to the **Selection** tool (V) and click elsewhere on the Artboard, then switch back to the **Pen** tool (P) and continue. Another, quicker, way, is to do it the way the pros do. Temporarily toggle

to the last used **Selection** tool by holding down the CTRL/CMD key, and click anywhere on the Artboard. Release the mouse button and then release the modifier key.

5. Click at Point C, and then click at Point D. Do not hold the SHIFT key down when you do this, as the angle of the sail is not an increment of 45 degrees. Then SHIFT+click on Point E, and to close the sail and constrain the line to a straight line again, click back on Point C. When you move your cursor back to Point C, Illustrator will be giving you a hint that you are over the beginning of the line. Do you notice the circle very close to the base of your cursor? This indicates that you are about to close the path. The main sail, at the rear of the yacht, can be completed in the same manner. Finally, try drawing the hull as well.

Not too bad was it? You're wondering what all that fuss was about, and I'm sure you noticed that in many instances it will be quicker for you to use the **Pen** tool to create a desired shape than one of your regular primitive tools.

Case Study: Drawing Marine Flags with the Pen Tool

Let's take a few moments to practice these skills before we move on to the more complex option of drawing curves with the Pen tool. You remember those simple marine flags we started drawing in Chapter 3, I'll bet you had a look at a few of those odd shapes and wondered how you were going to create them with rectangles, ellipses, and the like! Now you know the answer, we'll use the Pen tool to draw some of them now, just to consolidate these skills. As Marine Quest is a company which will be offering both sailing and diving, it makes sense that we get Flag A done, because its special meaning is to indicate that there is a diver down in the water.

The A Flag

1. Open up the file Flags.ai again. This is the same flags file that you started working on in Chapter 3 when you were creating those basic shapes, and Chapter 4 when you were using color. You'll remember that I created views that would allow you to zoom in directly on the flag in question? This time the flag we'll be doing is Flag A. From the View menu choose Flag A in the bottom section of the menu.

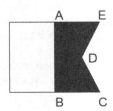

2. Ensure that you have **Smart Guides** on, this will help you to identify the guides that have been placed for you, and make sure that you have a black stroke and no fill selected.

3. Look at the flag carefully and you'll notice that it is created from two distinct shapes, a rectangle on the left – which will be easy for you to draw – and then an odd, irregular shape on the right which we can easily draw with the **Pen** tool. Create the rectangle first, and then you must deselect the rectangle – remember that tip on holding down CTRL/CMD and clicking away from the selected object.

4. Follow the letters shown opposite in the screenshot – note these letters are not in your flags file, because I realize that you may often want to try these skills without direct instruction from me. But if you are following – click at A and then SHIFT+click at B to constrain the line to an increment of 45 degrees, then SHIFT+click at C for the same reasons. Click at D and then E, but do not hold down the SHIFT key when you do it as these lines are not at increments of 45 degrees. To complete the shape, move the cursor over your original starting position, A, wait for the cursor to show a little circle below the base of the pen (indicating that you are going to be closing the path) and SHIFT+click.

5. You might just wish to complete this flag with color. The left-hand rectangle is white, and the odd shape on the right is blue. The swatches are in the Swatches palette for you.

The B Flag

1. Switch to the view for the B Flag.

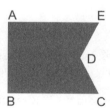

2. You'll notice that the shape is pretty much the same as the right-hand side of the previous flag. I think I can safely presume that you'll be able to complete this one without much instruction. The only tips I'll be giving is to remember to hold down the SHIFT key when you click for lines that are obviously increments of 45 degrees. Also, watch for that little circle at the base of the pen cursor when you return to your starting point to ensure that you are closing the path.

3. Color this flag red.

Flag 1

In addition to the rectangular alphabet flags, there are also 10 numeric flags, in the shape of pennants – just the job for the pen tool!

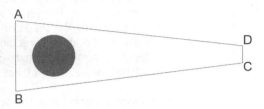

1. Switch to the view for Flag 1, and notice the new shape we have to draw here. You'll need to draw the pennant first, and then the circle, so that the pennant does not hide the circle – you know about stacking order. Once again, I've put the letter clues here, but not in the actual file.

2. Click at A, SHIFT+click at B to constrain the line, then click at C, SHIFT+click at D to constrain the line, and click back at A to close the path, keeping an eye on the cursor for that tell-tale circle again.

3. Draw the circle. If you look closely, you'll notice that there is a little X marking the center. Draw the circle from the center, using the X as a guide. Color the pennant white, and the circle red.

Feel free to go on to any of the other flags if you have time to practice. Look particularly for those ones with irregular shapes that you would have difficulty creating with the basic shape tools you used in Chapter 3.

Working with Curves

Before getting stuck into curves, let's ground ourselves with the different types of anchor points Illustrator uses. Essentially, it creates two distinct types:

- **Corner Anchor Points**: In the illustration on the right, there are two path segments, joined by three Corner Anchor points. Notice that the lines between the anchor points are straight.

● **Smooth Anchor Points**: The Smooth Anchor point is shown here. It is the central black point on the straight line, marking where that line joins the smooth curve. Two direction lines spring from it, which can be controlled like bicycle handlebars, thereby manipulating the shape and strength of the curve.

Illustrator also has the ability to create hybrids of these two. Have a look at the cloud shape below:

This is one of those typical hybrid shapes, similar to the heart shape you met in Chapter 2. We have curved lines, so they'll have direction lines, but you'll notice that where they meet there is a sharp corner. So here we have a Corner Anchor point, which has these direction lines. But there is a subtle difference with the way in which the direction lines will react. When we move one of them it will move independently of, and not affect, its adjoining handle.

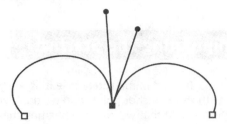

There's another hybrid you will meet in your exploration of Illustrator. We can get Corner Anchor Points that only have one handle – for the curved path segment which is either entering or leaving the anchor point.

Have a look at the two hollow anchor points in the diagram below and you'll notice that each only has one handle relating to where the line is curved. Now I'll let you into a little secret for dissecting how these lines work, and for drawing your paths a little later on.

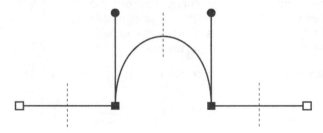

Now, I want you to look at this a little differently. Let's assume that anchor points always have two handles hiding inside – whether or not those handles are visible is what determines what type of anchor point you have and the shape of the line.

Look at the diagram above and notice the dotted lines I have drawn – these are marking half of the path segment going into the anchor point, and half of the segment coming out of the anchor point. That's essentially how we plot our anchor points, realizing that the anchor point controls the half of the line segment going into the point, and the half of the segment directly after the point. Have a look at that first solid point – the first half of the line going into the anchor point is straight, therefore it does not need a direction line, whereas the second part coming out of the anchor point is curved, and it does need a direction line. Similarly look at the second solid point. The first half of the segment going into the anchor point is curved, and therefore it needs a direction line, but the second half, the part coming out of the anchor point is straight, and therefore it does not need a direction line. Do not be too concerned if this concept still seems a little tricky. You'll get a chance to push and pull those direction lines in a few minutes, and we will also revisit this half and half concept when we begin to draw lines ourselves.

Exercise: Manipulating the Starfish

Open up your `Pencil.ai` file and immediately save it as `Penplay.ai` on your hard drive. We're going to fiddle with those anchor points and we don't want to damage your original creation. You might think it odd that we are manipulating these anchor points before you have actually started to consciously draw **Corner** and **Smooth** anchor points, but this little exercise serves two purposes. It will make you more familiar with how these anchor points are going to work, and also make you very much aware that it does not matter how and where you initially place your anchor points, because we can always come back and modify them later!

1.   Switch to the **Direct Selection** tool and click on your starfish outline to make the anchor points on the path visible. Note that the anchor points

are displayed as hollow squares. This indicates that they are not selected. If by chance you happened to click on an anchor point when you selected the path, that particular anchor point is displayed as a solid square. If no anchor point is active, click on one now.

2.   Zoom in closely on the edge of the path and have a little play with the anchor points to try and refine your path.

3.   Click and drag on an anchor point to reposition it slightly to improve the outline.

4.   Pull gently on a path segment between two anchor points and watch how it behaves. It will depend on what type of anchor point is at each end of the segment, but if there are direction lines, notice how they move as you pull and push on the segment.

5.   Be brave. Select a direction line, drag it along its existing angle and notice how the curve responds. Keep the direction line the same length, and move it to change its angle in relation to the anchor point, and again, watch how the curve responds. Do not worry if you distort the outline slightly. You may well be back to make it perfect.

Drawing Curves with the Pen Tool

The most accurate method of creating smooth, flowing lines in Illustrator is to use the **Pen** tool which allows you to place anchor points where you wish upon a path.

Creating Simple Curves

Unlike when you were placing **Corner Anchor points**, and you clicked with the **Pen** tool on the Artboard, to create a **Smooth Anchor point**, you click and drag with the **Pen** tool in the direction you want the line to go. This little instruction is telling Illustrator that you want to be able to drag those hidden direction lines out of the anchor point. Have a look at the diagram below, which was drawn from left to right using **Smooth Anchor points**. This is a very simple curved line drawn by placing Smooth points at certain points along the path, and then dragging in the direction in which we wish the path to go.

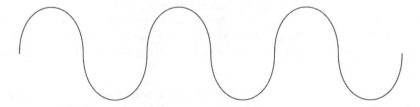

Now you may be wondering how I managed to tell Illustrator in which direction I wanted the path to go. The arrows that have been added to the diagram below now show you both where the **Smooth Anchor points** were placed, and the direction in which I dragged as I placed the anchor points.

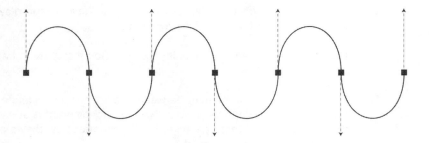

So, how does Illustrator know when to start making the line go up and down? Here's where we get back to that half and half story I mentioned earlier. Have a look at the diagram below and note the dotted lines I have used to segment the paths between the anchor points. At the first anchor point, I clicked and dragged up, and so the line went up, but at the second, I clicked and dragged down, and you'll notice that from halfway before the anchor point, denoted by a little star, to halfway after the anchor point, denoted by the arrowhead, the line went down.

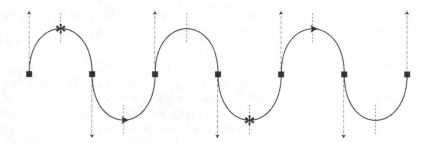

And that is the secret to placing these anchor points efficiently, knowing that as you do, you are drawing the half segment that goes into the anchor point, and the half segment that comes out of the anchor point. This is because all anchor points have two direction lines, although sometimes they aren't visible, as when we create simple **Corner Anchor points**. The important thing is to realize that one direction line is controlling the half segment just before the anchor point and the other is controlling the half segment after the anchor point.

Just a little bit more about these direction lines before we get onto a short practice exercise. The direction lines control two aspects of the curve – its **strength** and **direction**.

In the diagram below, the anchor point placed at Point A was dragged fairly strongly up, and thus that part of the path segment reflects a deeper curve – notice the first dividing line I have placed on the path segment. At Point B, I clicked and dragged only for a short distance, and hence the curve is not as deep. Granted, it may seem deeper than it should be, but we have to remember that it has to join up with the path segments created by the adjoining anchor points.

At Point D, I was no longer dragging directly upwards, but up and right, and notice how the curve is slanting to the right. At Point E, I clicked and dragged down and to the left, and you'll notice that from the dividing line before the anchor point, to the dividing line after the anchor point, that the line is going down and left. Once again the segment has to interact with the directions given to the segments before and after by the adjacent anchor points, but you can definitely see that it is going in that direction.

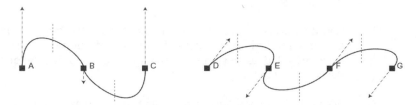

With all the previous examples, you may have noted that I was always clicking and dragging in the opposite direction to the previous point – and you may think that that always has to be the case! So, just to prove you wrong, here's a typical S-curve:

You'll notice that at each of the anchor points I clicked and dragged upward, and so immediately before and after the anchor point, the line is forced into a vertical climb. But Illustrator has to cope with this and keep these lines joined, and that is the downward stretch that you see between each anchor point. It's Illustrator managing to make sense of your demands, by saying 'if they want to make the line go up again, I guess, I'll just have to take it down a bit first'.

Exercise: Drawing Simple Curves

Let's put what we have just learned about creating simple curves into practice. Concentrate on where you are placing the anchor points, and the direction in which you are dragging. As you do, try to visualize which way you are telling the curve to go.

1. Open the file called Curves1.ai. Ensure that your Fill is set to None and the Stroke can be any color. Having no fill just makes it easier for you to see what you are doing, and to trace the curves beneath the path you are drawing. If you have Smart Guides on, I'd switch them off for the moment and also ensure that you do not have Snap to Grid on either. For both of these remember you go to the View menu to check whether they are active.

2. Choose Curves1 from the View menu. Select the **Pen** tool (P) and click and drag upwards at the first point on the left, using the direction lines I have provided as a guide for the direction and length of the curve. Release the mouse.

3. Click on the second anchor point and drag downwards, once again using my direction line as a guide. Notice how as you are dragging, that the line segment before the anchor point is starting to come down. Initially you may find it a little disconcerting that the segment after the anchor, which you are already drawing, only becomes visible once you plot the next anchor point.

4. Continue clicking and dragging at each anchor point, following the direction lines until you get to the end of the line. You must deselect before you go onto the next part of the exercise, otherwise Illustrator will continue to play 'join the dots' for you! Deselect by choosing Deselect from the Select menu (CTRL/CMD+SHIFT+D) or by holding down the CTRL/CMD key and clicking anywhere on the Artboard away from your art.

5. Switch to the Curves2 view. Here we will look at how the length of the direction line influences the depth of the curve. Click and drag upwards at the first anchor point, at the second, click and drag downwards, but do not make the direction line too long. Notice how this affects the curve. Complete by clicking and dragging upwards on the third point.

6. Remember to deselect before you go onto Curves3.

7. Switch to the Curves3 view. In this example, we will concentrate on how the direction of the line controls the direction of the curve. At the first point on the left, click and drag up and to the right, following the direction guideline. You'll only see the effect that this has on the line after you position the second anchor point, so let's do that now. Click and drag down and to the left on the second square. Notice how the first part of the path segment was being drawn towards the right, and then the half of the segment before the second anchor point is being dragged down and to the left. Complete the line by placing the two remaining anchor points and dragging in the directions as indicated by the guides. Deselect this line and move onto Curves4.

8. Curves4 is that S-curve example I discussed before you began this exercise. At each point click and drag upwards to force the path into a climb. Notice how Illustrator makes the path go down for you, so you can tell it to go up at each click and drag.

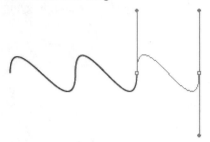

9. Save the file. You might just want to come back and edit some of those curves a little later on after you have learned more about how they work and how to manipulate them.

Drawing Mixed Paths

Okay, so now you've got a 'handle' on how to draw those simple curves, and you've also had practise drawing straight lines, but you know that shapes are not that simple. They are rarely composed exclusively of either straight or curved lines, many of them will be a combination of both, and it's about time we learned how to create these combinations. Look at the puzzle piece below, and I'll talk you through the shape:

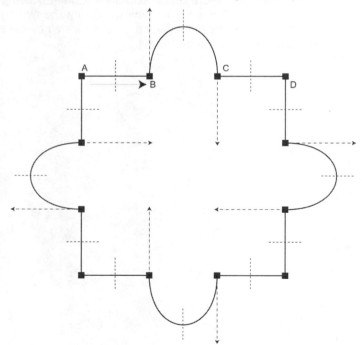

As you'll notice, there is a combination of **Corner** and **Smooth** Anchor points. The illustration was started at Point A and continued in a clockwise direction. At Point A, all I wanted was a simple Corner point with no direction lines, so I just clicked but did not drag with the **Pen** tool, but at the second point, it's all change. Think back to that half and half story. As you look at the Point B, note that the half of the line preceding the anchor point is straight, yet the portion after the anchor point is curved. This is going to be one of those hybrid corner points where we have one visible direction line – the direction line controlling the part of the segment after the anchor point.

Look at the Point C, and you'll see that this is the opposite of the previous anchor point. The part of the segment preceding the anchor point is curved, and will therefore need a direction line, but the part of the segment afterwards is straight, and therefore will not need a direction line.

How do we tell Illustrator that we want to create these hybrid anchor points? Think about it. As we created **Corner Anchor points**, we did one thing – we clicked with the **Pen** tool. This told Illustrator that we wanted a **Corner point** with no direction lines visible. It was effectively telling Illustrator to hide both of the possible direction lines. When we wanted a **Smooth Anchor point**, we clicked and dragged, and this told Illustrator to show both of the possible direction lines.

Now we want to 'talk' to the direction lines separately, firstly to the one that controls the part of the path segment preceding the anchor point, and then secondly to the one which controls the path segment after the anchor point. It needs to be a three-step process as we address the different direction lines, one at a time.

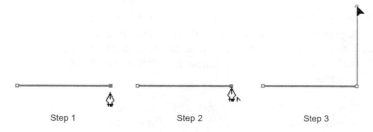

Step 1   Step 2   Step 3

Let's have a look at that three-step process used for creating Point B in our jigsaw puzzle piece.

- I click to create Point A, and then move to where I want to position Point B. At this stage I am 'talking' to the first of the direction lines – the one that controls the part of the line preceding the anchor point. I click, and by that instruction I am telling Illustrator that I want this segment to be straight.

- After releasing the mouse button, I move the cursor over the anchor point again. This time I am 'talking' to the direction line that controls the part of the segment that is drawn after the anchor point. Notice how if the cursor is positioned correctly, Illustrator tells me by displaying an upside-down 'V'.

- As the cursor displays, I click on the anchor point and drag a direction handle out of the anchor point. You recall I said that there were always two direction lines hiding inside anchor points and they would only display if we instructed them to do so. By clicking and dragging on that anchor point again, I am giving the instruction that I want that second direction line to display. Be aware that as you drag, you are not dragging the path, you are dragging a direction line, which is telling the path that in the next segment it must curve upwards.

A similar, but reverse procedure is used for creating Point C. This has a curved segment coming into it, and a straight path leaving the anchor point.

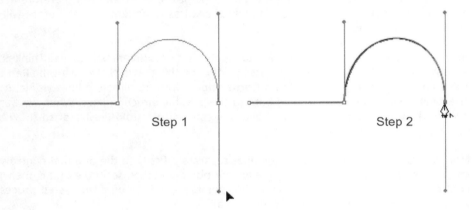

Step 1   Step 2

- To create the first part of the segment, I'm 'talking' once again to that first direction handle, and I click and drag to create a curved path. But the problem is that I now have two handles, because Illustrator has automatically assumed that I want to create a **Smooth Anchor point** because I have clicked and dragged.

- This is where the second instruction comes in, so to speak. I move the cursor over the active anchor point until it displays the upside-down 'V', indicating that I am about to convert this anchor point. I click – the instruction for a **Corner point** – and the handle is retracted. And I am able to continue by creating a straight-line segment.

Exercise: Drawing Combination Lines

Just as you were relaxing, taking all this new knowledge in and assimilating it, I'm here saying the best way to make it all seem clear is for you to try and create the puzzle piece yourself.

1.   Open the file called `Curves2.ai`. Notice that once again there is a guide for you to trace over, and there are also some additional details at the side, explaining how the anchor points have been color-coded. These colors have no special significance, I've just done it to try and make the process easier for you.

2.   Switch to the **Pen** tool (P) and make sure you have a Fill of None just to make drawing easier as you trace over the image. Having a solid fill would obscure the diagram below. Choose any color for your stroke.

3.   Point A is a red corner point, just click to place the point. At Point B – a green corner point – click to instruct Illustrator to create a straight segment. Release the mouse. When the cursor changes, click and drag on the anchor point to create a curved segment after the path. Drag the direction line straight up using the arrow line as a guide. If you wish to make sure the direction line is perfectly straight, hold down the SHIFT key as you drag.

4.   At Point C – a blue corner point – click and drag in the direction of the arrow guide to create an initial curved segment. Release the mouse. Move the cursor over the active point, and then when the cursor indicates that you are in **Convert Anchor point** mode, click to force Illustrator to retract the handle.

5.   Those are the three types of anchor points you'll meet in this exercise, so let's just re-cap what you'll do at each:

- Red – click to place a simple corner point.

- Green – a corner point with a straight segment preceding the anchor part, and a curved segment following the anchor point. Click and release the mouse. Move the cursor over the active anchor until it changes to the **Convert Anchor** point cursor. Click on the anchor point and drag out a direction line in the direction you would like the curve to go. Release the mouse.

- Blue – a corner point with a curved segment preceding the anchor point, and a straight segment following it. Click and drag in the direction of the arrow guide to create an initial curved segment. Release the mouse. Move the cursor over the active point, and when it indicates that you are in **Covert Anchor** point mode, click to retract the direction line.

6. Continue in this manner until you return to Point A. When the cursor indicates you are about to close the path by showing a small circle at the base of the **Pen** icon, click and release the mouse.

A Final Variation on Drawing Mixed Paths

You recall that cloud shape I showed you a few pages back – where we had curved paths going into sharp corner points. As there were curved lines, we can safely assume that there are direction lines, but where they meet there is a sharp corner. This is a third type of **Corner Anchor point** – with two visible direction lines, that act independently of each other, unlike the direction lines that act in tandem in **Smooth Anchor** points.

Once again, creating these hybrid **Corner Anchor** points requires a two-step process as we 'talk' initially to the direction line controlling the part of the path before the anchor point, and then to the direction line controlling the segment after the anchor point. Have a look at this diagram below, and I'll talk you through it:

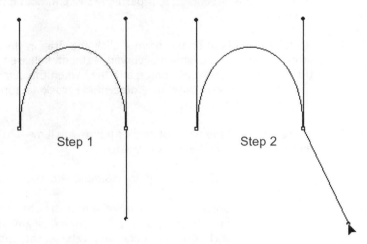

Step 1   Step 2

- In Step 1, after placing the initial point, click and drag down to tell Illustrator that you want the first part of this anchor point's path segment to curve downwards.

- In Step 2, without releasing the mouse, hold down the ALT/OPTION key, which indicates to Illustrator that you want to convert the second direction line. You are then able to swing it and place it independently of the first direction line.

Release the mouse and then release the ALT/OPTION key. It does not matter if you release the mouse key, before you start to swing the handle. Just hold the ALT/OPTION key down, grab the direction line and drag it round. It's easier to do it in one movement, as it saves you having to reselect the direction line, and run the risk of being presented with a horrid dialog box when you miss!

Exercise: Drawing Clouds

In this little exercise you'll get a chance to draw a cloud shape and practice getting those curves just right.

1. Open the file called Curves3.ai and you'll see that cloud template ready for you to practice your skills.

2. As before to make life a little easier, ensure that your Fill is set to None, and **Smart Guides** are not on.

3. The starting point is the red arrow at Point A. Click and drag following the arrow guide, and then release the mouse.

4. This is where it gets a little tricky. At the next point click and drag down in the direction of 7 o'clock, but do not watch where the mouse is going. Your focus is with the direction handle being created for the part of the path segment going into the anchor point. As you drag, you'll notice how you are dragging in the opposite direction to swing the direction line into position. Once you are happy with the placement of that direction line and the curve that is being formed, hold down the ALT/OPTION key and swing the direction line to line up with the second handle direction line emanating from that anchor point. Release the mouse and then the ALT/OPTION key.

5. Move to the next point, click and drag in a direction that is close to 9 o' clock, all the time watching the placement of the direction line being formed for the part of the line going into the anchor point. Press the ALT/OPTION key in when the curve is correct, and swing the handle round to match the other direction line.

6. Release the mouse and then the ALT/OPTION key.

7. Continue doing this, clicking and dragging in the opposite direction and then ALT/OPTION swinging that split handle. If you place an anchor point in the incorrect position, just hold down the SPACEBAR and drag to move it – just like you did with those basic shapes earlier. Release the SPACEBAR when the anchor point is in the correct position, and continue as before.

8. When you get to the last point – the place at which you began – hold down the ALT/OPTION key before you click and drag to create the curve.

9. Save and close the file.

Tips for Drawing Curves

Keep the following guidelines in mind to help you draw any kind of curve quickly and easily:

- To draw a curve, click and drag with the mouse button in the direction in which you would like the curve to go, and release the mouse when the angle and strength of the curve is to your liking. To continue the curve, click and drag elsewhere in the image. Illustrator will play join the dots for you.

- To split a pair of direction lines "on the fly" – as you are drawing the path – click and drag to create your curve, and then without letting go of the mouse button, hold down the ALT/OPTION key and drag the direction handle to a new position.

- To pull a handle out of a corner point "on the fly", place the point simply by clicking, then click directly on the anchor point, and drag a direction handle out.

- To force Illustrator to retract the second direction handle in a curve point whilst you are drawing the path, click again on the smooth anchor point immediately after placing it on the Artboard.

- Always drag the first direction point in the direction of the bump of the curve, and drag the second direction point in the opposite direction to create a single curve. Dragging both direction points in the same direction creates an "S" curve.

- When drawing a series of continuous curves draw one curve at a time, placing anchor points at the beginning and end of each curve, not at the tip of the curve. Use as few anchor points as possible, placing them as far apart as possible, because anchor points are information, and if you put unnecessary points in your file it will become more complex than needed.

- A further tip is to always choose the **Direct Selection** tool (A), and then the **Pen** tool (P) before you start to draw. Doing so will mean that you can easily toggle to the **Direct Selection** tool by holding down the CTRL/CMD key to access the tool used most recently, and consequently you can tweak your curves as you draw them without having to change tools.

- One of the niftiest options out is the ability to reposition an anchor point as you are drawing. Often as you begin drawing, you'll place your anchor point in the wrong position, and that will make it difficult for you to drag and get your curve correct. If your anchor is in the wrong position, don't let go of the mouse but hold down the SPACEBAR to reposition the anchor and when it is in the desired position, release only the SPACEBAR. Continue to drag the direction handles to create the angles of your curve.

Case Study: Using Bezier Curves to Create a Starfish

In previous chapters you started slowly building up the components that George and Lucy visualize you using in their Marine Quest corporate identity, and I think a company that is based around the sea, sun, and water needs a starfish or two on those glossy pages and web sites.

Now a real chance to practice drawing those Bezier curves. A few pages ago, I mentioned that you may find the **Pen** tool difficult to handle initially, but I also encouraged you to persevere with it. It is for this reason that we have chosen to redraw a shape with which you are already familiar. You'll complete this section of the exercise with a few directions as to how to place and drag the anchor points, and then later on, you can practice by tracing over a seahorse image, with limited help.

Open the file called Pen.ai. You should feel at home with this familiar starfish, but now you are going to recreate it far more economically and possibly more accurately. As your prowess improves, you will find that when you draw with the **Pen** tool, your curves will become smoother and more accurate.

Let's have a quick look at how the instructions have been included. The little colored squares around the edge of the shape are indicators to show you where to position your anchor points. Note that they are color-coded again to help you differentiate between the different types:

- The gold squares indicate that the anchor point is one of those smooth curves, where the direction lines function like bicycle handlebars.

- The green squares indicate corner anchor points, but not in every instance in this particular exercise; the corners have two direction lines projecting from each anchor point – similar to those you created in the cloud exercise.

- The little lines with circles at the end of each one are to indicate the positioning of the direction lines and direction points.

When you are finished with the starfish, save it and keep the file open. Now open the 03pencil1.ai starfish file that you created earlier. Compare them by looking at the smoothness of the curves and the number of points on each one. Remember you are trying to be as economical with the number of points as possible. Aspects that you are looking to compare are the smoothness of the lines that you have managed to create using the **Pen** tool as opposed to those lines created with the **Pencil**, and also the number of anchor points that have been created in the two illustrations. Remember, unnecessary anchor points mean unnecessary information in your files – and you want to keep these files as lean and clean as possible, right from the beginning.

When you are finished scrutinizing the files, save and close both of them. And you're on to the last challenge of the chapter – drawing a seahorse!

Case Study: Drawing the Seahorse

We know you're up for the challenge and this exercise certainly is one. I've given you a pretty complicated shape to draw – a seahorse with all its sharp edges and curved lines. It is a tough assignment, but excellent practice – it really is sink or swim time. Remember that it does not matter if your initial shape is less than perfect. You can always reshape by manipulating the positioning and direction of the anchor points and direction lines.

So open that Seahorse.ai file, settle back down, and face the challenge head on. You'll feel proud of yourself when you've accomplished it.

When you have completed the file, save it onto your hard drive again. We are going to be doing some wonderful things with that seahorse in the future. If you don't think yours is quite up to scratch, don't despair, as I will supply a completed one for you to use in later chapters as well.

Manipulating and Modifying Paths

As you've been learning all about how to draw with the **Pen** tool effectively, I bet there's been one nagging thought at the back of your mind. That fear of what happens if you put a point down in the wrong place, or put the wrong type of point down, or even miss out a point altogether. Does that mean you'd have to scrap the path and start again? Of course not, you know by now that Illustrator always has a few tricks up its sleeve to make your life easier.

Adding and Removing Anchor Points

It's extremely unlikely, even as you become more and more proficient with using the **Pen** tool, that you'll always be totally happy with every path you draw. With this in mind, there are two more variations of the **Pen** tool that we can use to add or remove anchor points from a selected path. Did you notice the use of that word – selected – it's very important! The path that you want to manipulate must be selected if these tools are to work.

The two tools we use to modify the number of anchor points on a path are the **Add Anchor Point** (+) tool – which is the pen icon with a little plus sign next to it – and the **Delete Anchor Point** (-) tool.

To add an anchor point to a path, ensure that the path is selected and with either the **Pen** tool or the **Add Anchor Point** tool, move your cursor over the path, and then click to add the new anchor point.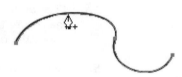

Removing anchor points from a path follows a fairly similar procedure. The path must be selected, and then with the **Delete Anchor Point** tool (-) or the **Pen** tool move the cursor over the point you wish to remove and click. If you're using the Pen tool, observe the + and - signs appear beside the icon.

Case Study: Creating a Banana Leaf

Here's an optional piece that you might find a use for in your case study at a later stage. George and Lucy have given you a fair amount of direction about the graphics they would like included in the materials, but they are always open to suggestions from you – so you might just want to show this to them:

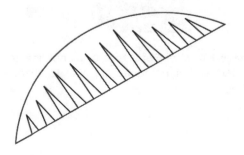

1. Open the file Banana.ai, and you'll see that a very basic leaf shape has already been drawn for you, but it bears scant resemblance to a banana leaf. Below that is a trace template for you to work with. Select the line and you will notice that there are anchor points at the base of each spike of the leaf but you are always missing that additional one at the apex. We'll place the additional anchor points and then drag them into position.

2. Select the **Direct Selection** tool (A) and either the **Pen** tool (P) or the **Add Anchor Point** tool (+).

3. Hold down the Ctrl/Cmd key to temporarily switch to the **Direct Selection** tool and select the line, and then release the Ctrl/Cmd key and you will be back at your selected tool – either the **Pen** tool (P) or the **Add Anchor Point** tool (+).

4. Click on the path between the two points. If you are using the **Pen** tool, make sure that the cursor has changed to indicate that you are directly above the path by adding a plus sign to the cursor.

5. Hold down Ctrl/Cmd key to temporarily switch to the **Direct Selection** tool and drag the anchor point into position. Release the Ctrl/Cmd key.

6. Continue in this manner until you have added and repositioned all the required additional points. If you wish to color the leaf, there is a radial gradient already in the Swatches palette that you can use, or you can create your own if you are keen for a little revision. Remember to use the **Gradient** tool (G) to fine-tune how the gradient is applied.

7. Save and close the file.

Converting Anchor Points

As often as you wish you had either placed an additional anchor point or that you had placed too many, you'll also be thinking that you should really have placed a **Smooth Anchor** point at that place, or a **Corner** with handles. So how do we convert them? The time has come to use that last of the **Pen** tools, and then from you to hear from you that you can actually do it more efficiently if you use keyboard modifiers.

Using either the **Convert Anchor Point** tool, or by holding down the Alt/Option key when we are over a selected anchor point, we are able to change the characteristics of that anchor point.

What you are going to do here is really just a continuation of how we create the various anchor points in the first place.

If you need to convert from a **Smooth Anchor** to a **Corner Anchor**, select the line, and then with either the **Convert Anchor Point** tool (or the **Pen** tool with the Alt/Option key depressed), click on the anchor point to retract those handles. When you created simple Corner points you clicked, now to convert a point you click on it with the **Convert Anchor Point** tool or the **Pen** tool with the Alt/Option key depressed.

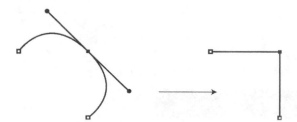

If you wish to convert from a **Corner Anchor** to a **Smooth Anchor**, ensure that the line is selected, and then with either the **Convert Anchor Point** tool (or the **Pen** tool with the Alt/Option key depressed), click and drag on the anchor point to pull out those hidden handles. Sometimes you may drag in the wrong direction and the line gets twisted. Don't let go of the mouse and just swing the direction lines round in the opposite direction. This is a similar action to when you created a **Smooth Anchor** point, and you clicked and dragged to show the direction lines. Now to convert, you click and drag with the **Convert Anchor Point** tool or the **Pen** tool as explained above.

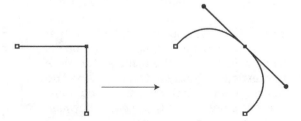

To convert from a **Smooth Anchor** to a **Corner Anchor** with direction lines, select the anchor point to display its direction lines. Then with either the **Convert Anchor Point** tool (or the **Pen** tool with the Alt/Option key depressed), click and drag on one of the direction lines to split them. Switch to the **Direct Selection** tool if you wish to continue reshaping the path, because sometimes staying on this **Convert Anchor Point** tool can result in you converting the point again by mistake.

So, just like when you converted a **Smooth Anchor** point to a **Corner Anchor** point with direction lines as you were drawing, hold down the ALT/OPTION key and drag on the direction line and not the anchor point.

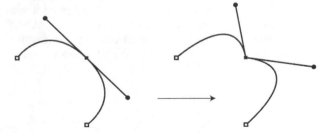

Anchor Points Exercise

Before I set you a task, which will really push you from being a yacht hand to skipper of your own boat, we'll have a little practice with a simple file:

1. Create a new file by choosing File>New (CTRL/CMD+N) and accept the defaults as we'll not be saving the file.

2. Select the **Rectangle** tool (M) and draw a perfect square by holding down the SHIFT key as you drag. The fill and stroke that you use are your own choice.

3. You'll notice, as you have previously, that this shape has four corner anchor points by default. To make the shape a little more interesting choose Object>Path>Add Anchor Points. This will insert additional anchor points exactly halfway between each of the existing points.

4. Select the path, and with the **Convert Anchor Point** tool (or the **Pen** tool with the ALT/OPTION key depressed), click and drag diagonally on the point at the top right-hand corner. This will convert that point from being a **Corner Anchor** point into a **Smooth Anchor** point.

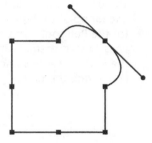

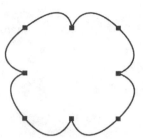

5. Continue doing this to the four corners of the square until your graphic is similar in shape to the diagram here:

6. To revert to a square shape, click – but do not drag – on the four corner points with the **Convert Anchor Point** tool (or the **Pen** tool with the ALT/OPTION key depressed). The direction handles will be retracted, and your rectangular shape will return to nearly its original condition. Keep the path selected.

7. Finally, choose the **Delete Anchor Point** tool (-) or use the **Pen** tool, but make sure that the cursor then changes to indicate the minus sign when you are over a point. Click on the four points we added with the **Add Anchor Points** command, and you are back where you started. Close the file, there is no need to save it.

Case Study: Creating the Fish

We need starfish, we need seahorses, we'll need shells, and of course we'll need a few fish to place strategically in our publications. This is a chance for you to really put yourself to the test with those manipulation skills. You may recall that in Chapter 3, I showed you an illustration of a fish composed of simple shapes and forewarned you that you would be creating this fish! That time has come, and it's going to need a fair amount of time and some strong concentration, so if you need a break, I'd suggest one before we tackle this task!

Your mission – should you wish to accept it – is to convert the lowly combination of rectangles, polygons and circles which previously made up the outline of this fish – into something that more closely resembles the type of fish we would be excited to see if we were underwater. Do not be concerned if you find this task challenging – it is supposed to be! I know how eager you are to become master of your own vessel, and be warned, I'll be constantly pushing you in that direction, each time setting tasks that exact just that little bit extra from you.

1. Open the file called `Fish.ai`. What you see is a very rough outline (your shape) and a refined fish tracing shape (my shape)!

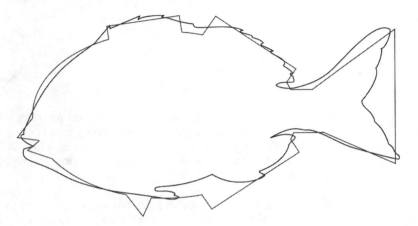

2. What you need to do is call all those manipulating skills you have been learning into action and re-define this shape so that it more closely resembles mine.

3. I'll give you a few pointers, but from then on, you're on your own!

4. Make sure that the path is selected if you want to edit it.

5. Use the **Pen** tool interactively to admit, remove, and manipulate individual anchor points.

6. Try to use as few anchor points as possible.

7. Remember when you are manipulating **Smooth Anchor** points, the direction lines act in tandem, and you'll have to keep an eye on the direction lines on both sides of the anchor point.

8. Select the **Direct Selection** tool before you begin to manipulate the shape. This way you can hold down the CTRL/CMD key to toggle to the **Direct Selection** tool if you need to reposition an anchor point or manipulate those direction handles.

9. When you have finished the file, save it. It will come in handy a little later on! If you found this exercise taxing, don't worry, I bet you're not alone. But manipulating anchor points until they are perfect is such an important skill in Illustrator, that all that sweat you've just been through will pay dividends in the end with cleaner, leaner, files!

Summary

Wow! What a major session, but pat yourself on the back, you are now well under way to becoming an accomplished Illustrator user. With perseverance, there is nothing that you cannot draw. You have the skills, and you have the natural talent of course, now all that's missing is the practice. If you found working with **Bezier** curves a little foreign, I urge that you continue to practice as much as possible, as it does become much more intuitive in time. A good way of practicing is to scan in simple images from children's coloring books and to trace them. From now on, it's warp speed as you cruise through chapters, adding to your arsenal of creative and manipulative tools.

6 Transforming Objects

What We'll Cover in this Chapter:

- *Using the Bounding Box to carry out transformations*

- *Using the Transform Tools including Scale, Reflect, Rotate, Shear, Free Transform, and Reshape*

- *Resetting the object's point of origin*

- *Repeating Transformations*

- *Using the Transform Palette*

- *Liquefy Tools including Warp, Twirl, Pucker, Bloat, Scallop, Crystallize, and Wrinkle*

- *Warp Effects*

  - *Using Envelopes with Meshes, Objects, and Warps*

  - *Manipulating Envelopes and setting Envelope Options*

▶

This chapter covers a plethora of tools, techniques, and almost 'magical' steps that will transform your simple shapes into impressive, mathematically correct artwork. Why transform objects anyway? In the last chapter you were introduced to the creation of circles, squares, stars, and straight lines. If you look around the room you will notice that not many things in the real world are pure circles, stars, and squares. Of course many objects contain elements of these basic shapes, but the finished article is often an irregular, indefinable shape. The tools and techniques you are about to learn will enable you to use the basic shapes, and turn them into recognizable, useful objects that have a role to play in everyday life.

We will also be looking at the process of duplicating artwork. One of the great things about computers is that when you create an object once, if you want 36 more of the same thing, it's a simple case of a few clicks. We can do cut and paste in Illustrator, but in addition there are other techniques that take cut and paste to a whole new level.

All the transformations we do will be done mathematically. The important thing to note is that because these vector shapes are already mathematically defined there will be no loss in quality when you resize or rotate them. Any bitmap images however will still be adversely affected from a quality point of view after being transformed. This is the great benefit of vectors and so ideally suited to logos and artwork that will be required at different sizes.

It has been decided that the Marine Quest logo will include a ship's wheel. The logo will need to be produced in a variety of sizes, the smallest being on a business card and the largest being on the front of the main office. A version will also be required for the web site. Over the coming exercises, you will be introduced to each of the transformation tools using simple examples to get the concepts into your stride. Then you will be able to use what you have learned to create the finished elements of the logo. The elements created here will carry through to the next chapter, each building until our artwork is ready for publishing.

Let's begin by looking at one of the basic elements of transforming objects.

The Bounding Box

We first looked at the **Bounding Box** in Chapter 2. We are now going to look further at how it can help you to make fast transformations.

1. Create a new document in the default size. Either RGB or CMYK is all right. If you haven't changed any preferences, this document will still be measuring in inches.

2. Create a square measuring 2 inches. Apply a red fill and a black stroke.

3. Select the square with the **Selection** tool. If you cannot see eight hollow squares surrounding the object, your Bounding Box is hidden. If this is the case, you will need to make them visible. If your Bounding Box is visible you can skip step 4.

4. Go to View>Show Bounding Box. The Bounding Box can be hidden if you no longer need it by going to the View menu and selecting Hide Bounding Box. Keep it visible as we are going to use it.

The benefit of having the Bounding Box visible is that you can resize and rotate the object without having to go to any other transformation tool. The process of re-sizing objects is called **Scaling**. We are going to do that to the selected red square now.

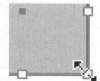

5. Make sure the square is still selected. Place the cursor over the bottom right hollow square and the cursor will change to a double-headed black arrow. Click and drag towards the center of the square. As you drag, the square will reduce in size. Unless you drag in a perfect diagonal line, the square will be reduced non-proportionately. To overcome this, keep the SHIFT key pressed as you drag and the square will keep its proportions. This keyboard shortcut is applicable to any shape you create.

6. Using the same point, drag away from the center this time. This will increase the size of the square. Again, holding down the SHIFT key as you drag will keep the proportions.

7. Try repeating this process on each of the corner hollow squares. As you drag each time, you will notice the hollow point opposite to the one that you are dragging remains fixed.

The other four hollow squares situated between each corner will also allow you to scale. These are primarily designed to scale an object non-proportionately, but again using the SHIFT key in conjunction will override this.

The other transformation you can make with the Bounding Box visible is **Rotation**. So, let's rotate the square.

1. Place the cursor near any of the hollow squares making sure it is on the outside of the shape. The cursor will change to a curved double-headed arrow. When you see the cursor change, click and drag either clockwise or counter-clockwise depending on which way you would like to rotate the square. Drag it about 45 degrees.

2. The Bounding Box rotates with the square. This can make it difficult to assess further transformations, so we are going to Reset the Bounding Box so it sits on a level plane once more. This can be done after each transformation so you are always working with a Bounding Box on a level plane. Go to Object>Transform>Reset Bounding Box.

3. By dragging to rotate an object you are making a free rotation, in that it is not conforming to any specific angle of degrees. If you would like to introduce a little precision to this process, the SHIFT key can be used once again. We will rotate in 45-degree increments this time. Place the cursor near one of the hollow points and look for the curved double-headed arrow to appear. Now drag clockwise or counter-clockwise while keeping the SHIFT key pressed. The square will rotate, but snap at 45-degree increments.

More than one object can be transformed at a time with the Bounding Box visible.

1. Create another object close to the original square.

2. Select both objects and you will see the Bounding Box surround them both. Transformations can now be made in the same way as above and both objects will be affected.

Although Illustrator is a great application for freehand drawing, it really excels in fine precision. This leads on to looking at how the Transform tools can make precise transformations easier.

Transform Tools

In many cases you will want to scale an object by a set amount, either using measurements or percentages. So, the first tool we are going to use is the **Scale** tool, which provides a quick and easy way to scale by percentage.

The Scale Tool

We are going to use the same document that you have been working in up until now. I'm going to introduce another element, so delete the square you have been working with and we need to add some guides.

I know you remember this from Chapter 2, but just in case, here's a recap. If the rulers are not visible, bring them up from the View Menu. The rulers should still be in inches. If you have previously changed them, you can get back to inches by double-clicking the ruler and setting inches from the preferences box that opens up.

1. Drag a guide from the vertical ruler from the left and position it at the 4-inch mark. Then drag a guide from the horizontal ruler at the top and position it

at the 6-inch mark. This gives you guides that cross very close to the center of the page.

2. In the last chapter we looked at drawing objects from the center. We now need a square drawn from the center using the point where the blue guides meet to start the square, so this step is a bit of a recap. Set the fill color to red and stroke color to black from the toolbox. Select the **Rectangle** tool and place the cursor over the point where the guides meet. Hold down the ALT key and drag towards the bottom right of the page. As you drag, press the SHIFT key to constrain the rectangle to a square. The size of the square doesn't matter, estimate about two inches. Remember not to release the ALT and SHIFT keys until you release the mouse.

Your screen should now look similar to the image below.

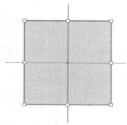

3. Select the square and then double-click the **Scale** tool in the toolbox.

4. In the Scale tool dialog box that opens, you have the choice of Uniform or Non-Uniform scaling. Uniform scaling will keep the proportions of the square. We are going to reduce the size of the square by half. Keep the Uniform option selected and type 50 in the scale box and click OK.

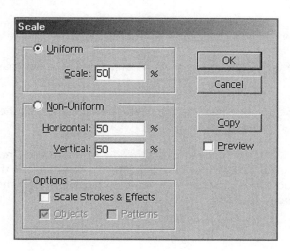

Notice how the reduced square is still centered on the guides. This is because the square has been scaled from the **Point of Origin**, which is the center of an object by default. We will look in more depth at the point of origin shortly, but for the moment, let's increase the size of the square.

5. Make sure the square is still selected and then double-click the **Scale** tool again. This time type 150 in the Uniform Scale box. This brings the square back to its original size.

Making a Scaled Duplicate

The scale tool also allows you to duplicate shapes at a specific percentage size. We are going to create a second smaller square just by using the scale tool.

1. With the square still selected, double-click the **Scale** tool.

2. In the dialog box type 75 in the Uniform Scale box.

3. Click the Copy button instead of OK.

A second square now sits on top of the first at 75% the size of the original. If you want to see what has happened more clearly, click a yellow color from the swatches palette. The inner square is already selected and so becomes yellow. This is one of the easiest ways to create a precise duplicate offset from the original shape.

Point of Origin

The **Point of Origin,** briefly touched on a moment ago, is a common element to all transformation tools. Any transformation must be transformed from a preset point. By default, this point is the center of the object. This is not always the desired point for the transformation, so you have the option to change the point of origin to any point on the screen.

We are now going to change the point of origin of the square.

First delete the yellow square that was duplicated. You now have just the red square and the guides.

1. Select the square on the page. This time just click the **Scale** tool in the toolbox once – **don't** double-click.

2. A new icon appears in the middle of the red square. This defines the point of origin. You will not be able to see it clearly because the blue guides are partially obscuring it, so we will hide the guides just for a moment so you can see the point of origin.

3. Go to View>Guides>Hide Guides. This does not delete guides, only hides them from view. Now you will be able to see the point of origin icon, so we will bring the guides back.

4. Go to View>Guides > Show Guides.

5. To reset the point of origin, keep the ALT/OPT key pressed and click the top left corner of the red square. The Scale dialog box appears again. Type 75 in the Uniform Percentage box and click OK. The square has now been reduced in size and but has also shifted away from the original center as depicted by the blue guides.

Using this method allows you to specify any point on the screen as the point of origin, but the true strength of changing the point of origin is best demonstrated when carrying out a **Reflecting** transformation.

The Reflect Tool

To understand what the **Reflect** tool is doing, let's start with a basic object and then we will use that knowledge to create the first element of our ship's wheel logo.

The **Reflect** tool allows you to flip an object so you are left with a mirror version of the original. A head on view of a cyclist with right arm stretched out becomes a cyclist with left arm stretched out. If the left arm of the cyclist was meant to be out, why not draw it that way in the first place? This tool holds a secret – it really becomes useful when you want to reflect a duplicate of the original shape, because suddenly you have a tool that draws perfect symmetrical objects. Imagine drawing an elaborate Grecian vase or a candlestick, or the Taj Mahal. Even the most ungifted amateur artist could have a fair attempt at one half of the subject. The difficulty arises when you have to draw the other half exactly the same. With the **Reflect** tool, this is a walk in the park.

Let's begin by looking at the basics of how the **Reflect** tool operates, by flipping single objects, and then we can begin on the Marine Quest Logo.

1. Create a new CMYK document using the default sizes.

2. Create a triangle using the **Polygon** tool in the middle of the page with a radius of 1.5 inches. Use a yellow fill and a black stroke.

3. Now drag a guide from the top horizontal ruler and position it at the base of the triangle. Your screen should look similar to the picture here.

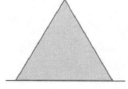

First we are going to flip the triangle upside down.

4. Select the triangle, and then select the **Reflect** tool.

It shares the same toolbox position as the **Rotate** tool, so you will need to keep the mouse pressed on the rotation tool and then select the **Reflect** tool from the flyout that appears. Once the **Reflect** tool has appeared, double-click it. This opens the **Reflect** tool dialog box.

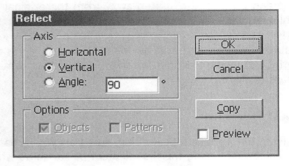

5. Drag the dialog box to a location on the screen so you can see the artwork on the page. You can drag it by clicking and dragging from the top title bar.

You will see the **Point of Origin** icon in the middle of the triangle. It doesn't look like the true middle of the triangle. Shapes like triangles have a virtual square or rectangle that completely encompasses them. The point of origin is the middle of this virtual square in this case. It is from this point that the triangle will be reflected.

6. In the dialog box make sure the Preview box is checked and the Vertical radio button is selected. The triangle shows no change on the page. It has actually flipped, but it has flipped it across a vertical axis running through the middle of the point of origin. Because it is a symmetrical shape in the vertical axis, we see no difference.

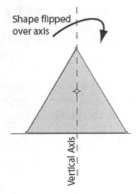

7. Now, click the Horizontal radio button. This turns the triangle upside down. We see this because the triangle has been flipped over a horizontal axis running through the middle of the point of origin.

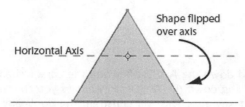

Reflecting Duplicate Shapes

Let's take this one step further. Rather than flipping the triangle, what if we want to flip a duplicate of the triangle and leave the original where it is? Visualize the triangle as the pyramid and the guideline as the River Nile. The reflection in the river would be the duplicate flipped upside down.

Clearly that is not going to happen with the point of origin being where it is. We would need to move the point of origin to somewhere on the guideline and have the pyramid flip across at that point.

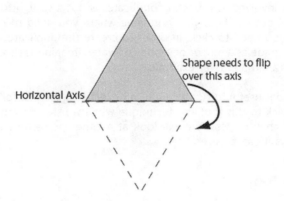

Let's set up the point of origin so we can see a reflection of the pyramid in the river.

1. Click the Cancel button on the **Reflect** tool dialog box to close it.

2. Select the pyramid. Then select the **Reflect** tool. Immediately you will see the point of origin in the middle of the pyramid. This is what we need to change.

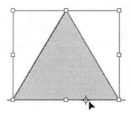

3. Click anywhere on the blue guideline to reset the point of origin.

4. Hold down the ALT/OPT key and the cursor changes to a double-headed arrow. Holding down the ALT/OPT key allows you to create a duplicate. Hold down the SHIFT key also. This will constrain the duplicate to flip across the guide over a perfect horizontal line. With both keys pressed, click anywhere on the blue guide. The duplicate is reflected across the horizontal guide.

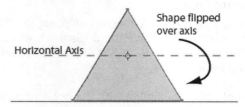

The process involved in reflecting duplicates is not a straightforward one. The guides are not essential but will help you in judging where you need to reset the point of origin to and where you need to click, in order to create the duplicate. It will also help you if you think of the guide as a mirror or a body of water. Imagine seeing the reflection in the water as in the pyramid and river example.

You may find it useful to run through this exercise again just for the sake of familiarity. We will come back to this tool and technique when we start to create the Marine Quest logo later in this chapter. Now we will look at another powerful transformation tool and the creative ways it can be used.

The Rotate Tool

Like all the tools in this section, the simple descriptive name of this tool hides its true power. We will start as before with a simple example of the **Rotate** tool.

1. In a new blank document create a rectangle 2.5 inches high by 0.5 inches wide. Apply a yellow fill and a black stroke. Select the object.

2. Select the **Rotate** tool from the toolbox. If you have just been using the **Reflect** tool it will be hiding the **Rotate** tool as they share the same location in the toolbox.

It should be no surprise to see the point of origin appear in the middle of the yellow rectangle.

3. Place the cursor close to the rectangle and click and drag clockwise or counter-clockwise. This is the same as when you used the Bounding Box at the beginning of this chapter. Holding down the SHIFT key as you drag will constrain the rotation to 45-degree angles.

We are now going to change the point of origin. You will probably be quite comfortable with this by now. You should still have the rectangle selected and the point of origin at the center of the rectangle.

4. Position the rectangle so it is vertical on the page. Then click the bottom edge of the rectangle to reset the point of origin.

5. Place the mouse near the rectangle again and drag in a circular manner as before. Now the rectangle rotates from the bottom edge like the hand of a clock. The diagram below shows the new point of origin at the bottom of the rectangle and the arrow describes the direction to drag.

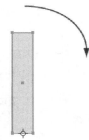

That's OK for simple rotation if you are not looking for anything precise. If you do need to rotate the original or a duplicate by a certain degree, then a different technique needs to be used.

Rotating by Precise Degrees

Your rectangle may be at an odd angle now so return it to its original form by going to Edit>Undo Rotate.

1. Select the rectangle and click the **Rotate** tool in the toolbox to select it.

2. Here's the part that makes all the difference. Hold down the ALT/OPT key and click at the bottom edge of the rectangle as you did before so the Rotate dialog box appears. Type 20 in the Angle box and click OK. The object is rotated at an angle of 20 degrees from the new point of origin.

3. Hold down the ALT/OPT key and click the same point of origin to open the Rotate dialog box.

4. Leave the number as it is in the Rotate box and click the Copy button this time. Now the duplicate is rotated at 20 degrees from the last object, based on the same point of origin. The original will stay where it is.

We will use this technique in earnest when we come to create the ship's wheel for our logo.

The Shear Tool

The final tool in this section is the **Shear** tool. To shear an object is to skew or slant it. How much use is it? Like all Illustrator tools, it has a role in life and its purpose cannot be underestimated. It may not be as ubiquitous in its functionality as its cousins in this section, but let's have a look at its uses.

To get a handle on its basic operation, let's start with a blank page and a rectangle. Fill with a color of your own choice and make it 1 inch wide by 2 inches high. Position it towards the bottom left of the screen.

1. Select the **Shear** tool. It shares the same toolbox location as the **Scale** tool. The point of origin will appear in the middle of the object.

2. Position the cursor above the rectangle somewhere and slowly click and drag to the right. I say slowly because the transformation can look a little erratic while it is happening. Also try to keep the cursor in a straight line as you drag. Holding the SHIFT key will also constrain the transformation as long as you hold a fairly straight horizontal line as you drag.

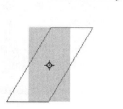

If you would rather skew the shape by using a precise measurement, you can bring up the dialog box as with the other tools. Use the Edit>Undo command to return the rectangle to its original shape.

3. Select the rectangle and double-click the **Shear** tool. In the dialog box enter 45 in the Shear Angle box. This achieves the same result, but without the erratic movement.

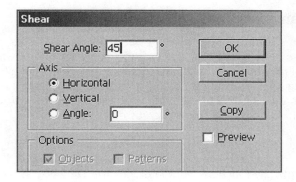

The result is a skewed shape. So what do you do with it? You can do all the things you have done so far, such as change the point of origin and create duplicates. That combination with this tool is ideal for casting a shadow. That's what we will do now.

Casting a Shadow

Return the rectangle to its original state. We need to reset the point of origin to a new location.

1. Make sure the rectangle is selected. Click the **Shear** tool in the toolbox and you will see the point of origin appear in the middle of the rectangle. Hold down the ALT/OPT key and click the bottom left anchor point of the rectangle to reset the point of origin. This also opens the **Shear** tool dialog box.

2. Type 45 in the Shear Angle box and click the Copy button. Leave the Axis set to Horizontal as shown in the screenshot above. As with the other tools, a duplicate is produced at the desired angle.

3. The duplicate is stacked in front of the original so you will have to send this to the back in order to see the effect.

Finally change the fill color to a dark gray and you have cast a convincing shadow.

The Free Transform Tool

The **Free Transform** tool does what the Scale, Rotate, and Shear tools do at a basic level. It also does something else that is very useful and a lot of fun, which we will look at in a moment. You may think, "Why do I need a tool that does what all the others do?" Well, if you are doing a lot of rotating, scaling, and shearing, you can just use the one tool and you are saved a lot of trips to the toolbox. It also means if the **Bounding Box** is switched off, you still have a fast way to make adjustments.

Let's take a quick tour of this tool. How about a new square to try it out?

The rotate and scale functions work in exactly the same way as their named counterparts. The shear function though, requires a keyboard shortcut to get it to work.

1. Select the square and then select the **Free Transform** tool in the toolbox.

2. Click on one of the top handles of the **Bounding Box** and start to drag to the right. As you drag, press CTRL+ALT/CMD+OPTION. Don't press the keys until after you start to drag, otherwise it will not work. If you click and drag the side handles you can drag up or down to shear vertically.

The other little trick up its sleeve is perspective.

Perspective

Stand at one end of 5th Avenue or Bond Street and look down the road as far as the eye can see. The buildings all appear to get smaller, the further you look and eventually diminish into the distance. This point is the **Vanishing Point**. On paper, drawing straight lines that meet at one end identifies this point. As the lines converge, they define the apparent size an object should be at any given distance. The accuracy of the scale results in a correctly proportioned drawing.

Open the file called Perspective.ai from the download folder.

These red and white stripes will be our building-lined street. I want to create the illusion that we are looking down this street and would expect the stripes to stretch out into the distance and come closer and closer together.

1. Select the red and white stripes, and then select the **Free Transform** tool.

2. Click the top right handle of the striped object and start to drag downward. As you start to drag, press SHIFT+ALT+CTRL/SHIFT+OPT+CMD. Drag as much as you need to achieve the effect. It is important you start to drag before pressing the keyboard keys, as it will not work otherwise. Also, stop dragging and release the mouse button before releasing the keyboard keys when you finish.

Your artwork should now look like the image here.

If you were standing at one end of an airport runway looking down it, you would see perspective slightly differently. There are no buildings to give the sense of reducing scale, but the grass verges at either side of the runway would appear to be drawn together until they finally meet at the vanishing point in the distance.

1. Select the blue and white striped object, and then select the **Free Transform** tool.

2. Click the top right handle of the striped object and start to drag to the left, pressing SHIFT+ALT+CTRL/SHIFT+OPT+CMD as you drag, as before. Drag as much as you need to.

The figure here shows the result you should get – a beautiful, technically correct perspective drawing.

You now have almost every skill you need to start work on the ship's wheel part of the Marine Quest logo. A little freehand creation will be required to create the spokes of the wheel. Anyone who feels they are not artistically inclined at this stage should not run for cover. The whole idea here is to create professional, attractive artwork and not be limited by how artistically gifted you may or may not be. The tool I am going to guide you through now is a long-standing member of the Illustrator toolbox and yet is relatively unknown. It could transform the quality of finished work and save hours in aborted attempts.

The Reshape Tool

The idea behind the **Reshape** tool is as the name suggests, reshaping things. You've already seen and practiced with other tools that effectively "reshape" things, so why another one? Well, this tool does it a little differently. It allows you to reshape paths and objects with a little more fluidity than the standard methods you have learned so far. More fluidity does mean less accuracy though, but there is always a trade off. What you lack in precision editing, you gain in expression and freedom of movement. Let's try this out in a simple exercise first to get a feel for what it does and then we will use it to create the first element of our company logo.

1. In a new document create a simple square of about 3 inches, with no fill color and a black stroke.

2. This is a crucial point for this tool to work properly. You must deselect the square first, and then reselect it with the **Direct Selection** tool. Make sure the four anchor points around the square are white, confirming they are deselected.

3. Select the **Reshape** tool. You will find it in the same toolbox location as the **Scale** tool. Click on any segment of the square. A large square anchor point appears. This will be used to reshape the segment.

4. Using the same tool, click and drag the new anchor point you just made. You will find it moves fluidly, flowing like a piece of string. However, all the original anchor points are still firmly locked in place and cannot be moved. The only editable part of the object is the segment to which you applied the anchor point.

5. Click again with the same tool on another part of the same segment. Now drag that point. Both of the new points now move in relation to each other. The fluidity still exists but, now you can make slightly more acute changes of direction.

Hopefully the purpose of the **Reshape** tool is starting to make sense as you use it. Take a few moments to add further points to different segments and see how they react with each other. I will emphasize again the importance of ensuring the object is selected with the **Direct Selection** tool only prior to clicking with the **Reshape** tool. If all anchor points are selected, the whole object will move rather than just the anchor points you intend to drag.

Let me now introduce a little more direction to this tool. I am not going to remove any of its fluidity, but I do have a specific object in mind. The moment has arrived where you need to create some real artwork that will be used as part of the Marine Quest logo. The ship's wheel I've been mentioning is the common linking symbol for the business's activities. Ships wheels are by tradition very elegant, ornate things, which is why there are as many wheels adorning the walls of restaurants and bars around the world as there are actually steering ships. Your task is to create the ornate spoke of this wheel.

Case Study: The Ship's Wheel (I)

Creating the Wheel Spoke

Perhaps you can see the potential problem area here. Your shape may not be symmetrical. The point I made earlier about fluidity and expression at the cost of precision is aptly demonstrated here. No doubt with a little more judicious clicking and dragging you could achieve symmetry, but why expend all the time and effort? You have already discovered and practiced the art of creating perfect symmetry, using the **Reflect** tool, when you flipped the pyramid. Now the benefit of what you learned in that exercise will be invaluable as we tackle the task of the ship's wheel.

It goes without saying that the ornate spoke of the wheel must be symmetrical. The **Reshape** tool is quite capable of creating the elegant curves, but professionally I would not even contemplate attempting to produce both sides of the spoke and hope to achieve a perfect symmetrical shape. It's not so much a case of ability, but more of available time.

Open the file called Spoke.ai from the download folder.

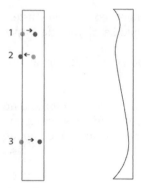

The finished one that I created is on the right of the page. The black outline rectangle is the object you will be using to create your version. To make life easy, I have created a template that shows you where to click and where to drag. The green dots show you which part of the black outline to click to place your anchor point. The red dot tells you where you need to drag to, to create the shape. The blue guides are just to help you click and drag with a bit more precision.

1. As always, select the rectangle with the **Direct Selection** tool.

2. Select the **Reshape** tool and click on the black outline above the green point at number 1.

3. Drag the anchor point to the red dot using the same tool.

4. With the **Reshape** tool click the black outline above the green point at number 2 and drag to the red point.

5. Repeat the process for number 3.

Your shape may look a little different from mine. It all depends on exactly where you click to place your point and how far you drag. If you are not happy with the final shape you can re-edit the anchor points or try it again from scratch. The important thing is that you understand how the clicking and dragging of the points defines the final shape.

Once you are happy with the shape, we are going to cut and paste it into a new blank document and move on to the next stage, which is to make it symmetrical.

6. Select your shape. Go to Edit>Copy. This copies your shape onto the clipboard.

7. Create a new CMYK document using the default page size.

8. In the new document go to Edit>Paste. This pastes your shape from the clipboard into the middle of your new document.

The ship's wheel will be a solid color. This half spoke has a stroke color and no fill so we will change that now.

9. Apply to the shape a yellow fill color and no stroke. The yellow is not the actual color we will use, but it makes it easier to see the point of origin for the next task in hand. The actual color will be applied later.

We are now going to reflect a duplicate to create the finished symmetrical spoke. You have already done this exercise with the pyramid, but I will outline the steps to help you along. Although not essential, you will find it useful to drag out a vertical guide and position it in line with the left edge of the shape. This becomes your imaginary mirror in which you will see the "reflection".

10. Select the object and then select the **Reflect** tool. We need to reset the point of origin first, so click anywhere on the blue guide.

11. Press the ALT/OPT key and the SHIFT key and click anywhere on the blue guide. You should now be looking at something similar to the image here.

12. Select both of the shapes and group them so they become a single entity. Finally, apply a big fill to the grouped shape.

Congratulations. We now have the first real element that will go to make up the company logo. Save this document in a folder on your computer calling it Myspoke.ai. We will be using it again shortly.

Creating the Wheel

We are going to move onto the next element of the logo now. Within the coming exercises I am going to introduce to you some new functions and techniques that will make this kind of work a lot more fun and highly accurate. You will also have to use some of the techniques you have learned already in this chapter, so you will be gaining experience in a real project as well as consolidating your new skills.

Open the file called Wheel.ai from the download folder. Just so you know what you are going to create, the figure here shows the finished wheel.

I have already started the artwork by creating guides that cross in the middle of the page. I have also created a black circle with a diameter of 4 inches. The circle's center point is positioned where the guides cross.

The wheel has a white, hollow center. We can produce this hollow center by creating a duplicate circle at a fixed percentage as you did earlier.

1. Select the black circle. Double-click the **Scale** tool. Type 80% in the Uniform box and click the Copy button.

The duplicate is also created from the center of the guides, at a size of 80% of the original. The duplicate is also black, so let's change the color.

2. Apply a white fill color to the smaller circle. Make sure you have no stroke applied.

Without too much effort you now have the rim of the wheel and all is perfectly geometric.

This would be a good time to save your file. Call it `Mywheel.ai` and keep the file open.

We are now going to incorporate the wheel spoke that you completed earlier. Open the file that you saved on your computer called `Myspoke.ai`. Now copy the spoke and paste it into the `Mywheel.ai` document.

Drag the spoke to one side of the page so it doesn't overlap the circle. You've noticed it's a little big? Not a problem. This is a vector so you can resize as often as you wish without losing quality. We are getting to a stage where some precise measurements are needed. This is always the case as components start to come together. So far you've seen two methods of re-sizing – dragging manually and scaling by percentage. The task here is to resize the spoke so it fits correctly within the wheel. This could be done visually of course, dragging as necessary. If you were given precise dimensions to reproduce, this method would be a little haphazard. The method we are going to use is by way of the **Transform Palette**.

Transform Palette

This palette allows you to apply position, scale, rotation, and shear to objects by a set of numeric values. I already have some dimensions and positions worked out for the spoke. You will be able to apply these values to the spoke by using the **Transform Palette** and the spoke will be perfectly sized and placed.

Case Study: The Ship's Wheel (II)

Postioning the Spokes in the Wheel

1. Go to Window>Transform to open the Transform palette in the bottom left of the screen.

2. Select the spoke and look at the Transform palette. The fields now show the values as they relate to the spoke. Let's break down the information in this palette.

The diagram on the left of the palette defines the point of the object from which values are taken. The center box, which is colored black, is the reference point by default. Look at the X and Y fields. These show the X and Y co-ordinates based on the center point of the spoke.

Now look at the **Info Palette** in the top right of the screen. The X and Y values are different to what you are reading in the Transform palette. The point from which the value was taken can account for the difference, as the Info palette measures from the top left of the object.

Go back to the Transform palette. We are going to change the point from where the value is taken.

3. Using the diagram on the left of the palette, click the top left white box. This now turns black and becomes the new point of origin for measurements. Take a look at the Info palette again and you will see that the values are now exactly the same.

Change the point of origin back to the middle square again by clicking the point on the diagram.

In addition to the X and Y co-ordinates, you will also see W (Width) and H (Height) fields, and on the bottom row Angle and Shear.

We are now going to use the Transform palette to resize and position the spoke all at once.

4. With the spoke selected, type the following values into the Transform palette.

- X: 4.25 in

- Y: 7.003 in

- X: 0.278 in

- X: 1.199 in

The spoke is now in position within the wheel. Do we repeat that process for each spoke around the wheel, taking measurements each time? No, we are going to use the rotation technique that you used earlier, but this time with an additional element that you will want to use again and again.

The first task is to rotate a duplicate of the spoke, but it won't be around its center axis, so we also need to change the point of origin.

1. Select the spoke.

2. Select the **Rotate** tool, hold down the ALT/OPT key and click the point where the guides meet in the middle of the circle. This opens the Rotate dialog box. Type 45 in the Angle box and click the Copy button. You have already performed this process. The next process is completely new.

To complete the wheel, it would not be a great hardship to repeat what you have just done, but there is a better way. We are going to tell Illustrator to repeat the last step you did using a menu command. The last thing you did was to rotate a duplicate from a given point of origin to a 45-degree angle.

3. Go to Object>Transform>Transform Again. That's all there is to it. In fact, if dragging the mouse to the menu is too much effort, let's use a keyboard shortcut to create the next duplicate.

4. Press CTRL +D/CMD + D. This produces the same effect.

5. Now press CTL +D/CMD + D five more times and you have completed the circular rotation of spokes.

This indispensable command will work on all the transformations you make with objects. The wheel is almost complete. The last elements will enable you to get some practice with the techniques you have learned so far.

Duplicating the Inner Circles

We need two small center circles in the middle of the wheel. Let's create this circle at a preset size and have it drawn from the center of the guides again.

1. Select the **Ellipse** tool. Position the cursor over the center cross of the guides. Hold down the ALT/OPT key and click. This opens the Ellipse dialog box. Type 0.9 in the Width and Height boxes. Click OK.

2. Apply a black fill to this circle and make sure there is no stroke.

In the same way as you treated the large outer circle of the wheel, we need a smaller one that will be the hollow centerpiece of the wheel.

3. Select the black circle you just made, then double-click the **Scale** tool. Type 80 in the Uniform Scale box. Click the Copy button.

4. Apply a white fill to the duplicate circle just created.

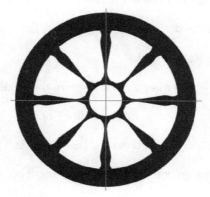

The last elements that we need to add are the handgrips that run around the outer edge of the wheel. This is a perfect shape for the rounded rectangle tool.

Creating the Wheel Handgrips

1. Select the rounded rectangle tool, and then click once on the screen to open the dialog box. Enter the following values.

Width: 0.25
Height: 0.6
Corner Radius: 0.167

The position of the first handgrip on the wheel is the important one to get right as all the others will be created by duplicating and offsetting from this original. This handgrip will sit on top of the wheel at the 12 o'clock position. This means it will need to have the same X co-ordinate as the spoke immediately below it, so it looks as if it is a continuation of the spoke. The information we need then is the X co-ordinate of the 12 o'clock spoke. To do this, select the spoke and note down the X co-ordinate as displayed in the Transform Palette. The X co-ordinate reads 4.25 inches in my example.

2. Select the rounded rectangle handgrip, and then enter the value you made a note of, for example 4.25, into the X box of the Transform Palette. The Y co-ordinate can be positioned by eye, judging how much the handgrip would protrude on a real ship's wheel. I used a Y co-ordinate of 8.2, which looked convincing.

The handle should now be positioned on the top of the wheel.

All that remains is to rotate and duplicate the handle at 45-degree angles around the perimeter of the wheel. You're an old hand at this now. Give it a try yourself or if you'd prefer, follow the steps in summary below.

1. Select the handle.

2. Select the **Rotate** tool.

3. Press the ALT/OPT key and click where the guides meet.

4. Enter 45 in the Angle box and click Copy.

5. Press CTL/CMD + D six times for six duplicates.

You can now clear the guides, select all the components, and group the artwork into one entity.

The ship's wheel is now complete. But although you have grouped the artwork, it still remains a collection of components within a group. To make it really efficient for printing it would be nice to combine everything into one object. We will cover this in the next chapter.

The tools and transformations we have been working on in this section so far might loosely be called "serious" in that we have created real-world, professional effects – the kind of artwork you see every day in print and on the Web. The set of tools I am about to introduce is capable of producing outlandish, ostentatious, abstract art. And yet, they are also capable of producing the most delicate and subtle of forms. Like everything in Illustrator, and most computer applications for that matter, it is not what the tool does, but what you do with it that matters.

Liquify Tools

Let's take a tour of what comes under the generic banner of the **Liquify** tools.

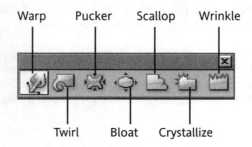

Warp   Pucker   Scallop   Wrinkle

Twirl   Bloat   Crystallize

The Warp Tool

The best way to understand these tools is to try them out. In a new document create a straight line that runs from the left to the right of the screen.

The **Warp** tool works by stretching objects and paths. Objects take on a very fluid property, becoming clay-like. There is a certain similarity with the reshape you used earlier, though there is less control here.

1. Select the **Warp** tool. All the **Liquify** tools are in the same location, so it would be a good idea to use the **Tear Off** to open this set as a separate toolbox.

2. With the **Warp** tool selected you see the cursor icon change to a + sign surrounded by a circle. Place the + sign beneath the line on the page and then drag upwards. As you pass over the line you will start to drag and bend it. Now place the cursor above the line and then drag downwards. The line will be pulled and bent downwards.

The amount of distortion will depend upon the settings. To change the settings double-click the tool in the toolbox. This opens the Options box below.

From here you can set the Width, Height, and Angle of the brush. The Intensity affects how pronounced the effect is – higher values render more elaborate results. Under the Warp Options settings, Detail defines the amount of points that appear on the object's outline. Higher values place points closer together. Simplify reduces the amount of anchor points without adversely affecting the shape.

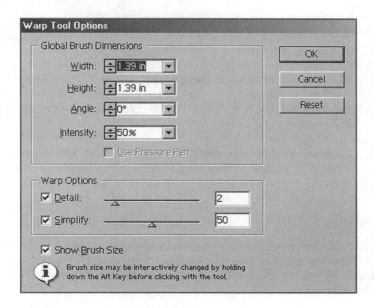

The Twirl Tool

This tool distorts objects in attractive swirls. We are going to use it to create a footer for some of the pages of the Marine Quest brochure.

Open the file called `Twirl.ai` from the download folder. The finished effect is shown in the bottom two examples. Both were made from a rectangle. You are now going to use the top rectangle to create a similar effect.

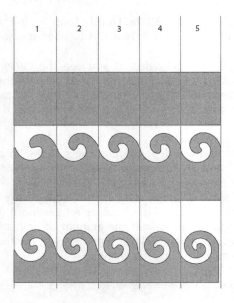

1. Select the **Twirl** tool.

2. Place the cursor between the guides in section 1. The guides have been spaced to accommodate the size of the tool exactly. Line up the horizontal of the cross with the top of the rectangle like below.

3. Click and hold for a second. The longer you click, the more it twirls. Try different click lengths for a different effect.

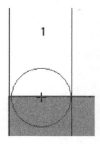

Pucker & Bloat

I'm going to tackle these two as a pair because they work well in conjunction with each other. The **Pucker** tool deflates an object by dragging anchor points towards the cursor. The **Bloat** tool inflates an object by dragging anchor points away from the cursor.

To demonstrate, we are going to create some flowers that will be used as a bed on menus in the restaurant.

Open the file called `Pucker_bloat.ai` from the download folder. You may not believe it possible, but all the flowers on this page were created from a simple star and distorted with the **Pucker** and **Bloat** tools.

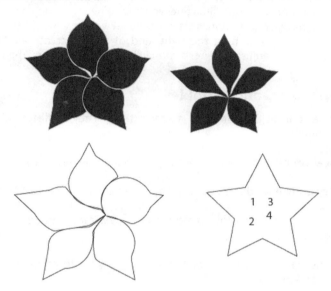

To get a feel for the tools, try them out first on the straight red line at the bottom of the page.

1. Select the **Pucker** tool. Click and hold just above the red line. The line is pulled toward it like a magnet.

2. Select the **Bloat** tool. Click and hold just above the red line. The line is repelled away from the cursor.

So let's do something useful with this tool. We are going to transform the star into a flower. The numbers inside the star show you where to click. Click in numeric order.

1. Select the **Pucker** tool. There is no need to select the star. Place the cursor over the number 1 and click for less than a second. The nearest anchor points will be drawn towards the cursor.

2. Click on the number 2. The longer you hold the mouse down, the more the anchor points are drawn towards the cursor.

3. Do the same with 3 and 4. Depending exactly where you click and how long you click for will have a bearing on how flowery your flowers look.

Now we are going to make the petals look more convincing and attractive.

4. Select the **Bloat** tool. Place the cursor inside one of the petals. Click for a fraction of a second. Imagine you are spraying a very expensive perfume or aftershave, so just short bursts. Gradually you can mould the petals into shape. If you are not getting the right kind of flower, create another star and have another go, adjusting where you click and the length of the click.

Scallop, Crystallize, and Wrinkle

The final three tools in this set all do a similar thing. They all distort the outlines so they become less uniform.

- **Scallop** randomly adds smooth, arc-shaped details to the outline.

- **Crystallize** randomly adds spiked, arc-shaped details to the outline.

- **Wrinkle** does the job of both the above, randomizing between smooth and spiked arcs.

Once again there is no substitute for trying it out. All the tools are best demonstrated by using them with a simple straight line.

1. Use the + sign as the "hot spot" of the tool, dragging it over the line.

2. Increase or decrease the affect of the line by double-clicking the tool in the toolbox and changing the settings.

Warp Effects and Envelopes

Warping an object is a very useful function for a variety of artistic purposes. Controlling how you warp an object with an envelope can take your vector artwork to a whole new level of realism. We are going to work through some examples of warps and envelopes so you can see just how powerful they are.

Flags feature heavily in the artwork requirements of Marine Quest. Flat plan flags look dull and lifeless. Flags blowing in the wind come alive. So, we're going to bring the Stars and Stripes to life with a bit of warping.

Open the file called `Warp_flag.ai` from the download folder.

1. Select the flag, which is a grouped object. As a grouped object all the objects within the group will be distorted accordingly.

2. Go to Object>Envelope Distort>Make with Warp.

3. The dialog box offers you a range of different envelopes to distort your shape. From the Style drop-down box, select Flag. Check the Preview box to see the effect. Drag the Bend slider to the left or right to increase and decrease the amount of bend. The central position creates the least amount of bend. The Horizontal and Vertical Distortion sliders produce perspective effects. Click OK when you have the effect you want.

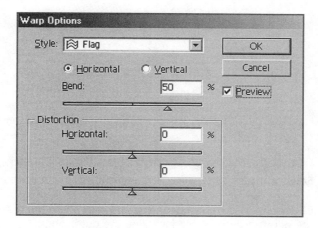

Try the other styles before closing the file.

As far as flags blowing in the wind were concerned, that was a little too uniform and obviously computer-generated for you. If you would like something with a little more free spirit the next option is for you.

Open the file called `Warp_mesh.ai` from the download folder. The top flag is my attempt at creating a flag blowing on one of those blustery days where the wind is everywhere. To do this I used a mesh and then manually moved the points. Have a go yourself with the flag at the bottom of the page.

1. Select the flag.

2. Go to Object>Envelope Distort>Make with Mesh. In the dialog box that opens, leave the default settings of 4 Rows and 4 Columns.

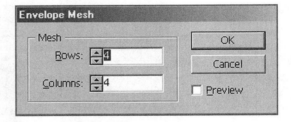

A blue grid appears over the flag. This is what allows you to edit the envelope and so affect the shape.

3. First deselect the flag, and then click on the edge of the flag with the **Direct Selection** tool. Make sure all the anchor points are white.

4. Click on individual anchor points and drag them to create bends in the flag. All the points are draggable including the outer ones.

Finally, you can create your own envelope by placing an object over the top of the thing you would like to distort.

Open the file called `Envelope_object.ai` from the download folder.

The green striped object is the object to be distorted. The white diamond sits on top. This is what we are going to use as the envelope. The final effect is shown in the picture here.

1.   Select both of the objects.

2.   Go to Object>Envelope Distort>Make with Top Object.

The result creates the impression of the bottom object wrapping around the top object. Different shapes will achieve very different results. Experimentation with different shapes will achieve many different and interesting results.

3.   If you want to get back to your original warped object, go to Object>Envelope Distort>Release.

Setting Envelope Options

The options allow you to define how closely the envelope is followed.

1. Go to Object>Envelope Distort>Envelope Options. The following options are available for you:

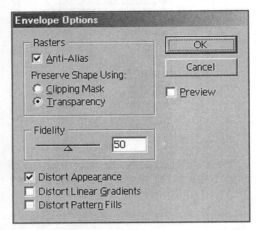

- Anti-alias – check the box to smooth the edges of bitmap images that have been distorted.

- Preserve Shape Using – refers to bitmap images again.

  - Clipping Masks – use a mask to preserve shape when distorted by a non-rectangular envelope.

  - Transparency – creates an **Alpha Channel**.
    (Both of these elements will be discussed in the next chapter.)

- Fidelity – slider defines how closely the object conforms to the envelope. Higher settings use more anchor points.

- Distort Appearance – affects the appearance of the object and any styles you may have applied.

- Distort Linear Gradients and Pattern Fills – these will be affected if their respective boxes are checked.

All the Liquify tools and Warp effects are deceptive in their power and function. The working examples you have just completed provide a structured approach in understanding the workings of each of the tools. With this understanding, you will be able to unveil their true potential through experimenting with your own shapes and ideas.

Summary

The knowledge you have gained in this chapter elevates you out of the level of creating basic shapes and into the domain of creating professional, efficient, and creative artwork. You are now able to create perfect symmetrical shapes and complex geometry with minimum effort and precision.

The Transform palette offers you the opportunity to make a number of manipulations to objects by specific values. You have learned to use this palette to good effect.

You have also been introduced to the weird and wonderful Liquify tools and Warp effects and learned how to exercise control over these powerful and often misunderstood elements. These are invaluable in producing real-world objects that would be difficult to create using any of the more conventional tools.

The ship's wheel logo that you produced will go forward to the next chapter for its finishing touches where we will also look at some of the more complex and visually rewarding elements of Illustrator.

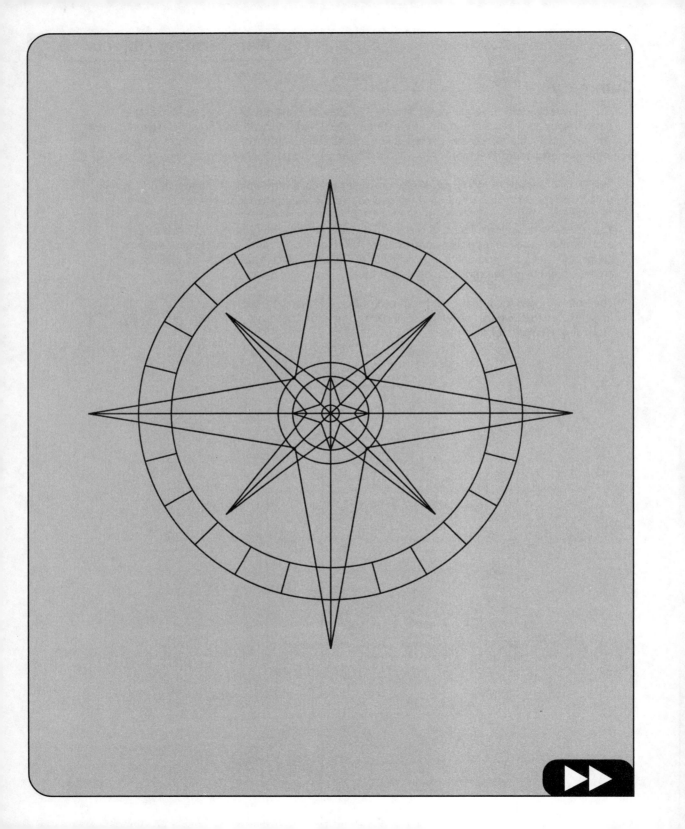

7 Creating Complex Shapes

What We'll Cover in this Chapter:

- Introducing the concept of Compound Shapes and Compound Paths

- Creating Compound Shapes with the Pathfinder palette

- Using the Compound Shape Menu commands

- Creating Complex Shapes with the Pathfinders

- Working with Compound Paths

- Using Clipping Paths

At this stage you should be feeling pretty proud of yourself. You've covered, and hopefully mastered, the basics of creating, coloring, and transforming graphics in Illustrator, and met some of the more interesting commands and features for manipulating them. Yet this is no time for us to sit back and rest on our laurels. The time has come for us to really push that envelope, and move on to bigger and better things – complex shapes.

Each day we are bombarded by an excess of visual material, coming from print, web, television, advertising hoardings. As a budding illustrator, I bet you've looked at some graphics and wondered how they managed to create them. In this chapter you'll start to look at images in terms of their component parts, and learn the skills behind creating all those complex shapes.

"The Whole is Different than the Sum of the Parts"

I recommend that if you are to get the most out of this chapter, and out of this book, you stop right now and look at an object near you. I want you to start slowing down and seeing the world around you in terms of squares, circles, polygons, arcs, and more, to see both positive and negative space, and to see the parts of the object, and not the whole.

For instance, take the ship's wheel logo you were creating in the previous chapter. It is a familiar shape – you would have recognized it immediately had you seen it in print or on the web. Yet, you now know that it's not a ship's wheel at all – but rather a combination of circles, rounded rectangles, and rectangles which have been manipulated. Furthermore, it is not only the shape of the component objects, but also the space between them, that makes up the overall form. The interplay of shapes, and both positive and negative space, is what allows us to perceive it as a ship's wheel – a recognizable object.

Once you start to see illustrations and graphics in terms of their component parts and not the total appearance, you will be in a position to start crafting those complex objects yourself using powerful Illustrator features such as the *Pathfinder* palette and effects, compound shapes, compound paths, and clipping paths, in order to create the final form.

Compound Shapes vs. Compound Paths

As this chapter proceeds, we'll increasingly refer to objects as either compound shapes or compound paths, so first we need to understand what we mean by these terms. Then we can get onto the real meat of the chapter and start making them. (A little aside here for those experienced Illustrator users who have picked up the book to get the skinny on all the new and improved features. Do not be tempted to skip this section, as Adobe, in their continual quest for the uber-illustration package, have radically reworked the way in which the *Pathfinder* palette works, and introduced the new concept of compound shapes.)

Compound Shapes

Compound shapes are essentially shapes consisting of two or more different objects. You may think you've already met them when we looked at grouping objects in Chapter 2. But no, there are differences between a group and a compound shape.

Think back to your schooldays: you were part of a group of students, you met each day in the same room, at the same time, ostensibly to learn the same things. When the class ended, you all left the room together – you functioned as a group, and even though you may well have dressed in a similar fashion, each one of you retained your individuality and independence. This, essentially, is how a group functions in Illustrator. We can take a mass of dissimilar objects, each with a different fill and stroke, and we can make them into a group, to scale, move, or whatever it is that we wish to do with them. Yet in grouping them, you do not change their inherent characteristics. You can still select them individually and assign different fills or stroke properties, or even transform the separate components.

To remind you how groups interact, and then to move on to comparing them with compound shapes, let's open the file called `Ed_and_al.ai` and have a look at it:

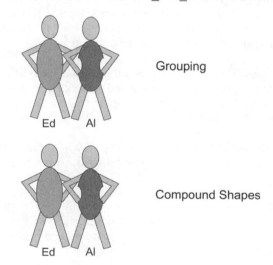

Grouping

Compound Shapes

We have two examples of Ed and Al for you to manipulate, and for this first part of the explanation, we'll concentrate on the top pair.

1. With the **Selection** tool (V) click on either Ed or Al. As you click, notice that you are selecting the entire 'person', not the individual component on which you clicked. Look also at the Appearance palette, choosing Window>Appearance if it is not visible. Notice how Illustrator is telling you that each character is actually a group of objects.

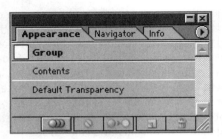

2. With the **Group Selection** tool – that's the white arrow with the little plus sign – click on individual components and re-color them. Since they are a group of objects, each element retains its distinct characteristics, even though when you select the group with the **Group Selection** tool, the entire group is targeted. By the way, you could also use the **Direct Selection** tool to select the components, but it is a little easier if you stick with the **Group Selection** to avoid inadvertently selecting an individual anchor point.

3. Select both Ed and Al and group them (CTRL/CMD+G) and now as you click on either one of them, both are selected, and can be moved or transformed as one. But they are still individuals, with separate arms, legs, and bodies, which can be colored differently when selected with the **Group Selection** tool.

4. Switch to **Outline** mode by choosing View>Outline (CTRL/CMD+Y) and you can clearly see those distinct components. Switch back to Preview mode (View>Preview or CTRL/CMD+Y).

With the concept of groups firmly established, we can now compare them to compound shapes and see how they differ. The clearest way for you to visualize the differences will be for us to create a compound shape from Ed and Al, and then compare how that differs from the group feature.

5. Select the second occurrence of Ed, and ungroup him by choosing Object>Ungroup (CTRL/CMD+SHIFT+G).

6. Display the Pathfinder palette by choosing Window>Pathfinder. Don't be too startled by all the icons you see on the palette, you will explore each and every one in this chapter.

With Ed still selected, choose **Add to shape area** – the top left hand icon on the Pathfinder palette.

He's turned a shade of green, and lost his internal outline. Notice that there no longer seems to be a black outline around his belly, even though if you look at the shape in Outline view, you can still see it. If you try using the **Group Selection** tool, you can still select it. And if you switch on **Smart Guides** (CTRL/CMD+U), and move the mouse over Ed, you'll notice that the individual components still become highlighted separately.

7. Have a look at the Appearance palette now – it should have changed to reflect the fact that you have selected a **Compound** shape. Deselect Ed, and turn Al into a compound shape as well by repeating the process. Illustrator uses the color on top of the stacking order to decide which color to use to fill the characters.

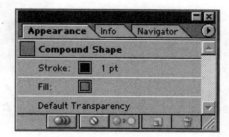

8. Visually, the only difference you are seeing is that both Ed and Al are each filled with just one color, although each one is filled with a different color to the other, because they are two separate compound shapes. We are going to combine them into one compound shape, but before we do that, take an educated guess at what color they will become now that you know how Illustrator assigns the color. Select both Ed and Al and combine them into a compound shape by choosing **Add to shape area** from the Pathfinder palette, and yes, now they both are colored the same.

9. Switch to **Outline** mode again (CTRL/CMD+Y) and note that if you compare the view of the grouped Ed and Al with the **Compound** shapes Ed and Al, in outline, they look essentially the same – they are both composed of those individual, original shapes.

10. With the **Group Selection** tool, select individual components of the compound shape. Using the **Group Selection** tool, SHIFT+click on all of Ed's limbs, and then choose the flesh-colored swatch from the Swatches palette. Remember if a palette is not visible on the screen, you can display it by selecting it from the Window menu. What happened? Yes, they're both as pink and unblemished as the day they were born.

So now you're thinking that we create compound shapes just so we can fill them with the same color? That seems an awfully long-winded and intricate procedure for achieving so little. You just know there has to be more to it than that.

1. Again, using the **Group Selection** tool, SHIFT+click on all parts of Al's body. We're going to modify her slightly so that she looks like she is talking to Ed.

2. Select the **Twirl** tool from the toolbox. It is located on the same flyout as the **Rotate** tool. Click on her torso, and drag slightly in an anti-clockwise direction, and you've accomplished that shape modification.

3. Before we draw our conclusions about the differences between grouped and compound shapes, let's do just one more thing. Ensure the compound shape is selected – remember the Appearance palette will tell you if you have a compound shape – and just cast an eye over all those highlighted anchor points and outlines you see. On the Pathfinder palette, locate and then click on the Expand button:

Notice the difference in that the overlapping internal outlines, visible when you had the object selected, have now completely disappeared. Switch to **Outline** view (CTRL/CMD+Y), and this will confirm your suspicions – wherever the filled areas overlapped, they have become one object. There are no longer component shapes that you can select. And finally, have a look at the Appearance palette – it should now be saying that you have a Compound Path selected:

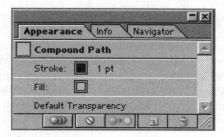

Right, now let's step back and view the differences between the objects you have created. If you look at the illustration below, the similarities and differences should start to become apparent.

Preview Mode

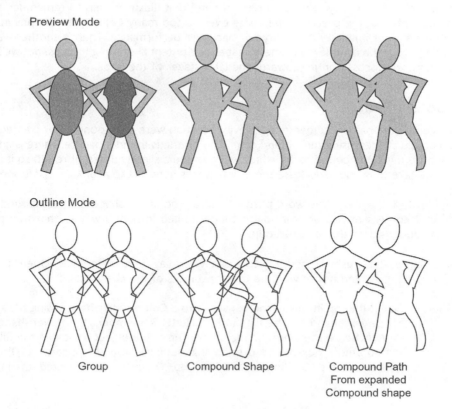

Outline Mode

Group   Compound Shape   Compound Path
                                       From expanded
                                       Compound shape

- In a group, all elements move together, but essentially always remain separate components.

- In a **Compound Shape**, the object is treated as one complete object, therefore having to have the same fill, and all overlapping outlines are removed. However the individual shapes remain 'live' within the compound shape, and can be selected using the **Group Selection** or **Direct Selection** tool. Once selected, these individual objects can be restacked, transformed, moved, or even deleted.

- When a **Compound Shape** is expanded, it becomes a **Compound Path**, and all the internal overlapping lines that formed the original objects are removed. But lines that originally demarcated open spaces within the shape remain. In our example above, note in Outline view how the overlaps have been removed in the body and arms, but the internal lines, which show the air between their arms, remain.

Essentially then, a **Compound Shape** gives you the best of both worlds, allowing you to create intricate shapes and to see them in **Preview** mode in their final form, while remaining free to make radical changes to the components. However, good things never come without a price; you need to bear in mind that Illustrator has to remember all the components and the overall shape, twice over, so too many **Compound Shapes** in a file may have a detrimental effect on your machine's performance. There's another warning coming about the complexity of these shapes and potential printing hiccups, but we'll save that until we discuss printing towards the later stages of the book.

Compound Paths

The compound paths you met in the previous section were compound paths created from compound shapes, using the Expand command on the Pathfinder palette. There is another way of forming compound paths, which will give you a slightly different result, so it is best that we take time and investigate these differences now, just to avoid any confusion later.

The greatest clue lies in the word **path** – there are no actual shapes in a compound path, rather it consists of two or more paths that are filled in such a way so that transparent holes appear where the paths overlap.

Once again, let's use Al and Ed to visually display that difference. Open the file `Ed_and_al2.ai`, and notice we have three instances of the characters.

1. Select the top instance, and convert it to a **Compound Shape**, using the Add to Shape command on the Pathfinder palette. Remember, it's the left-hand icon directly below the words Shape Mode. The entire object has taken the fill from the top-most object and overlapping outlines have disappeared in **Preview** mode. Switch to **Outline** mode (CTRL/CMD+Y) and as you expected, the internal

shapes still exist for you to manipulate. Remember to keep an eye on that Appearance palette as you perform these operations.

2. Select the middle instance. Convert this to a compound shape as above, and then expand it using the Expand button on the Pathfinder palette. Switch between **Preview** and **Outline** just to confirm that what you anticipated has happened.

3. Select the bottom instance, and choose Object>Compound Path>Make (CTRL/CMD+8).

   ■ The results look immediately different from any of the preceding objects. On first glance, three differences should be apparent:

      ■ The fill color is not that of the original top object, but the original bottom object.

      ■ The outlines across the body have not disappeared.

      ■ Ed has a hole in his top right shoulder, and at his hip.

Preview Mode

Outline Mode

Compound Shape   Compound Shape   Compound Path
                        from expanded   from menu
                        Compound shape

Let's look at those similarities and differences again:

- In a compound shape, the object is treated as one complete object with the same fill selected from the top most object in the stacking order, and overlapping outlines are removed. But the internal shapes stay live, and we can edit them as we wish by selecting them with the **Group** or **Direction Selection** tools.

- An expanded **Compound Path** made from a compound shape effectively swallows the original objects, and the only things remaining are the main external lines, and internal lines that demarcate open space. All lines that overlap the original objects are removed.

- When we create a compound path from the Object>Compound Path>Make command, the shape becomes one object, composed of two or more paths, and here are the major differences:

  - The fill is taken from the lowest object in the original stacking order.

  - Overlapping lines are stroked in the same weight, color, and style as that original bottom object.

  - The original shapes have disappeared although they can still be selected and modified by the **Group Selection** tool, but you cannot change appearance attributes, styles, or effects for individual components, and you cannot manipulate. You've not met styles and effects yet, so we'll draw your attention to this difference again at a later stage.

  - Overlapping paths cause holes in the object – hence Ed's shoulder and hip.

We'll fully explore the concept of **Compound Paths** made through the menu command a little later on in this chapter. They are an important part of Illustrator, used for creating intricate logos, and even as the basis of fairly complex **Clipping Paths**.

Creating Compound Shapes with the Pathfinder Palette

Our next port of call on the palettes route is the all-powerful Pathfinder palette, which we'll use extensively in this chapter as we continue to build our components for our case study. Let's take a look now at the function of each icon in turn.

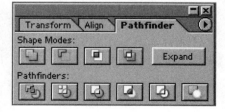

Note that the palette has been divided into two sections, Shape Modes and Pathfinders. The Shape Modes are what we will use to create our compound shapes. You've seen them in action already, where we basically create new shapes from old, swallowing up the original. The Pathfinders in the bottom row function differently, as they essentially divide overlapping areas of the selected objects into separate, non-overlapping, grouped objects.

Shape Modes

There are four icons and one button under Shape Modes on the Pathfinder palette, and reading from left to right, they are:

- **Add to Shape Area** – using this feature traces the outline of all the selected objects so that they appear to be one single object, and fills the shape with the color of the topmost object.

- **Subtract from Shape Area** – takes away the front objects from the lowest object in the stacking order. If you had four shapes on top of each other, **Subtract** would take away the area covered by the top three shapes from the bottom shape. The remaining shape is filled with the color of the bottom object.

- **Intersect Shape Areas** – using this feature, the shape that will remain is that area common to all the selected shapes, and it uses the color of the original top object.

- **Exclude Overlapping Shape Areas** – this is essentially the opposite of **Intersect** in appearance. Whereas **Intersect** kept only those areas common to the selected shapes, **Exclude** removes these overlapping shape areas and makes them transparent. Note that this fills the remaining shape with the original top object's fill color.

- And finally at the extreme right there is an Expand button, which you would use if you were happy with the selected shape and wished to convert it from being a compound shape into a compound path and thus remove all those internal overlapping shapes.

Have a look at the little diagram over the page to help clarify what is going to happen if you use these Shape Modes buttons on a couple of circles. Bear in mind that in the example I have only used two shapes, for simplicity, but you are definitely not limited to two shapes. This file has been included in the exercises folder as Shape_modes.ai, so feel free to open it and have a play with the shapes.

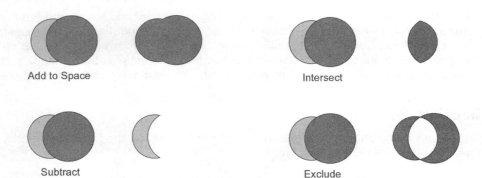

Add to Space   Intersect

Subtract   Exclude

You already know the background about these compound shapes, that the individual objects still exist, and can be transformed and modified by selecting them with the **Group Selection** or **Direction** tool, so you may wish to take some time transforming the component shapes after you have selected them with either the **Group Selection** or **Direct Selection** tools.

Then to accept your changes, and remove all the internal overlapping shapes, make sure you have selected your compound shape and press the Expand button on the Pathfinder palette.

Compound Shape Menu Commands

As you may already have noticed, Adobe realizes that we do not all approach work in the same way, and it allows us this freedom of choice by sometimes duplicating commands in different areas of the application interface. When we deal with compound shapes, we can also access commands on the Pathfinder palette context menu, so lets have a quick look at those relevant options now, before we go on and practice. To display the context menu, click on the arrow on the palette as illustrated below:

   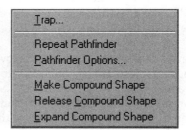

Notice that there are three commands relating to compound shapes at the bottom of the menu:

- Make Compound Shape – use this command if you have a number of objects that you want to weld together. By default, when you use the Make Compound

Shape command, Illustrator uses the **Add to Shape Area** method, but you can continue to edit the stacking order and shape modes of the individual components as you will practice in the second part of this chapter's case study.

- Release Compound Shape – Illustrator will then release the shapes from their composite outline shape into individual components. A nice little safety net for us.

- Expand Compound Shape – this does exactly what the Expand button on the palette does; it removes all the internal lines and creates a compound path.

Case Study: The Ship's Wheel Logo (I)

Armed with these new skills, you are now in a position to continue refining that ship's wheel logo that you developed in the previous chapter. If you remember, the open spaces between the spokes on the wheel were essentially just an optical illusion – they were actually white circles. This is a common, and very bad practice, where we use what is frequently called 'electronic whiteout' to trick viewers into perceiving something as an open, transparent space. Not only does it mean that we would have problems if we wanted to place a graphic behind the wheel and have it visible through the spokes, but it also introduces extraneous materials into our documents, and we should always be trying to design lean, slick, effective designs.

Open the file called Ship_shape.ai. What you will see is that we have two instances of this ship's wheel logo each stacked in front of a wavy water effect. It's unlikely that the water effect will remain part of the finished design, we are just using it to prove visually that the wheel does not have transparent spaces at the moment. You'll also notice that I have placed a rather ugly red stroke around the shapes that make up the wheel. These will not remain, but have been included so that you can see more clearly what is happening as you use the various **Shape Modes**.

We have two wheels so we can repeat the process twice, using slightly different approaches, thus extending your knowledge and leaving you in a position of being able to choose your workflow to suit yourself in different situations.

1. Unlock the Wheel 1 layer from the View menu, and select it.

2. SHIFT+click on the white wheel (1) and the outer black wheel (2).

3. On the Pathfinder palette, choose the second option from the left – **Subtract from Shape Area**. You should now be able to see through to the water shape behind.

4. If you look at the center of the wheel, you can see that we still have an opaque white circle. Select the white circle (3) and the black circle (4). You may wish to have **Smart Guides** (Ctrl/Cmd+U) on, so that you can be sure you are targeting the correct circles.

5. As with the shapes above, you have a white circle overlapping the black circle to give the illusion that the space between is transparent, but you know it isn't, so choose the **Subtract from Shape Area** icon once more.

6. You should now be able to see through to the water shape in all the areas of the wheel that were previously white, but we've not yet finished with our manipulation of the wheel logo.

7. It's not a complete object yet, is it? This is why I placed the red stroke on the objects, just to prove my point beyond any reasonable doubt. It's still a mass of components creating an optical illusion. With the **Selection** tool, marquee drag around the wheel to select all the components. Do not worry about the water, I have placed it on another layer and locked that layer so you will not be able to inadvertently select it.

8. On the Pathfinder palette, choose **Add to Shape Area**, the first icon on the left. Notice how all the internal red lines, which showed us where the individual shapes were, have now disappeared.

9. We know that because we are using **Compound Shapes**, those internal shapes are still there for us to manipulate independently if we wish. Have a look in **Outline** view on the View menu (Ctrl/Cmd+Y), and switch back to **Preview** mode. Remember that if you have a look at the Appearance palette, Window>Appearance, Illustrator will be telling you that you have a compound shape.

10. We are totally happy with our logo as it stands now, and so to reduce the overheads on our machine, let's commit this shape as a final. Click the Expand button on the Pathfinder palette, or if you wish, choose Expand Compound Shape from the palette context menu.

11. Switch to **Outline** view again, note that all those overlapping shapes have been removed, and you now truly have a ship's wheel. Glance at the Appearance palette now, you'll see it says Compound Path

12. If you wish to remove the distracting red outline, please feel free to do so. You may remember this skill from your chapter on color, but just to jog that memory:

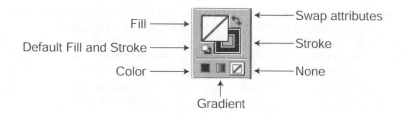

Fill → Swap attributes
Default Fill and Stroke → Stroke
Color → None
Gradient

13. Let's have a look at the final wheel now, without all those distracting numbers. Display the Layers palette (Window>Layers, or use the F7 function key shortcut). Click the eye off in the Layer called Instructions. Save the file.

Having successfully achieved the creation of your ship's wheel, let's consider another reason why the use and creation of **Compound Paths** from your final compound shape is a good idea. In the illustration below, the wheel on the left is the compound shape before we applied the Expand command, while the wheel on the right is a compound path created by using the Expand command. From a purely visual point of view, you can see that the graphic is much cleaner after we have expanded it.

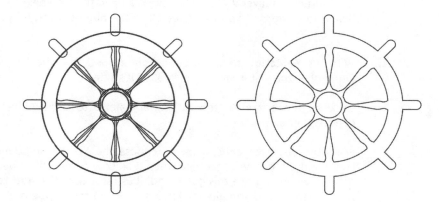

But there is more:

- Converting it into a compound path will mean that Illustrator does not have to remember all the component shapes, and therefore your machine will run a little faster.

- From a technical, printing position, it is also often advantageous to convert to compound paths. Note I said that it is **often** advantageous, but not always. This is because sometimes our compound paths can get so complex that imagesetters will have problems printing them, but we will cover that and solutions to it in the chapter on printing. What I want to mention at this point is the fact that we are always trying to keep our files as lean as possible, and that can often be measured by the number of anchor points and objects in our illustrations. So to prove the fact that the file on the right is smaller and simpler:

- The compound shape has 220 points and weighed in at 173kb.

- The expanded compound shape has 150 points, a reduction of anchor points by just over 30%, and is 166kb. Granted the difference in file size is not that significant at the moment, but this is a simple file. Imagine the comparative difference in size, as your files get more and more complicated.

Case Study: The Ship's Wheel Logo (II)

And now let's do it all again, using a different approach. I want to show you that you can adapt your approach dependent on your workflow, and, I want to give you a little revision on this important concept.

1. Choose Wheel 2 from the View menu, and on the Layers palette make the Instructions layer visible again by clicking in the area next to the layer label. Don't worry if you don't see all of the numbers yet, they'll appear a little later on.

2. With the **Selection** tool, marquee drag around the wheel to select it. Remember the water layer is locked, so it's safe.

3. Click on the arrow on the Pathfinder palette to display the palette's context menu.

4. From the displayed context menu, choose the Make Compound Shape command. Do not be concerned when it all goes black. This is because by default, when you use this command, Illustrator uses the **Add to Shape Area** method, and you already know that when this happens, everything becomes colored with the fill of the top object. You should be seeing all those numbers now.

5. If you're wondering how you will be able to select the parts you need, now that you cannot clearly see them, I have two suggestions to make it easier:

- Switch on **Smart Guides** (CTRL/CMD+U) so that the objects highlight as you move the mouse over them, or...

- Switch to **Outline View** (CTRL/CMD+Y) so that you can see the outlines. Bear in mind that when you are in **Outline**, you must click on an object's outline if you wish to select it.

6. With the **Group Selection** or the **Direct Selection** tool, SHIFT+click to select wheels 5 and 6, the center circles. On the Pathfinder palette, choose Subtract from Shape to make the hole at the center of the wheel. Then repeat the process on circles 7 and 8.

7. Choose the Expand button on the Pathfinder palette, and we have a ship's wheel again.

Just two further points about creating compound shapes:

- Occasionally you will try to apply a Shape Mode to some objects, but Illustrator will not play ball. No progress bar, no error message, no indication of what might be wrong. If this is the case, have a look on the Appearance palette. If it is saying that you have a group selected, that could be the answer to your problem. Illustrator does not seem to like converting groups into compound shapes. To solve it, just **Ungroup** (CMD/CTRL+SHIFT+G) and re-apply the **Shape** Mode.

- Sometimes you may be so confident that your design arrangement is what you want, and you can't be bothered with making it into a compound shape and then converting it into a compound path with the Expand command. To shortcut this process, hold down the ALT/OPTION key when you click on your chosen **Shape Mode** icon. For the moment, I'd not suggest that you did this too often as although you can still use the **Undo** command, you may find you have lost your original shapes by the time you realize that you want to modify it further.

Creating Complex Shapes with the Pathfinders

In this section, we'll have a look at the second row of icons in the Pathfinder palette, aptly called the **Pathfinders**. Remember that lines as we know them in the real world, are called paths in Illustrator; therefore what these Pathfinder filters do is look at the selected shapes we have stacked, and find where the paths overlap. Then they divide the overlapping areas of the objects into separate, non-overlapping, grouped objects, which you can further modify by using the **Group Selection** tool. How they divide objects, and what the resultant shapes will be, is dependent on which one of the icons we select, so without further ado, let's unwrap their secrets.

The icons on the palette are not labeled, but if you hover your mouse cursor over the icon, then the tool tip should display, telling you which icon would be selected. (If your tool tips do not display, choose Edit>General Preferences (CTRL/CMD+K), and check that there is a check mark in the Show Tool Tips check box.)

There are six icons under Pathfinders on the Pathfinder palette, and reading from left to right, they are:

- **Divide** – divides all the overlapping shapes into separate filled shapes or faces (a term used to describe an area which was not divided by a line segment when the objects were stacked.)

- **Trim** – removes any area of a filled object that is hidden by another object in the stacking order; additionally it removes the strokes from all objects. It is very useful for cleaning up complex artwork where large areas of detail have been covered by other elements in the stacking order.

- **Merge** – similar in function to the **Trim** pathfinder, **Merge** will remove any of those hidden objects and strokes, but it goes one step further. If it finds two overlapping shapes that are the same color, it will merge these identically colored shapes into one shape.

- **Crop** – as with **Trim**, **Crop** also removes underlying shapes and all strokes, but it also uses the shape of the top object as a cookie cutter, and any artwork areas that fall outside of that shape are discarded.

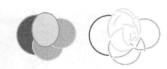

- **Outline** – when you use the **Outline** command, think of it operating in a similar fashion to the **Divide** command. It divides objects into their component faces, but where it differs is that it discards the original strokes and uses the fill color of the original objects as the stroke instead. You may be a little surprised when you first use this command as it looks like everything has disappeared. Check the stroke weight on the stroke palette and set it to a weight that is both visible and suitable. Where would we use this feature? Believe it or not, it can be very useful when you are stuck for ideas in a zany logo design. Its real technical strength is for **trapping** some artwork, which will be covered in the chapter on printing.

- **Minus Back** – this will subtract all the objects that fall behind the top object from the shape of the top object. Experienced users may remember that this operation used to be on the top row of the palette, but that was before the introduction of those wonderful **Compound Shapes**.

We have included a file called `Pathfinders.ai`, which you can open and use as a practice sheet before you continue using them on your case study a little later on. Better to take a few moments and get these ideas clear in your head before you apply them to real work!

> *If you use Pathfinder filters to simplify and clean up your artwork before printing, save two versions of the file – trimmed and untrimmed. This means that should you have any late-breaking changes and edits, you can always return to the original file, do the edits and then pathfind again to clean up.*

Setting Pathfinder Options

Let's look at the **Pathfinder** options on the Pathfinder palette. To display the options, choose the context menu from the Pathfinder palette and then select Pathfinder Options. This will display a dialog box with three options on it, so this will not take us long to discuss. I know you're itching to get back to work.

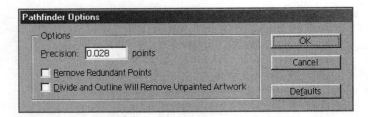

- Precision – the higher you set this value, the more accurately the **Pathfinder** command is applied, but there is a downside to this – it will take longer. In most instances I have not found a need to change the default value.

- Remove Redundant Points – a good option to choose. What will happen is that when the Pathfinder operation is performed, any duplicate points on top of each other will be removed. We're always trying to keep our illustrations as slick and lean as possible, so why have extra points left lying around if they are not needed?

- Divide and Outline Will Remove Unpainted Artwork – this is a personal choice and will change dependent on the particular artwork that you are working with. But what it means is that after the art has been divided or outlined, if there are any shapes that have neither fills nor strokes, they will be removed.

Case Study: Creating A Designed Compass Rose

You recall that simple compass rose we designed when we were learning about the line segment tool. Well, we showed it to George and Lucy, and they were quite happy with it. Now after seeing the great ship's wheel you have designed, they're even more impressed with your talents.

Recreating that compass rose will give you an opportunity to practice with the Pathfinder palette features, and the powerful transform tools you mastered in the previous chapter; and if no one is looking, maybe we'll sneak ahead and just add some final extra fancy bits too! The exercise will be quite an advanced one, requiring a high level of accuracy, but in case you're a little apprehensive, we've included a fair number of screenshots so that you can check your progress.

1. Open the file `Compass.ai`. As you start to create the compass rose, do not worry about the colors you use, we will color the file up later. To ensure that you create the shape as accurately as possible, we suggest that you have your **Smart Guides** active, View>Smart Guides (CTRL/CMD+U).

2. Select the **Ellipse** tool (L) and draw a perfect circle from the point at which the guides intersect to the circular guide you can see. To draw a circle from the center, remember that you hold down SHIFT+ALT/OPTION and release the mouse button before you release the keys.

3. Select the circle with the **Selection** tool (V), and check on the Transform palette that the circle is exactly 4 inches in width and height, and that its X and Y point are both at 0. If necessary, enter values here to change the size, but ensure that before you do so, the reference point is in the center as illustrated below.

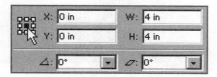

4. With the circle selected, switch to the **Scale** tool (S) and press ENTER/RETURN to display the Scale dialog box. Enter a value of 83 in the Uniform Scale field, and ensure that Scale Strokes & Effects is checked so that as you reduce the size, any stroke is reduced in weight proportionally. Select Copy to create a slightly smaller copy of the circle. Color this circle any color for the time being, and save the file.

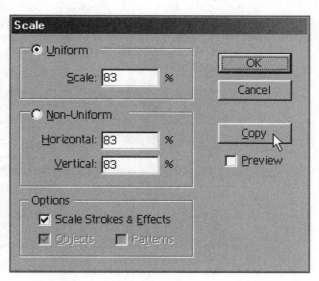

5. Switch to the **Line** tool (\). Position the cursor just above the top of the largest circle, where you see the guide number 1. Click with the mouse to display the Line Segment Tool Options dialog box. Make the line 4.5in long, at an angle of 270 degrees. This larger size is just a precaution to ensure that we have enough line length to effectively cut the shape later on.

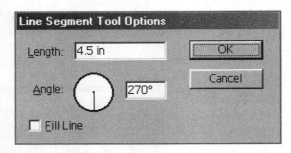

6. After you have created the line, check on the Transform palette, and set all the values to 0, except for the height, which should be 4.5 in.

7. Now we need to cut the shape into areas, so we'll power duplicate those lines and then use the **Pathfinder Divide**. With the line you have just created still selected, choose the **Rotate** tool (R) and press ENTER/RETURN to display that dialog box. We want to cut the circle into 24 equal pieces of pie. In the angle field type 360/24 because we know there are 360 degrees in a circle and we want to divide it in 24 equal segments. To see Illustrator perform the division for us, press TAB, and you should see that the value has changed to 15. Choose Copy to make one repeat of the line, our first segment:

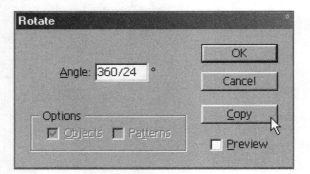

8. We need a number more, so you could either choose Object>Transform> Repeat Transformation, or, working smarter, depress CTRL/CMD+D until you see the shape is filled. You will not have to do this 24 times, because our line is longer than the radius so keep an eye on the screen. Another tip – when you are using the shortcut, keep the CTRL/CMD key down, and just press the D repeatedly. If you mistime your keystrokes, Illustrator may just hear D, and set your colors back to Default. Your illustration should look like this in Outline view:

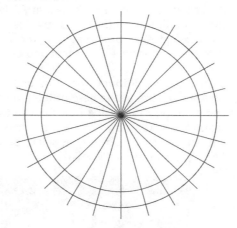

9. Save the file.

10. Now let's chop things up a bit, and get that rose growing. Select all the objects either by marquee dragging or being smart with a CTRL/CMD+A shortcut. On the Pathfinder palette, choose the **Divide** operation, it's the left hand one at the bottom of the palette – but you could use the tool tips to find that. Whenever you use **Divide**, the resultant shapes are grouped, so to select them, let's deselect the object and switch to the **Group Selection** tool.

11. We want to clear out the center segments, so select one and delete it. Once you have a clear spot, you can then marquee drag to select the others and delete them. Now save.

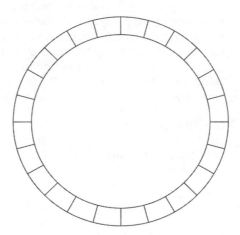

12. From the View menu choose the large pointer view at the bottom of the menu. We are now going to draw the North, West, South, and East pointers. With the **Pen** tool (P), click at the point marked A, SHIFT+click at B, click at C, and then click back at A. Before you click at A, ensure that there is a little closed circle at the base of your pen cursor so that you are closing the path. Again, I know you are using **Smart Guides** (CTRL/CMD+U) to make sure that you are totally accurate.

13. Switch to the **Reflect** tool (0), and with the pointer still selected, ALT/OPTION+click at the base of the pointer, to set the point of reflection and to display the dialog box. Choose to rotate on the vertical axis and select Copy. You now have two pointers. Move the reflected one to the left, so it joins onto the first, select both and group them by choosing Object>Group (CTRL/CMD+G).

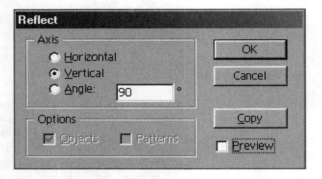

14. Save the file. In fact, it is a good idea to save the file as often as possible. There's no automatic backup for us here.

That's North done, but we now need the West, South, and East pointers.

15. With the grouped pointers selected, choose the **Rotate** tool (R). ALT/OPTION+click at the base of the pointer to set the point of rotation. In the angle field type 360/4, because you know you want a total of four pointers. Choose Copy to make one repeat of the pointer, and then CTRL/CMD+D to repeat the transformation until you have all four pointers. Select them and group them. Do not do a **Select All** command, as you have other objects in the illustration that are not visible at the moment.

16. Drag the pointers by the center to the center of your circle. To be absolutely sure, check on the Transform palette that when you have positioned the pointers, they are sitting at 0 on both the X and Y-axis. Save the file (again!).

Your illustration should look like this in Outline view:

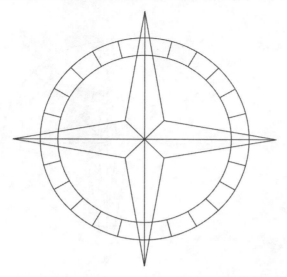

Now to create the little pointers. This should again provide an opportunity for you to think ahead and then confirm that you had the process all lined up in your head and you were just waiting for me to confirm it. The more often you can try to pre-empt what I am going to say, the easier it will become as you consolidate your knowledge, so wherever you see the gap – go for it. Plus, as we progress through this book, and I assume that you have mastered skills, you'll notice that my instructions about 'old' skills will become more and more scant, forcing you to draw on previous knowledge.

17. Switch to the view small pointer and create the shape with the **Pen** tool (P). Four clicks and done. Just remember to check that your cursor shows you are closing the path.

18. Create the other half of the pointer by choosing the **Reflect** tool (O) and ALT/OPTION+click at the base. It's on the vertical axis and you want a copy. Don't forget to group these two objects after you have created them.

19. To create the other three pointers, switch to the **Rotate** tool (R), ALT/OPTION+click at the base of the pointer and enter your value – remember how many degrees in a circle, and you want a total of four pointers. Don't forget to press Copy, then repeat the transformation (CTRL/CMD+D) until you have four and group them too. Save the file.

20. Drag the pointers by the center to the center of your circle, and check the Transform palette for accuracy, once again we are looking for values of 0 on both the X and Y-axis.

Check that your file looks like this:

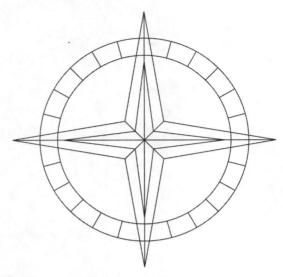

21. Hold on, we want those little pointers to point between the big pointers. Select the smaller grouped shape, switch to the **Rotate** tool (R), and enter a value of 45.

22. One little problem still, we want the smaller pointers to peak out from behind the bigger pointers. Select your small pointer group and choose Edit>Cut. Select your large pointers and choose Edit>Paste in Back (CTRL/CMD+B) to place them the small pointers behind them. Save your file once more!

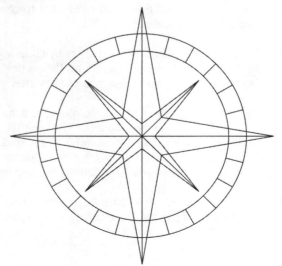

We're nearly finished. A few more shapes to add, some minor tweaks, a few pathfinder operations, some coloring, and then a reward for all this hard work.

For the next part of this exercise I suggest you work in **Outline** view (CTRL/CMD+Y) because we have some detail to do, and working in outline just makes it so much easier to be accurate.

For the center of the rose, I have created a series of guides for you which will become visible if you choose the center rose view. You'll create three circles and one four-pointed star, with only a few tips from me. In this instance, your shapes do not have to be identical to me, use the guides and these tips:

- Draw the largest circle first and then work in towards the smaller shapes to get the stacking order correct.

- Use the center guides and draw circles from the center (ALT/OPTION+SHIFT), or use the outer guides and just draw perfect circles (SHIFT).

- Use the Star tool to draw the four-sided shape. Use the UP and DOWN arrows to get four sides, and press CTRL/CMD when the inner radius is where you want it; and SHIFT to keep it pointing North. Do not try to exactly re-create my star shape, the revision of the finger skills is far more important.

- Once you have created the shapes and you are happy with them, group them and move them to the center of the rose, once more using the Transform palette check that you have them at 0 on the X and Y-axis. Save the file. It should now look like this in **Outline** view.

We're nearly there. Have a look at the Swatches palette. In addition to the normal basic colors, there are two colors for you to use. We've created two global process colors, so that if George and Lucy change their mind about colors or design, changing it will be easy. In fact we've chosen two arbitrary colors.

1. Display the Swatches palette, and then through the context menu, ask Illustrator to display the swatches in List View:

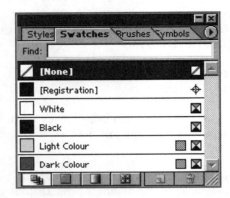

2. Working through the document, with the **Group Selection** tool, color alternate shapes with the light color or the dark color. Open the file Compass_color.ai to have a look at how the file has been colored up.

3. To give you a bit of artistic license at this stage, let's just play with those global process colors. Remember to double-click on the Light Color swatch in the Swatches palette to display the Swatch Options dialog box. Ensure that the Preview checkbox is on, and play with the color. Repeat for the Dark Color until you have a color combination that you personally like. It does not matter what colors you choose, because being Global Process colors, we can fiddle to our heart's delight until George and Lucy finally make up their minds!

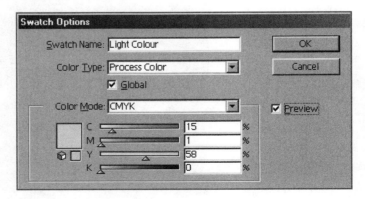

That's it, you're done! I know it was a mammoth task, but if you stuck with me through all of that, take a moment to congratulate yourself. What we did in that assignment was to work through many of the skills that you have learned thus far. A major revision exercise, just for some consolidation.

Shall we close the file down then, and move on? Before we do, let's look at features still to come, a reward for sticking with me through the exercise.

- Select all of the objects in our illustration (CTRL/CMD+A), and set their stroke to Black. Go to the Window menu and display the Brushes palette. Ensure that all your components are still selected, and then click on the brush as indicated in the screenshot below. There, doesn't that look better? You've just used an **Art Brush**, and they're great for giving a more organic feel to our computer generated artwork, but we'll be learning more about them a little later on. Save and close this file, and we're now ready to move on.

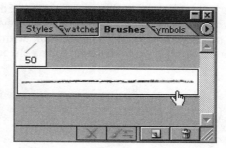

Using Pathfinder Effects

Do you recall that I suggested that **Pathfinders** should be used with care because they were destructive? They can consume your original shapes and if you need to go back and re-edit your work after you've used them, you might find it rather difficult. This is where **Pathfinder Effects** can be used, to prevent losing any original work.

Pathfinder Effects can be found in the View menu. They work in the same way as other effects, in that an **Effect** is not permanent until you **Expand** it, so you can play without fear of damaging your document until you get the look you want. Although this sounds like a dream come true, there are problems associated with the use of any Effect, so they'll be covered in more detail in the chapter on **Filters and Effects**.

Working with Compound Paths

At the beginning of the chapter we discussed the difference between compound shapes and compound paths, and also the difference between compound paths created from compound shapes, and compound paths created using the menu command.

Making and Releasing Compound Paths

To create a compound path, an object that consists of two or more paths, of course you first need to draw two or more paths. These paths can overlap, or they can be completely separate, it depends entirely on your design.

Once you have created your paths, select them and choose Object>Compound Path>Make. If at any stage you wish to manipulate or modify the shape of the component paths, you must select them either with the **Group Selection** or **Direct Selection** tools (A).

To release your compound paths, in other words, to return them to their original separate shapes, ensure that the compound path is selected with the **Selection** tool (V), and then select Object>Compound Path>Release.

Controlling Transparency in Compound Paths

Were you concerned earlier on in this chapter, when Ed had a hole in his shoulder and hip? Either you want no holes, or you fancy holes wherever the paths overlap – I've never much cared for half measures myself. Have a look at the illustration below, and note in the right-hand side graphic how all the overlapping shapes have been made see-through:

Non-Zero Winding Fill Rule   Even-Odd Fill Rule

This effect is achieved very easily using something called the **Even-Odd Fill Rule.** All we are going to say is that although the **Non-Zero Winding** rule is the Illustrator default, the **Even-Odd Fill** rule is a little easier to understand and far more predictable. Let's have a go at that.

1. Open the file Ed_and_al3.ai. You have two ready made compound paths, created using the Object>Compound Path>Make command.

2. Select the compound path on the right of the page – the one with the label Even-Odd Fill Rule.

3. Display the Attributes palette by selecting Window>Attributes. Click on the **Even-Odd Fill Rule** as indicated in the screenshot below, and now every other region within that even-odd compound path is a hole, irrespective of the path's direction.

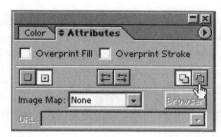

> *Path direction basically means that a path always has a direction, it is either clockwise or anti-clockwise, and we can use this to our advantage if we want a midway point – with some of the overlapping paths transparent, and others not.*

4. With the **Group Selection** tool, click on one of the component shapes on the left-hand side graphic, and look at the Attributes palette once more. Things have changed; the **Non-Zero Winding** rule is selected, and two other icons have become available – they are to do with the selected path's direction. In order to make the overlapping area become transparent, select the icon that is not highlighted. Depending on the selected path's direction, either one of the icons could be active.

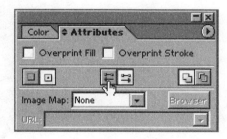

Editing Compound Paths

There may be a time when you want to slightly or even drastically alter the shape of the transparent area within a compound path.

To move an element within the group:

- Click and drag on it with the **Group Selection** tool. Remember you must click and drag without releasing the mouse button when you select the component, otherwise Illustrator will hear two clicks and select the rest of the group.

- Choose the **Direct Selection** tool and click on anchor points and modify their position or type.

Have a little play with these shapes and their transparent areas. Then take a short break, have that coffee, and we're off again to create a fishy story with compound paths.

Case Study: A Fishy Story

In this exercise we will quickly create a shoal of fish and then convert them into a compound path, which we could then color or use as a frame for our next exercise where we introduce you to clipping masks.

1. Open the file called `Fish_story.ai`, and notice that we have one fish already drawn as a starting point for this exercise.

2. Create a shoal of fish by duplicating the fish as many times as you wish. This shoal should have a fairly random appearance, so you can copy and paste using the Edit>Copy (CTRL/CMD+C) and Edit>Paste (CTRL/CMD+V) commands, or you can ALT/OPTION and drag to create duplicates, or use any other procedure which suits you at this point in time. Ensure that some of the fish are overlapping, although do not worry too much about their final positioning, as you will be able to edit it once you have created the compound path.

3. Pushing that random feature a little more, let's scale, rotate, and distort some of the fish, using any of the skills that you learned in your chapter on transforming objects. To get a totally random effect, I used the Transform Each command from Object>Transform:

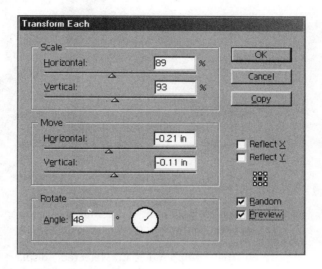

4. Once you have a shoal that appeals, select them all and choose Object>Compound Path>Make.

5. Fill the compound path with the gradient that is stored on the Swatches palette, or make your own gradient if you wish. Set the stroke to none.

6. You may be looking at the compound path, and asking what's exciting about that. But we're not finished yet.

7. With the compound path selected, display the Attributes palette, Window>Attributes and click on the **Even-Odd rule** icon as indicated below. Now you have fish that are transparent where they overlap:

8. Want to change it a little more? With the **Group Selection** tool, select individual fish and reposition or transform them as you wish. Just remember that as you do this you must click and drag in one movement, otherwise Illustrator will hear that second click and presume you want to select the entire group.

Try switching back to the **Non-Zero Winding** rule, that's the icon just to the left of the **Even-Odd rule** on the Attributes palettes and then with individual fish selected, choose the **Reverse Path direction** icons to change the direction of the path of that fish.

You could also edit the shape of individual fish by selecting anchor points with the **Direct Selection** tool (A) and having a little play there. Have some fun: experiment with the overlaps and then save the file, because we are going to use it in the next exercise as well.

Using Clipping Masks

Clipping masks are the last aspect that we will consider in this chapter on creating complex shapes. Essentially a clipping mask crops your artwork so that you can only see the part of the artwork when it shows through the shape above it.

They're handy for creating and repositioning artwork, because unlike the **Crop** pathfinder you met previously, using a clipping mask does not destroy the artwork outside of the shape, it merely hides it. However, I would always suggest that after you have used a clipping mask to position your artwork and you are happy with the final result, you release the mask and then use the **Crop Pathfinder**, especially if the file is very complex and you are hoping to export it to place it in a page layout application like Quark Xpress.

The other great use for clipping masks is that we can use them to give our photographs irregular shapes. What we do is get our photo, place an irregular shape on top of it; tell Illustrator to make it into a clipping mask and you only see what we want you to see.

We can also make clipping mask sets and semi-transparent masks using other features in Illustrator like the Layers palette and the Transparency palette, but more about that in later chapters as well.

Creating a Clipping Mask

To create a clipping mask, you need at least two objects – the shape, which can be either a simple or a compound path, into which you wish to clip your artwork, and your target artwork, which could be a collection of objects or a photograph. For the sake of simplicity, I would always suggest that in this new stage, you keep your objects on the same layer.

- Ensure that the clipping shape is on top of the other selected objects.

- Choose Object>Clipping Mask>Make. The target artwork will then only appear inside the original shape that you created.

- Your shape will have lost its original fill and stroke characteristics, and is now set to none. If you wish to have a stroke on the shape, select that shape with the **Direct Selection** tool and then assign a stroke in the weight and color you wish.

Releasing a Mask

Okay, you've changed your mind and no longer want the artwork inside the mask, but how do you get it out of that shape again. It's simple really:

- Select the mask with the **Selection** tool – this will select both the masking shape and the contents, because they are grouped.

- Choose Object>Clipping Mask>Release, and it will all pop out of the shape again.

- The clipping shape, that big shape you used to determine what part of your artwork would show, now has a fill and stroke of none if you did not apply a stroke and fill after you created the clipping mask. But you know enough about this application now to be able to apply a fill and stroke without any instruction. The only hint I can give is that you may have to work in Outline view to initially select the clipping shape.

Modifying your Mask

You've created your mask, but the underlying artwork or picture is not in exactly the right position in the mask and you would like to move those contents around a little, or add another object to the mask, or even remove one of the objects. Does this mean that you have to release the mask, re-master the artwork and then re-mask it? No. Adobe have put in place features that will let us do this ad infinitum:

- To select a component of the mask so that you can reposition it within the clipping mask, select that object with the **Direct Selection** tool (A), being careful to avoid anchor points so you don't distort the shape and then move it as you wish. (You could use the **Group Selection** tool here, but if you do make sure you click and drag in one movement.)

- If you wish to add another object to your mask, select that object with the **Selection** tool (V), and move it roughly into position over the mask. You know you can always reposition it later, but it's just a good idea to get it nearly there. Then cut that selected shape, Edit>Cut (CTRL/CMD+X). Select an object in the mask with the **Direct Selection** tool (A) and then either Edit>Paste in Back (CTRL/CMD+B) or Edit>Paste in Front (CTRL/CMD+F) depending on whether you wish to paste it behind or in front of the targeted object.

- If you wish to remove an object from the mask, simply select it with the **Direct Selection** tool (A) and cut it, Edit>Cut (CTRL/CMD+X).

There you go. There is more that we could teach you about the intricacies of masking, but as we've already mentioned we'll be discussing them again and again in later chapters as we get more competent. For now, let's go and practice those skills.

Case Study: Masking our Fish Story

Okay, so we've created a compound path and filled it with a gradient fill, nice, but what else can we do? What would it look like, if instead of a basic gradient fill, we clipped a photograph into it? Let's have a look:

1. Open the file called Fish_story.ai that you created in the previous exercise, and save it immediately as Fish_clip.ai by choosing File>Save As (CTRL/CMD+SHIFT+S) as we do not want to overwrite our original file.

2. Zoom out until you can see the photograph that I placed on the left-hand side of the scratchboard.

3. Drag the photograph until it is behind your fish compound path:

4. Select both the compound path and the photograph, and mask the photo into the shape by choosing Object>Clipping Mask>Make:

5. Remember that you can reposition the photograph once it is inside the mask by choosing it with the **Direct Selection** tool (A) and then moving it.

6. Also remember that you can change how the compound path is acting by switching the path attributes on the Path palette and also by manipulating the shape and position of the individual fish in the compound path.

7. If you feel that the mask lacks definition because it has no stroke, select the path with the **Direct Selection** tool (A) and assign a stroke.

8. Once you are happy with the overall appearance of this graphic, save it and close it.

Summary

As a designer, you now have to start seeing the parts, instead of the sum if you are to be successful. We've just explored some pretty complex tools. I hope that you're now looking around you at all those objects made up of circles, rectangles, and other shapes, and running through your head how you would create them.

If time is on your side, why don't you try creating a few of those objects you see? Remember, it's not important if your shapes are not absolutely perfect life-like renditions of the said articles, what is important is practicing those methods and thinking the problem through.

In the next chapter we stretch those skills even further, when we introduce you to the complexity in shading with the use of blends and gradient meshes.

8 Creating Painterly Effects

What We'll Cover in this Chapter:

- *Using the Blend tool, including blend options, expanding a blend, and morphing*

- *Using the Gradient Mesh tool*

- *Printing artwork created using blends and the Gradient Mesh tools*

Creating painterly effects was virtually unheard of in a vector application up to a few years ago. In this chapter you are going to learn how this is now possible by getting to grips with some of the newest and most exciting creative tools in any vector application. During the exercises that follow you will gain an understanding of the fundamentals of the **Blend** and **Gradient Mesh** tools, and how they can be used to transform your work.

When we think of vector artwork as opposed to bitmap artwork, there is a tendency to think of flat, solid areas of color. Typically this would include company logos, graphs, and primitive style artwork. To break up this flatness, we have gradients, but these too have a very computer-generated feel to them and follow a consistent radial or linear pattern. If Van Gogh had been able to sit at a computer and paint, he would probably have had an overwhelming desire to run his finger over the screen and mix up the colors.

From the earliest cave drawings through to the renaissance and on to the great works of the 20th Century, man has been blending color to create realistic or more expressive art. The term I use, blending, is no coincidence. It is my subtle attempt to introduce you to the power and creativity of the aptly named **Blend** tool.

The Blend Tool

This is exactly what the Blend tool does. It blends your colors together in a way that the gradient tool could never hope to achieve. But to say the Blend tool merely blends two colors together is like saying a Swiss army knife is used just to cut string.

So what effects is the Blend tool capable of producing?

- As you have just discovered, it can simulate the effects achieved with an airbrush, either in real life or within a bitmap program such as Adobe Photoshop. This can give the impression of highlights and shadows or form and depth.

- It can be used as a cloning or duplication tool for fast creation of patterns or any situation where an object is required multiple times.

- It can be used to morph two or more objects. Morph? I hear you say. If you've ever watched one of those old werewolf or Jekyll and Hyde movies, you've seen one of the earliest examples of morphing. Morphing is the transition of one shape into another. I should point out that the Blend tool isn't going to turn out Hollywood blockbuster effects, but it will provide you with an instant collection of independent shapes and colors that transform between two objects and are all controlled by you. That's not to say you can't export these shapes out to an animation program such as Macromedia Flash and begin your movie-making career in that way.

It's time we rolled our sleeves up and put this tool through its paces. We're going to start with the most basic use of the **Blend** tool – using it to create multiple duplicates.

1. In a new document with units set to **pixels,** create a square of about 50 pixels with a red fill and no stroke.

2. Position the square somewhere in the top left of the screen.

We're now going to duplicate it.

3. With the ALT/OPTION key pressed, use the **Selection** tool to drag the red square to the opposite side of the screen. The original stays where it is and a duplicate is dragged. By pressing the SHIFT key as you drag, the duplicate will be constrained to the same x-axis, in other words, dragged in a straight line. It is important that you release the mouse button before releasing the Shift key as the duplicate will not be constrained otherwise.

Your screen should now look similar to the one below.

4. Double-click the **Blend** tool. The **Blend** tool shares the same position as the **Auto Trace** tool in the toolbox so if it is not visible, keep the mouse button pressed with the cursor over the **Auto Trace** button and the **Blend** tool will appear from the fly-out, as shown here.

5. The Blend Options box opens offering three choices. From the Spacing drop-down box select Specified Steps. Type 4 in the number field to the right of the drop-down box, leave the Orientation as it is, and click OK.

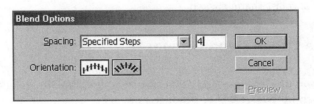

6. The cursor now changes to display the **Blend** tool icon. Click anywhere on the main body of the first red square that you created, then click the second red square.

Four duplicates are created equally spaced between the two squares. The six shapes become one entity and can be moved as one object.

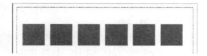

Editing the Blend

You have complete control over this process. Let's change the number of duplicates.

1. Make sure the blend is still selected on the artboard, and then double-click the **Blend** tool from within the toolbox. This opens the Blend Options box again. Type 3 in the number field and click OK.

The blend updates on screen. You should now have five red squares.

Although the duplicated shapes cannot be edited independently within the blend, the original shapes can be changed in a number of ways, which therefore affects the blend as a whole.

2. Deselect the blend. Using the **Direct Selection** tool, select the first red square. You can now reposition this square anywhere on the screen and the whole blend will redraw itself to follow the position of the moved square.

3. Make sure the first square is still selected. Now change the color of this square to yellow.

Each shape changes to a different color, gradually transforming from the first color to the last color. If you change the number of duplicates, you will increase or decrease the number of shades accordingly. The idea of changing the color in this step is to demonstrate how the blend gradually transforms from one condition to another, based on the first and last shape clicked.

Using the Other Blend Options

Besides Specified Steps, there are two other options that can be chosen in the Spacing drop-down box of the Blend Options dialog box. We are going to look at each of these options and the effects they produce now.

Smooth Color

As well as defining a pre-determined number of duplicates, you can allow Illustrator to generate the optimum number of duplicates automatically. This results in a continuous blend of smooth color, hence the name.

- Make sure the blend is selected on the artboard, and then double-click the **Blend** tool. From the drop-down box in the Blend Options dialog box select Smooth color. The number field becomes disabled because Illustrator works out how many duplicates are required to generate a smooth continuous tone of color. Click OK to close the dialog box and watch the blend update on the page.

Specified Distance

The final option allows you to determine how much space exists between each duplicate.

- Again, make sure the blend is still selected and then double-click the **Blend** tool. From the drop-down box, select Specified distance. If the document is set up as measured in pixels, the value you enter in the number field will relate to pixels. Type 72 in the number field and click OK.

There is now a gap of 72 pixels between the left edge of the first square and the left edge of the next square in the blend.

Undoing a Blend

Once a blend has been created it can just as easily be uncreated, leaving you with your two original shapes.

To undo the blend, make sure it is selected on the artboard. We are going to use the menu commands at the top of the screen. Go to Object>Blend>Release.

Now you are back where you started with the two original squares.

Creating Irregular Blends

When you click on the main body of the shapes, not an edge or anchor point, Illustrator creates exact duplicates. By clicking a non-corresponding edge or anchor point of a shape, it is possible to create a sequence of irregular shapes. Let's try that now using the same two squares that you have just released from a blend.

1. First set up the **Blend** tool to use the Specified Steps option with a value of 8. You should remember that you do this by double-clicking the **Blend** tool in the toolbox.

2. Place the cursor over the bottom right anchor point of the first square. A small x will appear near the cursor to signify you are over an anchor point. Click when you see this x.

3. Place the cursor over the top right anchor point of the second square. A + sign appears to signify you are over an anchor point again. Click this anchor point and the new blend is created.

You should now have a sequence of eight irregular shapes, each one a gradual transition from its predecessor. These irregular shapes have been created because you clicked on non-corresponding points.

Take a few moments to experiment by clicking on different non-corresponding edges and anchor points. The results are not always easy to predict, but that makes it all the more fun.

Expanding a Blend

There may be a shape within the blend that you would like to edit or use in another piece of artwork. As we have seen, the blend becomes one entity and only the original shapes that were blended can be edited. However there is a way around this limitation. **Expanding** a blend allows you to access the independent shapes for editing or even using elsewhere.

We'll use the last blend that you created.

1. Make sure the blend is selected, then go to Object>Blend>Expand. The blend won't look any different, but it will now react differently.

2. Deselect the blend, by clicking elsewhere on the artboard or by using the keyboard shortcut CMD/CTRL+SHIFT+A. Now, using the **Direct Selection** tool, you can click on any of the intermediate shapes and move or edit it.

By expanding the blend you lose the ability to edit the original shapes and thereby update the blend as a whole.

Using Blends with Strokes

If you are like me, there will be times when you sit and ponder your credit card. I ponder the fabulous intricate design it has – the same kind of mind bending geometric patterns you see on bank notes and certificates. You know what's coming up next don't you? Yes, we're going to forge credit cards and currency. No! Only kidding. I am going to show you one of the techniques they use to create those intricate patterns and you can decide how you choose to use that information.

Let's set up the artwork to create a complex design. We are going to use techniques that use the absolute minimum amount of manual labor. Speed and accuracy are our goals so we'll use all the automated assistance that Illustrator offers us.

We need a simple 1-point line weight stroke that runs horizontally from the left to right of the screen.

1. Select the **Pen** tool and click once in the top left of the screen.

2. Hold down the SHIFT key and click again in the top right of the screen, roughly parallel to your first click. Holding the SHIFT key constrains your second click, resulting in a perfectly straight horizontal line.

Your screen should look similar to the one below.

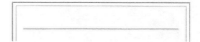

Next we need to convert this into a perfect wavy line. We are going to cheat here and have a sneak preview at one of the **Filters** that you will be looking at in detail later, in Chapter 10.

3. Select the line, then go to Filter>Distort>Zig Zag. (You will see two Distort menus. Select the first one).

4. Enter the values as shown below.

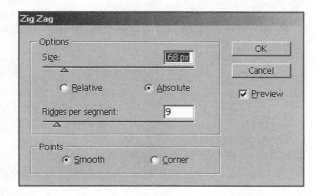

5. Now we are going to duplicate this wavy line. Using the **Selection** tool, click the wavy line and start to drag it, holding down the SHIFT and the ALT/OPT key. The

SHIFT key constrains the duplicate to a perfect vertical as you drag and the ALT/OPT key creates the duplicate. Drag it about two thirds of the way down the screen. Remember to release the mouse button before the keys.

Your screen should now look similar to the one below.

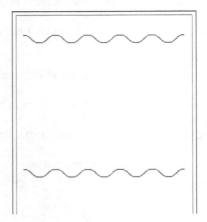

6. Set up the **Blend** tool option to use Specified Steps with a value of 40. The amount of steps you specify directly relates to the distance between the two objects you are blending. The closer together the objects are, the more densely packed the blend will be.

7. Place the cursor over the right-most anchor point of the top wavy line. When you see the x appear by the cursor, click.

8. Now place the cursor over the corresponding right-most anchor point of the bottom wavy line. Click when you see the + sign appear and your screen should change to look like the one below.

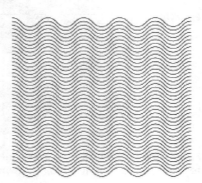

Let's give it a nice subtle change of color.

9. Using the **Direct Selection** tool, select the top wavy line. Now change this to a bright red stroke color.

10. Again using the **Direct Selection** tool, select the bottom wavy line and change its color to blue.

Try experimenting with different numeric values in the blend options box and different styles of stroke.

The shapes don't have to be parallel to each other. Offsetting the strokes can create some of the more interesting stroke blends.

1. Create your artwork similar to the image below using the **Rotation** tool to rotate one of the lines about 45 degrees. Use two different colors for the stroke to give the effect more impact.

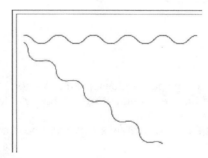

2. Now create the blend by clicking on the corresponding anchor points, first at the right-hand end of the top line, then the right-hand end of the bottom line, and using about 40 steps again. The finished result can be seen in the picture below.

Because the distance between the two strokes differs at either end, we see a densely packed blend at one end and a more spaced out effect at the other. The amount of steps remains constant throughout.

Hopefully, you will be getting all sorts of creative ideas about the many ways you could use the blend tool. In fact you might be on a roll right now. Let's keep the momentum up and create the illusion of a 3D wire frame object. But Illustrator is a 2D program, I hear you say. This is not possible! You're quite right. It is a 2D program but our 3D will only be an illusion, just like everything that lives in your computer.

Simulating 3D objects with Stroke Blends

We'll start by creating a 3D look cylinder.

1. Create an oval with a stroke and no fill and duplicate it so you have a screen looking similar to the image on the right:

2. Set up the **Blend** tool to use Specified Steps with a value of 40.

3. Click the right-most anchor point of each of the ovals with the Blend Tool and you have a 3D looking wire frame object. Easy when you know how.

What if this was a flexible hose following a nice smooth curve? You can have a blend follow a pre-defined path that you create. We'll use the cylinder you have just created to try this.

4. Using the **Pen** tool, draw a curve and position it as in the screenshot below.

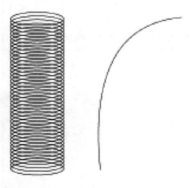

5. Select both the blend and the curve, then go to Object>Blend>Replace Spine. This surgical sounding command simply applies the blend to the path. However, it's not following the natural flow of the path. So let's fix it so the blend bends with the path just as a flexible hose would.

6. With the blend selected, double-click the **Blend** tool to open the Blend Options box.

7. You may have wondered what the railway track type of diagram called Orientation is for. Click the diagram on the right. This aligns the blend to the path as opposed to the page. Click OK and now it looks like a flexible hose.

Case Study: Marine Quest Certificates

Let's use the skills you have gained so far to create a piece of artwork required by Marine Quest. As clients engage in the various diving and yachting activities, certain levels of competencies will need to be demonstrated. These levels are graded and once accomplished, certificates of merit will be awarded. Certificates need to look official and intricate and what better method could we use than the blending of strokes that you have just learned.

In this exercise you will also be able to consolidate, in a real world situation, some of the skills you have learned from earlier chapters.

Open the file called `Certificate.ai` from the download folder.

The file has been started for you. The pale blue rectangle is the background. Take a look in the layers palette in the bottom left of the screen. You will see a layer called background. This is where the blue rectangle resides. This layer is also locked. You know this because of the padlock icon to the left of the layer. Locking the layer is a good idea as you won't be able to drag it out of position by mistake. The top layer is called guides. I used these to line up the original rectangle. This is also locked and hidden, as we no longer need the guides.

The only active layer is the one called artwork – this is the layer that you will be working on. This layer already has a rectangle with a white stroke and no fill. This will be used to create a border for the certificate. First we need to make a smaller duplicate of this rectangle and then blend them together.

1. Select the rectangle. Double-click the **Scale** tool in the toolbox. In the dialog box type 86 in the Uniform Scale box and click the Copy button.

You should now be looking at two white outlined rectangles, one inside the other as in the image below. The two black outlines are the artboard and page tiling lines, which you see on all documents.

2. Double-click the **Blend** tool and set it up to apply Specified Steps using 3 steps.

3. Click on an edge (but not an anchor point) of the outer rectangle, then on an edge of the inner rectangle. The image here shows a corner section of the completed blend border.

Now we will create the intricate background using a blend of wavy lines as you did earlier.

4. Select the **Pen** tool and click once in the location as shown in the image below.

5. Hold down the SHIFT key and click parallel to where you just clicked on the opposite side.

You should now have one straight line that runs from the left of the inner rectangle to the right of the inner rectangle.

We are going to use the same filter you used previously to turn this into a wavy line.

6. Select the line and go to Filter>Distort>Zig Zag. Type the values as in the image below.

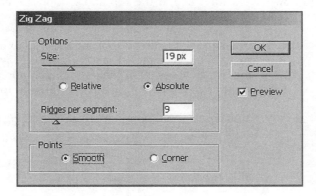

The page should be looking like the one in the picture below.

We need a duplicate of this line at the bottom of the certificate, so let's get some more practice with the **Transform Palette**, but this time we will use a neat shortcut to create duplicates and position them.

If the Transform Palette is not in the bottom left of the screen you can open it by going to Window>Transform.

7.   Select the wavy line. In the **Transform Palette** type 1.555 in the Y box. Hold down the ALT/OPT key and press the ENTER key. This creates a duplicate of the selected object and positions it at the Y location as defined by the number you typed. The measurements stated have been quoted to ensure consistency. I positioned the original by eye. Make sure your ruler hasn't been changed from inches to something else as these figures are based on inches.

So you now have a wavy line at the top and a duplicate at the bottom. All we need to do is create a blend between them.

8.   Double-click the **Blend** tool and set it up to use Specified Steps using 35 steps. Then, click the left anchor point of the top wavy line followed by the left anchor point of the bottom wavy line. You can click either anchor point of course as long as they correspond for both lines.

If all has gone to plan you should be looking at something like the image below.

It needs one more element to give it that certificate look. Rather than describe it, take a look at the image opposite. Let's create this in a new document and then we can copy and paste it into our certificate. This is the time that all computers choose to crash, so before anything else, save your certificate file calling it Mycertificate.ai.

1. In a new document create an ellipse measuring **0.8 in** width and **3 in** height. Apply a black stroke, with 2-point line weight and no fill. You have applied black just so you can see it on the white page. We will change it to white later.

We are going to change the point of origin prior to rotating a duplicate, just as you did in Chapter 6.

2. Select the **Rotation** tool. Hold down the Alt/Opt key and click the bottom anchor point of the ellipse. This resets the point of origin and opens the Rotate box.

3. Type 10 in the Rotate box and click the Copy button. You have told the program to rotate a duplicate at a 10-degree angle based on the new point of origin.

4. And now the fun bit. Press Ctrl/Cmd + D. Each press will repeat the last procedure. You can keep the keys pressed and the repeats will continue to produce. Repeat the procedure until you have a complete circle like the one shown at the beginning of this section.

5. Select the whole piece of artwork and group it. Then copy it.

6. Now back to your original file called Mycertificate.ai. Paste the artwork into this document. All you need to do is change the color of the stroke from black to white and position it in the middle of the page.

Who wouldn't feel proud of hanging this on the wall? Of course, there is something missing – the text. Don't worry, in Chapter 13 you will be looking at the text tools in depth.

Time to get some practice with another aspect of blending.

Morphing

Morphing, as you now know, is the process of changing one shape into another. Let's look at some practical examples. A nice easy example is the monthly lunar cycle. Creating a diagram of the moon's phases could be a laborious task, but we'll let the Blend tool automate the process for us.

First we need the starting and finishing phases of the moon. No prizes for creating a full moon, a simple circle will do. The new crescent moon is a little trickier. We're not going to waste time trying to draw it manually. We can use the Pathfinder palette. You will learn about this in detail in Chapter 10, but in this exercise lets just skip ahead a little to make our lives easier.

1. Create a circle on the left hand side of the page using the **Ellipse** tool, by clicking and dragging, holding down SHIFT to constrain your shape to a perfect circle.

2. Create two more circles on the right hand side of the page with the same dimensions as the first one, by clicking on the artboard and pressing OK in the Ellipse options box when it appears.

3. Click on the **Selection** tool in the toolbox, or use the shortcut V, and move one circle over the other as in the screenshot below.

4. The top circle should still be selected. Make sure both circles are selected by clicking on them with the **Selection** tool and holding down SHIFT.

5. If the Pathfinder palette is not visible, got to Window>Pathfinder.

6. Use the **Minus Back** option from the Pathfinder palette, by clicking on the icon on the bottom right.

This will cut the top circle away from the bottom circle, leaving you with a crescent moon.

Now that we have the required artwork, we're ready to go.

1. Position the two moons at opposite ends of the screen as you did with your first blend, so that you have the full moon (circle) at one end and the crescent moon that you just made at the other end.

2. Double-click the **Blend** tool and set it to Specified Steps. Enter 6 in the number box and click OK.

3. Now click the main body of each shape in turn to generate the individual moon phases.

It should be stated that while the two shapes will always complete the transformation between each other, there is no guarantee that the effect will be beautiful or even lifelike. The success is largely dependent upon your choice of shapes and their similarity to each other. Good examples would be a submarine and a shark, like in the screenshot below, or the profile of a man's face and the profile of an eagle. Both examples are similar enough to render a pleasing transformation.

You are not limited to two shapes. Try blending a whole sequence of shapes by clicking on each object in turn. The number of steps you specify will be created between each pair of shapes. A word of warning though, make sure you have a healthy supply of RAM, as the more shapes you blend, the more system resources are swallowed, often making it a very slow process.

Using the Blend Tool for Airbrushed Effects

So far, all the blends we have created have been between shapes in different locations on the screen. I'm betting that you are wondering what would happen if we blend two shapes that overlap? What we achieve is a very subtle transition of color – similar to the way an airbrush would work.

But, isn't that what the Gradient tool does? I know you know the answer to this rhetorical question because I outlined it earlier, but it's worth mentioning again as it's an important distinction. Whereas the gradient tools must follow a preset geometric pattern, linear or radial, the Blend tool can literally bend and weave a shape and depict a more lifelike illustration. Imagine one of those big 1950s American cars with rounded chrome bumpers. The Blend tool used in this way would be the best method to realistically illustrate the rounded, reflective form of the bumper. This technique has been the mainstay of computer illustrators and commercial artists since drawing on a computer began.

To get some practice with this technique we could start by drawing a photographically realistic 1950's Chevrolet, or we could draw an orange. We're going with the orange. Once you've mastered the basic technique, you'll be able to draw the Chevy on your own.

Drawing an Orange

Imagine an orange sitting on a table. We know it's round-ish in shape. How do we know? The light falling on the orange will provide all the information you need to assess that the orange is a sphere. If the light source is coming from the top right of the orange, the orange will have a small highlight somewhere on its upper right. As your eye moves away from the highlight, you will notice the orange becomes progressively darker in color as it is exposed to less direct light. What we are actually talking about is simulating a 3 dimensional shape again. This is the effect we are going to create.

1. Let's begin by creating an orange shape. The **Ellipse** tool will do. Make the height around 300 pixels so it's big enough to work with comfortably. It should be orange in color and have no stroke. This is the first object to be blended.

We now need to create another object to complete the blend. This will be the highlight. You've probably come to realize that I'm a great advocate of not wasting time doing something manually, when the computer can automate it for us.

2. Select the orange, and then double-click the **Scale** tool. From the Scale dialogue box select the Uniform option, type 20 in the percentage box. Click the Copy button.

3. Change the color of this scaled down shape to a pale yellow, and then position it somewhere on the top right of the original orange shape, similar to the picture here.

4. Double-click on the **Blend** tool and set the Spacing to Smooth Color, and then use the blend tool to click the small yellow shape followed by the large orange shape.

5. If you are not happy with the position of the highlight, using the **Direct Selection** tool, you can drag the yellow shape anywhere and the blend will redraw itself.

This is actually a very easy blend and not too different from what the gradient tool might achieve. Let's try something a little more demanding.

Blending Stars

Drawing stars is easy because we have a **Star** tool. Stars and other heavenly bodies have a soft glow around them that fade into the deep blue of space. So the **Blend** tool will help us out again here.

1. Start with a letter size page set up in portrait format. Draw a rectangle half the size of the page and position it on the top half of the page. Give it a fill color of very deep blue/black.

We're now going to work in the bottom half of the page.

2. Select the **Star** tool. If you can't see it, it resides in the same tool well as the oval tool. Keep the mouse button pressed over this tool and it will appear from the fly-out.

3. Click on the bottom half of the screen and the Star dialogue box will appear. Set Radius 1 to 0.667in, Radius 2 to 0.13in, and Points to 4, and click OK.

4. The star should be filled with the same color blue as the large rectangle. If not, use the **Eyedropper** tool to do this quickly and to save you guessing which is the correct color to use.

5. Select the star. Double-click the **Scale** tool and using the Uniform option, set the percentage to 25. Click the Copy button. A 25% scaled down duplicate now sits in the center of the original.

6. The duplicate on top is still selected. Change the color to white.

7. Double-click on the **Blend** tool and make sure Spacing is set to Smooth Color. Because the shapes are very small and there is not much space between them, you will find it easier to place the cursor over the top anchor point of the inner star. When the X appears by the cursor, click. Then place the cursor over the top anchor point of the outer star and click when you see the + sign appear. The blend is now formed between the two shapes.

8. Now, using the **Selection** tool, drag the whole star blend so it sits on top of the blue rectangle.

So maybe NASA won't offer you a job in the imaging department based on this, but you're on the right track.

Printing Blends

Whilst blends offer a valuable addition to the Illustrator arsenal, from a printing point of view they are not without problems. A problem that can manifest is **Banding**. This is visible on the printed page as bands of color, rather than one long continuous tone. The bottom line is, the more complex the blend, the greater the potential for printing problems. One way to alleviate this potential problem is to expand the blend. You already did this earlier in the chapter in order to be able to use one of the shapes within the blend. From the file menu, go to Object>Blend>Expand. This process converts the blend into individual objects. The blend will not look any different but it will make life easier from a printing point of view.

The following points will also help to minimize the problems of banding when printing blends.

- Use shorter blends wherever possible. The optimum length will depend on the colors you use, but try keep the blend less than 7.5 inches in length.

- If you must use a long blend, use light colors. Dark colors are best kept for short blends. Banding is most apparent between dark colors and white.

We will be looking deeper into the processes and problems of printing in Chapter 15, Preparing for Print.

The Gradient Mesh Tool

Think back to the orange you created. You created a fairly convincing highlight. As in the real world, areas around the highlight begin to darken. In the case of a sphere, if there is only one source of light and there are no other reflective surfaces around the sphere, the side opposite to the source of light becomes draped in shadow. The more spherical the object, the broader and darker the area of shadow will be and that's what our orange lacked. It didn't show any shadow towards the bottom left. In the real world this is the most common form of interplay between light and shadow that we see everyday. Take a look now at some objects that surround you. Depending on your environment you will see this light and shadow relationship in varying degrees.

I'm describing a simple form of light and shadow — one light source, a simple, perfect sphere and no reflective surfaces. Most objects are far more complex than this. Take a look at your wristwatch or a telephone. There's probably more than one light source — natural light and perhaps a lamp or a reflection from a shiny table. The shapes follow different angles and there are dips and crevices. Imagine describing this complex array of shapes, light, and shadow using the Blend tool. I'm not saying it's impossible, far from it. In fact, at one time this was the only way to illustrate such scenes. The problem is the time it would take to create the artwork. It quickly ceases to be an artistic endeavor in the true sense of the word from a painter's perspective and starts to become a mathematical problem. Rather than using one blend, multiple blends are used. The process is a painstaking one and does involve a certain amount of trial and error. Sharp jagged points are always lurking if two blends do not interact smoothly.

So is there a solution? Yes. It's called the **Gradient Mesh** tool. It sounds mathematical doesn't it? Well it is, but you don't have to worry about that. Illustrator takes care of all the math and leaves you to be creative and play with colors and shapes.

Let me dispel a myth first. It's called the Gradient Mesh tool, but forget about basic gradients. It is a far superior cousin of the standard gradient tool, and is much more closely related to the Blend tool that you now know. Think of it as an automated blend tool. If we were to draw the orange with the Gradient Mesh tool, you would only have to create one shape. All the other shapes which would account for the highlight or highlights (there could be more than one) and shadow areas would be created automatically. You just need to tell Illustrator where to put them and what color they should be. Is it really as easy as that? Well, almost. You just need to know first of all what you would like to do and then how to achieve it. And that's exactly what we are going to do now.

Using the Gradient Mesh Tool

You're probably expecting an orange again. Well I think you have now graduated beyond the orange so we're going to create a cherry. That's not so demanding you may think. Well in fact it's several degrees of magnitude more complex than the orange. First of all it's not going to be a simple oval. The cherry will have a little dip where the stalk goes. This irregular shape will create a mammoth problem for the blend tool as the shapes try to interact with each other. However, the Gradient Mesh tool will make child's play of this. We could also add a small green unripe area that merges into the highlight and shadow area seamlessly. It's not as difficult as it sounds. You'll even enjoy doing it.

We need our basic cherry shape first. Rather than trying to use the pen tool to create the outline, we're going to start with a simple oval and edit it to give us the shape.

1. Create an oval 162 pixels wide by 134 pixels high. Give it a red stroke and no fill.

2. We're going to flatten the top of the oval. Deselect the oval. Then use the **Direct Selection** tool to select the topmost anchor point. Make sure only this anchor point is selected. Drag the anchor point down a short distance to match the picture below.

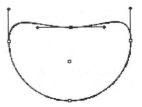

The anchor point now reveals its two blue direction handles, like the handlebars on a bike

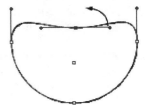

4. Still using the **Direct Selection** tool, select the **direction point** on the right and drag it up and to the left. The arrow in the diagram below shows you which way to drag.

5. Using the **Convert Anchor Point** tool (you will find this within the pen tool location) select the left **direction point** and drag it up and right. This is a mirror version of what you did with the first control point. You should end up with a shape that looks similar to the one below. Don't worry if yours looks a little different. The final shape depends on how far you drag with the handles. You can always tweak them to fine tune the shape if you really want to.

Your shape has a red stroke and no fill. The reason I said use a stroke color and no fill was because it is easier to select individual anchor points when you are editing the shape if you only have a stroke. Now we are finished editing we're going to transpose the stroke and fill, all with one simple keystroke.

6. Select the shape with the **Selection** tool. Press the SHIFT key and X. You now have a red fill and no stroke.

7. You can choose your own red color if you wish. I've used the RGB model:

```
R: 222, G: 0, B: 0
```

You will find it useful have to the Color Palette accessible now as we can mix colors quickly from there.

We've done the groundwork. Now we can use the **Gradient Mesh** tool. It is possible to apply a Gradient Mesh from the **Object** menu but you will find it much more intuitive using the tool from the toolbox in this instance.

8. Select the **Gradient Mesh** tool.

The cursor changes to tell you the tool is active. Click towards the top right quarter of the cherry as shown below. By doing this we are saying this is where we want our light source to appear to be coming from.

You should now see blue crossed guides on top of the shape. The shape has been divided into four quartered segments, though it is still one shape. Effectively you have a mesh, hence the name. There is no difference to the shape visually though.

If you look closely, you will see the point you clicked is the only one that is blue. All the other points are white (deselected). Take a look at the fill color box in the toolbox. This shows red, the same color as the cherry. We are now going to change the fill color, which will change the color of the selected anchor point. Use the Color mixing palette, as it will give you more control.

9. If the color palette is not visible, go to Window>Color. Make sure the anchor point you identified as blue is still blue and selected. Now click in the white square from the color palette.

If you didn't know better, you would probably say you were looking at a blend. Deselect the object and take a look at the top of the cherry where the stalk goes. That little v-shaped dip is blending in perfectly with the rest of the cherry. With the blend tool, that would be the first problem area.

Gradient Mesh Points

Let's analyze this object a little further. Using the **Direct Selection** tool, click on the edge of the cherry. It's important you click right on the edge, otherwise all the anchor points will become selected as one entity.

Around the perimeter of the cherry there are a number of white anchor points. These are the same as normal anchor points, as each consists of a pair of direction handles. These handles have the same function as they do with any Illustrator object.

We are going to edit the highlight using the anchor points to achieve different effects of light. Whenever you are working with Gradient Mesh objects, always use the **Direct**

Selection tool to select the points. Only use the main selection tool if you want to reposition the whole object.

1. Zoom in a little closer to your cherry. Using the **Direct Selection** tool, click on the edge of the cherry, making sure all the anchor points are white.

2. Now click on the anchor point you created. You should see four direction handles emanating from the anchor point - two from the vertical axis and two from the horizontal axis.

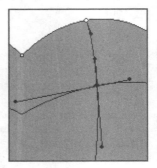

3. Click on each control point in turn and drag it left, right, up, and down to get a feel for how it is affecting the shape. As you shorten the handles by dragging them towards the central anchor point you will notice the pale color reduces. You are actually making the white shape smaller, similar to the way the blend tool works. This however is far more subtle in its effect.

To achieve an obvious change in light, you will need to change the color that emanates from the anchor point.

4. Zoom out again so that the whole cherry is visible. Select the same anchor point making sure no other points are selected. Using the color palette apply these RGB values:

        R: 232 G: 227 B: 197

This is a soft pink and makes the light appear less harsh and more diffused. Try a few different shades to see the overall effect before resetting the above values.

We have the light, now we need the shadow. The shadow should be as subtle as the light so we are going to apply the color to several points at the same time.

5. On the left of the cherry edge there will be about four anchor points around the perimeter (depending on how round your shape is). Select any one of these points with the **Direct Selection** tool, then hold down the SHIFT key and select the others. In the image below, the arrows signify which anchor points were selected on my shape.

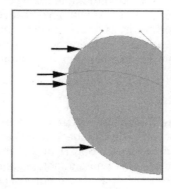

6. Using the Color Palette, enter the following color:

R: 131 G: 25 B: 0

A deep red color now begins to emanate from points you selected. Again, try other colors to see the effect, then re-enter the above values.

To finish off, we are going to add a small green unripe area. Attempting to do this with the Blend tool would cause all sorts of confusion, but it is easy with the Gradient Mesh.

7. Select the **Gradient Mesh** tool and click in the bottom left quarter of the cherry.

This adds a further mesh point and is ready to receive another color.

8. Apply the following green color to this point:

R: 0 G: 154 B: 0

Removing a Gradient Mesh Point

If you decide you don't want the green unripe area after all, and want to return to your previous stage, all is not lost. Points can be removed as easily as they can be applied. Follow the next step to remove the green point you just made.

9. Select the edge of the cherry with the **Direct Selection** tool so you can see the anchor points.

10. Select the **Gradient Mesh** tool. Hold down the Alt key and place the cursor over the point you want to delete. You will see a Minus sign appear next to the cursor. Click when you see this and the anchor point will be deleted, leaving the rest of the mesh intact.

You could continue to work on this, fine tuning color and moving shapes around until you have sculpted the final effect. As with any creative endeavor, knowing when something is finished is often as difficult as knowing where to start and the Gradient Mesh is one of those tools where you want to keep trying out more things. It's at that point that things can quickly degenerate into a complex mess of lines and colors.

Complex Structures

Let me demonstrate this by way of creating a piece of artwork that will be used within Marine Quest's brochure. The Caribbean waters around Grenada are teeming with brightly colored tropical fish and so it is only right that the brochure should be liberally scattered with them. Rather than using photographs, we are going to use one particular vector fish. This way we can use the fish as a common linking theme throughout the brochure and reproduce it at different sizes without any quality loss. We don't want a 2D cut out shape, but rather something with a little more subtlety of color, so the Gradient Mesh Tool is ideal for this style of image.

Open the file called `Fish_GM.ai` from the download folder.

You will recognize this from the last chapter. Now it's time to breathe some life into it. The fish at the bottom of the artboard is the finished thing that you are going to attempt yourself. That soft orange in the middle of the fish that blends outwards helps create the illusion of the roundness of the fish's body and removes the flat 2D effect. But before we go any further, I have to warn you that this is where even the all-powerful Gradient Mesh

Tool is going to come unstuck. The problem is the complexity of the shape of the fish. Remember all those anchor points around the fins and tail that provide the realism to the shape. Those are the same points that will cause all the problems.

You can judge for yourself now. The plain yellow fish at the top of the artboard is the one you are going to work on.

1.   Select the fish.

2.   Select the **Gradient Mesh** tool and click somewhere in the middle of the fish's body. This creates your mesh and already you can see a less than simple mesh. The true difficulty will be seen when applying color to the new point you have just created.

3.   Apply an orange color to the anchor point. This is when the realism disappears, particularly around the bottom right edge of the fish.

This doesn't mean you can't use the Gradient Mesh tool for more complex shapes. It just requires a different strategy. The underlying concept of everything you have done so far hasn't changed. Creating difficult shapes is simplified by building your final object as a collection of independent components. This is how you created the fish in the first place. Rather than attempting to turn the whole fish into a Gradient Mesh, we will combine a number of Gradient Mesh components.

Using Gradient Mesh Components

Open the file called `Fish_components.ai` from the download folder.

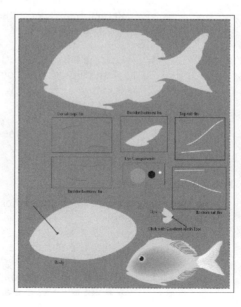

Here's the same fish in "kit form". I have drawn the components already – these are simple shapes or strokes. By placing these shapes on top of the main fish body, the desired effect will be achieved.

The Fish Body

First, we'll start with the "oval" type shape and create a gradient mesh object using the orange color that I have prepared in the swatches palette.

1. Select the object labeled "body".

2. Select the **Gradient Mesh** tool and click the point as defined by the arrow.

3. Apply the orange color from the swatches palette.

When the other components are complete, this can be dragged over and positioned on the main fish body and the two will appear to blend together.

The Fish Mouth

Next we'll do the mouth. This is small, so zoom in so you can clearly see it.

1. Select the mouth.

2. Select the **Gradient Mesh** tool and click the point as defined by the arrow.

This time we do not want to change the color of the center anchor point that you just created. We are trying to create a soft red at the ends of the lips only.

3. Deselect the lips, then reselect using the **Direct Selection** tool. Remember click on the edge of the object only or all of the anchor points will become selected.

4. Use the **Direct Selection** tool to select the four anchor points at the end of the lips. I have placed red dots approximating where your anchor points will be. (This is a similar process to when you applied the shadow edge to the cherry.)

5. Now that the anchor points are selected, apply a red color from the swatch palette.

The Eyes

The eye components are all together inside a black box. The blue circle will have a Gradient Mesh applied.

1. Select the blue circle.

2. Click in the center of the circle with the **Gradient Mesh** tool and apply a white color to the anchor point.

3. The black circle is the pupil. Drag this on top of the blue one and position it in the middle.

4. The small white circle will give the impression of a glassy reflection. Drag this on top of the other two. Use the original fish as guidance for where to place it.

The Fins

The rudder fin below the fish has a soft orange color that blends into the yellow from the edge of the fin. We are going to use The Gradient Mesh to apply this color, but this time we will use the menu command rather the tool in the toolbox. This is just an alternative way of applying a Gradient Mesh and is fine if you just want to highlight the edges of an object as we do in this case. Any shapes requiring a more irregular distribution of light and shadow will benefit from using the Gradient Mesh tool in the toolbox as you did with the cherry.

1. Select the yellow rudder fin.

2. Go to Object>Gradient Mesh. The dialog box opens and allows you to define the size of the mesh.

   - The Rows and Columns fields allow you to define how many horizontal and vertical sections you would like to create over the object.

   - In the Appearance drop-down box, you have a choice of To Edge, which applies a white highlight to the edge of the object. Center, which applies a white highlight to the center of the object and Flat, which applies the original object color evenly over the surface, so no highlight is visible.

   - The Highlight percentage box defines the amount of highlight with 100% being maximum white and 0% is no highlight.

3. Set Rows to 2, Columns to 2, Appearance to To Edge, and Highlight to 25, and click OK.

We are going to apply orange to the edge anchor points.

4. Deselect the fin. Using the **Direct Selection** tool select the four anchor points on the bottom edge of the fin.

5. Apply an orange color to these points. You should now see a pleasing soft wash of color spread out from the edge of the fin.

Now it's just the thin lines for the fins to be done. These do not use the **Gradient Mesh** tool. This is a chance for you to get some more experience with the **Blend** tool. We will work on the white tail fins first. The top and bottom fins will be treated as two separate blends. First we will work on the top half of the tail.

6.   Double-click the **Blend** tool and set it up to use Specified Steps with 7 steps.

7.   Click the left anchor point of the first stroke, then the left anchor point of the second stroke.

Now do the same with the bottom half of the fins using the same settings.

Finally, repeat with the red rudder and dorsal fins, which go at the top and bottom of the fish. This is a blend again and will be treated as two different blends. Use 10 steps for each of these blends. Click the left anchor point of each stroke as you did with the tail fins.

OK, that's all the components complete. Now it's a simple case of assembly. Drag the oval body portion into place first. Use the original sample as guidance for positioning.

Now drag the lips into place. The eye is made of three separate components, so it will be a good idea to group these first. And finally, move the various fins.

Using this technique, you have all the power of blends at your disposal without any of the potential problems created by an over-complex object. It does require a little study prior to beginning your work session. It is all too easy to start clicking and hoping but in the long term this will take longer than taking a few moments to assess how you can simplify your object.

My process of analysis with the fish began by deciding, first of all, what effect I wanted to achieve. Once I had a clear picture in my mind, I drew the large oval shape, which immediately took the intricate fins out of the equation. The lips also needed a subtle red tinge, but the area covered was very small. So I decided to make a shape just for that portion, making sure there was sufficient room for the yellow and red to mix without them meeting too abruptly.

Here's your chance to be creative with the Gradient Mesh tool. Another element that will be repeated on the brochure will be a flower. We need this flower to be scaleable also, but not to be flat in color.

Open the file called `Flower_GM.ai` from the download folder.

The bottom flower has been completed using the Gradient Mesh tool as an example. Each petal and leaf section is one element. The shapes are quite simple so this is a much easier task compared to the fish that you just worked on.

The top two flowers are ready to practice on. Try different color combinations to change the effect. If you get carried away, remember it is easy to remove an anchor point with the Gradient Mesh Tool by holding the ALT key and clicking the point you no longer want.

Printing gradient mesh artwork

We've come a long way from filling simple shapes with solid colors. With the kind of power demonstrated in blends and gradient mesh objects, it would be easy to dismiss the more "basic" objects and color fills in favor of these later tools. As any designer would testify, it's not always the most colors or the most special of special effects that makes the most successful design. All the tools in Illustrator have a valid role to play at a given time. Beyond the considerations of color and style there is another vital element that must be considered when assessing which tools to use. Is the artwork going to be viewed on a screen via the Internet or a presentation, or will it be printed? Printing on paper will not always deliver what you see on screen. Of course if you are creating artwork for the Web, this will not affect you, but in many cases artwork will be required in a printable format and another format optimized for the screen.

Banding, as mentioned previously, is a potential problematic source for Gradient Meshes as well as blends. In fact, the points made earlier with regard to printing blends can equally be applied to printing Gradient Mesh artwork. However there is an additional consideration when you come to print a Gradient Mesh object.

If you are intending to print Gradient Mesh artwork on PostScript level 2 printing devices, you will encounter problems. Gradient Mesh artwork is designed to print on PostScript level 3 printing devices, however, even these can have difficulty printing what you see on screen.

If this is a likely scenario you could consider taking the following route.

1. Go to File>Document Setup. Choose Printing & Export from the pop-up menu at the top left of the Document Setup dialog box.

2. Select the Compatible Gradient and Gradient Mesh Printing option. Click OK.

Only use this option if you do not intend to print on a PostScript level 3 printing device. The speed of printing can slow down as a result of this.

Although this process is a recommended one, it is far from ideal. What actually happens is a conversion from the original vector art to a bitmap in JPEG format. Converting the artwork to a bitmap for final printing is not a problem, but the choice of format may be though. The JPEG option, as we will see later on, can introduce a loss in image quality.

A preferable route therefore is one of the following:

- Use the File>Save As command to save the artwork as an Illustrator **EPS** format.

- Use the File>Export command to export the artwork as a **TIFF** format.

Both of these options will be expanded on in depth in Chapter 15, Preparing for Print.

Summary

In this chapter you have learned how to create artwork using the Blend and Gradient Mesh tools to a professional level. By combining these new skills with techniques that you learned in earlier chapters, you have been able to complete real world projects, for example, the certificate and tropical fish. In addition to the obvious accomplishments of creating attractive artwork, you have succeeded in producing the work in an efficient and cost effective manner. The fact cannot be ignored that commercially, even the most awe-inspiring work will be of little use if the deadline to deliver it is not met.

The value of the Blend and Gradient Mesh tools cannot be underestimated. While file sizes will grow dramatically and caution must be applied with regard to print, used judiciously and in the right context there is little to equal them in terms of sheer impact and the "wow" factor in a vector application. In the next chapter, we continue the theme of "wow" factor tools as well as looking at professional techniques for more efficient working.

9 Creating Artwork Efficiently

What We'll Cover in this Chapter:

- The Symbol Sprayer and related Symbolism tools

- Calligraphic Brushes

- Scatter Brushes

- Art Brushes

- Pattern Brushes

- Using Styles

We need to speed up the construction of the material, and also to move away from the feeling of computer-generated artwork. To this end, we're about to introduce you to an entirely new arsenal of tools that will help matters. They'll never know that in addition to making Illustrator do all the math for you when you create your graphics, you've now put it to work as an effective production tool generating artwork at a speed which has them staggered.

Without further ado, let's introduce these tools and get you going on the rest of your case study. Deadlines are looming.

What are Symbols?

Symbols are one of the great innovations of Illustrator 10, designed not only for effective print production, but also for the creation of those assets that you may need for your Flash animations. For all you designers who have one foot in the print world, and the other in web design, who've been waiting to hear how the latest release of Illustrator is going to help you speed up the creation of your animations, this is one of those features.

For those of you who have no experience of web design, Macromedia Flash is a powerful program for designing animations small enough in file size to be distributed via the web. This was where the concept of symbols and instances was developed. A standard workflow method for producing animations in Flash is to create your artwork in an illustration package, and then import it into Flash to be animated. As Flash is now such a widely used tool, companies like Adobe, producing illustration packages, have been keen to develop Flash compatibility. The concepts also have benefits for you in terms of workflow and storage, even if your work is not destined for web delivery.

Before we go any further, let's explain briefly what we mean by the concepts symbols and instances, and how they can be of benefit to you in both the print and web design fields.

A **symbol** is an object stored in the **Symbols Palette** and then re-used in your document. Each time you place an occurrence of that object on the page, it is known as an **instance**. Each **instance** that you place on the Artboard is then linked to the **symbol** in the Symbols palette. So you can have many instances, all from the same symbol. If you modify an instance, only that specific instance will change, but if you modify a symbol, all the instances of it will also be modified.

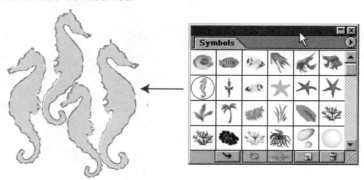

So how does this benefit us in print design? Take for instance a design scenario where you have been commissioned to create artwork for a shampoo company. They want you to create a spring meadow effect, with thousands of tiny green leaves, sprigs of grass, and spring flowers. So off you go, creating this artwork, painstakingly drawing and placing each component, shading each one slightly differently, just to produce the impression that this is not a computer-generated piece of work.

Five days, and 20 000 components later, you have an enormous file. Unfortunately, the clients have changed their minds, and they now want to recreate the graphic as an autumn meadow with the deadline being eight hours. You realize that all 20 000 pieces have to be individually re-colored. A feat that is impossible to achieve manually in eight hours. If only you had used symbols to create the artwork. All you would have had to do was edit and replace each symbol in the Symbols palette, and all the occurrences of the graphic – those **instances** – would have been automatically updated.

If you're not convinced of the versatility of this feature, in addition to the basic **Symbol Sprayer** tool, Illustrator has a series of **Symbolism** tools which allow you to gently – or not so gently – vary the color, size, screen, rotation, and other characteristics, so that each little instance will look as if it was hand-crafted and hand-placed by you. The best part of this is that using symbols and multiple occurrences of instances will reduce your file size.

The web designers amongst you may well be asking if these symbols and instances are the same as the symbols and instances that I use to create my Flash animations. Yes, they are, but a small warning is that using the **Symbolism** tools can result in you creating a fair number of symbols for your Flash files, so we must use these features with care if we are designing for the Web. Don't worry, I'll make sure that you know all the benefits and pitfalls so that you can design armed with the knowledge you need.

Before we discover the **Symbolism** tools, there's just one more bonus I want to point out, useful for both web and print designers. Have you ever wanted a virtual library of your associated graphics, so that you can access them with ease, rather than repeatedly having to search for files to use in your current document? With the Symbols palette you can do just that. Symbols palettes from one document can be opened while you are working in another document, and the artwork can be simply dragged from one palette to the other, or directly into the new document.

The **Symbol Sprayer** and its associated tools are powerful, with many options and functions. We'll introduce you to the basics of the tool in this chapter, but to really get the best out of it, you'll need to practice on your own.

Creating Symbols

The first thing we need to do before we can actually start using these symbols is to create some symbols of our own. Granted, Illustrator does ship with a few symbols for you to use, and the Default_CMYK or Default_RGB samples are loaded whenever you create a new file, but it is far more gratifying to start creating your own symbols, especially as you are already armed with all the knowledge to create wonderful, expressive graphics.

You are not really limited in the type of artwork that you can place in the Symbols palette. In fact you can use any of the types of graphics you have created so far in your exploration of Illustrator – simple graphics, graphics with gradients and blends, gradient mesh graphics, compound paths, groups, and the still to be discovered brushes, graphics with styles, graphics with effects, and even text.

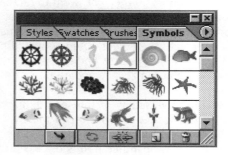

To actually convert a piece of art into a symbol, first ensure that the Symbols palette is visible. I'm sure you already know how to display a palette, but just to remind you, you go to the Window menu and select the one you want. Once the palette is visible, simply select the graphic on the page and either drag the artwork into the Symbols palette, placing it wherever you wish it to appear within the palette, or click the **New Symbol** button at the base of the palette, or choose New Symbol from the Symbols palette menu. Mission accomplished, and the new symbol appears proudly in your palette ready for multiple uses in your document.

Once placed on your Artboard, this instance can be modified with any of the **Symbolism** tools, in addition to any of the ways you've learned thus far, but more about that a little later. For the moment, let's concentrate on getting some symbols onto the Artboard.

Case Study: Building a Virtual Library

As we move closer to the assembly of your project, the time has come to start organizing all those assets which you may need for use in your publications for Marine Quest, and what better way to manage these graphics than to use the Symbols palette as a virtual library. This way we can store all the graphics we'll need in one place, to use in whatever piece we are producing. We'll be collecting all the graphics you have made thus far, so whenever I refer to a file and you have your own completed version of that file, use the updated one.

1. Create a new file. Name and save it as `Marine_Quest_library.ai`. The size and orientation of this document does not matter, as you will never physically be putting any graphics on the Artboard. We are just going to use this file as an assembly plant.

2. With this new file open, display the Symbols palette and then the Symbols palette context menu. We're going to clean up the palette by removing the existing default symbols. Choose Select All Unused from the menu. This will highlight all the unnecessary symbols in the palette, and then you can either drag them into the trash can at the base of the palette – the **Delete** icon – or click on the **Delete** icon, and answer Yes to the warning display, or, my personal favorite because I'm big on working smarter and not harder – hold down the ALT/OPTION key as you click on the **Delete** icon. This shortcut removes all the symbols without you having to respond to a warning dialog box. Illustrator presumes that because you have gone to the trouble of holding down the ALT/OPTION key as you execute this command, you know what you're doing!

> *Try using this shortcut whenever you are deleting objects from a palette in both Illustrator and Photoshop and in other Adobe products.*

3. Open the file called `Ship_shape.ai`, which should contain your finished logo. Tile the two open files so that you can see both of them, and in `Ship_shape.ai` ensure that you can see the logo.

4. Drag the logo into the `Marine_Quest_library.ai` file and close the `Ship_shape.ai` file. In `Marine_Quest_library.ai`, drag the logo from the Artboard onto the Symbols palette. Delete the logo from the page – remember I said we were not going to actually place any artwork on the Artboard in this document, but that we were going to use it as a virtual library.

5. Open the files `Shape_fish.ai`, `Seahorse.ai`, and `Starfish.ai` and place these in your Symbols palette as well. In fact, open all the files that you have created thus far and place them in the Symbols palette following the process outlined above.

6. Save the file.

7. To speed up the process a little, additional graphics created for the project are stored in a file called `Stocking_fillers.ai`. Open that file as well, and drag all the graphics that have been placed on the symbol library into your Marine Quest document. Sneak a peek at the Symbols

palette, and you'll notice that all of those graphics have been magically added to the palette. This is because once a graphic has been identified as a symbol and placed as an instance in any document, copying that instance to another document will automatically add it to that target document's Symbols palette – in this case the Marine Quest Library document. Save the file.

8. Another file called Little_wishes.ai contains further graphics. We'll access these symbols in a slightly different way. With the Marine Quest file still open, select Window > Symbol Libraries > Other Libraries and locate the Little_wishes.ai file on your hard drive. Notice that the Symbols palette for that file is opened, and not the actual file.

9. Click on the symbol in the top-left corner, and then SHIFT+click on the symbol in the bottom-right corner, so all the symbols are selected.

10. Drag them into your Marine Quest Symbols palette, and close the Little_wishes Symbols palette.

As you continue working though the exercises in this book, I suggest you always drag a copy of the completed art into your Marine Quest Library. This way, you'll have all the required artwork at your fingertips whenever you have the Marine Quest Library file open.

Placing Single Instances

Now that you have successfully created some symbols, let's get down to the business of actually placing them on the Artboard and building illustrations. There are three ways in which you can place a single instance of a symbol in your document:

■   Select the symbol in the palette and then drag the symbol to the desired position on the Artboard.

■   Click on the **Place Symbol Instance** icon at the base of the Symbols palette to place an instance of the symbol in the middle of the Artboard.

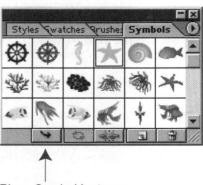

Place Symbol Instance

- Choose Place Symbol Instance from the Symbols palette menu.

Placing Instance Sets

To place multiple instances of the same symbol simultaneously – an **instance set** – which you can then manipulate and edit as a whole, use the **Symbol Sprayer** tool, located at the left of the **Symbolism** tools flyout.

Select the **Symbol Sprayer** tool (SHIFT+S) and then select a symbol in the palette, and click and drag on the Artboard. Where you place the mouse, and which symbol you use, is not that important, as this is our Marine Quest Library file and the only content that is of any interest to us is that stored in the Symbols palette. We'll be constantly spraying, modifying, and then deleting as we come to terms with these tools.

As you release the mouse, do you notice that a bounding box surrounds the selected instances that you have just drawn? This is an indication that what you have just created is an instance set. To add a different symbol instance to that instance set, choose a new symbol from the palette, and click and drag with the mouse again in the same area. Do you notice how the bounding box indicating the instance set has grown larger to accommodate the new instances?

Deselect the current instance set, and then click and drag over the same area. Notice that when you release the mouse, you have created another, separate instance set, which can be moved and manipulated separately.

Take a deep breath. There are many options to come, and you're not expected to remember immediately how each one of them will affect how the **Symbol Sprayer** will add instances to your document. What we are aiming for here is a general understanding of the power of the tool, and an understanding of the concept that you do, in fact, have great control over how and where these instances are placed. This is not apparent at the moment, so let's dive in, and discover that hidden treasure.

Controlling the Symbol Sprayer Tool

The first thing we need to do is confront you with a very large options dialog box, and then work our way systematically through the various options, illustrating how each one works. To show the Symbolism Tools Options dialog box, double-click on any of the **Symbolism** tools.

The first options we will discuss are those relative to the **Symbol Sprayer** tool as it's important that we control how we place the initial symbols before we begin to worry about modifying and transforming those symbols at a later stage. Make sure that the aerosol can on the extreme left of the dialog box is highlighted. Do not worry if the settings you have are slightly different from those shown below, all will be revealed in a moment.

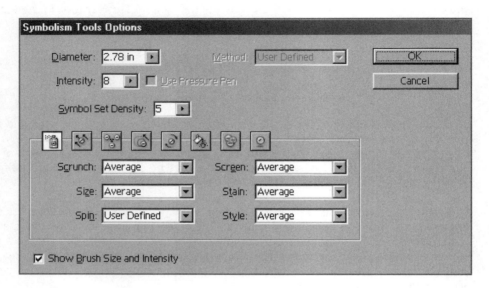

Diameter

As you placed some symbol instance sets previously, did you notice a large round icon on the page? This was the Diameter setting in practice. So what does this do? Let's have a look.

Select a symbol, set the Brush diameter to 1 inch, and click and hold the **Symbol Sprayer** tool down on the page for a few seconds. As the number of instances grow, you'll notice that they take absolutely no regard of the size of that brush diameter. That's because it does not directly control the size of the instances.

Rather the brush diameter is used if we set the Scrunch, Size, Spin, and other options visible in the screenshot above to Average. What this means is that when we add a new instance to an existing active instance set, the **Symbol Sprayer** looks around within the area covered by the brush diameter to determine how it should reproduce the instance.

For example, place two instances and resize one slightly smaller with the **Symbol Sizer** tool. When we go to place another instance, the **Symbol Sprayer** will take the average size of the symbol instances that fall within the diameter of the brush, and create this new symbol instance accordingly.

Exercise: Brush Diameter and Average

This is a really important concept and crucial to your understanding of how the tools are going to interact, so I suggest we take a little time out and see the concept in action.

1. Open the file Average.ai, and notice the various instance sets already created on the Artboard.

2. Select the leaf symbol from the Symbols palette, and with the **Selection** tool (V), select the first instance set at the top of the Artboard.

3. Display the Options dialog box by double-clicking on the tool in the toolbox, or by pressing ENTER/RETURN with the tool selected. Ensure that the setting under Size is set to Average. With the **Symbol Sprayer** tool (SHIFT+S), click to add a few more leaves to the instance set. Notice that the instances created are the same size as those that already exist.

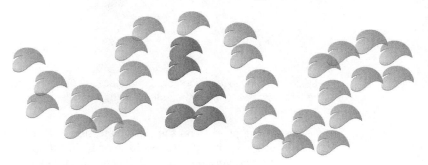

New leaves added are the same size as the others in the set

4. Deselect this set. Select the second set, containing slightly larger leaves, to display its bounding box. You'll notice that I've left a space in the middle of the instance set for you to spray in some more leaves.

5. Select the **Symbol Sprayer** tool, and ensure that the diameter of the brush is really large so that it encompasses all of the leaves in that set. Do not worry if it happens to cover any other instance sets as well, that does not matter as this is the selected set.

> *To increase the brush diameter, you can double-click to display the options, set a larger diameter, close the dialog box, see that the brush size is not yet big enough, and then repeat the process until your brush is large enough. Alternatively use the [key to decrease the size of the brush, or the] key to increase the size of the brush interactively without having to go to the dialog box.*

6. Click to add an instance or two – and note they are the roughly the same size as the surrounding ones. Deselect this instance set.

7. Select the third instance set. Note that in this one, I have a number of groupings all within the same set, all at different sizes. Reduce the size of your brush diameter so that it overlaps only onto the large leaves on the left, and then place a few more instances to the right of the large leaves. They should be similar in size to the large leaves, but the exact size will depend on the size of the brush diameter, because remember it is averaging the size of the instances within the diameter of the brush.

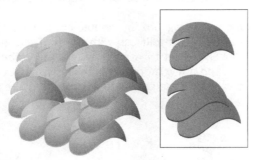

Notice how the leaves added are large, because the brush diameter overlapped the larger leaves to the left; and thus averaged their size in the new leaves

8. Repeat the process on the right-hand side where there is a collection of smaller leaves, but this time add the new instances to the left of the small leaves – and you guessed it, your new instances should be similar in size to those leaves.

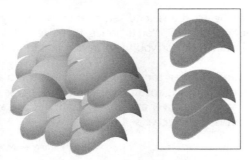 

Note that large leaves are added where there were large leaves in the adjacent area falling under the expanse of the brush diameter; and similarly, small leaves were added where the adjacent leaves were small

9. Now, change the size of the brush diameter so that it is overlapping some of the large leaves and some of the smaller leaves. With that brush diameter, Illustrator looks at the different sizes and averages them out. If you spray with the tool now, your new leaves should be sized somewhere in between the size of the large leaves and the small leaves.

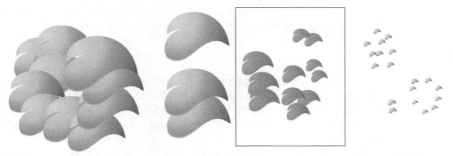

New leaves added are an average of the size of surrounding leaves under the brush diameter

That concept of how both the brush Diameter and Average work should be a little clearer now. It was important that we took that minor detour because whenever we discuss any of the **Symbolism** tools, they will feature very prominently. Now let's get back to the dialog box.

Intensity

For the **Symbol Sprayer** tool, the easiest way to explain the concept of intensity is to imagine that you have an aerosol can in your hand. If the intensity value is set low, this is equivalent to lightly pressing on the nozzle, so just a little bit of paint – in this case our instances – is escaping. Conversely, if you set the value to maximum, your finger's got that nozzle fully depressed, and paint is spraying out frantically. Select any symbol from your Marine Quest Library file, and spray-paint that page, changing intensity as you go. This concept will also become important as we use the other **Symbolism** tools to manipulate our instance sets.

Density

This means how closely packed the individual instances are within the instance set. The higher the value, the more closely packed the instances will be, and the lower the value, the more space between each individual instance. To continue the spray paint analogy, the higher the density, the closer you are to the wall, and the lower the density, the further away, so paint sprays over a wider area but with less intensity. This setting applies to the density of the entire set, so if you change the value, all instances within the set will rearrange themselves according to the new value. The best way to see this in action is to spray a number of symbols into an instance set, then double-click the **Symbol Sprayer** tool to display the Options dialog box. Move the slider and notice how the symbols attract or repel each other. When you first start using the **Symbol Sprayer**, my suggestion is that you do not worry about setting the density before you start to spray unless you have a very clear idea in your mind that you want the instances close together or far apart. It is far easier to spray a few, and then with the instance set selected, interactively change the Density setting until you have what you want. Then you can carry on spraying.

Note that if you want to overlay additional different instances, you must deselect this set and start another instance set, otherwise the new instances will merely push the other instances away in an attempt to maintain the current density setting.

Methods

As for the methods shown in the dialog box below, we'll have a quick look at some of the more obvious ones now, and leave you to play with the other settings once you've worked through the other **Symbolism** tools and had a chance to create and modify some of your own instance sets. You'll find it easier to understand them then! Without getting too concerned, I tend to set all the methods to Average so that they can pick up the settings of previously created instances, except for the Spin option, for reasons that will become apparent.

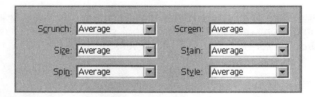

Let's just have a look at the Spin and Stain options before we go on.

- In the Options dialog box, ensure that Spin is set to Average and click and drag in a circular action to add instances to the page. Deselect the mouse, and note the orientation of the leaves. It should be exactly the same as the orientation of the original symbol in the Symbols palette. Now change that Spin option to User Defined, and repeat the circular drag. Notice the difference? That looks a little more dynamic, doesn't it?

- In the same dialog box, ensure that Stain is set to Average, and then choose a different fill color. Click and drag, and your instances remain the same color as the symbol in the palette. Now switch to User Defined, and your instances are now fully stained with the color you chose. This approach is a little heavy-handed, so we'll be looking at more subtle ways of staining with other tools a little later on.

These symbol instances – irrespective of whether they are single instances or instance sets – are exact copies of the original symbol in the palette and are linked to that symbol. This is similar to the concept of global process colors, with which you are already familiar. Consequently if you edit the symbol, all instances of that symbol will be automatically updated. Which brings us back to that sorry story about the spring-like meadow and the editing of all 20 000 objects – if only symbols had been used to create the artwork, the update and edit would have been easy.

Case Study: Building the Brochure Cover (I)

Lucy and George have decided that for the cover of their brochure, they want something that looks handcrafted, painted, and unusual. Great – what you had already half-designed in your mind's eye was this really classy, understated cover, with a few carefully chosen photographs, and now you have visions of having to create those 20 000 leaves yourself. But armed with the knowledge you've already discovered about the **Symbolism Sprayer** Tool, you're not as daunted as you would have been an hour ago.

The cover illustration will be a vista, with the viewer looking through the foliage to a secret, unspoiled bay. The file, `Brochure_cover.ai`, has already been started for you – a few blobs for mountains, a blue area for the ocean, a brown bit for the beach, and a solid blue area for the sky; nothing anything remotely resembling breathtaking.

But what you make of it is really up to you. We know that you are juggling between learning new skills and practicing 'old' ones. If you have the time, you might want to consolidate some of those skills you have learned in previous chapters by possibly:

- Applying some gradient fills, blends, or gradient meshes to the mountains, beach, and water.

- Adding a subtle linear or radial gradient in the sky.

However, if time is not on your side and you need to press boldly on, just imagine what you would do if you had time, and let's start using the **Symbol Sprayer** to develop the foliage.

1. Display the Layers palette (F7) and have a look at the layers that have already been created. As this is going to be a fairly complex file, we have already created a number of layers for you. Remember a layer must be active, unlocked and visible for you to work on it. In this file, there are layers called Guides and Instructions, which we have created to help you develop the scene. Switch their eyes off in the Layers palette whenever you want to view your illustration without these distractions.

2. The first thing we will do is start to build the foliage at the base and lower right and left-hand sides of the picture. Have a look at the diagram above, and notice the guide and the label Leaf Area. This is a rough indication of where the foliage should be placed. Do not be concerned if some of your instances wander outside of this area – all will be corrected in due course.

3. Select the **Symbol Sprayer** tool and choose one of the leaf samples in the top row of the Symbols palette. Ensure that the Leaf Area layer is unlocked, visible, and active. Set the **Symbol Sprayer** options to the levels indicated in the screenshot below:

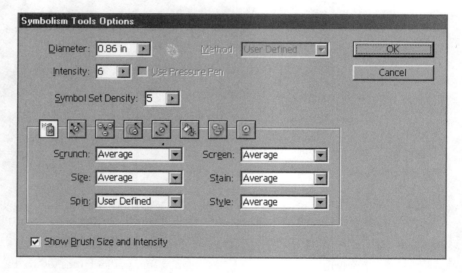

4. Click and drag with the **Symbol Sprayer** within the demarcated area. Make your clicks and drags fairly small and move the mouse in a circular fashion so that the leaves are not all standing in a row like soldiers. Do not try at this early stage to entirely cover the area with leaves – we are going to build this up subtly, so that it looks like we have placed them individually.

5.   Deselect the instance sets at various times to build up different sets to which you can apply different settings. I suggest you create a minimum of three instance sets; one for the base, one for the left and one for the right. The screenshot below is intended only as a guide, to give you some idea of how many leaves we will place, nothing more.

If you feel your leaves are too closely packed, or too far apart, select the instance set you would like to modify with the **Selection** Tool (V) and then display the **Symbol Sprayer** options by double-clicking on the tool, or by pressing ENTER/RETURN with the tool selected. Change the Density values dynamically by moving the slider and keeping an eye on your illustration. When you are happy with the result, close the dialog box.

Select a different symbol leaf and one of your instance sets with the **Selection** tool (V) and then switch to the **Symbol Sprayer** and repeat the process, but don't crowd them. We still have so many toys to play with! But what you have seen here is that you can create mixed sets of symbol instances by using the **Symbol Sprayer** tool with one symbol and then using it again with another symbol.

If you put down some instances you don't want, keep the set selected, and with the ALT/OPTION key depressed, click and drag over them with the **Symbol Sprayer** and they are gone! Save the file, but don't close it, we'll be back in a moment once we have discovered what the rest of the tools in this set do.

Using the Symbolism Tools

Earlier, as I was singing the praises of the **Symbol** tool in the hypothetical creation of the meadow scene, I said that although these instances were all linked to a symbol in the Symbols palette, you would be able to manipulate them in such a way that no-one would know that your 20 000 objects were all related to each other in some way, manner, or form. This is where we discover these inside tricks. We are about to use the rest of the **Symbolism** tools to manipulate instances by changing their density, color, location, size, rotation, transparency, and style.

Before we return to our brochure cover illustration, I suggest you create a sample file, just to practice these skills. Create a number of mixed instance sets on the page, just ready to be transformed by you. Remember that when you create mixed instance sets – sets with instances from different symbols all in the same grouping – only instances of the symbol selected in the Symbols palette will be affected. Bear in mind that the size of your brush and the intensity set in the Options dialog box will have an effect on what you are doing, so you might want to keep an eye on that and change it at various times to see the impact that the changes have on it

The Symbol Shifter

I know it sounds like a character out of a sci-fi television series, but it really isn't. What the **Symbol Shifter** does at the simplest level is – yes you guessed it – it shifts instances within an instance set.

Select one of the instance sets on your sample page and with the **Symbol Shifter** selected, gently nudge by clicking and dragging, to reposition certain instances within the set. When you initially placed your instances in your brochure cover, I told you not to be concerned if there were errant instances that wandered outside the suggested boundaries. Well, now you know how you can get them back in shape.

The **Symbol Shifter** can also be used to change the stacking order of a symbol within the selected instance set. If you want to bring a symbol forward, hold SHIFT+click on it with the **Symbol Shifter** tool, and if you want to send it backwards, hold down ALT/OPTION+SHIFT and click on the instance.

Did you notice that in the mixed instance sets only some of the instances were being affected – those instances formed from the same symbol? You can spray down masses of different types of fish for example, and when it comes to manipulating them with the **Symbolism** tools, only one type of fish will get transformed. If you want to affect more than one instance type, SHIFT-select in the Symbols palette those symbols you wish to affect.

The Symbol Scruncher

Sometimes you may wonder who dreams up the names for these tools, but I guess even though they may sound a bit odd, they give you a clear indication of what they are going to do. The **Scruncher** scrunches! Not any clearer? In plain English, the **Symbol Scruncher** pulls symbol instances together or pushes them apart.

Ensure that one of your instance sets is selected and with the **Symbol Scruncher**, click or drag in the area where you want to pull the symbol instances toward each other. To push them apart, hold down the ALT/OPTION key and click or drag.

The Symbol Sizer

The function of this tool is pretty obvious, so let's look at how we *control* sizing.

With the **Symbol Sizer**, there are a few options to control how the sizing takes place, so let's have a look at that Symbolism Tools Options dialog box again.

The options for Diameter and Symbol Set Density have been covered previously when we discussed the options for the **Symbol Sprayer**, as was Intensity, but with the **Symbol Sizer** selected, Intensity will refer to how quickly or slowly these instances change size.

At the top right hand area of the dialog box, you have a choice of three methods:

- Average gradually smoothes out the sizes of the symbol instances. Remember that this is relative to the size of the area covered by the brush diameter.

- The User Defined method will gradually increase or decrease the size. The speed at which this happens will depend on what level of intensity you have chosen. If you depress the mouse, the instances will grow in size, whilst if you hold down ALT/OPTION as you do this the instances will get smaller.

- With Random selected, as you click or drag some leaves will get bigger, others will get smaller.

In the lower half of the dialog box, there are two optional checkboxes:

- If Proportional Resizing is checked, as the leaves are scaled, they will remain in proportion to their original shapes.

- Checking Resizing Affects Density will move symbol instances away from each other when they are made larger and move closer together when they are scaled down.

Note that if you opt to hold down the SHIFT key shortcut and you are making instances bigger, they may disappear. This is because they have got too big for you to maintain a density while preserving scale, so they have been removed. Nothing to worry about, it's just a bit disconcerting when your leaves disappear, so I thought I had better tell you about it.

The Symbol Spinner

Another of those self-explanatory tools – it's all in the name! You know that this tool is going to allow you to rotate your instances, and you're waiting for me to give you the low-down on how you can control what it does!

The only options available here are those methods which you have previously met in other **Symbolism** tools, so we'll mention them briefly, because you have probably already formed an understanding of how they will react here:

- Average will gradually smooth out the orientation of all symbol instances. To test this out, make your brush diameter pretty large, choose the Average method and click and hold the mouse down. Watch how those arrows swing round to the same direction. The speed at which they swing and the number of instances affected will depend on your chosen Intensity setting and Brush Diameter.

- Going for control? Then choose User Defined as this allows you to change the rotation in accordance with the direction of the mouse cursor.

- Using Random changes the direction randomly. This one is fun to watch. It's like being at one of those game shows where you swing the big wheel and wait anxiously to see whether you have won a prize, as the arrow swings round. Just click and hold the mouse down.

The Symbol Stainer

This tool changes the color of the instance by mixing its original color with the color you have chosen as the present fill color on the toolbox, or wherever it is you like to change your fill color.

Once again we have those three methods that allow us to control how the staining will happen:

- Average will average out the difference of the colors beneath the brush diameter. Don't try this option until you have stained a few instances using either of the other methods, otherwise the instances are likely to all be the same color, so although Illustrator will be doing all this averaging for you, you're likely to see nothing because they were all the same color to start with!

- User Defined will gradually stain the color of the instances below the brushes diameter with the fill color you have chosen. The more often you click in the same area, or the longer you hold the mouse down in an area, the greater the degree of colorization.

- Random changes the colorization and the amounts of colorization randomly. Great for designing confetti, or perhaps something like flowers or tropical fish, where you want a multicolored effect.

Hold down the ALT/OPTION key as you click to remove some of that tint color, and restore the original color to your instance. Hold down the SHIFT key to keep the amount of staining applied constant.

> *Although this tool is very useful, caution is needed, especially for designing for the web. In addition to using masses of machine power and larger Illustrator files, the Symbol Stainer tool is one to steer clear of if you are creating files for Flash animations or SVG graphics. Huge files and myriad symbols are the result. Not exactly what you are looking for when preparing web files, is it?*

The Symbol Screener

In the world of print, when we apply a screen to something, it normally means to make it lighter. It's similar here, with an added bonus! Not only do they get lighter, but they also get transparent!

I'm not even going to discuss the methods because I think you have got the idea of how they work by now, so we'll just say that you can use Average, User-Defined or Random. Once again, if you go to far, the magic ALT/OPTION key held down in conjunction with a mouse click or drag will help you restore some of the instance's opacity.

The Symbol Styler

This is the last tool we're going to have a brief look at before we go back to our case study and really get to grips with this tool. The **Symbol Styler** applies selected styles to the instances. 'We are going to cover styles a little later on in this chapter, so I'll just say that a style is a user or pre-defined set of attributes which you can quickly apply to objects. Bear with me – we'll be discussing them just a little later on.

Yet again we have the optional methods with which you are familiar, and the use of the ALT/OPTION key to reduce the amount of styling added, and the SHIFT key to keep the amount of styling applied constant. But, we have a big caution as well. Before you go and play with this tool, please remember you must choose the **Symbol Styler** tool before you click on a style in the Styles palette, otherwise the style will be applied to the entire instance set.

Enough theory for the moment, let's go and develop that case study further. There is a little more that I want to show you about the Symbols palette, but that can wait until we've had a chance to really explore these **Symbolism** tools.

Case Study: Building the Brochure Cover (II)

I know you are itching to get going. When we were last working with this illustration, we had laid down two different types of leaves in at least three different instance sets. We'll now build on from there. Remember that you can change the options for each of the tools by pressing the ENTER/RETURN key at any point with the tools selected. I'll not be prescriptive about sizes and placement of leaves, so just modify those options as you see fit.

1. Let's first move some of those errant leaves back into the fold. Don't get too hung up on where they are and putting them all neatly inside the guides. We need to allow for a little natural freedom here. Select the

instances set with the **Selection** tool (V), and then select the **Symbol Shifter** – we're going to shift some leaves. In the Symbols palette, select just one of the leaf symbols you previously placed in this set, and gently nudge them into position. Remember that the brush diameter and intensity will affect how and which specific instances react. You should note that the only leaves reacting are those that are instances of the symbol active in the palette.

2. Now SHIFT+click in the palette to select both symbols you have used, and notice as you work with the **Symbol Shifter**, both leaf instances react. You may notice that you need to constantly SHIFT+click to select multiple instances in the Symbols palette, and you may think that this is a bind. Just think of it as a little insurance that Adobe built in to stop you changing the wrong instances by mistake.

3. Switch to the **Symbol Scruncher**, ensure that the instance set and the related symbols are both selected and then move the instances as you wish. Hold down the ALT/OPTION key if you wish to repel instances from the cursor. Use the brush diameter and intensity to suit your needs.

4. It will all start to look a little more natural if we have leaves of different sizes, so let's put the **Symbol Sizer** to work. You have the instance sets and the relevant symbols selected in the Symbols palette, so I'll not harp on about that any longer. With the **Symbol Sizer** click or drag to scale the instances up, and ALT/OPTION+click to scale them down. Of course, after all that scaling you may want to do a little Shifting and a little Scrunching – be my guest.

5. Now you want to play with the big wheel – the **Symbol Shifter**. Even though many of the instances should already be pointing in diverse directions because of our initial **Spin** option with the **Symbol Sprayer**, we've moved and scaled instances, so a little refinement may be needed here.

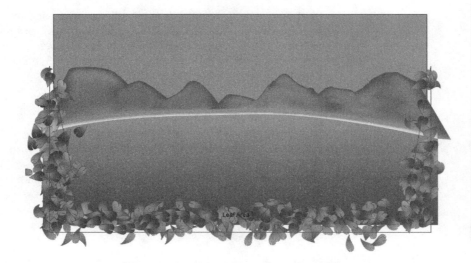

6. On to staining some of those leaves. Choose yourself a nice bright, yellow green for a starter. I'm just giving helpful hints here – ignore me if you wish and choose your own color. Set your options for the **Symbol Stainer** by choosing the tool and pressing ENTER/RETURN to display the Options dialog box. Click on the selected instance sets to stain the active instances within the set, remembering that if you stain too much, you can always ALT/OPTION click to remove some of the staining. Switch your fill colors if you wish and continue to stain leaves.

7. Save your file.

Now that you have the base of the foliage in place, deselect all the instance sets, choose another leaf symbol and proceed to create another instance set on top of the existing sets. It's often easier to work this way, layering set upon set to get the effect you want. What we are looking for is some fairly dense foliage at the base and sides.

Continue laying down instance sets with various leaf symbols, manipulating them as you wish until you have a fairly dense base of foliage along the bottom and sides of the file. Do not worry about the odd errant leaf wandering into the water – this adds just that little degree of spontaneity that we want. You have a fairly good idea of where we want to place the leaves so it might be a good idea to switch off the guides and instruction layer so you can see the file without any interference.

I know exactly what you're thinking! You've got the foliage down thick and heavy – and you've played with all those symbolism tools, but you want a dash of bright, contrasting color. After all, what's a tropical paradise without a smattering of wonderfully bright, sweet-smelling flowers?

8. From the Window menu, choose Symbol Libraries > Other Library and open the file called Casablanca.ai. There is only one symbol in this file, a wonderful flower, just the thing to add a bit of zing to our leaves. Copy the symbol from the palette into your Symbols palette.

9. On the Layers palette, locate the layer called Flowers and make sure it is visible, unlocked, and active. Select the **Symbol Sprayer**, depress ENTER/RETURN to set your options and spray some flowers along the base and up the sides on top of the foliage. Use the other **Symbolism** tools as you see fit to modify the instances.

10. Save the file.

I know there were some of you, who pressed for time, decided not to embellish the water, mountains, and sky, and now you're looking at this illustration develop and wishing you had. Don't worry, you can still do that in your own time, but I have a little more explanation to give you regarding symbols, and then I'm off to show you how to draw palm trees.

Managing Symbols

Recall that spring meadow scenario I mentioned at the beginning of the chapter, and how I said not only creating, but also editing with symbols would make our life so much easier? Let's have a look at a few of the options in the Symbols Palette that will make our managing of symbols and instances a little easier.

Imagine you have a bright green spring colored leaf, and you now – as a result of the client's change of mind – need to change this to rich autumnal shades throughout the document. It really is a cinch to automate this entire process with just a little forethought.

You have to make ground level changes to your document, so follow these steps carefully:

- Drag a single instance of a symbol from the Symbols palette onto the Artboard.

- Break its link with the original symbol by either choosing **Break Link to Symbol** from the palette menu, or by clicking on the button in the Symbols palette.

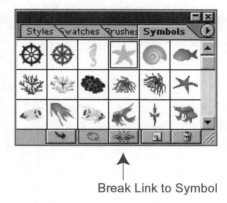

Break Link to Symbol

- Edit the graphic, as you see fit.

- Then either, select the symbol you want to redefine in the Symbols palette, and choose Redefine from the palette menu, or ALT/OPTION-drag the new symbol into the Symbols palette and release it once it is over the symbol you wish to replace. All the symbols in your illustrations are automatically updated!

Accessing the Symbolism Tools

Adobe has realized that when we are spraying with the **Symbol Sprayer**, there's every chance we may then want to change to the **Shifter**, the **Sizer**, the **Screener**, or any of the other **Symbolism** tools. And that's going to be a whole load of mouse walking if we constantly have to keep going to the toolbox to switch tools.

To see this in action, first select one of the Symbolism tools. Then, hold down the ALT key and right-click with the mouse. Keep the mouse button down, and drag the cursor slightly and you should see an image similar to the one below. Move the mouse over the tool you want, the cursor icon will change to that tool; and your new tool is selected!

Using Brushes to Stylize your Paths

There are basically four types of artistic brushes that you can use in Illustrator. Before we start our investigation, let's display the Brushes palette (F5), so that you can learn to identify them.

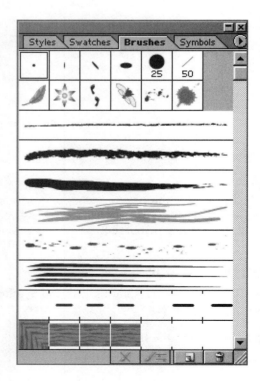

- **Calligraphic** brushes, those brushes in the top row of the palette, are used to create strokes, which should look like you have drawn with a calligraphic pen. This option is especially useful for drawing 'hand-drawn' sketches.

- The **Scatter** brushes, those brushes in the second row of the screenshot, 'splatter' copies of an object along a path drawn with the paintbrush, pencil, pen tool, or any of your primitive shape tools. We'll be using it to scatter a few clouds into our wonderful tropical sky, and possibly a few palm trees along the shore's edge.

- The **Art** brushes, those horizontal brushes below the scatter brushes in the palette, are useful for individually placing unique copies of artwork onto the Artboard. In our instance, we would have more than likely used the art brushes to place individual copies of the flowers onto our illustration, so that we could have made each one unique, well, that's before they gave us the power of symbols of course. But in this instance, we'll be using the Art brushes to place some palm trees along the edge of our illustration for our brochure cover.

- **Pattern** brushes, located towards the bottom of the palette and easily identifiable by the little cross marks in the palette, are used for painting patterns – made of individual **tiles** – that repeat along the length of a path.

Painting with the Paintbrush

Although you can paint paths with a number of the drawing tools you have already learned to utilize, this seems like an ideal opportunity to introduce you to another drawing or painting tool, the **Paintbrush**.

Before using the **Paintbrush** tool, you have to tell Illustrator which particular brush you would like to paint with, so you'll need to select one from the Brushes palette (F5). To start with, I'd suggest you choose one of the simplest brushes, the calligraphic brushes from the top row, and in a sample file, click and drag to create a proud sweep across the Artboard.

I know you're just dying to try them out, so go ahead. Select a **Scatter** brush and draw a swash across the page, noting how the objects are scattered and rotated left and right of the path you drew. Try an **Art** brush, and notice how the object follows the shape of the line you have drawn. Finally, select a **Pattern** brush to see how the individual tiles stack up to form a patterned path.

Now let's have a look at the options for the **Paintbrush**, and I'll give you some hints for using it effectively. Display the tool's options, by either double-clicking the tool, or hitting ENTER/RETURN.

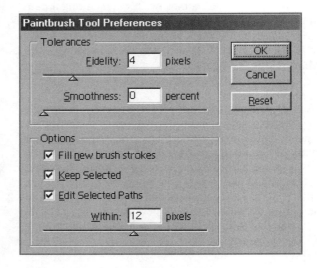

Some of these preferences may seem fairly familiar – yes – they do bear a certain similarity to those you saw earlier when you first met the **Pencil** tool, so let's use this not only as an introduction to the **Paintbrush**, but also as a refresher for those **Pencil** tool options. You may also wish to refer back to some of those illustrations in Chapter 3 showing how smoothness and fidelity affected the shape of the path.

- For the Fidelity value, you are indicating how far the stroke you are drawing can wander away from your original action in order to draw a smooth path. Remember there is always a trade-off; the higher the value, the smoother the path, but the less true it will be to the stroke you made with the paintbrush. The lower the value, the closer Illustrator will try and replicate your mouse actions, but this path is likely to have a few kinks in it, and will be more complex with more anchor points.

- For the Smoothness value, once again the higher the value, the smoother and simpler the path will be, but possibly not that close in resembling the path you drew. The lower the value, the more kinks you'll retain, but the line is likely to be more complex with more anchor points once more.

- The Fill new brush strokes option can be a little confusing at first. You draw a path with the paintbrush, and you look at it and it seems filled. In actual fact, it is not. When you draw using one of the paintbrushes you are placing objects along a line, irrespective of which particular type of brush you use. This command is talking about the area in-between the beginning and end of the stroke.

Fill New Brush Stroke
Option checked

Fill New Brush Stroke
Option unchecked

- The Keep Selected option determines whether or not the path remains selected after you have released the mouse button. It is useful to keep this checked if you find that you battle to draw a complete line in one movement and need to constantly add to the end of the existing path you have drawn. It just saves you having to re-select the path each time you want to continue the line. On the other hand, it can be annoying if you are drawing a number of brushstrokes really close to each other, and Illustrator keeps joining them because the previous line was still selected.

- Similar in frustration value is the Edit Selected Paths option. It's useful to be able to draw over and reshape your brushstroke if it was not drawn exactly how you wished, but a real pain if you are trying to draw a number of lines close together, because Illustrator thinks you want to keep re-drawing the same path. An option is to keep the boxes checked, and if you find that you need to draw another line near to the existing one, just make sure it is not selected.

As with the **Pencil** tool, if you wish for the path to be closed automatically, hold down the ALT/OPTION key, and when the path is the shape you want, release the mouse button and then the keyboard modifier.

Although the paths drawn by the **Paintbrush** may look very different in appearance, they are in actual fact paths, which have been stroked with an object. This means that they can be transformed with any of the tools you have previously met, and that individual anchor points along the path can be selected and manipulated, although it's often much easier to switch to **Outline** view on the **View** menu (CTRL/CMD+Y) to do this. I know you've already worked out that if you can manipulate a **Paintbrush** stroke as you would any other path, then it follows that you can apply a **Brush** from the Brushes palette to any shape you have drawn. You're looking a little quizzical, so I'll just remind you of that compass rose we drew a few chapters back, that conglomeration of rectangular and circular paths. Remember, we added that brush stroke to give the compass a slightly organic feel. Why not have another go at the brushing a path seeing that we're here learning about them!

Case Study: Stroking the Seahorse

As we move closer towards that time when we will begin putting the components of this case study together, it's a good idea for us to revisit some of our earlier artwork and see if there isn't something we could do to it to enhance it. That's exactly what we'll do with our seahorse.

1. Open the file Seahorse.ai. If you look closely, you might notice there's a bit of trickery afoot here. You have used the gradient mesh tool before, and you know that when a mesh is applied to an object, that object loses its stroke. So, how come this seahorse has an outline? We've simply got two copies there, exactly on top of each other. The lower one has a gradient mesh; the upper has a blue stroke with no fill. You see, there is a way around every limitation you feel a program might place on you – it just demands a little cunning sometimes!

2. As the objects are exactly on top of each other, you'll have to be very careful to ensure that you select the seahorse with the stroke and no fill. Switch to the **Selection** tool (V), and carefully select the outlined seahorse. Check that you have the correct one selected by looking at the Appearance palette. It should be telling you that you have an object selected with a 1 pt blue outline and no fill. If you selected the incorrect seahorse, deselect, and try again.

3. Let's first try applying a **Calligraphic** brush to the seahorse. You might find the one on the extreme top-left really does not make much of an impact. Try another one and see if you get a better effect.

4. Move down to one of the **Scatter** brushes in the second row. Again some interesting effects, but possibly not exactly what we are looking for, although you may be surprised once we start editing these shapes in the next section.

5. Again, move down to the **Art** Brushes, and try a few of these options, and then finally try the **Pattern** brushes.

Even with an odd shape like this, we can get an interesting effect with an odd **Pattern** brush. But they just don't fit. Keep this file open. You'll use it to experiment on as you edit the brushes, and the final choice of brush will be yours.

Modifying Existing Brushes

In this book, we'll not explicitly tell you how to create your own brushes, but if you have a look at the options for modifying brushes, you'll soon get the gist of how to control them, and then making your own will be easy. In addition, before you run off thinking that all these default brushes are awful, and you just have to create your own, on the CD that your Adobe Illustrator came on there is an Illustrator Extras folder containing hundreds of really good brushes waiting to be used. We'll make sure you know how to open a **Brush Library** before the end of this chapter, but for the moment let's see if we can find any use for those in the default **Brush Library** – you might be pleasantly surprised.

Essentially there are two ways in which we can modify a brush that we have already applied to an object. The first method changes only the options of a selected object, while the second will make changes to the brush in the Brushes palette, which will then be applied to all new strokes, but we will be given the option whether we want to apply it to our existing strokes as well.

- To change the options only for the selected brushed objects, choose Options of Selected Object from the Brushes palette menu, or click the **Options of Selected Object** button in the palette.

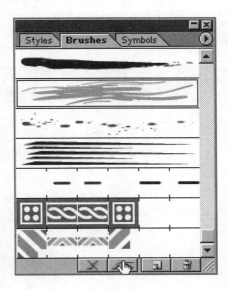

- Change the options, and click OK. Only the selected objects that have been brushed with this particular brush will be changed. Any previous or future objects painted with the brush will use the original attributes of the brush, as these have not actually been changed.

- If you wish to change the attributes for all future paths stroked with a particular brush, and possibly the paths you have already brushed, double-click on the target brush in the ∫rushes palette. Dependent on what type of brush you have chosen to edit, a dialog box will be displayed, select your options and then click OK. Illustrator will ask you whether you wish to Apply To Strokes, to change those you have already created as well as new paths, or you wish to Leave Strokes to leave those paths unchanged and apply the brush only to new paths or brushstrokes.

Modifying a Calligraphic Brush

We'll look at how to modify each of the certain types of brushes, because this is a really good way for you to play with the options and get familiar with them. Thus, when you decide the time has come to create your own brushes, you'll be ready. These options dialog boxes are big, and possibly a little daunting, but don't let that put you off. We'll take it pretty slowly at first, and then as various options repeat themselves in different boxes, we'll start to pick up speed.

To display the Calligraphic Brush dialog box, first select the seahorse, and apply a calligraphic brush – I chose the second one from the left, but you can choose whichever one appeals. I'll get a little more prescriptive later. You don't need to select artwork and apply a stroke before you modify a brush, but half the fun (and knowledge) comes from actually seeing what changing the different options does to the brush.

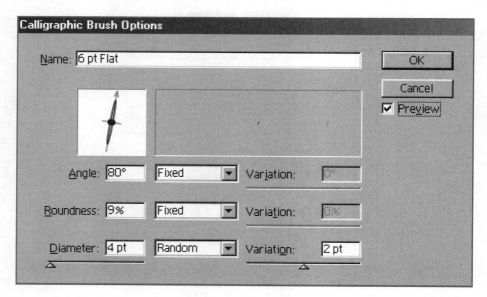

Don't let any of these options intimidate you – especially all those degrees and percentages. The key here is seeing in real-time what changing those values does to your brushstroke – so make sure you have clicked the Preview box on the right of the dialog box.

Look at the little diagram at the left of the dialog box that is the shape of your present brushstroke.

- To change the angle, click on the arrow and drag it to another direction. Notice that as you do so, the angle in the Angle field has updated to reflect the change, as have the little icons in the right-hand area of the dialog box. Have a look at your seahorse too.

- Change the roundness of the brush by clicking and dragging the little balls located halfway down the icon, once again note how the values and the display update dynamically. And the seahorse has changed again.

- Drag the Diameter slider to change the width of the brush, and again, look to see how the brushstroke is being affected.

To the right of the value fields, you'll notice a little drop-down menu with three options, which allow you to control the variations you have set in roundness, angle, and diameter:

- Fixed uses the absolute value chosen by yourself.

- With Variation, you need to enter a value and the value applied to the object will vary within the limits you have set. For example, if you set a weight for Roundness of 9%, the greatest amount of variation you could choose would be 9%; and the resulting line could vary from anywhere between 0% to 18% (9 % either side of your value). Of course, you don't have to choose the full rate of variation, I'm just showing you that you cannot exceed the value – after all you couldn't have a line less than 0% in roundness.

- Choose Pressure if you are lucky enough to have a pressure-sensitive graphics tablet, and the variations will react to the pressure you apply with your pen.

Modifying a Scatter Brush

Before we look at this dialog box, ensure that you have applied a **Scatter Brush** to your seahorse. I'm suggesting you go for the one on the right of the second row, called ink drop. Also choose a new stroke color, not a fill color – because there's a little bit of color magic hidden in there too.

Double-click to display the dialog box.

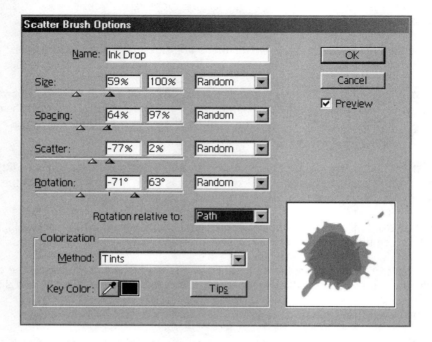

Make sure you've got Preview checked and keep an eye on that screen. We're going to try and get as many of those ink splats as possible inside the seahorse for an interesting effect. On the right-hand side you see familiar options – Fixed, Random, and Pressure. All the options for this brush have been set to Random. To the left you see the Features, with value fields and sliders. Look closely at those sliders and note there is a center point for each one. For Size and Spacing, the center is 100%, whilst for Scatter and Rotation, the center is 0%, and you pull the sliders to affect the extent to which you wish to allow variation. For example, in the Size field, these blots can vary in size randomly from 59% of their original size to 100% of the original size.

In those four fields, there should be only one that may be posing some problems – just what does Scatter mean? This seahorse is a closed path, you'd agree with that? Well, all Scatter does is determine how far away from that path on both the left and the right of the path, it can drop down shapes. Thus the greater the percentage of scatter allowed, the further away from the path these objects will appear, and vice-versa. If I wanted them to follow the path exactly, I'd set the method to Fixed and the Scatter to 0%.

Rotation relative to Page or Path, just determines that in accordance with the values set in the Rotation option, whether they rotate in relation to the horizontal axis of the page, or in relation to the direction of the path that you are stroking.

You recall I suggested that you choose a different stroke color before we started to play with this brush? Have you noticed how the ink splats have changed to reflect that color? That's because the Colorization method at the base of the dialog box was set to Tints. This means that your brushstroke will always be tinted the color chosen by you as the stroke.

There are four colorization methods:

- None – the color of the stroke will not affect the brushstroke, it will remain whatever color it was when it was first created.

- Tints displays the brushstroke in tints of the stroke color. So black in the artwork becomes the color you have chosen as a stroke, and all other colors become tints of that color, except white – white remains white.

- Tints and Shades re-maps the brushstroke colors in tints and shades. Unlike in Tints, where any black in the brushstroke became the tint color, with Tints and Shades, black remains black and everything between becomes a blend from black to white using the stroke color.

- Hue Shift uses the most prominent color in the brush artwork, and shifts all the colors round in relation to it. Hue Shift does work well for colorful brushes, but the results you get are sometimes quite wacky.

Modifying an Art Brush

Let's apply an **Art Brush**, and have a look at those options. I'm at a loss for which brush to suggest here, so I've chosen one that at first glance doesn't look like it will suit this particular subject, the Scroll Pen Variable Length. This is just to prove to you how versatile these brushes are!

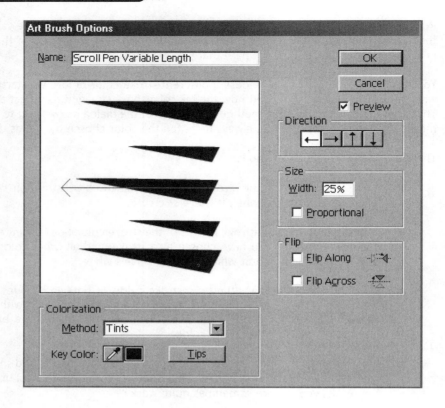

Ensure that Preview is on and let's have a look at how we can modify Art Brushes.

- The four directional arrows on the right indicate the direction in which the art will be drawn. An easy way to make sense of this is to remember that the arrow always marks where the stroke will end.

- Below that we have the Width – and you've worked out what that does, but what is the Proportional option? It just means that the longer you make your stroke, the fatter the art brush will become. The brush stroke will keep its original proportions.

- Below that we have the options for flipping the brushstroke on the path either horizontally or vertically.

- At the bottom left we have our colorization methods, which work exactly the same as they do in the previously discussed **Scatter** brush.

Modifying Pattern Brushes

This is the last type of brush, and the one that is really going to prove to be the greatest surprise in this little exercise. So, once more, for the last time, with our seahorse, let's apply a pattern brush and display those options. I chose Classical, the lilac one, and came up with some interesting results.

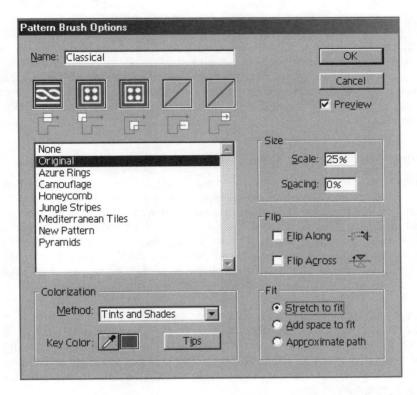

With Preview on, I immediately scaled it down to 25% as the patterns were far too large for this intricate shape. Below the Scale option is an option for Spacing, which, if we entered a value, would create spaces between our tiles.

Flip Along and Flip Across have very little effect on this regular, rectangular pattern, but they would show an effect if our pattern was more irregular.

The Fit options determine how Illustrator interacts with the tiles to make them fit round the shape we have selected – you know how they say that you can't put a square peg in a round hole – just let Illustrator at the top!

- With the Stretch to Fit option, the tiles in the pattern will be gently stretched so that no space appears between them.

- With Add Space to Fit, our tiles will remain their original size, and Illustrator will shift them along, adding space in between the tiles to get that perfect fit.

- In the Approximate Path, our instruction to Illustrator is that when dealing with rectangular shapes, it cannot stretch our tiles, nor can it put space in between the tiles, but it can place the pattern slightly inside or outside the path if this will help it maintain the even tiling we require.

Finally, the tiles that dominate the left-hand side of the dialog box deserve a mention! As a pattern brush is essentially a series of tiles, stacked closely together to give the illusion of one continuous design, we need to have tiles for every type of kink our path is going to have – hence we have tiles for the beginning, the end and length of a path, and to provide for rectangular shapes and sharp corners in paths, we also have inside and outside corner tiles.

Creating Your Own Brushes

Although an in-depth explanation of how to create every type of brush is beyond the scope of this book, I think that if I show you how to make a simple brush, and you take that knowledge and couple it with what you have learned about modifying existing brushes, you'll be in a very strong position to come back and start creating your own personal brushes for use in your artwork. Let's look at how to make a basic brush, and then you'll have a chance to practice these skills by creating and then painting with your very own Palm brush on your brochure cover illustration.

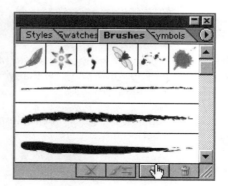

The first thing you'll need to do is create the shape that you wish to use for your art brush. I've just chosen a very simple triangular shape here, with a hybrid Corner Anchor points to give it a little bit of shape. Using this shape as a starting point might also give you a fair idea as to how I created the palm leaf shapes you'll meet. Note that the shapes you create for brushes cannot have gradient fills or gradient mesh fills.

With the shape selected, choose New Brush from the Brushes palette context menu, or click on the **New Brush** icon at the base of the Brushes palette.

After you have told Illustrator that you wish to make a new brush, another dialog box will appear, where you choose what type of brush it is that you wish to make.

As it is an **Art** brush that we wish to make, check the New Art Brush option and click OK or press ENTER/RETURN. The next dialog box you see will be very similar to the dialog box you saw when you were learning about modifying brushes. There are two differences however; you have an opportunity to name the brush here, and there is no preview box. This is because there is nothing on the Artboard for you to preview as you make changes. It is for this reason that I always suggest that you accept the defaults immediately. When you have done that, paint some examples of the brush onto your Artboard, with different directions and different lengths.

Once you have a few examples of your brush on the page, then it's time to modify it to suit your purpose. This you may recall is achieved by double-clicking on the brush in the Brushes palette to display the Art Brush Options dialog box. It does make sense to do it in this order, because with those examples on the page, you'll get real-time previews of how the changes in direction or size will affect your brushes. Alternatively if you alter the options as you first make the brush, you have little guidance as to how these changes will affect the brush.

Using Brushes and Brush Libraries

I mentioned earlier in this section that Illustrator ships with a large number of pre-built brush libraries that you can use, and I promised to show you how to get them into your files.

You may recall how we opened up another document as a **Symbol Library** in the section of the Symbol tools. It's exactly the same procedure. Select Window > Brush Libraries > Other Libraries and locate the **Illustrator Extras** folder on the Illustrator CD, inside that folder is where you will find all these goodies. The CD also ships with an Adobe Acrobat file with small thumbnails of all the brushes, so you can have a look at that before you randomly search through all the Libraries for a brush that might not be there.

Once you have opened the **Library** you want, drag the brushes you wish to use from the Library palette into your Brushes palette and there they are ready for use.

You may find that some of the brushes just don't fit your needs, but with a little editing they would be perfect. If this is the case, simply drag a copy of the brush from the Brushes palette onto the Artboard, ungroup it – they will always be automatically grouped – edit it and then drag it back into the Brushes palette.

Some of these brushes appeared deceptively simple as we placed them on the page, but they may actually be made up of hundreds of intricate items and blends, and spraying copious numbers across your artwork may result in a very large file and a printer's nightmare. Use them judiciously and speak to your printer about the file before you send it in. They may be able to give you some advice.

Case Study: Building the Brochure (III)

If you have closed your brochure cover file, open it again as we're just going to add some clouds and some birds to the sky to add a little bit of interest in that area.

1.   Ensure that the Clouds and Birds layers are unlocked, active, and visible.

2.   Select the **Paintbrush** tool (B) and check that you do not have a fill selected – remember it is the stroke that affects the color of brushstrokes if the **Colorization** methods are set to anything other than None.

3.   From the Brushes palette, select the Clouds scatter brush. If you are finding it difficult to see which is the Clouds scatter brush, display the Brushes palette context menu by clicking on the area at the top right hand corner of the palette.

4.   Choose List View from the options to display the names of the brushes as opposed to thumbnails of what they look like.

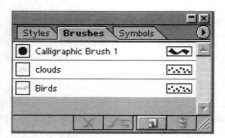

5.   Sweep across the sky with your **Paintbrush**. Do not worry about the placement of the clouds or their size initially. You know you can edit the shape of the path directly with the **Direct Selection** tool (A), and you can also change the attributes of this selected brush by choosing Options of Selected Object from the menu or from the bottom of the **Brushes** palette.

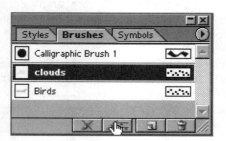

6. As we're only editing the selected objects, the options dialog box that appears is slightly different from the one you saw previously when we were modifying the scatter brushes. This is because only some of the options are available for what we are doing.

7. Manipulate your options, with the Preview button selected, until you are happy with the clouds. Remember it is a sunny, tropical sky advertising this wonderful holiday, so the clouds can neither be too big nor too abundant.

8. Repeat the above procedure, this time using the birds scatter brush that is in the Brushes palette and save the file.

Case Study: Making Palm Leaves for our Brochure Illustration

You had practice using Art brushes, but how about we take it to the next level and make our own Art brush that we can use it to paint some palm leaves onto our illustration as well.

1. Open the file called Palms.ai. You'll notice that I have already created the palm leaves for you, but if you look carefully you may also have an inkling of how I created those base shapes.

2. Before we create our own brush, we'll clean the Brushes palette of all those brushes we do not need first. Choose Select All Unused from the context menu on the Brushes palette, and when the brushes are highlighted bold, ALT/OPTION+click on the Trashcan at the bottom of the palette. This will remove them without supplying a warning dialog box.

3. Select one of the branches – each one is already a grouped object – so if you use the **Selection** tool (V), you will select all the components.

4. From the Brushes palette context menu, choose the first option, New Brush, and select Art brush in the dialog box that appears.

5. Once you have done this, the following dialog box will appear, but as I've suggested previously, do not worry about selecting options here until you have placed a sample brush on the page. Name the brush Palm Leaf 1, and set the Colorization Method to Tints and Shades. Remember Tints and Shades re-maps the brush stroke colors in tints and shades with black remaining black and everything between becoming a blend from black to white using the stroke color. Click OK, or press ENTER/RETURN.

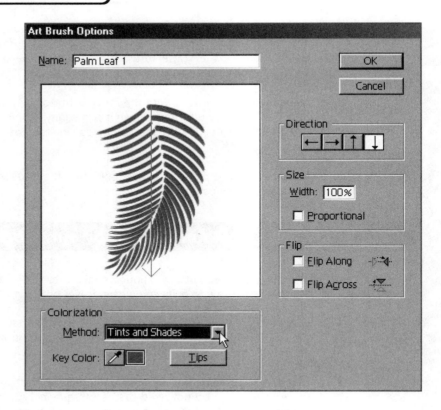

6. As we have chosen to use Tints and Shades as our Colorization method, choose a green for your stroke, and a fill of none. Select the Palm shape that you originally used to create the brush, and then select the **Paintbrush** (B) and the Palm leaf you have created in the Brushes palette. Paint a number of strokes on the Artboard to use as samples when you modify the brush. Double-click on the Palm brush in the Brushes palette to display the Art Brush options dialog box. Ensure that Preview is selected and make changes as you wish.

7. When you close the dialog box and the warning about changing the brush strokes appears, choose Apply to Strokes, and you have one palm leaf ready for use in your brochure cover illustration.

8. Create a second palm leaf Art brush, and close and save the file, noting carefully where you save it as we'll need to access its Brush library in a moment to use in our brochure illustration.

9. If your brochure cover illustration file is not open, open it now.

10. We need to access those brushes that you have created, and we'll do it in exactly the same way as earlier to access symbols from other files. From the Window menu choose Brush Libraries > Other, and then locate your palms file. A small palette with the palm art brushes in it will appear. Drag the two brushes into your Brushes palette and close the palms palette.

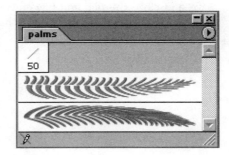

11. Now we'll start painting those palm leaves across the top of our illustration. Remember we have chosen Tints and Shades as the colorization method, so choose a bright green, for your stroke, from the Swatches palette, and a fill of None. On the Layers palette, make sure that you are working on the Palms layer; and that it is both unlocked and visible.

12. Choose a Palm brush from your Brushes palette, and paint a few palms at the top edge of the illustration. Switch brushes and stroke colors as you continue to place additional palm leaves. Remember if you want to make all the palm leaves from one brush a bit larger, double-click on the brush in the Brushes palette to display the Brush Options dialog box. However, if you only want to change the size of the selected brushes, choose the **Options of Selected Object** icon from the base of the Brushes palette.

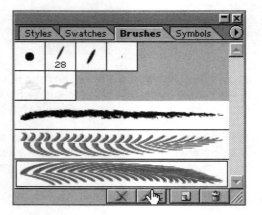

13. Continue painting with the brushes, changing stroke color until you have pretty much covered the top area and a little down the sides. You may wish to reposition your clouds and birds if they have got hidden behind the trees! Just make sure you're working on the correct layer!

14. Save and close the file, and have a break before you go on to the next section, or just sit back and admire that artwork!

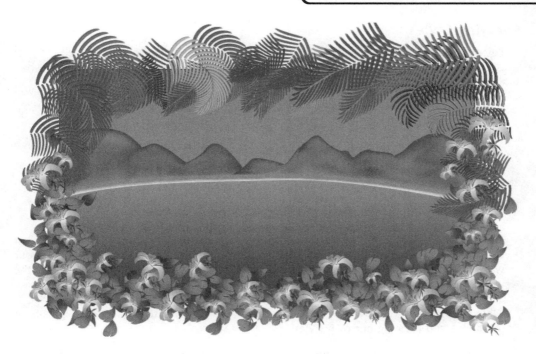

Introducing Styles

And so on to our last section of this chapter on creating your artwork efficiently. I'm sure you'll agree with me when I say that the preceding two tools have really shown you ways in which you can speed up production and get those clients off your back, while at the same time maintaining a sense of spontaneity and energy in your illustrations.

Let's have a look at **Styles** and then we'll wrap this chapter up. I mentioned **Styles** earlier when we discussed the **Symbol Styler**, and gave you an explanation, which may not have left you any clearer about what they are, so I'll try again here.

Essentially **Styles** are an effective way of storing presets for coloring up and styling your art quickly and consistently. Take for instance, your web design that you will be developing later. If you know that every button is going to have a gray fill with an orange 4-point border, the quickest way to develop all those buttons would be to create and save a style in the Styles palette and then apply that style to the buttons as you draw them. No need for fiddling and choosing fills and strokes each time you had to color a button.

Granted, you could use the **Eyedropper** and **Paintbucket** to copy objects' attributes and paint them onto other objects – in this hypothetical case, our buttons – but **Styles** are so much more powerful. They can contain any combination of color, fills, gradients, transformations, and strokes, but still to come in this book, they can also contain **Effects** – from the Effect menu, transparency settings, and even **Blend modes**.

Applying Styles

Let's have a look at that Styles palette, as I'm sure you're dying to see what all the fuss is about.

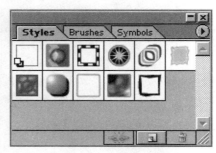

Adobe has kindly supplied us with some sample default styles, but once again, I'd not get too excited about them. In fact I'd even warn against using them unless you want your wonderful artwork to end up looking the same as millions of pieces of artwork around the world, but using them to understand how styles work is a good starting point.

What we'll do is create a little rectangle and apply a style to it, and then go about modifying and creating our own styles.

1. Create a new sample file, and with the **Rounded Rectangle** tool selected, click and drag on the page to create a shape that very roughly suggests the shape of a web button.

2. From the Styles palette, select the **Scribbly Fawn** option, which is the style in the top right-hand corner of the palette.

There you go, you've just applied a style – although admit it, if you used this as a design for a web button you might well be looking for a new job! The real interest in what we have done is in what is showing up on the Appearance palette, and in wondering what happened to that rounded rectangle! All will be revealed in due course, although if you're the inquisitive type, switch to **Outline** View (CTRL/CMD+Y) and have a look! Let's for the moment presume, that you like the color of the strokes and fill, but can live without the Roughen and Scribble & Tweak filter. Click on the Roughen detail in the Appearance palette and drag it into the **Trashcan** at the bottom of the Appearance palette. Do the same with the Scribble & Tweak, and we have the strokes and the fills and our rounded rectangle. You've just applied a style and then removed some of its characteristics.

Creating and Modifying Styles

Anxious to keep your job, you decide that you had better build your own style of web button and take it to the boss to impress him. So you plumb for the over-used, drop-shadow effect. You just know I'm trying to warn against over-zealous use of the drop-shadow, don't you?

1. Select your rounded rectangle with the **Selection** tool and then go to Effect > Stylize > Drop Shadow. Accept the default settings, and one button with a drop shadow.

2. Let's just imagine that the boss is thrilled with the button, and wants you to use it throughout the web site – all 3000 pages. You need to save this style. Although there are a number of different ways in which you can achieve this, possibly the simplest way is to just drag the object with the style applied to it into your Styles palette. Do that, and notice how it has been added to the end of the Styles, or if you placed it over existing styles, how it has neatly slotted itself in order.

If when you are dragging the style into the Styles palette, you wish to overwrite an existing style, hold down the ALT/OPTION key as you drop the object over the style that is no longer required. There is an added bonus here as if other objects had already been tagged with that style they would automatically have been updated with the new attributes.

Unlinking Styles

There may well come a time where you want replace a style so that it updates all but a few of the objects that are presently tagged with those style attributes. What you need to do is unlink the objects from the style, and that's as easily said as done – not often you hear that from a designer, is it?

Select the object you want to unlink from the style and depress the icon at the base of the Styles palette.

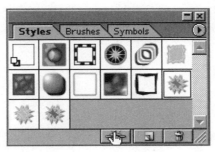

Alternatively, with the object selected, choose Break Link to Style from the Styles palette menu.

Using Style Libraries

You've seen it before when we discussed symbols in this chapter; and then I reminded you when we looked at **Artistic** brushes, but just in case you hadn't noticed, there at the base of the Window menu is an option which will allow you to open the Styles palettes from other files and use them in this file. It's exactly the same procedure as before. Select Window > Style Libraries > Other Libraries and locate the file with the styles that you want.

Once you have opened the Library you want, drag the styles you wish to use from the Library palette into your Styles palette and there they are ready for use again.

You should start developing these libraries – **Symbol**, **Brushes**, **Styles**, and even **Color** libraries, containing assets that you will require often. It's just like building a portfolio of your work, but these little libraries can prove even more useful!

Summary

At the beginning of this chapter I mentioned a hypothetical nightmare – a client changes a job at a ground breaking level. Not so hypothetical really, it happens all the time! Now that we've shown you how to use the **Symbolism** tools, the **Artistic** brushes, and the **Styles**, you should be in a position to not only plan your work a little more effectively, but to take advantage of the functionality that these tools will give you in producing that artwork and staying ahead of those deadlines! That hypothetical nightmare, when it does happen to you, will not be too much of a nightmare after all.

In the next chapter, we'll back off a little and let you have some fun with the **Filters** and **Effects**. But remember filters are often over-used in artwork, and the secret of good use of a filter, is making everyone wonder how you achieved what you did, not their guessing immediately which filter it was that you used.

10 Filters and Effects

What We'll Cover in this Chapter:

- *The concept of Filters and Effects*

- *Saturating, Desaturating, Adjusting, Converting, and Inverting Colors*

- *Converting Objects to create the Marine Quest catering image*

- *Mastering Destructive Filters and Effects including Pucker and Bloat, Scribble and Tweak, Twisting, Roughening, and Rounding Corners*

- *Using the Appearance Palette in Conjunction with Effects*

- *Creating Soft Edge Effects including Drop Shadows, Inner Glows, Outer Glows, and Feathered Edges*

Filters

To understand what a filter is, think of one of the spotlights at a theatre pointing down at the stage. The spotlight projects white light but the director wants to create an atmospheric midnight scene. The lighting operator places a sheet of blue transparent film over the light, which allows light to pass through, but now projects a blue wash over the stage, creating midnight. The original object is still visible, in this case the light, but the filter has added its own unique quality and changed the final visible result.

What I have just described is a very simple filter. Illustrator is capable of this effect through its own filters, but also so much more. Objects you create can be distorted so dramatically and completely that you no longer recognize the original. Often the complexity of the final image disguises the simplicity of using the filter. Over the years, this has become one of the problems in using filters. The relative ease with which a filter can be applied has led to a saturation of filter effects in books, magazines, and on the Internet. The ubiquitous "drop shadow", once a subtle way of emphasizing text, has been overused to the extent where today it's use is often questionable unless graphically justified.

The real question self-respecting designers should ask themselves is "when do I use filters and when do I avoid them?" Broadly speaking, if the finished result has "this is a filter" stamped all over it, perhaps alternative ideas should be sought. With the exception of the obvious filters such as the drop shadow mentioned earlier, the secret in using filters well is to aim to disguise the fact that you have used a filter in the first place. Artwork in print or on the Web is no different than in the movies. The audience is disappointed and laughs mockingly when they see the hero leap from a helicopter, knowing he has been superimposed over a false background. This kind of telltale sign is visible in many of the more popular computer application filters and results in an amateurish, false image.

Combining multiple filters unveils their true strength. By carefully and thoughtfully applying one filter over another, the fact that you have used filters can be completely disguised, resulting in a piece of artwork that allows the viewer to judge the work on its own merits rather than being distracted by the identifying features of any given filter or effect.

In the exercises within this chapter we are going to be investigating some of the filters and effects available with Illustrator 10 and using many of the results in a real world situation to create artwork for Marine Quest's publicity. The filters will be used in a way that optimizes your time and takes the drudgery out of laborious tasks to achieve a given desired effect. Hopefully, by the end of the chapter you will have joined the school of thought that uses filters because they benefit the current project as opposed to using filters "because you can".

Before we get started, a few ground rules.

The Filter Menu

Open the file called `Adjust_colors.ai` from the download folder.

1. Select the orange sail of the yacht.

2. Go to Filter, which expands the Filter menu. The menu is divided up to three sections:

- The top section allows you to reapply and adjust the settings of the last filter you applied.

- The middle section lists all the filters that can be applied to vector artwork with the exception of Pen and Ink>Photo Crosshatch. As you drag the cursor over these headings a further sub menu appears offering further selections.

- The bottom section can only be applied to bitmap images and we will be looking at these in Chapter 14.

We will be concentrating on the middle section of the menu for the present. So, let's begin by looking at some of the control you have in changing colors through the filters.

Saturate

The artwork of the yacht at the top of the page has been created with a range of fairly muted colors. If you decide after completing your work that you would like the color to have more impact, one quick and easy option is to saturate the color. Let's give this a try.

1. Select all the artwork that makes up the yacht image including the sea, sky, and sun.

2. Go to Filter>Colors>Saturate to open the Saturate dialog box, which has a percentage box and a slider to adjust the Intensity.

The Saturate filter darkens or lightens the colors by increasing or decreasing the percentage of color in the object. This filter will also work with spot colors by changing the tint percentage. In this instance we are going to darken the colors by saturating them.

3. Drag the slider to the right. Check the preview box to see the effect on screen. If you want to lighten or desaturate the colors, drag the slider to the left to see the result. When you have seen the various effects, drag the slider to 80, or you can type 80 in the number box, then click OK.

In this exercise, you saturated or desaturated all the colors at once. If you only want to change the color of one object, just select that object. This filter is quite simplistic in that it only allows you to lighten or darken. It doesn't help if you want to change the hue though. For that we need to use the more flexible Adjust Colors Filter.

Adjust Colors

To demonstrate this we are first going to change the hue of the sky from its current sky blue color to a deeper, purer blue. This document has been set up in RGB mode. The sky blue appears that color because it has a large proportion of green in it, making it less than a pure blue. To remedy this we will subtract some of the green from the object.

1. Select the blue sky rectangle.

2. Go to Filter>Colors>Adjust Colors. This opens the Adjust Colors dialog box. Check the Preview and Convert check boxes to enable them.

As you might expect, the dialog box gives you the option of adjusting the colors. In this case as the image is in RGB mode, there are sliders and percentage fields for Red, Green and Blue.

3. Drag the Green slider to the left to read −24. This has reduced the amount of green in the object, resulting in a purer blue color. It has also made the sky very similar in color to the hull of the yacht. So let's change the color of the hull. Click OK to confirm the sky color change.

4. Select the hull of the yacht. Go to Filter>Colors>Adjust Colors.

5. Make sure the **Preview** and **Convert** check boxes are checked. Drag the green slider to the right to read 40. This adds green. Drag the blue slider to the left to read −46. This subtracts some blue and results in a fairly bright green color.

Finally, we will make the sea a more inviting tropical aqua color.

6. Select the sea. Go to Filter>Colors>Adjust Colors. Drag the green slider to 29 and the blue slider to 31. This increases the amount of both colors taking us closer towards pure cyan resulting in a very vibrant aqua color.

Convert to Grayscale

Many publications are printed in grayscale rather than color for a number of reasons. Cost is one, and artistic considerations could be another – with this book of course it's artistic considerations. If you have existing color artwork that is going to be printed in a grayscale publication, this filter will carry out the process quickly for you.

1. Select the red to yellow concentric circles in the bottom half of the page. This is what we are going to convert to grayscale. Go to Filter>Colors>Convert to Grayscale. The intensity of each color is converted to a shade of gray of the same intensity, so the original effect is unchanged, and only the color is removed.

This filter converts CMYK files to Grayscale or Grayscale to CMYK. It also converts RGB files to Grayscale or Grayscale to RGB.

Inverting Colors

The Invert Colors filter produces a negative version of the selected artwork by inverting the color values. For instance pure black is converted to pure white. Pure blue is converted to pure yellow, pure red to pure cyan, etc. We are going to try this filter out on the yacht artwork, which has a variety of color values.

1. Select all the artwork that makes up the yacht scene.

2. Go to Filter>Colors>Invert Colors. There is no dialog box associated with this filter to apply settings. The original color values are automatically inverted.

Filters are not just about color changes though. A filter can just as easily be applied to an object to manipulate its shape in some way. You should recognize some of the filters we are about to look at from earlier exercises. These filters also have a counterpart in the toolbox that offers an additional way of applying the effect.

Free Distort Filter

When you were applying perspective effects to objects in Chapter 6, you used a tool called Free Transform in combination with some keystrokes. This filter gives you the same result, but allows you to preview an outline of the envelope before confirming the effect.

Open the file called Free_distort.ai from the download folder. We are going to distort this shape to create the illusion of looking at it as if it was receding into the distance.

1. Select the striped object.

2. Go to Filter>Distort>Free Distort to open the dialog box showing an outline preview of the shape. The handles in each corner are draggable and will be used to create the shape of the perspective you want to achieve.

3. Drag the top right handle down and the bottom right handle up to create a shape that tapers towards the right hand side of the page, and then click OK.

Once you have distorted a shape, you can distort it again and the new distortion will be based on the current shape. We'll do that now to see how it works.

4.   Select the object again and go to Filter>Distort>Free Distort. This time drag the top left handle up and the bottom left handle down to accentuate that taper even further. Click OK.

Clicking the Reset button in the dialog returns the draggable handles to their default position allowing you to edit the shape again with greater distortions.

The picture below is my finished shape. Yours may look a little different depending on how much you dragged each handle.

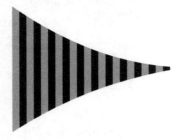

Round Corners Filter

When you were discovering the basic shape tools such as the ellipse, polygon, and rectangle, you were also introduced to the highly useful rounded corner rectangle tool. Had you created a whole heap of standard rectangles and then realized you should have been creating rectangles with rounded corners, the rounded corner rectangle tool would have been little use to you. It can't convert existing rectangles, so that's where the round corners rectangle comes in.

Open the file called `Round_corners_filter.ai` from the download folder.

Let's see how this works using the blue rectangle as an example.

1.   Select the blue rectangle.

2.   Go to Filter>Stylize>Round Corners. This opens the dialog box. The Radius refers to how rounded the corners will become. The higher the value, the more rounded the corners will be. This document is in inches, so the values you type in this box will also be in inches. Type 0.35 in the Radius box and click OK.

You probably guessed what you were going to see but don't think of this filter as purely a method of rounding corners on rectangles when you forgot to round them in the first place. The other shapes I have created in this file all have sharp corner points. They can all be changed to varying degrees resulting in very different objects depending upon the value you apply to the radius.

> **3.** Select each object on the page in turn and apply the Round Corners filter, but try different values. 1 and 1.5 will give you a more pronounced effect.

OK, you've had a little practice with some of the filters and are starting to see the kind of things they do. We haven't used them in anger yet and that's what we are going to do now with a real project. As well as producing some actual artwork for Marine Quest, the next exercises are going to have you following the path and thought processes I outlined at the beginning of the chapter. Namely, using filters in combination, thereby disguising the individual filters and producing an original piece of unique artwork.

It goes without saying, but I'll say it anyway – the more you know about how a filter acts, the more opportunities you will find to use it in a meaningful way and as a time and work saving device. The brief I am about to pass on to you will demonstrate what I mean.

Marine Quest Design Brief

The company wants to use an image that will be associated with all the catering aspects of the business. This includes such things as the cocktail bar and beach bar, the restaurant and dining onboard the yacht, and live-aboard dive vessel. After looking at a number of possibilities, the image that was decided upon was a Strelizia Reginae flower, commonly known as a Bird of Paradise flower. The flower has strong associations with the Caribbean and its bright colors and distinctive shape will create a powerful and lasting image. Because the image is going to be used as a kind of signature, it was decided that the final image should definitely not be photographic, but be stylized almost as an icon of strong distinctive shapes, but still being recognizable as the Bird of Paradise flower. There should also be just the suggestion of hand drawn lines, avoiding anything too obviously hand drawn and anything too obviously computer generated. And just to top it all, it needs to be ready to go to print within the hour.

So what are the options? We could get busy with the pen tool producing the outline of the flower and working it up from there. But we are going to take a different approach, one that will render the finished art and can be timed in terms of minutes rather than hours.

The knowledge of what shapes to start with and the thought processes in linking filters with those shapes will come with experience. There is also a fair degree of experimentation, but as you practice more you will find you need to experiment less.

We are about to cover a range of different filters and revisit some of the tricks you have learned already.

Case Study: Creating the Strelizia Flower

Open the file called `Strelizia.ai` from the download folder. At the bottom of the page is the completed flower that you will be creating.

1. Select the larger of the two crescent shapes. The smaller one will be used later.

2. Go to Filter>Distort>Pucker & Bloat. Where have you heard those words before? Yes, you have used these options, but in a different way. These tools are also in the toolbox under the liquefy group. You used them to create a different kind of flower in Chapter 6, but the results, while having a degree of controllability, were quite irregular and invited far more experimentation. Under the filter category, Pucker and Bloat share one filter heading. Both options are encompassed within this one filter and the results are far more uniform and possess a greater element of predictability.

The Pucker & Bloat dialog box opens. Dragging the slider to the right invokes the Bloat side of the filter. Make sure the Preview box is checked. As you drag further to the right slowly you will see the crescent changing. The concept of "inflating" the shape is still obvious, as it is with the Bloat tool in the toolbox, however the uniformity and symmetry of the changing shape are the dominant features this time.

Drag the slider to the left and we invoke the Pucker element of the filter. Now we see the "deflate" or concave concept working. Once again, the fundamental principle of this filter is no different to its toolbox namesake, but the uniformity and symmetry offer a very different result. Now you know what the filter does, let's apply a setting that will take us closer to our goal in creating the Strelizia.

3. Drag the slider or type −169 in the percentage field. Click OK to close the dialog box and apply the filter. Your object should now look like the image below.

If you are in an imaginative mood at present, you may see a glimmer of how this is going to end up looking like a Strelizia already.

Although you can see a number of different shapes that have been created from the crescent, we still have only one object. We need to manipulate the shapes independently, which means we need to break the object up into its component parts in some way. Sounds like a perfect task for the Pathfinder Palette that you have been using. If the Pathfinder Palette is not open, open it now from the Window menu.

4. Make sure the object is still selected. From the Pathfinder Palette, click the Divide button. Although the shape looks no different, you will see some extra anchor points appear around the object. Each shape that makes up the main object has been separated into its own independent object. All the objects are grouped though, so next we need to ungroup them.

5. Make sure the objects are selected and then ungroup them using the Object>Ungroup command. Deselect the objects by clicking on a blank part of the screen with the Selection tool and then you will be able to click on each individual shape independently.

The downward pointing object needs to be rotated almost 180 degrees, so it is pointing upwards. This will be one of the main flower heads. As we have done so many times already, we are going to change the point of origin of this object before we rotate it. Zooming in a little closer, about 400%, will show you an image similar to below. The new required point of origin has been marked on this image by the end of the gray arrow.

6. Select the **Rotate** tool, and then with the ALT key pressed, click the point as marked on the picture in above. This opens the Rotate dialog box. Type 190 in the Angle box and click OK. Your artwork should now be looking like the picture below. Zoom out so you can see all the artwork.

We are going to rotate this object again so we have two flower heads.

7. With the object still selected, reset the point of origin to the same place as last time, remembering to press the ALT key when you click. In the Rotate dialog box type 32 in the Angle box. Click the Copy button to create the duplicate. This is what you should now be looking at now.

Thinking back to the original brief, it was requested that the flower should be neither too hand drawn nor too computer generated in its style. At present it's leaning to towards perfect computer generated art, so we need to roughen it up just a little. No better time to take a look at the Roughen filter.

Roughen Filter

This filter works by adding anchor points and shifting them by different degrees, so your perfect artwork starts to look less than perfect. How rough is entirely up to you. Let's try it out.

1. Select the object you just rotated. Go to Filter>Distort>Roughen. The Roughen dialog box opens. Here's what the different settings in the dialog box are going to do.

- Size – unsurprisingly affects the amount of distortion to the object. Higher values result in greater distortion.

- Relative – applies a distortion of an amount based on a percentage of the size of the object.

- Absolute – applies a distortion by a fixed specific amount.

- Detail – defines how many details per inch. Greater values result in greater distortion.

- Points-Corner – select this option for a more jagged effect.

- Points-Smooth – select this option for a smoother, more rounded effect.

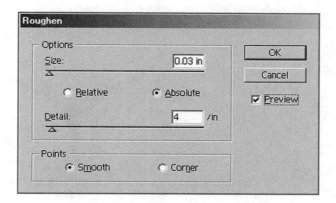

2. Set Size to 0.03in, choose the Absolute option, set Detail to 4, and choose Smooth Points. Click OK.

We'll also apply the filter to the object on the lower left.

3. Select the object on the left and apply the roughen filter using the same settings as last time, except set Size to 1 and Detail to 4.

Here's where we are up to so far. You should have something similar to the picture below.

This would be a good time to color the individual objects. All the fill colors to be used are already in the swatches palette. Use the completed flower example as a guide for applying fill colors to what you have completed so far.

Pucker & Bloat Filter with Different Settings

The central flower head of the Strelizia is a complex and delicate shape. We are going to use the smaller of the two crescent shapes and transform it, resulting in a startling likeness to the actual flower head centerpiece.

1. Select the crescent.

2. Apply the Pucker & Bloat filter with a value of −75. This is the shape you will be left with.

3. Color this shape blue using the blue in the swatches palette and then position on top of the flower using the finished example as a guide.

4. Zoom in to the bottom central portion of the flower, about 1000%, so you can see the elements as in the following picture. The small objects highlighted in gray in this picture are not required as part of the artwork, so delete them all.

We now need to place the stem of the plant in position. I have already created this by using the pen tool to draw a simple shape. This is ground you have already covered, but if you would like to try creating the stem yourself you can use mine as a guide.

5. Position the stem in place, using the completed example as a guide.

And there you have it. Although in real life you would have to tidy up the file a little before sending it off to the printers, the purpose of completing this project has been to demonstrate that filters can be used to create real objects and even quite standard real world shapes that might be difficult or time consuming to create using manual tools and techniques. They certainly should not be thought of solely of as a way of adding special effects and abstract images.

Looking at the finished work, it would difficult for anyone to view the picture and categorically state it has been produced using filter A or B and that is the whole idea that is so often missed. In your early stages of learning, you will find it beneficial to experiment. The more shapes and combinations of shapes you can use, the more ideas you will get. Note keeping is paramount. I have dozens of fabulous images that I would like to reproduce and share with the world, but I can't because I didn't keep notes of the steps I took and trying to backtrack is unproductive and futile at the best of times.

Let's continue this theme of what we could unofficially call 'Filters by stealth'. However, we are now going to look at another category known as Effects.

Effects

What you did in order to create the Strelizia flower with filters, you could just as easily have done using effects. So what's the difference between filters and effects? Once you apply a filter, you have changed the object for good. (We know that's not true because you can undo what you just did, but for the sake of understanding the difference, let's assume undoing a step isn't an option.) When you apply an effect to an object, the effect is recorded as a step in the Appearance Palette. If you decide you do not wish to keep an effect, you simply delete it from the Appearance palette. It doesn't matter in which order you applied the effect, even if it was several steps ago, you can still remove it without affecting anything else in the object.

An effect does not change the underlying artwork, only its appearance. For instance a square will still be a square no matter how many effects you apply to it. It won't look like a square, because the effects you apply will alter the appearance. At the root, the original square is still there and for that reason it is possible to remove some or all of the effects and see your square just as you created it in the first place. Applying a filter by contrast will change the underlying artwork. In the example of the square, any filters applied will destroy the square leaving only the new distorted artwork.

We are now going to work with both the effects and Appearance palette in combination, but we are going to use them to create actual artwork required by Marine Quest. Once again we will aim to use the effects with the same considerations we paid to filters, that is, ensuring they do not obviously look like pre-set effects, but rather create a unique, attractive piece of work that also saves us time and manual labor. Here's the assignment.

Marine Quest Design Brief 2

Each month, Marine Quest will send personal invitations out to their regular clients to join specific charters, events, or special dinners and dances. The invitations need to have a strong degree of personalization, almost achieving the tone of a hand-written note to a friend. Images and color play a strong role on all the companies literature and the invite is no exception. Because of the personalization needed, it is important that the graphics should look as if each one was painted or drawn by hand. There must be no computerization visible within the image. Each event will require different graphics each month, so a realistic and efficient, from a time point of view, formula needs to be found.

Case Study: Creating a Banana Plant

The first "hand drawn" style graphic required is a banana plant. So, with no time to waste, let's get started.

Open the file called Banana_palm.ai from the download folder

Banana plant leaves have a characteristic ragged, weather beaten look to them. This is what we need to put across, as well as creating the feel of a hand-drawn piece of work. The example at the bottom of the artboard is the finished result you will achieve. The green ellipse is the shape that you will be using to create the finished work. Before beginning, let's analyze the Appearance palette that I mentioned a moment ago.

The Appearance Palette

The Appearance palette is indispensable when working with the Effects menu, as doing so can often be an experimental endeavor, so it allows you to try out ideas without committing to them.

The Appearance palette will be on the top right of your screen by default. If it is not open, you can display it by going to Window>Appearance. Select the green ellipse shape, and then look at the Appearance palette.

The palette gives you certain information about the selected object. It tells you the object has no stroke and also that the fill is green. At present that's all it tells you because you haven't applied any effects yet.

We will be checking the Appearance palette throughout this project and learning what else it does as our artwork develops.

Modifying Basic Shapes with the Convert Point Tool

The ellipse has rounded edges at the left and right. To create a more realistic pointed edge to the leaf we are going to convert the anchor points at the right and left to corner points. This is a process you have carried out before, so try it yourself, or if you would like some guidance, follow the next step.

1. Deselect the green ellipse if it is selected. Now select it with the **Direct Selection** tool, making sure to click on the edge of the ellipse so all the anchor points appear white.

2. Select the **Convert Point** tool from the toolbox (in the same location as the Pen tool). Click the anchor points on the left and right as in the picture below.

This new shape gives us a better starting point from which to build the leaf shape. Now we are going to apply an effect for the first time.

The Twist Effect

1. Select the ellipse and then go to Effect>Distort & Transform>Twist. As you have the menu expanded have a look at the various options. You will recognize many from the filter menu. These are exactly the same as their filter namesakes, the difference being, as explained earlier is that you can remove the effect without harming the artwork.

2. In the Twist dialog box that appears, type 35 in the Angle field, this is 35 degrees. Click OK.

Now that you have applied an effect, let's go back to the Appearance palette. The palette has a new section added to it called Twist. This refers to the effect you just applied to the objects.

The next step has nothing to do with the project, but is to illustrate what happens when an effect has been applied to an object.

3. Create a square on the page, any size. Notice something unusual? Your square also has a twist applied to it, as would a rectangle, a star, or any other shape where a 35-degree twist would be noticeable.

By default, the attribute you applied to the original ellipse is maintained when new shapes are drawn. So, if you don't want every shape you draw to have the same effect as the one you just applied, we need to disable this function.

4. Click the **New Art Maintains Appearance** icon at the bottom left of the Appearance palette. This now allows you to draw new shapes in their standard format. Try it out. Draw another square and that is precisely what will be created, a normal square. Now that you know how to override this function, you can delete the square that you created for testing and we'll get back to our project.

We're going to perform an old trick now. Rotating a duplicate around a new point of origin. This will give us the circle of leaves.

5. Select the green ellipse. Select the **Rotate** tool and with the ALT key pressed click the left anchor point of the ellipse.

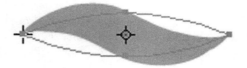

6. Type –45 in the Angle box and click the Copy button. You now have a duplicate of the original object at an angle of –45 degrees.

7. Press CTRL/CMD + D six times to complete the shape as in the figure below.

Time to try another effect. This effect will aim to achieve the ragged look found on banana leaves.

Scribble and Tweak Effect

I know it doesn't sound like a serious effect, but I promise it is. As with the Pucker and Bloat filter, there are two elements to this effect. Scribbling randomly distorts objects by moving anchor points away from the object. Tweaking randomly distorts objects by moving anchor points on the object by a specific amount. You define this amount yourself.

1. Select all the leaves then go to Effect>Distort and Transform>Scribble and Tweak.

There are similarities between this effect and the Pucker and Bloat filter you used previously in terms of the dialog box settings.

- Horizontal Amount – defines the distance to move points on the horizontal axis.

- Vertical Amount – defines the distance to move points on the vertical axis.

- Relative Option – applies a distortion of an amount based on a percentage of the size of the object.

- Absolute Option – applies a distortion by a fixed specific amount.

- Modify Anchor points – when this option is checked, the original anchor points move as part of the effect. Deselecting this option keeps anchor points in their original position and the filter is applied to the rest of the object.

- Modify "In" Control points – when this box is checked, this option moves control points that lead into anchor points on the path.

- Modify "Out" Control points – when this box is checked, this option moves control points that lead out of anchor points on the path.

2. Ensure the Preview box is checked to see what you are doing. You will notice as you change the horizontal and vertical settings, the image changes radically. As with other Filters and Effects, higher settings result in greater distortions. By unchecking the Modify Anchor points check box, the original anchor points are held in place, which attempts to maintain the basic structure, at least as far as the anchor points are concerned. When you have practiced with the settings and get a feel for what they are doing, set the Horizontal amount to 0.14in, the Vertical amount to 0.11in, select the Absolute option, and check all of the boxes in the lower half of the dialog box.

It is important to note once again that there is a random function going on here, so your artwork probably won't look exactly the same as mine, but the basic principle is the same. The word "tweaking" in this filter is aptly named, as a fair degree of tweaking may well be necessary in order to get the effect you are looking for.

Let's take a look at the Appearance palette again now that you have applied another effect. You will see another addition to the palette. The Scribble & Tweak effect now appears. The advantage of using this palette with the effects may become apparent at this stage. The Appearance palette is also acting as a notebook of what you have done to an object. If we returned to this file months later and forgot how the effect was achieved, just by selecting the object and looking in the Appearance palette you would have all the effects listed.

We can also use this same palette to edit effects. Let's assume you want to change the degree of twist from 35 degrees to 38 degrees.

1. Select all of the banana leaves. In the Appearance palette, double-click the panel that is labeled Twist. This opens the Twist dialog box with the value you entered previously. Type 38 in the box and click OK. The effect is now updated.

For the purpose of seeing how easy it is to remove an effect if you decide you no longer want one, we will apply an effect and then delete it from the object.

2. Select the banana leaves. Go to Effect>Distort & Transform>Roughen. This is one we used when creating the Strelizia, but at that time we applied it as a Filter, not an effect. Apply any settings. In fact, really destroy it with a high setting, and then click OK.

Take a look in the Appearance palette and you will see the addition of the Roughen effect. Your banana leaves are probably looking a little hurricane damaged also, so let's remove the effect. Keep the objects selected.

3. From the Appearance palette, there are two ways to remove an effect. Do either of the following.

    -   Select the effect labeled Twist. Click the black arrow button in the top right of the palette to reveal a pop-up menu. From this menu select Remove Item.

    -   Drag the effect labeled Twist to the bin in the bottom right corner of the palette.

Any of the effects can be removed in the same way irrespective of the order in which they were applied.

We are almost done – just one more touch to apply to the leaves to give then a hand-drawn look. We are going to draw upon some of the experience you have already gained in your work with the paintbrush. Some black rough lines as an irregular outline would complete the feel, so the paintbrush is the ideal tool. There is no drawing involved as the artwork has already been created. We can just apply the brush as a stroke.

Open the Brushes palette if it is not visible. You will find it under the Window menu if it has been closed down. You will see two brushes in the Brushes palette. We are going to use the thicker of the two.

1. Select all the artwork that makes up the banana leaves, then click on the brush from within the Brushes palette.

The brush is applied as a black outline. How it appears will depend on the actual shapes of your leaves. If it is too thick in any one area or doesn't appear in others, you could try applying the thinner brush from the swatch palette.

Finally, to help lift it off the page we are going to use a drop shadow effect.

2. With the leaves selected go to Effect>Stylize>Drop Shadow. Leave all the default settings in the dialog box as they are and click OK.

The bunch of bananas in the example was created using the same techniques. Have a go at producing this yourself. It starts with a single crescent shape. I then used the roughen effect to get the hand-drawn effect. Then duplicate the banana and apply the brush.

Your artwork should be similar, though not an exact copy, of the example in the file. It is important to remember that the Scribble & Tweak effect is a random filter, so if you don't have the look you were after it's a case of truly "tweaking" the Scribble and Tweak.

What is really important is understanding the relationship between the Appearance palette and the effects and how they differ from the filters. This project has been designed to give you that experience and help you make important decisions before starting any work.

One unfortunate consequence of applying many of the filters and effects is the eventual size of the file, in particular with the Drop Shadow. Producing a number of duplicates in varying shades creates this effect. Each duplicate will add to the total file size. In fact any filter or effect that produces a large number of anchor points will have a detrimental effect on the size of the file. This can be problematic for print, but can also be a problem for artwork for the Web, not due to the number of anchor points, but the number of colors and arrangement of shapes, as you will see when we cover this subject in Chapter 16. Regardless of your intended method of output, it is wise to be aware of the potential problems that can arise from an over use of filters and effects. It takes us back to the opening paragraphs of this chapter when the reasons for using filters and effects were discussed.

As long as the use is justified and contributes to the artwork without attaching a disproportionate overhead in terms of file size or file complexity, then the benefits outweigh the disadvantages.

Convert to Shape Effect

Many of the filters and effects we have used have what is known as a destructive effect. We can't take that description too literally as we have used destructive effects such as Pucker and Bloat and Scribble and Tweak to actually create real objects from nature as opposed to destroy. But in its most basic context, the filters are destroying what was a perfectly good square, ellipse, crescent, or some other geometric shape. The effect we are about to look at now has the opposite effect. It takes any shape and converts it into a rectangle, a rounded corner rectangle, or an ellipse.

Open the file called Convert_shape.ai from the download folder.

We will convert all three shapes on the page to one of the available options within this effect.

1. Select the star. Go to Effect>Convert to Shape>Ellipse.

Although you selected Ellipse as the original option, it is not too late to change your mind and choose another option. The drop-down box at the top of the dialog box offers all the choices again, Ellipse, Rounded Corner Rectangle, and Rectangle.

The options for Absolute and Relative have exactly the same meaning as with the other filters and effects covered earlier. Absolute allows you to define a new fixed size irrespective of the size of the object at present while Relative creates the new shape relative to the current size of the object. The shape can also be made smaller by applying a negative number.

2. Choose Ellipse from the Shape drop-down menu, choose the Absolute option, and enter 1.5 in the width and height fields. Click OK.

As with all applied effects, the underlying shape has not been changed, as explained earlier. The appearance has changed, but the original outline of the star is still visible when the object is selected. Take a look at the Appearance palette and you will see this effect has been added and can just as easily be removed in the same way as you removed effects earlier, leaving the original star shape unchanged.

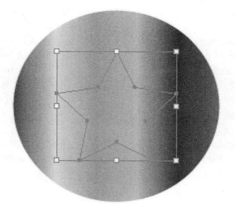

3. Select the blue ellipse on the page. Convert this to a rounded rectangle. From the dialogue box choose the Relative option, and enter 0.25 in the Extra Width and Extra Height fields. The only addition to the dialog box with this option is the Corner Radius setting. It works in the same way as when you create rectangles with the round corner rectangle tool. The higher the number, the more rounded the corners will be. Set this to 0.50in.

4. Select the purple shape, and convert it to a rectangle. Leave the default settings. You will notice the Corner Radius box is disabled when converting to rectangles.

Soft Edged Effects

We have seen repeatedly that vector artwork lends itself well to crisp edges and flat areas of color, with the exception of blends and gradient mesh objects. So soft edged effects would seem to be out of place within a vector environment. As with blends and gradient mesh objects, what the viewer sees is an illusion. The impression of a blurry, soft edge is produced by an additional bitmap image, either as a transparent bitmap or a bitmap inside a mask, as you created in Chapter 7. You have already seen one example of a soft edged effect when you applied a drop shadow to the banana plant. There are three other effects that fall under the same category – **Inner Glows**, **Outer Glows**, and **Feathered Edges**. We are going to take a look at all of these now, but a word of warning again with regard to file size. As with the drop shadow, the addition of a bitmap image means an unavoidable consequence is a larger file size. For that reason, all the considerations stated earlier should be taken into account.

Drop Shadow

You have already applied this effect but we are going to look a little closer at the options you have in controlling the result.

Open the file called Drop_shadow.ai from the download folder.

Drop Shadow overkill is not as prevalent as it was in the mid 90s, but it still exits, both on the Web and in print. But the reason for looking at this file is not simply to demonstrate why you shouldn't use too many shadows, it is also to illustrate a fundamental and more natural point. The question any designer should ask is "where is the light source coming from?" On the page, the light is apparently coming from everywhere. So let's look at how to control the appearance of shadows.

We are going to apply a drop shadow to the fly graphic at the foot of page. The picture below shows the fly before the shadow has been applied.

1.   Select the fly graphic. Go to Effect>Stylize>Drop Shadow.

Let's analyze the options in the Drop Shadow dialog box. Check the Preview box so you can see the settings taking place.

- Mode – Anyone familiar with Adobe PhotoShop will recognize this as blending modes. The concept in Illustrator is the same. Blending modes let you vary the ways that the colors of objects blend with the colors of underlying objects. In this case, the object is the fly and the underlying object is the shadow. We will stick with Multiply in the Mode drop-down box, as it has the effect of multiplying the color of the shadow, which is black by the color of the fly. Multiplying any color with black produces black. Think of this effect in the real world as painting one watercolor brushstroke over another, each time to multiply the amount of paint so the color becomes darker.

- Opacity – The higher the setting, the darker the shadow. 0% is completely invisible.

- X and Y Offset – These settings change the apparent distance of the selected object above the page as well as the location of the light source. Increasing the X Offset value moves the shadow to the right. Decreasing the X Offset value moves the shadow to the left.

Increasing the Y Offset value moves the shadow to the top of the page. Decreasing the Y Offset value moves the shadow to the bottom of the page.

- Blur – This softens the shadow, creating the difference between a hard cast shadow and a subtle, vague blur. Higher settings create softer shadows but if you go too high, the shadow will completely disappear. A zero setting produces a shadow with no blur at all.

- Color and Darkness – Darkness is the default option. This applies percentages of black as the shadow color, with higher percentages resulting in a deeper shadow. Select Color if you want to define the color of the shadow. This can often result in greater realism as few shadows are pure black and often contain an element of the complimentary color to the color of the object that is casting the shadow.

2. Click OK to accept the default settings. The picture below is the fly after applying the Drop Shadow.

If you wish to change the shadow, because you applied it as an effect, all you have to do is double-click the Drop Shadow label in the Appearance palette and the dialog box opens with the current settings.

Drop shadows can be very subtle and sophisticated if the right combination is found. As with all effects experimentation is called for. Before we move on, try changing the color of the text in the page to white and then adjust the shadow so the offset is very small. The idea of white text on a white page doesn't seem to make much sense on the face of it, but the subtlety of the shadow changes the effect completely.

Outer Glow

An outer glow would describe the effect you see as a halo around the moon or an eclipse of the sun. You created a similar effect when you applied a glow around a star in the Blends section of Chapter 8. Let's do the same thing now using the Outer Glow effect.

Open the file called Outer_glow.ai from the download folder.

1. Select the yellow crescent moon. Go to Effect>Stylize>Outer Glow to open the Outer Glow dialog box. There are far fewer options here than in the drop shadow dialog, but there are similarities.

The Mode option works in exactly the same way. Screen is the default option for this effect. Once again the mode is a combination of the color of the top object, in this case, the moon, and the color of the underlying object, which is the glow. The glow color has been set to a pale cream color. The square box next to the Mode drop-down displays this color. The Screen mode always results in a lighter color, which translates as a glow.

Opacity defines how visible the glow is, with higher values creating a stronger effect.

Blur creates a softer edge and appears to spread the glow out over a greater area. Lower values give a more realistic and pleasing effect.

2. Set Opacity to 100 and Blur to 0.21in Click OK. The picture below shows the effect that these values will create.

Though the effect is convincing, it is often better when applied to dark objects against a dark background. The black circle will serve to create a solar eclipse effect. Apply the same effect to the black circle, accepting all the default settings in the dialog box.

Once an effect has been applied, it is locked to the object, so you can freely move the object around irrespective of the background color. Try positioning your solar eclipse in various places on top of the gradient at the bottom of the page. In many ways this has greater impact than when placed over a solid color object.

Inner Glow

The result of this effect is the same as the outer glow except it places the glow on the inside of the object rather than the outside. Once again, the effect is applied by way of a bitmap. However the bitmap is placed inside a mask, the object itself defining the shape of the mask.

Open the file called Inner_glow.ai from the download folder.

One interesting use of the Inner Glow effect is to make gradients look a little less uniform and computerized. This works particularly well with radial gradients. The circle on this page has been filled with a white to black radial gradient. This depicts a planet reflecting a single source of light. Many spherical objects, particularly those with reflective surfaces, often display a ring of light just inside the circumference. This light area also serves to form the spherical shape to the viewer's eye. We are going to use the Inner Glow effect to simulate this band of light and therefore strengthen the image and form of the planet.

1. Select the circle. Go to Effect>Stylize>Inner Glow. In the dialog box that opens, the only differences to those we have seen with the other Stylize options are the Center and Edge options. Center applies the glow so it emanates outwards from the center of the object and Edge applies the glow to the outer edge and emanates in towards the center.

2. Leave the Mode as Screen, set the Opacity to 70, the Blur as 0.25in, and leave the Edge option selected. Click OK.

If you need to fine tune the settings, double-click the Inner Glow label in the Appearance palette to reopen the Inner Glow dialog box.

Feathering Edges

Feathering edges is really the fundamental principle behind drop shadows and inner and outer glows. To "feather" an edge is to soften or blur it. If shadows and glow effects didn't exist, we would still be creating the effects but we would be calling it feathering edges. The effect creates a transparent bitmap in the same way as shadows and glows, so watch that file size again.

Open the file called Feather.ai from the download folder.

1. Select the red circle. Go to Effect>Stylize>Feather. The simple dialog box offers only one option, the Feather Radius. The value you enter in this box defines the distance over which you want the feathering or fading effect to take place. Higher values increase the amount of feather, which results

in a softer edge, however it also reduces the apparent size of the original object.

2.   Check the Preview box in the dialog box so you can see the results as you change the number. Enter a low value first, 0.10. Then steadily increase the value by using the arrow buttons within the number box. When you have seen the effects, type 0.25 in the box and click OK.

3.   Reposition the red circle on the different colored backgrounds in the page. You will notice the background color makes no difference to the effect. We still see the soft edge and the circle appears to blend and merge into its background regardless of the color, just as a shadow would.

The picture below shows the circle after the Feather Effect has been applied. The circle has been positioned so it equally straddles the different shades of backgrounds.

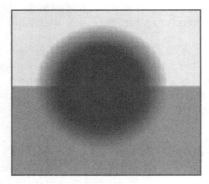

Summary

The filters and effects development department of any graphics software company could arguably be the busiest, most fun and obscure department in the whole company. As I have stressed, experimentation is the key. Knowing the underlying principles behind each filter and effect reduces much of the guesswork from your experiments and provides a greater degree of control, thereby saving you time and improving your chances of achieving the desired look.

In this chapter you have learned about the role filters and effects play in everyday artwork, their limitations and strengths, and the consequences of using them with regard to file size and potential printing problems. You also now know how to create artwork elements by combining a number of filters and effects to produce complex shapes efficiently while at the same time disguising the fact that filters were used.

The Appearance palette plays a valuable role when used in conjunction with effects and you learned how to get the best out of this combination for fluent effective editing.

In the next chapter you will learn more about the blending modes that we touched on this chapter when you applied the drop shadow and glow effects. Blending modes feature strongly in Adobe Photoshop, as do another set of features that you will cover, in the form of Opacity masks. You will also learn about a fairly recent innovation to Illustrator, Transparency.

11 Creating Transparent Art

What We'll Cover in this Chapter:

- Displaying Transparency in your file

- Applying Transparency to simple Objects, Groups, and Layers

- Using Transparency Knockouts

- Applying Transparency to individual attributes

- Introduction to applying Blending Modes

- Introduction to using, editing, and applying Opacity Masks

In this chapter we are going to familiarize you with the concept of creating transparent graphics in Illustrator. Although it is often thought that transparent images are the unique preserve of raster applications like Adobe Photoshop, vector applications, especially powerful ones like Illustrator, are more than capable of producing those subtle effects.

In the previous chapter when you were using filters and effects, you may well have been using transparency effects without realizing it and when you used the Symbol Screener on your brochure cover, once again transparency was being used!

The concept of transparency opens up a whole new world of printing considerations, so you really need to be aware of whether you have incorporated it into your illustration. Although these printing concerns will be mentioned in this chapter, they will be covered in detail in the chapter on printing. I urge you to read that discussion very closely if you don't want any of those unpleasant surprises when your artwork goes to print.

Also, there is so much more power and control that you can gain by learning more about transparency, blending modes, and opacity masks, which will take your illustrations to an entirely new level and enable you to create artwork with a subtlety that you never thought possible. Although an in-depth study of all the transparency options available within Illustrator is beyond the scope of this book, I will make sure that you can begin using these features creatively and efficiently.

Displaying Transparency

Before we actually start discussing how we can add transparency to our Illustrator publications, it would be useful if we could ask Illustrator to show us just exactly where the artwork is in fact transparent. We achieve this by displaying the **Transparency Grid**, which by default will display a checkered background grid indicating the transparent areas.

By this stage you should be familiar with the idea that anytime you wish to change the way in which artwork is being displayed on the screen, you can access a relevant command from the View menu. To display the Transparency Grid, Go to View > Show Transparency Grid (CTRL/CMD+SHIFT+D) and conversely to hide it, you would choose View > Hide Transparency Grid (CTRL/CMD+SHIFT+D).

Furthermore, if you don't particularly like the way in which the Transparency Grid is displaying, for example it does not provide enough contrast with your illustration, and you need to change either the size or the color of the blocks, you can do this by changing the settings in your Document Setup. To display your transparency settings, choose File > Document Setup. The Document Setup dialog box will appear, and from the drop-down menu at the top left-hand corner, choose Transparency.

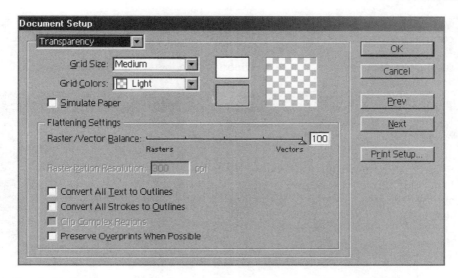

From the screenshot, you will see that you are able to change both the size and color of the Transparency Grid, by clicking on the relevant drop-down menus and making a selection. If none of the preset grid color combinations suit you, click on the colored squares to the right of the menu to make your own selection.

The Simulate Paper option gives you an opportunity to see how your transparent areas will look when they are printed onto colored stock. You choose your paper color by clicking on the top swatch, the one adjacent to Grid Size, and select a color similar to your paper stock from the Color Picker that appears. This onscreen simulation of the paper color will only happen if you are not displaying your Transparency Grid.

For the moment, we will presume that we are working on white stock, and therefore have no need to simulate white paper onscreen because the Artboard is white. However, it is worth bearing in mind that this is not entirely correct when we talk about working in CMYK. Setting Illustrator to simulate even white paper will give us a much clearer idea of how the document will print. So, as a rule of thumb, I'd suggest that you always set Illustrator to simulate your paper.

In the lower part of the dialog box, we have a number of features which relate to how transparent art will be flattened for printing. We'll be discussing this feature in some depth in our chapter on Preparing for Print.

Applying Transparency

Let's have a look at how transparency works and how we apply it. Depending on whether we are working with groups or individual objects, and whether these objects are on the same or different layers, using transparency can result in some very different effects. So we'll start, as we always do, from the ground up, introducing more and more complex concepts as we progress.

Display the Transparency palette by choosing Window > Transparency (SHIFT+F10).

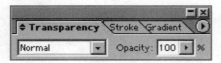 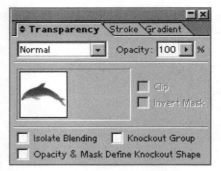

If your palette looks like the one on the left-hand side, from the palette context menu choose Show Options and Show Thumbnails. It should look a little more interesting now, although it will only display a thumbnail if there is an object selected on the Artboard.

> *If at any stage your palette looks smaller, or devoid of features that you are sure you remember seeing elsewhere, have a look at the palette context menu, there may well be a* Show Options *command that will display more features.*

Applying Transparency to Simple Objects

Open the file called `Transparency1.ai`. In this first example, we have four starfish and a colored rectangle on a single layer, with a stacking order of the rectangle being at the back with Star A in front of it, and then Star B, Star C, and finally Star D at the very front.

I've started using Views again, because our art is going to get pretty complex in this section, and you will find you need to zoom in to work on the details, and then zoom out to admire your handiwork. It seems a good idea to re-introduce that skill here. We will show you how to create your own views a little later in this chapter.

As we will be working with Transparency in this exercise, now would be a good idea to ensure that you are displaying the Transparency Grid by choosing View > Show Transparency Grid (CTRL/CMD+SHIFT+D). Notice how the checkered grid appears where there is no artwork, showing that the background is transparent. We'll be keeping an eye on this grid and how it keeps us informed as we progress through the chapter.

1. From the View menu choose the view Stars as Individual Objects.

2. Select Star A, and set the Opacity to 40 by using the slider from the drop-down menu on the Transparency palette, or enter the value in the field to the right of the drop-down menu.

Notice how you can now see through Star A to the rectangle behind.

3. Select Star B, and set its Opacity to 40% as well. Now you can see through Star B to both Star A and the rectangle below. Notice how where the two stars overlap, the color is darker. When you are using transparency, the opacity of overlapping objects will become accumulative.

4. Repeat the process for the two remaining stars. You'll notice that in the areas where more than two stars overlap, the color becomes even darker.

But the grid really isn't telling us much about the transparency of these objects. That is because behind the starfish there is this solid, opaque rectangle.

5. On the Layer palette (F7), locate the layer called Stars as Individuals, and click the triangle to the left of the layer name to expand that layer. You'll notice there are four stars and a rectangle on that layer. In the column on the Layer palette which indicates whether a layer is visible or not, click on the eye next to the rectangle object. The eye will disappear, the rectangle becomes invisible and you should be able to see the transparency grid through the stars. This indicates that the stars are not opaque. Keep an eye on this grid throughout the exercise, and make objects and layers invisible at certain times just so you can see how the grids keep you informed. Make the rectangle visible again, by clicking to display the eye next to the rectangle object in the Layer palette.

6. Now select those four stars again, and change their Opacity back to 100%. Select and you will see that they have all reverted back to being opaque.

7. Reselect the stars and set the value back to 40%, and you'll see those overlaps again. This point that I have just proved to you may seem rather silly, but it will become apparent when we select the stars in groups and on layers a little later on in this exercise.

8. Deselect the stars, and set Star C to an Opacity of 60%. Now select all four stars in that grouping again and have a look at the Transparency palette. Notice the Opacity field is blank. This is because you are asking Illustrator to tell you the Opacity value of mixed objects, and it cannot choose one value – so it shows you nothing. Whenever you have objects of mixed appearances selected, Illustrator will either return a blank field or a question mark.

That's basic transparency dealt with, but what if you wanted the stars not to be transparent to each other, and only to interact with the rectangle underneath?

Controlling Transparency with Groups

Remaining with the same `Transparency1.ai` file, let's have a look at the second grouping of stars and rectangles.

1. From the View menu choose the view Stars as a Group.

2. With the **Selection** tool (V) select Star A. All four stars are selected simultaneously, which should be a giveaway that the four stars have been grouped. You know that you could also look in the Appearance palette to check whether what you have selected is a group.

3. With the group selected, set the Opacity to 40% on the Transparency palette. What you'll see is that whilst the stars do not show as transparent where they overlap the other stars in the group, they still interact with the objects below.

Consequently, you can draw the conclusion that if you have a group of objects, which you wish to remain at complete opacity with relationship to each other, but to interrelate with other objects beneath them, the answer is to group those initial objects. Also notice how the color of the background objects is apparently affecting the color of the semi-transparent stars.

However, this is only true if you target the group as a whole with the Selection tool. This is helpful as there will be times when you wish to group objects so that you can transform them together, but you want to be able to control their transparency relationship with each other on an individual basis.

You can use the **Group Selection** tool to target the individual stars.

1. From the View menu choose the view Grouped – modified individually.

2. With the **Group Selection** tool, select Star A. Look at the Appearance palette to check whether you have the individual star selected. It should look like the screenshot here.

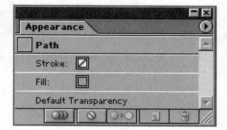

3. With Star A selected, set the Opacity to 50% on the Transparency palette. Notice only this star has reacted. Select each of the remaining stars in turn, and change their Opacity to values you desire. Notice that even though they are grouped, because we have targeted them individually we can affect them individually, and they still interact with the objects below.

4. Now return to the Stars as a Group view. With the **Group Selection** tool, select Star B, and look at the Transparency palette. It might be surprising that the Transparency palette tells you that the Star is at 100% Opacity, yet you know it isn't because you set the value to 40%, and it's very visible to you that the star is not opaque. Quite simply it means that this star is at 100% opacity for the Opacity level set for this group, which is 40%.

5. Now set the Opacity of this star to 40% and you will see that it becomes visibly lighter, because it is now 40% relative to the value it was, which was also 40%, so in actual fact this star is set to a value of 40% of 40%, or 16%.

6. Select the entire group, and change the opacity level back to 100%, and then select Star B with the **Group Selection** tool. It still reflects a value of 40%, which is now 40% of the group's value (100%).

The exercise might well have left you feeling a little confused. It's quite clever really, because you now know that you can get groups to interact with other objects, and to further interact with each other within the group. It also explains why sometimes when you select objects, the information displayed in the Transparency palette might seem a little misleading. So, as you begin to work more and more with transparency, keep this little exercise in mind.

Controlling Transparency with Layers

In addition to applying transparency values to individual objects or groups, you can also apply transparency at a layer level. This is useful if you want to change the transparency for all objects on a layer, and you will be setting them to the same value initially. Once again, we are still using that sample file – Transparency1.ai.

1. From the View menu choose the view Rectangle on separate layer. The object you are looking at here is that collection of four stars again, ungrouped, and on their own layer with the rectangle below them on another layer.

2. Display the Layer palette by choosing Window > Layers (F7). Locate the "stars on layer" layer.

3. On the Layer palette, click on the circle to the right of the layer name. Notice the rectangle to the right of the circle, indicating that the all the stars are selected. Of course, you can also see that they are selected by looking at the Artboard.

4. On the Layer palette, click on the triangle next to the layer "stars on layer". This will expand the layer so that you can see all the paths on that layer, and what you should notice is that every star path of that layer is now selected.

5. On the Transparency palette, set the Opacity value to 50%. As you had selected all the stars on that layer, they have all changed to reflect the new transparency. Additionally note, they are not interacting with each other. There is no visible overlap as there was when you earlier selected the individual stars – in fact, they are acting as if they were a group. Deselect the stars.

6. Click on the little circle to the right of the path label Star A. This will target that path, and you will see that you have it selected by the display of a colored rectangle to the right of the circle – of course, the selected star is also visible on the Artboard.

We could have selected the star directly on the page with the **Selection** tool (V), but as we start using Illustrator we often get stuck in one particular workflow pattern when there are often easier ways to work. So, I'm just reminding you about the Layer palette again, especially as you will soon be doing some very special things with layers in the coming chapters.

7. Have a look at that Transparency palette again, and once again it's reflecting 100%, because although that layer's Opacity has been set to 50%, this particular star itself is at an Opacity of 100%. It is the command you applied to the layer as a whole which is affecting its appearance.

8. With Star A selected, set the Opacity to 25% on the Transparency palette. Notice only this star has reacted because you targeted the path directly on the Layer palette, and the Transparency palette reflects 25% which as you already know is 25% of 50% or 12.5% of the original color.

You might well be thinking that you cannot trust the Transparency palette to reflect the Opacity values accurately, but it does. It's always telling you the opacity of what you have selected, but not that it may be a relative opacity because the object has also been targeted as a group or layer. We need to look elsewhere for that information, the Appearance palette.

9. Ensure that Star A is still selected – the one you have just set at 25%. Display the Appearance palette if it is not already visible.

Notice that the Appearance palette indicates that the star has an Opacity value of 25%, which you know to be correct.

10. Now click on another star in that particular collection, and look at the Appearance palette. The Opacity value is recorded as Default Transparency. That's because this object has the default transparency for that layer.

11. One final step with this little collection of stars. On the Layer palette target the "stars on layer" layer, and click on the circle to the right of the layer name. Make sure the rectangle becomes visible, so you know that you have selected those objects on that layer; and look at the Appearance palette. Notice it is now reflecting that you have a layer selected, and that the opacity of that layer is set at 50%.

Controlling Transparency with Layers and Groups

Let's target a group of stars that have been placed on a layer separate from the underlying rectangle, and see how they react to different opacity settings, and how you can keep track of what you have done by using the Appearance palette.

1. From the View menu choose the view Group – rectangle on sep layer. Here you have a group of four stars on their own layer with two rectangles below them on another layer.

2. Display the Layer palette by choosing Window > Layers (F7). Locate the G stars on layer layer, and click on the circle to the right of the layer name to select all the stars on that layer.

3. Set the Opacity for the selected layer at 75% – note I am saying layer, not group of stars. You are again targeting the opacity of a layer, and not the opacity of the objects on that layer, even though because they are on that layer they will be affected by any changes you make to the layer's opacity. As you expected, the stars have all changed to reflect that they are at 75% opacity, and because we targeted them at a layer level, they are not interacting with each other, but with the objects – in this case two rectangles – on the layer underneath. Deselect the stars by clicking elsewhere on the screen where there is no artwork, or going to Select > Deselect or using CTRL/CMD+SHIFT+A.

4. On the Layer palette, expand the layer by clicking on the triangle next to the layer G stars on layer. This will expand the layer so that you can see that there is a group on this layer. Expand the triangle again, to show that there are four stars in this group.

5. Target the group by clicking on the adjacent circle, and then have a look at the Transparency palette and the Appearance palette again. The Transparency palette is recording the Opacity of the group at 100% because the group itself is still at 100%. It is the layer that was targeted in the previous step, and the Appearance palette says Default Transparency because this group is at the default transparency value set for that layer.

6. With the group selected, set the Opacity value to 80%. As you are in actual fact setting the value of the group to be 80% of the already established value for that layer, 75%, the stars will get lighter and not darker.

7. On the Appearance palette, click on the word Layer, and the little white square will move to the left of it. The Appearance palette will reflect the opacity value for that layer. Double-click on the word Contents, and the Appearance palette will change to show you that on that layer, there is a group that has an opacity value of 80% applied to it. The little gray and white checkered square that appears on the Appearance palette that looks just like the Transparency Grid is Illustrator reminding you that you also have a level of transparency applied to this layer.

Now let's see what happens if we apply different opacity levels on an individual basis to the objects within that group, which already have an opacity level of 80%, on a layer with an opacity level of 75%.

8. Deselect all the stars.

9. On the Layer palette, target Star A by clicking on the adjacent circle or by using the **Group Selection** tool, and set its Opacity level to 50% – that's 50% (object) of 80% (group) of 75% (layer). When you look at the Appearance palette, you see that the path has an opacity of 50%, in a group where a level of transparency has been applied, on a layer where transparency has been applied.

10. Set the Opacity level for Star B to 60%, Star C to 70%, and Star D to 80%, ensuring that you target the stars directly either by using the **Group Selection** tool or the Layer palette. Keep an eye on that Appearance palette as you do this.

Using Transparency Knockouts

Let's say that in our particular instance, we wanted to set the individual components of this group at different opacity levels, as we have just done, but we did not want them to interact with each other, only with objects outside of the group. Ensure that you have the Transparency palette in an expanded view by going to the palette context menu, and selecting Show Options.

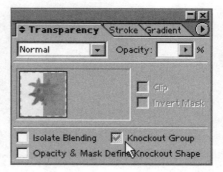

At the base of the palette, you should see an option that says Knockout Group, and at the moment it more than likely has a gray tick or dash in the box. Quite simply put, using the Knockout Group option prevents the elements of a group from showing through each other. If you look at the example that you have on screen, where we have applied different levels of opacity to the objects within the group, you can see through the stars to the other stars and see where they overlap. If we didn't want this to happen, we would make sure that Knockout Group was selected, in other words, it had a black tick in the square.

So why is there a gray tick or dash at present? It just means that the Knockout Group option is in a neutral position – it's neither on nor off.

- Use the Off option – blank checkbox – when you want to ensure that a layer or a group of transparent objects will never knock each other out, and you will be able to see through them to other objects within that group.

- Use the Neutral option – gray tick or dash – when you want to group artwork without interfering with any knockout behavior that you may have chosen for any enclosing layer or group. You may recall that as we have progressed through this chapter, you've seen how we can apply different opacity levels to objects, groups, and layers, and you also know that we can create groups within groups.

This means that we could have a group or layer which incorporated this object, and which had a different Knockout Group option applied to it.

■ Use the On option – black tick – when you don't want to see through objects within the group, so you don't want their transparency values to interact with each other.

Knockout Group Off   Knockout Group On

1. From the View menu choose the view Group – rectangle on sep layer if it's not already showing on your screen.

2. Select the group of stars, either by targeting them directly on the Layer palette or by using the **Selection** tool (V).

3. Cycle through the Knockout Group checkbox options by clicking a number of times. You are unlikely to see a difference between Neutral and Off and this is because this group of stars is not within another group or layer for which we have specified any Knockout options. However, when you check Knockout Group to on, you should see that you could no longer see through the individual stars within the group. Save and close this file.

Before we move on to discussing other aspects about transparency, let's briefly summarize what we have learnt about transparency in the preceding exercises:

- Transparency can be applied on a path-by-path basis, a group-by-group basis, or a layer-by-layer basis. Consequently, an object can have more than one transparency value applied to it at different stages.

- As we apply different levels of opacity to an object, the resulting appearance is always relative to the opacity value that has been applied to the layer or group of which it is a part.

- The Transparency palette always tells us the true opacity of a selected object, group, or layer but it is unable to indicate to us that this may be a relative transparency value.

- The Appearance palette will reflect the transparency level of the selected component, but it will also indicate whether or not that object is within a group or layer which has had an opacity value applied to it.

- By default, individual objects react to transparency in a different way from groups. However, we can always change the group components by targeting them directly either through the Layer palette or with the **Group Selection** tool.

- In a group where components have different opacity levels, we can instruct them to knock each other out by choosing Knockout Group on the expanded Transparency palette.

It might have seemed a very lengthy exercise, but I'm sure you now realize how easy it would have been to get yourself in a pickle about transparency, and why objects on the Artboard just didn't look correct. Remember that if at any stage you are concerned about the apparent transparency of an object, select the object, look at the Appearance palette, and slowly work your way back through the group and layer within which the object is located. This will tell you all you need to know.

Applying Transparency to Individual Attributes

What if you wished to change the transparency values of just the stroke or the fill – could you possibly do this? Yes, and very easily!

1. Open the file called `Transparency2.ai`, and go to the view called Individual Stars. With the **Selection** tool, select one of the stars in that collection.

2. On the Appearance palette, highlight the Stroke option by clicking on the word Stroke. Set the Opacity value on the Transparency palette to 50%. Note that only the stroke, and not the fill, has changed. This is because you specifically targeted the stroke on the Appearance palette.

3.   Target the object's fill by clicking on the word Fill on the Appearance palette, and set the Opacity for the object's fill to 25%. The object's fill has reacted independently of the stroke, and the two differing opacity values are reflected on the Appearance palette.

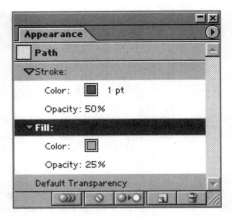

Now let's see what happens when we try to target only the stroke or fill for our group. Display the view Grouped Stars.

1.   Select the group with the **Selection** tool, and have a look at the Appearance palette. You may be a little disappointed, because there seems no obvious way to target only the stroke of all elements within the group, and if your group consisted of a few hundred objects, selecting each one individually and applying the desired stroke opacity would be a real bind!

2.   Double-click on the word Contents, to ask Illustrator to display the contents of the group, and you'll notice that you can now target either the stroke or the fill. Select the stroke by clicking on the word in the Appearance palette, and set the Opacity to 45%, then select the fill and set its opacity value to 40%.

Have you noticed that your grouped stars are actually interacting with each other as if they were independent stars and you can see the overlaps between the objects? If you don't want this to happen, remember to go to the Knockout Group option on your expanded Transparency palette and check that box.

Let's try that routine again on another group.

3.   Switch to the view Grouped Stars 2. Select the group with the **Selection** tool, and have a look at the Appearance palette. Once again it reflects that you have a group with contents.

4.   Double-click on the word Contents to ask Illustrator to display the contents of the group. You'll see that this time, no stroke or fill attributes are discussed, just a comment saying the contents of the group have a mixed appearance – in other words, they have different fills and strokes. In this instance, unfortunately, if you want to target their attributes individually, you would have to select the path either with the **Group Selection** tool or through the Layer palette as

before, and then make the necessary adjustments by selecting Stroke or Fill on the Appearance palette.

Before we move on to putting all these wonderful new skills to use in our case study, let's just recap again.

- We can target the individual attributes of an object and apply transparency to these by targeting them through the Appearance palette.

- Similarly, if our group contains objects with the same attributes, we can safely follow the same procedure.

- If a group contains objects with mixed fills and strokes and we want to target these, we need to do it on an object-by-object basis.

Case Study: Making Waves

George and Lucy have been back in the studio and they are thrilled with the way in which they see this concept developing. You're back working on that illustration for the brochure cover, which is nowhere near complete. Your point of focus at the moment is that stretch of water. Even with a gradient fill or a gradient mesh applied to it; it still seems a little flat. It has no texture, nothing interesting in it. We're going to solve that right now with a few of our old skills, and a little bit of transparency!

For this exercise you will need to open Waves.ai, and then either your brochure cover file which you developed in Chapter 9, or the Brochure_cover.ai file for this chapter. With the file Waves.ai visible on screen, let's get ready to draw in some waves to use as the basis of this texture.

1. Display the Brushes palette (F5), and then display the palette's context menu by clicking on the arrow at the top right hand corner of the palette. From the menu, choose List View to see the names of the brushes – or in this case – the brush. (I've tidied the file up by using the Select All Unused command and then placing those brushes in the trashcan to keep the file size smaller.)

2. Select the **Calligraphic Wave** brush from the Brushes palette, and then the **Paintbrush** tool (B) and ensure that you have a white stroke and no fill.

3. With the **Paintbrush**, draw broad strokes across the bay. You're not really looking for detailed wave strokes, just nice smooth, sweeping lines.

Ensure that every line overlaps off the edge of the water shape, or if you start one that does not go edge to edge, ensure that it meets up with another line.

4.   If you do not like your waves, do not delete them. Edit them either by ensuring that they are selected, and then drawing over them again, or by selecting anchor points and direction handles with the **Direct Selection** tool (A) and manipulating your paths. Your illustration should look similar to this in Outline View (CTRL/CMD+Y). You are not looking to faithfully reproduce what I have created, but all my lines overlap the edge of the water expanse, and on the right where I have a line that does not go from edge to edge, I have made sure it meets the other path. Check your illustration in Outline View, and if necessary make any further alterations.

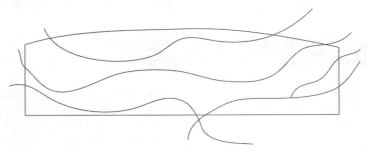

5.   We now need to select all the lines and the water expanse which you could do by choosing the **Selection** tool and marquee dragging over the components, or using your **Lasso** tool, or by choosing Select > All, (CTRL/CMD+A).

6.   With all the lines and the water selected, display the Pathfinder palette from the Window menu (SHIFT+F9) and choose Divide from the palette. It's the first one in the second row, under the heading Pathfinders.

You have divided the underlying shape of the waves you drew into a number of different shapes, and the gradient has been applied separately to each of the shapes. We're going to use transparency to make this even more interesting a little later.

7.   Switch to the Outline view and check that you do not have any superfluous shapes lurking outside the water's border. Notice on my illustration there are lines protruding from my shape, circled, and I don't want them. Whenever you use the Pathfinder, remember that Illustrator groups the objects, so with the **Group Selection** tool, select any of your extra line segments and delete them.

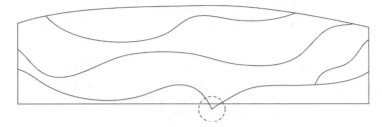

8. Save the file, but there is no need to close it as we will be coming back to it a little later in this chapter.

Now the time has come for us to get those waves into our cover brochure. Ensure that your cover brochure file is open, and arrange both files on the screen so that you can see them.

9. From the View menu choose Fit in Window (CTRL/CMD+0) for both files. The screen may be a little cluttered, and all we need for the moment is our toolbox and our Layer palette. Press SHIFT+TAB to hide all the palettes, but to keep the toolbox visible, and then press F7 to show the Layer palette. When you want all the other palettes to show, just press SHIFT+TAB again.

10. In the brochure cover file, make sure that the **Waves** layer is visible and active. Make all the layers above this layer invisible, by clicking and dragging in the column where the eyes appear, and lock them.

11. In the Waves.ai file, select the waves with the **Selection** tool – remember the object has been automatically grouped by the Pathfinder operation you performed a little earlier. Drag the waves across into your brochure illustration, but do not worry about where you position them for the moment. Release the waves, and minimize the Waves.ai window because we no longer need to see the waves, although we will be using them again a little later.

12. Switch on Smart Guides, and select these waves by the top left hand corner. Your mouse should indicate that you are over an anchor if you hover the mouse over that area for a while without clicking.

13. Drag the waves on top of the original water, and release the mouse when the Smart Guide indicates that you are over the anchor point in the corresponding part of the water. The objects should be perfectly aligned. You can switch all the layers back on now if you wish.

A little organization before we get started will make your life easier, because you want to be fairly zoomed in on the picture and if you have all the palettes back, the screen will be too cluttered.

14. On the Layer palette, ensure that all the drawing layers are visible but you don't need to see the instructions or guides, so you can hide these. Make sure all the layers except for the waves layer are locked and then press F7 to hide the Layer palette.

15. Display the Transparency palette by pressing SHIFT+F10. This will display the grouping, which includes the Gradient palette if your palettes are still in their default arrangement. If not, press F10 to display the Gradient palette as well. If the Gradient palette is with the Transparency palette, click and drag on the word Gradient to separate the palettes. You may well be switching from one to the other as you refine this water section, and it's much easier to have them both up there.

16. Switch into Full Screen mode by selecting the Full Screen option at the bottom of the toolbox, or by pressing the letter F twice. We've just freed up the screen from all unnecessary distractions so that we can get down to the task in hand.

17. With the **Group Selection** tool, select the wave closest to the shore, and set its opacity level to around 20-25%. Remember that if you used a Gradient fill as I have done, you can also refine the gradient by clicking and dragging with the **Gradient** tool (G) over the selected area. However, always remember to switch back to the **Group Selection** tool when you want to move onto the next wave.

18. I had roughly four waves, so I set the opacity at 25%, then 30%, then 35%, and then 40% as I moved away from the shore, But choose what levels suit your waves and their placement. Just bear in mind that we are going for a subtle, sweeping look in our waves, nothing too distinct, we just want to introduce a bit of interest here.

19. Switch the eye off next to the waves layer in the Layer palette to see the "before" waves effect and then switch the eye back on to see the "after".

20. Save your file and let's go back and learn some new skills to add more interest to these waves!

Using Blending Modes

As I said in the beginning of this chapter, the main reason for introducing you to transparency at this level was because you might already be inadvertently using it with effects and the Symbol Screener, and it was best that you were aware of it.

We don't have enough space here for a detailed discussion, but let's have a quick look at those **Blending Modes** on the Transparency palette, and explain the basic concepts behind what is happening. If you are an advanced Photoshop user, then these blending modes will be familiar to you.

Essentially when we are dealing with blending modes, we are blending the colors between two overlapping objects by targeting the specific object, layer, or group and then choosing a blending mode from the Transparency palette. Using different blending modes allows us to alter the ways in which that object's colors blend with the colors of the objects below it.

When talking about blend modes, it is useful to think in terms of base colors, blend colors, and resultant colors. Let's have a look at the illustration below. This shows the basic concept behind these terms.

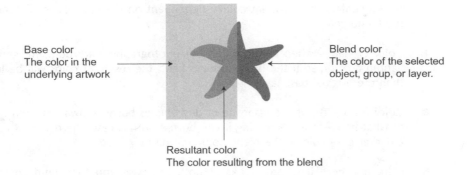

Base color
The color in the
underlying artwork

Blend color
The color of the selected
object, group, or layer.

Resultant color
The color resulting from the blend

Now let's have a quick look at the sixteen different blending modes available with Illustrator. Bear in mind that the explanations below are just a general guideline as to how each blending mode works, because the result you'll get will always be dependent on the color of the overlapping objects – the base and the blend colors as mentioned above.

As we work through these options, there are two sample files called `Blending_modes1.ai` and `Blending_modes2.ai` that you can use to experiment on because this is the only way in which you will become more familiar with these modes and have a fairly good idea of what to expect when you apply them.

- Normal – this is the default setting where the blend color, the color of the top object, does not interact with the base color, the color of the underlying object.

- Multiply – this mode multiplies the base color with the blend color, and your resultant color is always darker. Multiply is a good option to choose when you are trying to get the effect of a shadow overlaying an object.

- Screen – in the printing world we often talk about creating a screen, or a tint of a color, and this is what Screen does. It will always give you a lighter, bleached out color as your resultant color.

- Overlay – essentially a combination of Multiply and Screen. Overlay will darken the dark areas and lighten the light areas.

- Soft Light – this is supposed to change the colors as they would if you were shining a soft spotlight onto the artwork. The effect is a little similar to Overlay in that if the blend color, the color of the top object, is light, the resultant color will be lighter. Alternativley if the blend color is dark, the resultant color will darken.

- Hard Light – similar to Soft light, except now we are dealing with the apparent results of a harsh spotlight. Hard Light will multiply (make darker) or screen (make lighter) the resultant colors, dependent on the darkness or lightness of the blend color.

- Color Dodge – when we dodge in the photographic darkroom, we generally lighten a color, so if the blend color is light, the resultant color will be lighter than the original base layer.

- Color Burn – this is the opposite of dodging, as burning always darkens. Think of what happens to something if you burn it. In this case, the resultant color is a darker base color if the blend color was dark.

- Darken – here Illustrator looks at both the base and the blend color; and chooses the darker of the two as the resultant color.

- Lighten – this is the converse of Darken in that Illustrator looks at both the base and the blend color; and chooses the lighter of the two as the resultant color.

- Difference – this looks at the base and blend colors, and then subtracts the brighter color from the darker color. This results in the colors being inverted, with the more dramatic effects being achieved with a brighter blend color.

- Exclusion – this creates an effect similar to that achieved in Difference mode, but the contrast is lower.

- Hue – using Hue creates a resultant color with the lightness and saturation (gray values) of the base color and the hue (color) of the blend color.

- Saturation – the resultant color is one with the lightness and hue (color) of the base color and the saturation of the blend color.

- Color – using Color will give you a resultant color that is a blend of the base color's lightness and the blend colors hue and saturation.

- Luminosity – with Luminosity, the resultant color is a blend of the base color's hue and saturation, and the lightness of the blend color.

If that all seemed terribly complex, do not let it concern you. My most sincere advice to you is to play and experiment with the different modes until you get a feel for them. Take a few at a time and see if you can anticipate the result, remembering of course that it all has to do with the color of the two overlapping objects.

Having said that, you have acquired skills in the first part of this chapter that are of great relevance here as well. When you are experimenting with the blending modes, use those same procedures to check on the blending modes you have applied.

Isolating Blending Modes

You may also recall how when we studied transparency, we had the option to control how our group interacted with each other and with the items below by using the Knockout Group option on the Transparency palette. Well, we have similar control here. When you apply blending modes to objects in a group, the effects of the blending modes are normally seen on any objects that lie beneath the group.

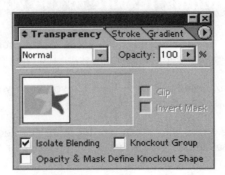

If we use the Isolate Blending command, we can change the behavior of the blending modes so that only members of the selected group are affected and the objects below the group remain unaffected by the blending modes. Have a look at the illustration below. Each group is comprised of a starfish and a rectangle, which are grouped together, placed on top of another rectangle.

Original   Isolate Blending not   Isolate Blending
                applied to group   applied to group

- On the left we have the original starfish and small rectangle, with no blending mode applied.

- In the center, a Screen blending mode has been applied to the star. Notice how the star is interacting with both the small rectangle with which it is grouped and with the larger rectangle behind it.

- In the third example, Isolate Blending has been applied to the star and small rectangle group. The star interacts with the small rectangle, which is within its group, but remains faithful to its original color when it overlaps the larger rectangle. This is because with Isolate Blending applied to the group, the blending mode affects only that group, and not the group's relationship with other objects within the illustration.

Case Study: Adding Texture to the Waves

I did promise earlier that we would make these waves more interesting than the flat expanse that they originally were. Let's apply some blending modes to our waves.

1. If you closed the `Waves.ai` file you were working with earlier, you will need to re-open it now.

2. Once again, with the **Selection** tool (V), select the waves and copy them to the clipboard by choosing Edit > Copy or CTRL/CMD+C.

3. Close the file, and switch to your brochure cover file.

4. Hide all the layers above the textured waves layer, to make alignment of the waves a little easier. Lock all the layers except the layer called textured waves, and target this layer by clicking on its name. When we attempt to paste the copied waves, Illustrator will know upon which layer we wish to place the waves.

5. Paste the waves from the clipboard by choosing Edit>Paste or CTRL/CMD+V. Ensure that Smart Guides are on, and drag those waves by the top left hand corner. Your mouse should indicate that you are over an anchor if you hover the mouse over that area for a while without clicking.

6. Drag the waves on top of the gradient waves, and release the mouse when the Smart Guide indicates that you are over the anchor point in the corresponding part of the waves. The objects should be perfectly aligned. Switch all the layers back on now and save the file.

You might be wondering whether we have just spoilt our magnificent transparent waves. We are about to do something wonderful with blending modes. First we need to find the patterns that I want to use with this illustration.

7. As the patterns were already part of the Waves.ai, we can access them easily by opening the file as a library, similar to what we did when we accessed symbols from other files. Choose Window>Swatch Libraries> Other Library·and navigate through your hard drive to where you saved the Waves.ai file and open that file. A small palette will appear on the screen, containing the swatches from the Waves.ai file.

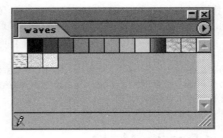

8. At the base of the swatches, you will notice that there are five rather bland looking black and white pattern swatches. SHIFT+ select these swatches and drag them over into your Swatches palette. Close the palette.

Before we start to work with the patterns and blending moments, let's just take a moment to reconsider the contents of the file. Ignoring all the non-water layers, we have one complete block of color on the water layer, then above that on the waves layer we have our divided gradient waves, and now on the textured waves layer, we have those gradients again at 100% opacity.

9. With the **Group Selection** tool, select each of your waves and fill each one with a different one of the pattern swatches. Do not be concerned about which pattern fill you use, you know that you can always swap them around once you get a feel for your design.

10. For each of these waves we are going to do two things – apply a blending mode, and change the opacity of the textured fill until it is barely discernible. You will find that at the low opacity values, which I am suggesting you use, you'll get pretty good results using Screen, Overlay, Soft Light, and Color Dodge. Keep those opacity values very low once again we are looking to add very gentle texture and life into the ocean.

11. Once you have an effect that you find tasteful, save the file.

Creating Opacity Masks

For the next part of the case study, I think it's time to add some dolphins to our illustration. We want to make it look as if they are jumping in and out of the water, and to give this any sense of realism they are going to have to be semi-transparent in places, as if they are partly submerged in the water.

Enter the mighty **Opacity Mask** – or for you Photoshoppers out there, think layer masks with a twist.

Once again, this is a pretty powerful and complex feature and we could fill a few more chapters on its use, so all we'll do here is teach you how to make a fairly simple opacity mask and to encourage you to learn more about this impressive application later.

Essentially an opacity mask will allow us to hide part of our artwork, using the lightness and darkness values of a mask. This means that we can draw artwork that seems to fade subtly in and out.

Creating Basic Opacity Masks

To illustrate what we mean by this, let's return to our starfish, and see how this feature really works. Open the file called Opacity_masks.ai.

In the left-hand column of the page, you see five purple starfish, each partially covered by a black box, which ranges from 100% black fill in the top box, to a 20% fill in the lowest box. A few moments ago, I said that an opacity mask allows us to partially hide our artwork, depending on the lightness and darkness of the mask.

1. On the Transparency palette menu, check to ensure that there is no tick next to the New Opacity Masks are Clipping command. As we are going to be building very simple opacity masks in this book, we won't be using this feature.

2. With the **Selection** tool, select the top starfish and rectangle as we need a minimum of two objects to form this opacity mask; one to be the masked object, the bottom one which in this case is the starfish, and another object to perform the masking, the top object which in this case is our rectangle.

3. Choose Make Opacity Mask from the Transparency palette menu. Notice that two things have happened. The lower part of the starfish that was covered by the black rectangle has disappeared, and the Transparency palette has changed to reflect that you now have an opacity mask on that object.

Look at the icons in the Transparency palette. On the left-hand side is an icon representing your original art, and on the right is the mask icon, the black rectangle. Between the two icons is a chain indicating that these two, the object and the mask, are linked, and therefore if you move the star, the mask will go with it.

4. Repeat the above step to all the remaining starfish and rectangles in this column. Do you notice that, as the mask gets lighter, more and more of the lower half of the starfish begins to show through the mask? This is because with opacity masks we partially hide our artwork, depending on the lightness and darkness of the mask, so the lighter the mask gets, the subtler the masking effect.

Masking with Colors and Gradients

You can use other colors in the mask, it's just that using black makes it easier for us to perceive the lightness or darkness of the mask. It also proves a nice correlation for all you Photoshop users who are familiar with layer masks and channels.

We can mix more than one color, like if we used a gradient fill. Where the fill is light, we will see more of the underlying object, and where it is dark, we will see less. In fact, you can create an opacity mask from virtually any artwork imaginable, including gradients, meshes, and patterns. However the more complex this mask becomes, the more likely you are to run into printing problems, so keep an eye on it and also consult with your commercial printer – more about the importance of that in the chapter on Printing.

1. With the **Selection** tool (V), select the top starfish and rectangle in the second column, then choose Make Opacity mask from the Transparency palette menu.

2. Repeat this step for the remaining objects in the column, ensuring that for the bottom three where the rectangle totally obscures the starfish that you do select both objects. Notice how the lightness and darkness values of the overlying mask determine how much of the masked object is visible.

Editing and Removing Opacity Masks

If you want to remove a mask, simply click on the masked objects, and choose Release Opacity Mask from the Transparency palette context menu, and the objects will be released back to their normal state.

Editing masks until they really suit our purpose and design is just as easy. There are just a few steps we need to remember as we do it otherwise it can be a little confusing. To edit a mask we must enter mask-editing mode, which we do by either clicking on the mask icon on the Transparency palette or by ALT/OPTION clicking on the mask icon.

In the first instance, you can edit the mask in place and see the effects of your changes as you make them, whereas with the ALT/OPTION alternative, you will view only the mask and not the rest of the document.

Have a look at this screenshot below:

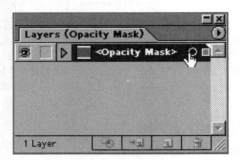

This is normally the moment when users think they have lost all their layers, but it is only because they are in mask-editing mode and need to return to normal mode before the layers display again. To do this, just click on the artwork icon on the left of the Transparency palette.

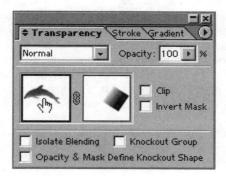

Once you are in mask-editing mode you can use any of the drawing tools, transform tools, fill options, and many of the filters to refine your shape and color content until the effect is what you want. Let's take a moment and practice on the objects in the third column of the Opacity Mask exercise before we move onto those dolphins.

1. With the **Selection** tool, select the top starfish and rectangle in the third column, and then choose Make Opacity mask from the Transparency palette menu.

2. On the Transparency palette, click on the right-hand icon, the mask icon, to enter mask editing mode. Keep an eye on that Layer palette for that all-important hint that you are in mask-editing mode! As you click on the mask icon, the mask shape will become active on the Artboard.

3. Experiment with different colors and different types of fills. Use the Transform tools to rotate, scale, and distort the masks. Try some of the filters and effects that you met in the previous chapter. All the time knowing that you are not distorting your artwork, you are manipulating a mask on top of the art; and you've seen how easy it is to release the objects from the mask.

4. When you're feeling confident, close but don't save the file, and we're ready to start on those dolphins.

Case Study: Disappearing Dolphins

Your brochure cover illustration is coming along really well. So well in fact, that Lucy and George are thinking that it might be used not only on the brochure, but also on a poster, postcard and leaflets. In fact they're looking to put it anywhere they can.

Nevertheless, you're looking at that bay, thinking it still looks rather bare, even with the texture and interest we have introduced into the water. It's about at this stage that you hear Lucy telling someone about the wonderful dolphins they always see when they go out for a sail, and George adding his little scuba bit of how great it is to watch them playing underwater. That's when the idea hits you to put some dolphins in the bay. So, you take the first dolphin, place it in the bay, and it looks terribly out of place, as it's not interacting with the water at all. You need it to look as if it is jumping out of the water which means that the tail has to fade away. This is when the opacity mask comes to the rescue.

1. Ensure that you have the brochure cover file open, and that all layers except the dolphin layer, are locked. Make the dolphin layer visible, and active by clicking on the layer name.

Remember that idea of a virtual library that we started building? In that library is our dolphin, ready for use.

2. Click on the dolphin in the Symbols palette and drag a copy of it onto the Artboard, roughly in the position that you would like. Break the link to the symbol by clicking on the **Break Link to Symbol** icon at the bottom of the Symbols palette.

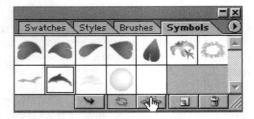

3. Scale and rotate the dolphin until its size and orientation is more in keeping with your idea. Then draw a rectangle over the base of its tail and rotate this until the angle seems right. You might find this easier if you switch to Outline view (CTRL/CMD+Y).

4. Fill the rectangle with a white to black gradient, and no stroke.

5.   Select both the dolphin and the rectangle and choose Make Opacity mask from the Transparency palette menu.

6.   Click on the mask icon to edit mask-editing mode. Make sure none of the option boxes are checked.

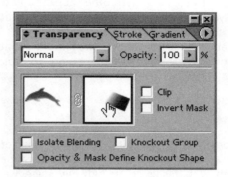

7.   With the **Gradient** tool (G) selected, click and drag within the rectangular area to modify the duration of the gradient. Remember that with the Gradient tool, you can control both the direction and the duration of the gradient. In opacity masks, when you paint with lightness, you allow the underlying object to show through, and when you paint with darkness, you hide the underlying object. In this particular case, let's surmise that we want the dolphin's tail to disappear. Drag diagonally from left to right, following the direction of the body, but release the mouse when you get to the tail. You should see a gradual fade towards the tail, as the mask passes from lightness, through shades of gray into darkness. You can apply the gradient as many times as you want until you are satisfied with the way the mask is being applied.

8.   Exit mask-editing mode by clicking on the artwork icon – in this case the dolphin – on the Transparency palette, and save the file.

9.   Add as many dolphins as you wish, scaling and rotating them before you apply an opacity mask. When you have finished, save the file. Press F twice to switch to Fullscreen Mode, press the TAB key to hide all the palettes, and CTRL/CMD+0 to fit the artwork in the window. Now sit back, fold your arms and survey the scene. You should be proud of your efforts, and to think there is still so much more to come in this book!

Printing Files Containing Transparency

At the beginning of the chapter I warned you that one of the reasons that we look at transparency at a Foundation level is because with all the effects and Symbolism Screener tools you may well be using transparency without realizing it. The problem with using transparency is the need to understand how it works when it comes to printing.

Essentially, when artwork contains transparency, Illustrator performs a process called flattening before printing the artwork. During flattening, Illustrator looks for areas where these transparent objects overlap other objects and divides the artwork into components – a little like you've seen the Pathfinder Divide function working.

The considerations that need to be taken into account will be discussed in a later chapter, so I'd suggest you hang on for a while before you rush out and have this artwork printed commercially.

Summary

Congratulations, you can definitely begin to think of yourself as a pretty accomplished Illustrator now, as you have been introduced to some fairly complex design features and come through with flying colors. At this stage we have built a fair number of the components for our case study, and in the following chapter you begin putting it all together.

I would suggest that in this chapter you really concentrate on getting those basic transparency skills firmly in your grasp, and see the Blending Modes and the Opacity Masks as the cherry on the top, material we've included just to whet your appetite.

12 Organizing your Artwork

What We'll Cover in this Chapter:

- *Setting Document Parameters and adjusting Page Boundaries*

- *Using the Print Setup box*

- *Changing the Page Zero Point and accurate placement of Guides*

- *Tiling Artwork*

- *Layout using the Align Palette*

- *Further Working with Layers*

- *Mastering the use of Smart Guides and changing Smart Guide preferences*

▶

We are now going to bring together some of the of artwork you have created so far and incorporate it into the setup of a number of pieces of publicity material for Marine Quest. During this chapter you will re-visit many of the elements that were touched upon in early chapters and explore them in greater depth.

It would be fair to say that the most interesting and creative aspects of Illustrator are embodied in tools such as the Gradient Mesh and Blends. The Paintbrushes allow you to exercise your freehand flair and the filters, styles, and effects offer a degree of experimentation and fun. When the completed work is ready for a public viewing, for example a business card, a T-shirt design, or a complete web page, the "A" team tools and commands cease to have a function. At this point, we must call upon more modest tools in order to make sure the final published work's appearance is what we originally intended.

When you're setting up, pages, rulers, guides, grids, and layers are the unsung heroes of professional artwork. These "behind the scenes" aids are responsible for the accuracy of layout. Without the assistance of these tools, your final document would be a very hit or miss affair. It is for this reason we cannot overlook the importance of understanding these tools and ensuring they are used in association with your artwork projects rather than relying on what your eyes tell you.

You already have a fundamental knowledge of these elements from what you learned in Chapter 2, but now we will use them in earnest to set up some documents. As we create the documents you will also learn how to master the finer points and use these tools quickly and efficiently.

The items required by Marine Quest are:

- A Business Card
- A large Display Poster
- A Web Page

You won't be required to create any artwork for these items. Some you have already done in previous chapters, other bits of artwork have been created for you. The focus on this chapter is preparing and bringing together all elements into a finished document ready for printing or the Web. In pre-computer times, a paste-up artist would have carried out this function, and the concept today is still the same. Accuracy and efficiency are the goals in this chapter.

Before we begin one of the projects, let's look at some of the fundamental aspects of setting up your document. You looked at this briefly, back in Chapter 1, so you will have seen some of the terms already.

Using the Document Setup Dialog Box

Create a new document using the default sizes. Once you have a new document open, you can edit the page to your required size. The fact that we have an **Artboard** and an **Imageable Area** means there are two things that can be set up within the document. Let's get some practice by changing the size of the Artboard and see what impact that has on the document.

Editing the Artboard Size

Go to File>Document Setup. When the dialog box opens, you will find Artboard is already selected from the drop-down menu in the top left of the dialog box. From the Size drop-down box, select A3. Click OK.

The Artboard size has now changed, but the printable page still shows the original Letter Size as defined by the dotted lines. It will only be possible to change the size of the printable page to A3 if the printer software installed on your computer is able to print to an A3 size. This of course means that the printer connected to your computer is also capable of printing A3 sheets of paper. The limitation is not within Illustrator, but the printer and software connected to Illustrator via the computer.

Let's run through this process, bearing in mind the computer you are using may not have the required printer driver installed to achieve the desired page size.

Using the Print Setup Dialog Box

Go to File > Print Setup. If you are working on a Mac, this option is called **Page Setup**. The drop-down box at the top of the dialog box tells you which printer driver this computer has installed, in the case shown below, a printer driver designed for an HP LaserJet 2100 printer. There is also a drop-down box labeled Paper, enabling you to specify paper size. If you have a printer capable of printing up to A3, you will be able to select A3 as the size from here. To make the change really obvious, select A5 as the page size, which is smaller than letter size. The Orientation label lets you set Landscape or Portrait. Leave the default, Portrait, and click OK.

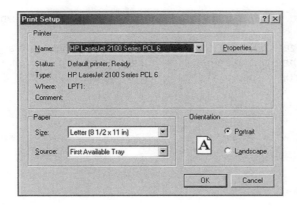

You should now be looking at the same size Artboard, set to A3 and a much smaller printable page set to A5.

Precision Layout Tools

You have had an introduction to many of the tools and aids in this section in Chapter 2. We are now going to further explore the capabilities of these tools, and good working practice, by way of a real exercise in setting up the parameters for a printed business card. As stated earlier, the artwork elements have been created for you. Your task will be to set up the layout in a professional and efficient manner ready to be finished off in Chapter 14 on preparing for print.

We will create a standard size business card based on 3.5 inches by 2 inches dimensions. For this example we are going to set up one card in the center of the page.

Open the file called `Biz_card.ai` from the download folder.

The rectangle with two colors in the center of the page is the start of the artwork. Select the rectangle and see what the dimensions are by looking in the **Info** palette. You will see this card is bigger than the finished size we want to produce. The reason for this is due to a factor called **bleed**. The bleed allows for a margin of error when cutting the artwork from the master sheet.

Let's get started. The first thing to do is display the rulers. (CTRL/CMD +R)

Make the new zero point the top left corner of the business card as in the picture below. When setting the point to an object as you are doing now, you will find the cross hairs at the tip of the cursor snap to the corner of the object.

The images I have included here are based on the finished business card with the text and logo in place. This is to demonstrate the context of the text and logo relative to the guides.

Using Guides

You will now need to place guides on the page to mark the bleed and the true finished size of the card.

1. From the vertical ruler, click and drag a guide onto the page. As you drag, keep the SHIFT key pressed. This forces the guide to snap to the increments of the ruler. Place the guide on the zero point of the top, horizontal ruler. This lines up with the left edge of the artwork. Your artwork and guide should look like the picture below. You may remember from Chapter 2 that guides lock by default when dragged onto the page. We are going to unlock them so they can be repositioned if necessary.

2. Go to View>Guides>Lock Guides. This will remove the check mark from the menu and unlock them.

Next, we need another three guides, one each for the top, bottom, and right edge of the artwork.

3. Drag another guide from the left ruler and position it on the 4-inch mark of the top ruler. This is the right edge of the artwork. Hold down the SHIFT key as you drag so the guide will snap into place on the 4-inch ruler increment.

4. Drag a guide from the top ruler and position it on the zero mark on the left vertical ruler.

5. Drag another guide from the top ruler and position it on the 2.5 inch mark on the left vertical ruler.

Your page should now look like the one shown over the page.

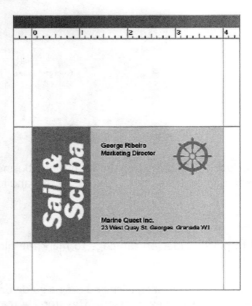

The next set of guides will define the actual card that will be cut out. In order to position these guides accurately we are going to use the Transform palette you came across in Chapter 5. If the Transform palette is not visible on the page go to Window>Transform.

> **6.** Drag another guide from the left-hand ruler and place it anywhere on the page. In the Transform palette, type 0.125 in the X box. This defines a one-eighth inch bleed from the left of the card.

> **7.** Drag another guide from the left-hand ruler, positioning anywhere as before. In the Transform palette, type 3.875 in the X box. This creates a one-eighth inch bleed from the right.

Now we need to do the same thing to create a quarter inch bleed at the top and the bottom of the card.

> **8.** Drag a guide from the top ruler this time, positioning anywhere on the page. In the Transform palette, type -0.125 in the Y box. In case you are wondering why you typed a negative number this time, bear in mind the page zero point is the top left of the business card. Any location above the zero point will be a positive number and locations below the zero point are negative numbers. You could of course have set the page zero point to the bottom left of the card, but for many people it is more logical to measure from the top left corner. It's a personal thing and you can make your own decision on this in your own projects.

9. Finally drag another guide from the top ruler and type -2.375 in the Y box of the Transform palette to position it.

We now have a full set of bleed and trim guides so we know the parameters in which we can work and the printer knows where he has to trim. Your work should now be looking like the picture below.

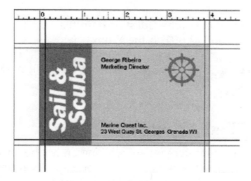

Save the current file you are working on to update the changes. Now that we have the working area of the card complete, we can start to add the elements that have been prepared for you.

Open the file called `Biz_card_components.ai` from the download folder. This file contains all the elements you need to complete the business card. Copy all the artwork from the `Biz_card_components.ai` file and paste it into your own file. You can now close the `Biz_card_components.ai` file.

Postioning the Elements Using the Transform Palette

The last thing to do is to position the elements. For efficiency we are going to use the Transform palette again. The finished business card picture in the book showed the Sail & Scuba text rotated 90 degrees, so that is the first thing to do.

1. Select the 'Sail and Scuba' text. In the Transform palette type 90 in the Rotate box and the figures in the X and Y boxes as in the picture below.

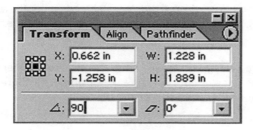

2. Select the ship's wheel. In the Transform palette type 3.36 in the X box and -0.647 in the Y box. These numbers are used based on a standard business card size.

3. Select the 'George Ribeiro...' text. In the Transform palette type 2.026 in the X box and -0.5 in the Y box.

4. Select the 'Marine Quest' text. In the Transform palette type 2.586 in the X box and -2.091 in the Y box.

Save this file calling it `Mybiz_card.ai`. You will be using it again when looking at trim marks in Chapter 15.

Working with Tiled Artwork

In many instances, the computer you are working on will be linked to a printer capable of printing a maximum paper size of letter size or perhaps A3 at best. Image setters can print full size posters, which would never be achievable on a desktop printer. Before sending a piece of work of this description to the printer it is often useful to see a proof of the work to get a feel for how it will look at full size. This is possible on your own desktop printer using Illustrator's tiling function. This function allows you to print the entire artwork on individual pages so you build up the picture like a mosaic.

Marine Quest has a poster measuring 17" by 28", roughly the equivalent of four letter size pages. Let's take a look at how we can tile this artwork and learn a few new techniques along the way.

Open the file called `Poster.ai` from the download folder.

Editing the Guide Preferences

The first thing we need to do is make the guides a little more visible. They currently merge into the background too much.

Go to Edit Preferences>Guides and Grid. There are two options in the Guides & Grid dialog box. We want to change the Color of the guide, so select Light Red from the Guides color drop-down box. The drop-down box labeled Style allows you to chose between guides that display as an unbroken line or a dotted line. Leave the style as it is and click OK.

Now the guides are clearly visible. We have a similar set up here as to when you did the business card in the last exercise. For the sake of simplicity, there is only one set of guides. These define the actual finished size of the poster.

Tiling Full Pages

You may be wondering where the dotted lines displaying the imageable and non imageable areas are. To make the file less confusing to view when you opened it, I hid these beforehand. Let's make them visible now.

1. Go to View>Show Page Tiling. Now the true size of the page becomes apparent. The dotted lines display a letter size page. If we were to print this document, all we would end up with is the top left corner. So the next step is check the size of the Artboard and set up the page tiling function.

2. Go to File>Document Setup. This is where we were at the beginning of the chapter. The Artboard has been set up to be 19 by 30 inches. In the bottom half of the dialog box you will see three options:

    - Single Page
    - Tile Full Pages
    - Tile Imageable Areas

The first option, Single Page, is set by default. This displays the dotted lines showing a letter page size as in the current document. The letter page was defined in the Print Setup box that you looked at, at the beginning of the chapter.

3. Select the second option, Tile Full Pages and click OK. This option will only display the dotted line border of a full page (as defined in the print setup box) provided it can fit onto the Artboard. In this case four pages fit fairly neatly onto the Artboard. It's not a perfect fit though. If we were to print these pages we would print a little more than was required. Look at the red guide that defines the right edge of the poster. It is just to the left of the dotted line defining our printable page. We will print more than is needed for the poster. However it is a very quick and simple way of printing a large format piece of work on a desktop printer for the purpose of a rough printed copy.

Tiling Imageable Areas and Moving Page Boundaries

There will be times when large format work does not fit exactly onto a set number of pages. Let's look at an example where another kind of tiling will be useful as well as a method for manually defining the boundary of the page.

Open the page called Large_palm.ai from the download folder.

The Artboard is 20" by 27". The tiling mode has been set to Tile Full Pages, the same as in the last exercise. This Artboard is not big enough to show more than two full pages, so the best we can achieve is the two pages you can see on screen defined by their dotted lines. Let's change the tiling mode to overcome this problem.

1. Go to File>Document Setup. Select the third option, Tile Imageable Areas and click OK. The Artboard is now divided up into a set of tiles, each tile being a page or part of a page in size. The entire Artboard is now printable, each on a separate sheet of letter size paper. The numbers that appear in the bottom left corner of each page are just for reference and do not print.

You can override the placement of the tiles relevant to the artwork. This might be desirable in many cases to prevent blank pages running through the printer or to prevent a very small element of artwork being printed on a single page, when it could be printed as part of another page. To demonstrate this potential problem, have a look at the image below. This shows the same scene as you have in your file on screen.

Because of the positioning of the artwork and the page tiling, the page numbered 1 will print even though there is no artwork on it. This is because it is the objects Bounding Box that defines whether or not it will print. The Bounding Box overlaps onto page 1 making that a printable page. Look at page 5, although this does have a small amount of artwork, it would be wasteful and time consuming to print this page when we could simply move the artwork or move the page boundary. Moving the page boundary is exactly what we are going to do now.

Select the **Page** tool. It shares the same toolbox location as the **Hand** tool. Click near the bottom left of the green artwork as in the picture below. As you click, you will see a double dotted rectangular line. This is the placement of the page that you are controlling.

It is as if you are holding the page by the bottom left corner. When you release the mouse, all the other tiled pages are displayed around it.

If you have ever tiled a kitchen wall, this is a similar principle – the first tile laid down is the critical one, as every other tile will be positioned relative to this one.

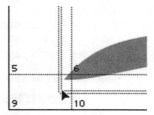

The idea from here on is to create the most economical formation of tiles so you don't end up with blank pages because the Bounding Box overlaps a page or a tiny bit of artwork that could fit on a page elsewhere. The following picture shows the finished tiling with the artwork fitting neatly onto four pages.

Using Layers

Layers, as we saw in Chapter 2, give you all the convenience of separating your artwork onto different independent layers that can be hidden, viewed, locked, combined, and a range of other clever options that make your life easier, particularly when working with complex artwork or artwork with many elements. A good working exercise of layers would be the production of a web page. We are going to lay out the Marine Quest web page using layers so you get some real working practice of how useful they really are.

First let's create a new blank document using the following settings:

- 760 pixels by 420 pixels
- RGB Color
- Landscape Orientation

There's little point using inches or centimeters here as our work will only be viewed on a screen and the only relevant measurement on screen is pixels. The size of our file is designed to fit comfortably onto a screen with a resolution of 800 by 600 pixels. Save the page calling it `Webpage.ai`. The completed web page can be seen in the image below.

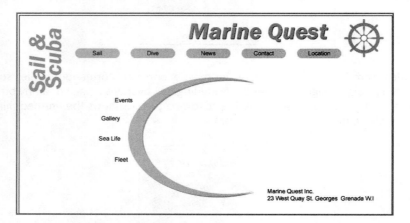

From this point on, we are going to be working with two files, the components file and the new one you have just created. Open the file called `Web_components.ai` from the download folder. This file contains all the bits that will make up the web page, but first we have to finish a few pieces off by aligning them correctly.

Using the Align Palette

Identify the 'Sail' button on the page. This button is composed of some text and a rounded rectangle. The word 'Sail' appears directly in the middle of the rectangle button. It's no coincidence, or good luck. Using the Align palette achieves this effortlessly and perfectly. So, let's make the other buttons.

1. Select the word 'Dive' and the rectangle immediately above it. These are the two objects we need to align.

2. If the Align palette is not visible go to Window>Align. The top row of this palette offers all the alignment options. Hover the cursor over each icon to see a label describing how the alignment will take place. We need to use two of these options in order to align our Dive button.

3. Click the icon second in from the left, **Horizontal Align Center** and the icon second in from the right, **Vertical Align Center**, in the top row. These icons center the selected objects horizontally and vertically respectively, which results in a perfect center alignment of our two objects.

4. Once they are aligned, make sure they are both still selected and then group them. Try using the keyboard shortcut. CTRL/CMD+G. This will make it easier to move them within the web page.

5. Follow the same steps to create the other buttons – 'News', 'Contact', and 'Location'.

Creating and Renaming Layers

Go back to your own file that you saved as Webpage.ai. We are going to rename the existing layer in this file and then create a new layer, which will be used for the buttons.

1. To rename a layer, double-click the layer in the Layers palette. Call it 'Background'.

2. Now to make a new layer, click the **New Layer** icon third from the left at the bottom of the palette. Name this new layer Top Buttons.

3. Create three more layers naming them Text, Logo, and Center Buttons. Select the layer called Top Buttons.

4. Now that the layers are set up, we need to copy and paste artwork between the two open files. Copy all the buttons from the components file into your new file. When you paste the buttons, they will automatically be pasted into the current active layer.

Using the Align Palette for the Buttons

We are going to use the **Align Palette** again to align all the buttons at the top of the page. We only need to position the first button and all the others will be aligned to it.

1. Select the 'Sail' button and, using the Transform palette, position it at X = 160, Y = 340.

Make sure none of the buttons are any higher on the page than the 'Sail' button. The highest object will be the one to which all others are aligned.

2. With the 'Sail' button selected, select all the other buttons. In the Align palette, click the icon labeled **Vertical Align Top**.

    All the buttons are now in one straight line, but they are not spaced evenly, so that is our next task. The Align palette will also do this for us. The second row of the Align palette offers the option to Distribute Objects, otherwise known as spacing evenly.

    We need to define the horizontal position of the last button in order to keep control over this process. The distribution of all the buttons will be based on the position of the button at the extreme left and extreme right. Select the 'Location' button and position it using the Transform palette to X position 612. There is no need to change the Y co-ordinate as you have already aligned this.

3. Select all the buttons, and then click the **Horizontal Distribute Center** icon in the Align palette, fifth from the left in the bottom row.

The final components can now be copied and pasted into the new file. Select all the artwork from the Web_components.ai file and paste them into the 'background' layer of the new file.

Dragging Artwork Between Layers

Layers are completely flexible making it possible to move artwork easily between layers. We are going to transfer all of the components that currently reside on the 'background' layer onto their own named layer.

1. Select the ship's wheel. The background layer becomes active. In this layer you will see a small blue square appear to the right of the layer name. This blue square relates to the selected artwork on the page. Place the cursor over this blue button and the cursor changes to a pointing finger icon.

2. Drag the blue square up to the Logo layer. This action transfers the selected artwork from its current layer to the layer on to which is dragged. On the Artboard, position the wheel in the top right corner of the page.

3. Use the same technique to transfer the 'Marine Quest', 'Sail & Surf' text, and address block to the layer called Text. By selecting all three of the text objects, they will be transferred at the same time. Position the objects on the page as in the example.

4. Finally select the four text objects named Events, Gallery, Sea Life, and Fleet. Transfer these text objects to the layer called Center Buttons.

Using the Align Palette to Distribute Vertically

Position these four text objects around the crescent using the original picture in the book as a guide. We will use the Align palette to distribute the text objects vertically, so they will be spaced evenly.

1. Select the four text objects.

2. In the Align palette click the **Vertical Distribution Center** icon, second in from the left on the bottom row.

We will be returning to the subject of the web pages and web graphics in later on in the book.

Releasing Artwork to Separate Layers

This function of layers is particularly useful when creating animated sequences. Artwork on one layer can be distributed across separate layers. Open the file called `Release_layers.ai` from the download folder.

The cloud, rain, and lightning are all one layer called Weather in the Layers palette. Each separate artwork component is housed in its own sub layer within the Weather layer. The small thumbnail preview on each sub layer allows you to identify the artwork that it contains and the word describes what it is. In this case the yellow lightning and the cloud are described as Path and the rain is a group, so we see the word Group.

We are now going to do two processes to separate each artwork piece on to different layers. Select the Weather layer. Click the black arrow button in the top right corner of the Layers palette and from the pop-up menu that appears select Release to Layers (Sequence).

This releases each item to a new layer. You now have three new layers numbered sequentially. Each layer contains one of the components. Expand each of the new layers by clicking the gray arrowhead button. This reveals the individual components again, showing the path and group.

Using Layers as Templates

This function of layers is perfect for when you want to use another piece of artwork or a photo as an object to trace around.

Open the file called `Template_layers.ai` from the download folder.

The bottom layer on this file is called fish. It is a normal layer and the fish picture in the layer can be moved as normal. We are going to prevent any editing of this layer and also prevent the layer from printing.

1. Double-click on the fish layer to bring up the Layer Options dialog box.

2. Check the Template check box to enable the Dim images to field. This allows you to put a number in the percentage box and the artwork on this layer will be dimmed accordingly allowing your own artwork to stand out with greater clarity. Leave 50 in the box and click OK.

The photo is now dimmed on the page and the layer is also locked as depicted by the padlock icon appearing in the fish layer. The icon next to the padlock confirms that this layer is a Template layer.

3. To return it to a normal layer, double-click the fish layer to open the layer options dialog box, then uncheck the Template check box. You will also notice a checkbox for Print and Lock. Unchecking the print box will also prevent artwork on that layer from printing. Checking the Lock option will prevent any editing from being carried out on that layer.

Duplicating Artwork Using Layers

If you have a large amount of artwork on a layer and wish to try out a few design ideas without affecting what you have already done, one of the easiest ways is to simply duplicate the entire layer. You can then edit as much as you wish without affecting the original layer.

Open the file called `Duplicate_layers.ai` from the download folder. We are going to duplicate everything on this layer. Select the layer, and then click the black arrow button in the top right corner of the Layers palette. Choose Duplicate "Sea" from the pop-up menu. A new layer called 'Sea Copy' is created which has all the same artwork as the original layer.

Alternatively you can drag the layer you want to duplicate onto the **Create New Layer** icon at the bottom of the Layers palette.

Flattening Layers

During the process of creating artwork, you may build a number of layers. Once you have completed your scene, there may be no reason to keep the many layers and you may find it practical to combine all the layers into one layer.

1. Open the file called `Flatten_layers.ai` from the download folder. The waves in this scene were built up on many layers. We will now flatten all the layers into one.

2. Double-click the top layer and in the dialog box that opens, rename it Final Scene.

3. Click the black arrow button in the top right corner of the Layers palette. Choose Flatten Artwork from the pop-up menu. Any individual components of artwork still remain independent, but they are all brought together into the uppermost layer, the one we called Final Scene.

Smart Guides

The Smart Guides provide a way to use an existing object as a point of reference for creating further objects that line up with the segments, anchor points, and center points of the reference object. Rather than dragging guides from the rulers manually, the guides are created in relation to the position of the cursor on the screen whenever you have one of the object tools selected. The guide is not permanent as it disappears as soon as the cursor is moved out of alignment. This dynamic interaction between objects and guides can be far quicker than using the conventional guides in many circumstances. Let's get some experience with smart guides.

Open the file called `Smart_guides.ai` from the download folder. The first thing we need to do is enable the Smart Guides.

1. Go to View>Smart Guides. A check next to the menu item means they are enabled already.

This file acts as a template demonstrating how the smart guides operate. The green rectangle in the middle of the page is the reference object.

The goal is to create a series of rectangles that all line up with certain segments or anchor points of the green rectangle. The red dotted line rectangles are provided as a guide to where you will be creating your own. The yellow dotted lines illustrate where the smart guides are going to appear. Let's begin.

2. Using the **Selection** tool, hover the cursor over the anchor points of the green rectangle. As you do so, you will see words appear describing the point over which the cursor is hovering. Anchor appears when you are over a corner point, Path when you are over the edge of the shape, and Center when you over the center point. Place the cursor over any yellow dotted line and the smart guide appears. Move the cursor away from the yellow dotted line and the smart guide disappears. The guide will only appear if you are directly aligned with one of the anchors, paths, or center point of an object. Place the cursor over a place where two yellow dotted lines cross over each other. Now two smart guides appear and the word intersection appears. This confirms that guides created from two different reference points on an object are intersecting each other.

We will now use the alignment information the smart guides give us to create some rectangles that are in perfect alignment with some point of the green rectangle.

3. Select the **Rectangle** tool. We are going to create a rectangle on top of the rectangle numbered 1. Hover the cursor over the yellow dotted line leading to rectangle 1. You will see the smart guide appear. Follow the dotted line, keeping the mouse in a straight line as you drag up the page until you come to the bottom left anchor point of the red dotted line rectangle. The word Anchor appears to confirm you are over the anchor point of the rectangle.

Now draw a rectangle using the red dotted lines as a guide. Your new rectangle is now in perfect alignment with the center point of the green rectangle.

4. Hover the cursor over the yellow dotted line that leads to rectangle 2 until the smart guide appears. This guide aligns the bottom right anchor point of the green rectangle with the top left anchor point of rectangle 2. When the cursor is held over the top left anchor point of rectangle 2, the word Anchor appears confirming you are over the anchor point. Now you can create your own rectangle using the red dotted lines as a guide again.

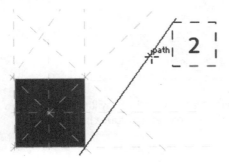

5. Continue this process for each of the other rectangles. Each time you will be aligning different areas of the rectangles, but they will all have some common reference points.

Once all of your objects are created, place the cursor over different intersecting guides and you will also see information referring to angles of degree at which the guides intersect. The angles at which smart guides are created can be defined in the smart guides preferences.

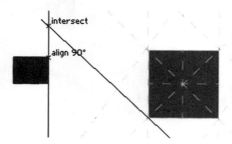

Setting the Smart Guide Preferences

1.   Go to Edit>Preferences>Smart Guides and Slices. In the dialog that opens the Angles drop-down box offers the options for the angles of degree for intersection. 90 and 45 are the default setting.

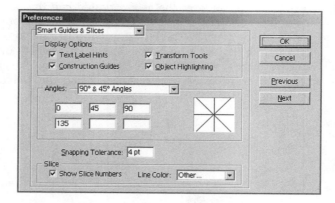

2.   Change this to 90 and you will see the preview window to the right of the drop-down box reflect your change.

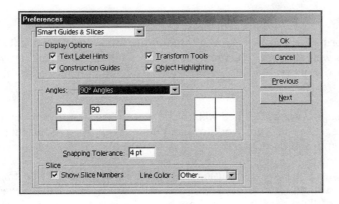

The six white number boxes below the Angles drop-down box display the angles that will be used to create smart guides. You can also type a number in this box to create customized angles. Type 279 in one of the empty boxes, then click on a gray part of the dialog box or another empty number box to confirm the addition and the preview window will show you this new guide angle.

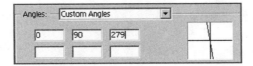

The Snapping Tolerance refers to how close the cursor must be to an object or point of alignment in order for the smart guide to become active. 4 pt is the default setting, so if your cursor is 5 pts away from the object or point of alignment, it won't create a guide. The lower the number, the more sensitive the smart guides will be.

There are a number of check boxes that can be chosen in the Display Options section. The following gives a brief explanation of each:

- Text Label Hints – displays information about the position to which the cursor is currently snapped, such as an Anchor Point.

- Construction Guides – allows you to see guidelines in the file as you use Smart Guides.

- Transform Tools – Smart Guides assist you when scaling, rotating, and shearing objects.

- Object Highlighting – highlights the object below the cursor as you drag around it.

3. Select the original setting of 90 and 45 and click OK.

Summary

This chapter has served to reinforce some of the fundamental concepts learned in earlier chapters as well as giving you some hands on experience of actual artwork projects. The Business card you created will be taken forward to when you set up the final parameters for print.

The knowledge you have gained will enable you to keep a track of complex artwork with greater ease, speed up your workflow, and understand the need to take into account the limitations imposed by printers.

In this chapter you have been using text objects that were created for you. In the next chapter you will be creating your own text and learning about the powerful text handling capabilities of Illustrator, not only from a word processing point of view, but as a truly creative text generation tool.

13 Creating and Formatting Type

What We'll Cover in this Chapter:

- *Creating copy with the various Type tools*

- *Formatting type at a Character level with the Type menu and the Character Palette*

- *Setting Type Preferences*

- *Formatting type at a Paragraph level with the Paragraph Palette*

- *Working with Larger Volumes of Text*

- *Creating Graphics from Type*

Although Illustrator is often thought of as a vector application, designed primarily for the creation of vector graphics, which you would then import into a print page-layout application, we have already seen that its scope goes far beyond this, in the production of graphics for web and print delivery. In this chapter, our focus is on the use of type within Illustrator.

We will continue on our development of the Marine Quest case study, with refinement of the logo and other components developed in the previous chapter, and we'll also get some of our brochure created in this chapter as well. So without delay, let's discover what Illustrator has to offer us in the way of type management.

The Type Tools

The first thing that will make you sit up and take note of Illustrator is the plethora of type tools you'll see when you expand the **Type** tool flyout for the toolbox:

Before we start, let's cut the number of type tools in half. Notice the arrows next to the icons and the different orientation of the text in the second half of the tool flyout – that should be a clue. The second set of three tools is essentially identical to the first three tools, except that they place text vertically instead of horizontally.

The Type Tool

This is the tool that you will find yourself using the majority of the time as you work with type in Illustrator.

With the **Type** tool, you have two means by which you can place type on the page. If you wish to place a label or a name on a business card for example, simply click with the **Type** tool (T) and begin to type. The result is the creation of a horizontally expanding line of text, which does not wrap unless you press ENTER/RETURN to force the text to another line:

Grenada is a rolling, mountainous island, covered with perfumed spice trees and extraordinary tropical flowers

The alternate means is to click and drag to create a 'text box' area. The width and height of this text box constrains the placement of text on the page. You create text boxes to hold larger volumes of text and paragraphs.

You may notice the columns in the screen below – I'll be showing you how to create them as well a little later.

Grenada is a rolling, mountainous island, covered with perfumed spice trees and extraordinary tropical flowers. Bordered by spectacular beaches, and dotted with picturesque towns, this lush island has long been a major source of nutmeg, cloves, ginger, cinnamon, and cocoa. In the interior of this volcanic island are cascading rivers and waterfalls, lush rainforests, and one of the most breathtakingly beautiful mountain lakes imaginable. The capital, St. George's, is widely held to be the loveliest city in the Caribbean. A pastel rainbow of dockside warehouses and the red-tiled roofs of traditional shops and homes surround its horseshoe-shaped harbour. Grenada's physical beauty is complemented by its rich history and vibrant, living cultural heritage. Local festivals, fairs, and markets remain an integral part of life on Grenada. Its centuries old spice plantations and rum distilleries still use traditional methods, emphasizing quality rather than quantity. Although the tourist industry has become more substantial in recent years, the island's easy rhythms and the friendly openness of its residents evoke an atmosphere that has long since vanished elsewhere in the Caribbean.

Have a close look at the cursor icon for the **Type** tool – do you notice the little crossbar a little way up from the base of the icon? When you start to click and drag, it is the position of that crossbar which determines the top of the text box, and not the position of the top of the cursor icon.

Another point to consider is how to resize a text box if it is too small or too big for your text. Use the Bounding Box to facilitate such changes. If you have switched the Bounding Box off, as many of us do, go to View>Show Bounding Box (CTRL/CMD+SHIFT+B).

If you wish to create another text area on a page, you must first de-select the text area that is active. Do this by choosing the **Selection** tool, and clicking anywhere on the page away from any components, or hold down the CTRL/CMD key to temporarily toggle to a **Selection** tool, and click on the page.

The Area Type Tool

Although the majority of your text may be placed inside rectangular text boxes, there will also be times when you want to work with text artistically and place it inside an irregular shape, so that the content of the text is enhanced by the shape which it makes on the page.

A word of advice about using the **Area Type** tool, though! Sometimes we tend to get carried away with our sense of artistic creativity, and forget about the larger picture and the aim of text, which is primarily to convey information. When you place text inside an irregular container, letter and word spacing can be erratic, and consequently aspects like readability are severely diminished.

If the text is difficult to read, people won't read it, no matter how pretty it looks on the page:

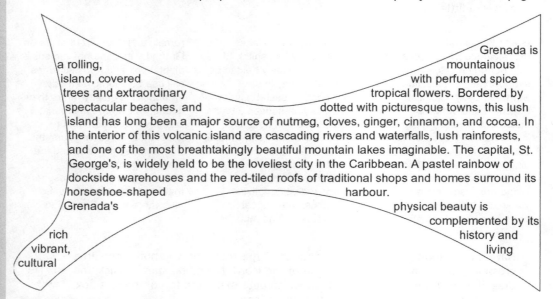

a rolling, island, covered trees and extraordinary spectacular beaches, and island has long been a major source of nutmeg, cloves, ginger, cinnamon, and cocoa. In the interior of this volcanic island are cascading rivers and waterfalls, lush rainforests, and one of the most breathtakingly beautiful mountain lakes imaginable. The capital, St. George's, is widely held to be the loveliest city in the Caribbean. A pastel rainbow of dockside warehouses and the red-tiled roofs of traditional shops and homes surround its horseshoe-shaped harbour. Grenada's Grenada is mountainous with perfumed spice tropical flowers. Bordered by dotted with picturesque towns, this lush physical beauty is complemented by its history and living rich vibrant, cultural

Placing Text Inside a Path

Before you place text inside an irregular shape, the first thing you'll need, of course, is an irregular shape! When you create this shape, you do not need to worry about whether it has a stroke or a fill, because both will automatically be removed when you place the text inside the container.

With that container selected, move the text cursor over the edge of the shape and notice what happens – automatically Illustrator detects the shape below and changes to the **Area Type** tool.

When you move the cursor over the selected path, again it is the little crossbar on the cursor icon that indicates exactly where you must click – line the crossbar up on the path and then click. The cursor will automatically appear within the path and you can begin to type.

There will be times though when you must select the **Area Type** tool and this is when the shape into which you wish to place the text is an open path, because Illustrator may erroneously presume that you wish to place the text on the path and not inside the path. Keep an eye on the cursor – it will always tell you how Illustrator is interpreting your instructions. With the **Type** tool, move the cursor over a selected path, and Illustrator will then indicate whether it thinks you want to place the text within or on the path by displaying the appropriate cursor. Hold down the ALT/OPTION key to temporarily access the other **Type** tool.

The Path Type Tool

The **Path Type** tool is very often used to give movement to text as illustrated in the text below, or alternatively, you may have seen examples where the text seems to follow around the outline of a circle, in logo design. In fact, you are going to create this! You now know what one of the components of this chapter's case study is.

As with the **Area Type** tool, overuse of the **Path Type** tool, and a lack of attention to letter and word spacing can often destroy what was essentially a solid design concept. As we discover the Character palette, you will learn ways of controlling this spacing, and make constant use of it to ensure that your type designs are esthetically pleasing.

Placing Text on a Path

As with the **Area Type** tool, you'll need either an open or closed path shape, which is selected before you can place the text on the path. With the **Type** tool active, if the path is open, the cursor icon will automatically change to indicate that you will be placing the text on the path. If it is a closed path, you should either choose the **Path Type** tool, or hold down the ALT/OPTION key if the **Area Type** tool is showing to tell Illustrator that you wish to place the text on the path.

Once again, notice the crossbar on the cursor. This must be lined up exactly on the path for Illustrator to place the text on the path. Additionally, the text will start from the precise point at which you clicked on the path. The cursor will automatically appear at that position on the path and you can begin to type.

If you place the text at the incorrect position, and want to change it, you can edit the position of the curve fairly easily on the path. Switch to the **Selection** tool – remembering not to use those singe letter shortcuts – and click on the path to select it if it is not already selected. At the beginning of the text, you'll notice an I-beam icon. Move your mouse over the I-beam and drag along the line to reposition the text.

The first few times you attempt to do this, you may find that you miss the I-beam, and move the path unintentionally. Choose Edit>Undo (CTRL/CMD+Z) to move the path back to its position, and try again. To change the orientation of the text so that it is placed underneath the path and going in the opposite direction, double-click on the I-beam. Also bear in mind that both the **Area Type** tool and the **Path Type** tool are placing type in relation to a path, and so to edit the shape of the path, you simply switch to the **Direct Selection** tool and select and then modify the shape of the path. The text will re-flow automatically.

Case Study: Refining the Marine Quest Logo (I)

As your skills grow, George and Lucy are always looking for ways to incorporate all these wonderful features in their company's publications, and they have a new request. They like the ship's wheel logo, and think it's a good idea to incorporate the Marine Quest company name within it, especially for instances where they just wish to place a small logo as opposed to the logo and a separate company name.

The logo has a circular appearance, so it seems logical that you could place the company name at the top of the ship's wheel, and then a catchphrase at the base, rotating the text on a circular path around the wheel:

In this first part of the exercise we'll just concentrate on placing the text on the paths so that it rotates around the logo, and explore some of the considerations in placing the text above and below the logo. Later on in this chapter, we'll return to the exercise and refine the placement and style of the text, so do not be concerned if your logo does not look like the one in the illustration just yet.

1.   Open the file called Logo.ai. Ensure that **Smart Guides** are on to allow you to perfectly align the circle as you begin to draw it. Switch to the **Ellipse** tool (L).

2.   Move your cursor over the position where the two guides intersect. Hold down the ALT/OPTION key to indicate that you wish to draw this shape from the center. Click to display the Ellipse Options dialog box and enter 0.934 in the Width field. Remember you do not have to re-type this value

in the Height field – simply by clicking on the word Height, Illustrator will copy the value into the field for you. Click OK to create the circle.

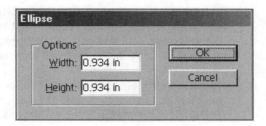

3. Display the Transform palette and check that the object's reference point is in the center of the icon, that the X and Y fields reflect 0 in to indicate that the center of the circle is at exactly 0, and that the W and H fields display 0.934 in. If these are not your values, you can correct them.

4. With the path selected, switch to the **Type** tool (T) and move the cursor over the path. Note that it automatically switches to the **Area Type** tool because you are over a closed path. As you don't want this, you can either choose the **Type on a Path** tool directly from the toolbox, or hold down the Alt/Option key so the cursor changes to indicate that the **Type on a Path** tool is selected.

5. Line the crosshair up at the position at the top of the circle where the guide intersects the circle and click to create an insertion point.

6. Type the words Marine Quest. Notice as you do, that the words are typed clockwise starting from the 12 o'clock position. We'll be back later to correct that, and to choose the font and type size.

7.   But now, the tricky work begins. We wish to place the words 'Sail & Scuba' at the base of the circle, but we need to make them go in the opposite direction so that they read left to right, and it is impossible in Illustrator to have two sets of words running in different directions on a single path, so we cheat – just a little. Ensure that the original path is selected with the **Selection** tool and copy it by choosing Edit>Copy (CTRL/CMD+C). You now have a copy of this text and path up on the clipboard.

8.   To make our life easier, we need to lock this original text otherwise we might keep selecting it. Choose Object>Lock>Selection (CTRL/CMD+2). The original Marine Quest text will remain visible, but we will not be able to select it.

9.   Now we'll paste a copy of that original text exactly on top of the visible path by choosing Edit>Paste in Front (CTRL/CMD+F). You may be fooled into thinking that this is just the original text, but remember we locked that one, and this pasted text should be highlighted, which indicates that it is selected. This means that it must be a copy.

10. This text needs to be manipulated so that it is running from left to right. Position your cursor, with the **Selection** tool selected, over the I-beam as indicated in the screenshot below:

11. Double-click on the I-beam and the text will move to the inside of the circle and run from left to right. You should now see that the original text still exists, and was perfectly hidden behind the pasted text. With the **Type** tool selected, click in the "Marine Quest" text on the left hand side of the circle and choose Select>All (CTRL/CMD+A) to highlight it. Note the other Marine Quest is not highlighted for two reasons – it is on another path, and it is still locked. Type "Sail & Scuba" to replace the second instance of Marine Quest.

12. Save the file.

Formatting Characters

In terms of characters, Illustrator's Character palette works in much the same way as any of the popular word processing applications. Font, character style, and character size can be manipulated in exactly the same way. However, here's a quick run down of the more layout-based issues which may not come up on the average document.

Leading

Leading (pronounced 'ledding') is essentially the space between lines in a paragraph measured from one baseline to the baseline below – so called because of the lead strips that professional typesetters used to hammer between lines of text all those years back.

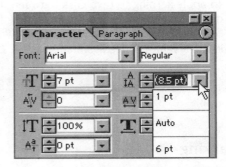

You may notice in the screenshot that there is an option called Auto, and also that the value which is at present in the field next to Leading icon has brackets around it. The presence of brackets indicates that the auto-leading value is being used, which is set at

120% of the font size in use. Once again you are not limited by the preset values, and you can also use the keyboard shortcuts, Alt/Option+Up Arrow and Alt/Option+Down Arrow, to increase or decrease the leading values, and increase that value by a multiple of 5 by adding the Ctrl/Cmd key to the combination. These values are also controlled by the initial values set in your **Type** Preferences.

In our brochure, we'll be upping that leading just a little, to give the impression that this is an exclusive and desirable venture. The aesthetics of a document are that delicate!

Kerning

Kerning is the spacing between character pairs, and so to apply a kerning value, we click in between the characters we wish to kern as opposed to highlighting them.

VA VA

In the text above, the characters on the left have not been kerned, whilst those on the right have. Many fonts today already have kerning pairs built in the font, but there are instances where you may find you need to kern character pairs manually to get the desired effect, especially if you wish to create a logo from letterforms, or have text placed on a path.

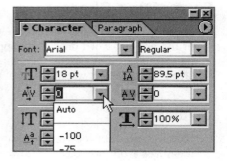

To apply kerning to text, click between the two characters you wish to kern, and from the drop-down menu on the Character palette either choose a preset value or enter your own, or use Alt/Option+Right Arrow and Alt/Option+Left Arrow to increase or decrease the kerning values. Once again adding that Ctrl/Cmd key will increase the multiple by 5.

Grenada Grenada Grenada
-100   0   +100

Tracking

Tracking is similar to kerning, in that you are adding or removing space, but this time it is to highlighted letters and words, instead of directly to character pairs. As tracking is applied to text, you must highlight the text before you attempt to apply any tracking values.

You would use tracking if you wanted to create an artistic effect with text in headings slightly more spaced than an auto setting would allow, or if you placed text along a path and noticed that the letters had become a little too cramped or too loose as a result of the shape of a path.

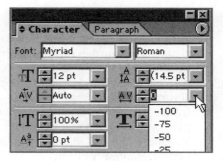

To apply tracking to text, highlight the letters or words you wish to track, and from the drop-down menu on the Character palette, choose either a preset value or enter your own. The shortcut is the same as that for kerning, ALT/OPTION+RIGHT Arrow and ALT/OPTION+LEFT Arrow, to increase or decrease the tracking values, and adding that CTRL/CMD key will once again increase the multiple by 5. The difference lies in what has been selected. If you click between character pairs, Illustrator knows that you want to apply kerning to the text, but if you highlight characters or words, Illustrator will assume that it is the tracking values that you wish to change.

Vertically and Horizontally Scaling Text

The options on the Character palette also allow you to scale text, but I would advise that you apply any scaling judiciously. Remember that the font has normally been designed for optimum readability and if you stretch and scale the text excessively, you will be destroying the very medium that you are using to convey your message.

Grenada   Grenada   Grenada

Vertical scaling at 150%   Horizontal scaling at 150%

In the examples above, I have applied either vertical or horizontal scaling. You can apply scaling along both axes on the same words, but this is a little pointless, as it would be far easier if you simply changed the font size.

If you wish to apply either vertical or horizontal scaling to your type, highlight the type and chose a value from the drop-down menu on the Character palette, click the UP or DOWN arrows next to the relevant scaling field, or enter your own value.

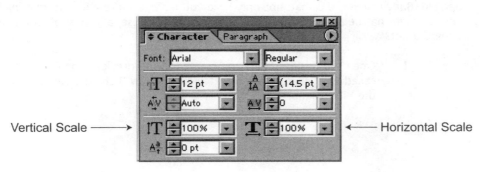

Vertical Scale ⟶   ⟵ Horizontal Scale

Baseline Shift

The last feature on the Character palette is the option to change the position of a character or word in relation to that line of text's baseline. You may remember that when I discussed leading, I said that it is measured from the baseline of one line of text to the baseline of the line below, but I did not really go into what the baseline was other than by illustrating it in a diagram. The baseline is the imaginary line on which text sits, excluding the length of the descenders, (downward tails on letters such as 'g') which go through the baseline. So by using baseline shift, you are moving the text up or down in relation to that imaginary line on which it was set. Once again, be careful about using baseline shift excessively. Reserve its use for one or two characters for artistic effect. If you find yourself having to baseline shift entire lines or paragraphs it may well be that your leading settings need attention.

In the example below, I wanted to kern the space between the C and the o, so that the word seemed to be enclosed within the letter C, but in order to do so, it was necessary to baseline shift the C downwards in order to line up the gap in the C with the rest of the word.

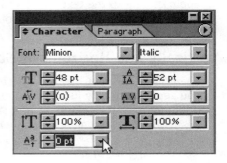

As with previous options on the Character palette, highlight the text you wish to affect and then choose the value from the relevant drop-down menu, enter your own value, or use the small arrowheads to the left of the value field to change the values incrementally.

Case Study: Refining the Business Card (I)

In the previous chapter, you accurately created a business card with text that has been supplied. But since you did that, not only have you learned more about formatting text, but also there has been a change in the choice of font in use, and possibly a few more changes afoot?

1.   Open the business card you created in the previous chapter, or the one called `Biz_card.ai`, and switch to the view Bizcard created for you on the View menu.

2. Before we begin to manipulate the file, let's set our **Type** preferences. Display the Type Preferences dialog box, and change the Size/Leading value to 0.5pt, as we will change the size of the text using both the Character palette and the keyboard shortcuts.

3. The set-up of your file should be exactly the same as this, so let's just check that Layer palette.

4. The guides and the bottom layer containing the rectangles need to be locked. You may wish to change the name of the bottom layer to Rectangles.

5. Ensure that the ship's wheel logo is on the art layer. If it isn't, move it to this layer, and then lock the art layer

6. Make the text layer your active layer.

7. The first text we'll edit is the Sail & Scuba grouped text on the left-hand side of the business card. As we will be applying the same text formatting to both of these text objects, it will be easier if we select them with the **Selection** tool. To select them, either click on the imaginary baseline of one of the words, or marquee drag with the **Selection** tool. With the objects selected, change the settings as shown below:

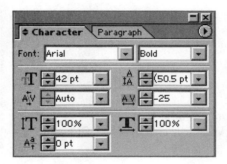

8. On the Transform palette, ensure that the reference point is set to the center location, and reset the position of the object to -1.25 on the Y-axis.

9. Now we'll move on to formatting George's name and his title. We'll do this by using the Character palette and also keyboard shortcuts. Select the **Type** tool (T) and click in George Ribeiro to create an insertion point. Triple-click with the mouse, to select the paragraph – which is effectively George Ribeiro because the ENTER/RETURN key has been pressed after his name to force the title onto a new line.

10. On the Character palette, ensure that the Font has been set to Arial (or Helvetica) and the style to Bold. Change the size to 11pt, using either the drop-down menu or by inputting the value yourself. You might wish to be brave and even try that CTRL/CMD+SHIFT+> keyboard shortcut to increase the size.

11. To increase the contrast between name and title, we'll reduce the size of the title – this time using the keyboard shortcut. Triple-click to select the title Marketing Director and using CTRL/CMD+SHIFT+<, decrease the point size until it is 8.5 pts. Ensure that the font is Arial (or Helvetica) and the style is set to Regular.

12. With the text Marketing Director still selected, type the words Dive Instructor. Notice that because you had the original text highlighted, typing new text replaces the original text.

13. We've built the contrast into the upper area of text, and now it's time to have a look at the bottom – the text that deals with the contact information. The first thing to do is to check the alignment of the two text blocks because even if it looks aligned on screen, there is always a chance that it is slightly out and this will be visible in print. Select both text blocks with the **Selection** tool and choose Horizontal Align Left from the Align palette:

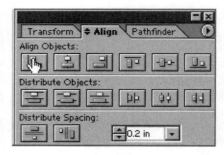

George Ribeiro
Dive Instructor

Marine Quest Inc.
23 West Quay St. Georges Grenada W.I

14. Select the text Marine Quest Inc. by triple-clicking with the **Type** tool and format it as follows:

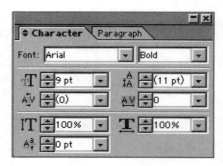

→ **Marine Quest Inc.**
23 West Quay St. Georges Grenada W.I

15. Select the address text and format that as Arial/Helvetica, size 8.5 pt, Style Regular. We also need to add some additional contact details for Lucy and George's international clients. To add the additional lines of text, ensure the end of the line by pressing END, and then press ENTER/RETURN to insert another line of text.

16. Type the telephone number +1473-555-5678 and then press ENTER/RETURN again to move to another line. Then type the web address, www.marinequestinc.com. Ensure that all the text for the contact details, excluding the name of the company, is formatted as Arial or Helvetica, size 8.5 pt, Style Regular.

17. Select all the lines in that text block, including the Marine Quest Inc. line, and then have a look at the Character palette. Notice how no values are being displayed for the Font, Style, Size, or Leading. This is not a fault with the application. The lines that you have selected contain mixed information for all of these aspects and consequently Illustrator cannot display the information.

18. The text looks a little too vertically spaced. With the text still selected, change the Leading value to 9 pt. You will have to enter the value in the field yourself, but because your measurement system is set to points for text, you need enter only the value, 9, and not the measurement system, pt.

19. The last remaining problem with the text seems to be that the web address seems to have more space above it than the previous lines in that block. The reason for this is that the web address contains no uppercase letters, and consequently that space gives us the optical illusion of being greater than the others. What we'll do to rectify this is use baseline shift on that last line. Double-click with the **Type** tool to select the web address, and then adjust the baseline shift to between 1.5 and 2 pt depending on your personal preference.

20. Select the contact details text block with the **Selection** tool, and then using the Transform palette, reposition the block so that the lower left-hand position is at -2.257 in.

21. Save the file as Biz_card2.ai and close the file. We will work on it again once we have completed our manipulation of the new logo.

Case Study: Refining the Marine Quest Logo (II)

With all these powerful character formatting tools, you are now in a position to complete that ship's wheel logo. We will also pull out a few tricks from the Paragraph palette as we go, just to get you employing those word processing skills in a design context!

1. Open the file called Logo.ai, which you used earlier in this chapter.

2. The first thing we'll do is correct the alignment of the text on the circle. We want Marine Quest at the top center, and Sail & Scuba at the bottom center. We could reposition the text by selecting the text with the **Selection** tool, and then dragging the I-beam that appears, but that would rely on our eye for placement, and we're going for accuracy here. Switch to the **Type** tool and click inside Sail & Scuba to create an insertion point. Display the Paragraph palette (CMD/CTRL+M) and choose Center alignment for the text. The text is now placed at the top center of the circle, but we need to move it to the bottom.

 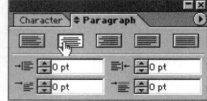

3. Switch to the **Selection** tool, and select the Sail & Scuba text object. Choose the **Rotate** tool, press RETURN/ENTER to display the Rotate dialog box and enter a rotation angle of 180.deg. Click OK to accept the value, and the Sail & Scuba text will swivel round to the bottom of the circle.

4. To move the Marine Quest text to the top center, you may need to unlock it first (Object>Unlock All). Select the text with the **Selection** tool, and then choose Center alignment on the Paragraph palette.

5. Select the Marine Quest text with the **Selection** tool, or use the **Type** tool and triple-click to highlight the text. Using the Character palette,

format the text as Arial Bold, size 18, and set the Tracking to -10 to tighten up the letter spacing around the circle.

6. Select the Sail & Scuba text and format it as Arial Bold, size 12 and tracking -8. Then finally, to place this text in its correct position on the circle, change the baseline shift to -9.83pt.

7. Look carefully at the spacing between individual letters in both sets of text, and determine whether there seem to be any unequal spaces. At first glance, I think that the space between the 'S' and 'a' of 'Sail' could possibly do with a little kerning, as could the space between the 'S' and 'c' of 'Scuba'. Remember that kerning is something that must be done with a very delicate hand. With the **Type** tool, click in between the two letters, making sure you don't highlight them, and then kern, using either the Character palette, or the keyboard shortcut ALT/OPTION+LEFT Arrow.

8. One final step, and our logo is finished. We need to color the text. From the Window menu choose Swatch Libraries>Other Library, and locate the Logo_colors.ai file. This will open a palette with the two spot colors used in the logo and other corporate materials. Highlight the text, and set the fill to the stronger blue, with no stroke.

9. Select all the objects and group them with Object>Group (CTRL/CMD+G). Save the file, and then take a break.

Case Study: Refining the Business Card (II)

Having completed the new logo design, you're eager to show it off to George and Lucy when they next visit the office, and you've decided that it might look good on a few of the components already completed. You're hesitant to make major changes to the completed articles, so we'll build in an escape hatch – just in case they're not keen on the new design. You'd hate to have to reconstruct materials at this late stage.

1. Open your business card, Biz_card2.ai.

2. Create a new layer called Logo Alternative and position it above the art layer in the Layers palette. Lock all the other layers.

3. We are going to drag a copy of the completed logo onto this layer. Arrange the two open files so that you can see the contents of both. With the **Selection** tool, select the new logo and drag it across onto the business card. Don't worry where you place it for the moment. Close the logo file.

4. Select the new logo and drag it roughly into position at the top right - hand corner of the business card. Switch off the eye next to the art layer.

5. Select the new logo and position it at 2.82 in on the X-axis and -0.208 in on the Y-axis, with the Reference Point set at the top left-hand corner.

6. Now we'll scale the logo to an exact value, and keep it in proportion at the same time. Type 1 in the W field, but do not press ENTER/RETURN yet. Hold down the CTRL/CMD key and then press ENTER/RETURN. Both values will change to 1, thus keeping the proportion of the logo intact.

7. Now with the new logo, you can display this option to George and Lucy when they pop in, and if they do not like it, you can delete the new layer, and set the art layer back to being visible. This saves you having to create multiple files to open and show the client. Just remember to delete layers you don't need. Save and close the file.

Working with Larger Volumes of Text

It is unlikely that we will ever use Illustrator as a total replacement for our page-layout packages as it lacks some of the necessary tools for handling the larger volumes of text in text heavy publications. However, it does already have some powerful features for managing text.

Importing Text

It is likely that the text you are going to use in your publication may have been already created in a word processing application. It's far more efficient to import the text into Illustrator, with the added bonus that in some file formats, any styling previously applied will be retained. Illustrator will import text from Microsoft Word 97, 98, and 2000 documents, Rich Text Formats, and plain text files, although with the plain text files, all formatting will be lost.

One of the most efficient ways to import the text directly into Illustrator is to create a text box by clicking and dragging with the **Type** tool, and then, with the insertion point within that text box, to choose File>Place and select the text file to be imported. Doing so this way ensures that the text is automatically positioned in the correct place. You can import without a text box active, but this does mean that you will have to resize and re-position the text box.

> *Always use the* Bounding Box *– which you access from the* View *menu –*
> *to change the size of text boxes, to avoid any inadvertent scaling or*
> *transforming of text.*

Setting Text in Rows and Columns

Obviously once you have imported a larger volume of text, it's unlikely that you would want to spend your time drawing numbers of different text boxes in an attempt to simulate columns of text on the page, and having your text in one long line makes it difficult for the reader. Luckily in Illustrator we have a feature for instantly creating rows and columns from our text.

With the text box selected, choose Rows and Columns from the Type menu. If the option is grayed out, it is likely that you either do not have a text box selected, or you have the **Type** tool, as opposed to the **Selection** tool, active.

Once you have opted to create either rows or columns, or both, you'll be faced by another dialog box:

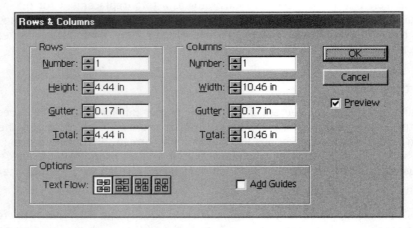

Essentially, the only factors that you have to worry about are how many rows or columns you want, and how wide you want the gutters (the gaps in-between) to be. Illustrator will fiddle the figures for the rest. At the bottom of the dialog box are a series of icons, which allow you to determine how you want your text to flow within the rows and columns.

1. Open the file called Columns.ai, and select the text box that is already there with the **Selection** tool.

2. From the Type menu, choose the rows & columns option. Ensure that Preview is checked, and try different combinations of Rows and Columns, changing the gutter widths and altering the text flow.

3. Click OK to accept the settings you have entered.

4. Select the text box once more, and set the rows and columns back to the original format by choosing Type>Rows & Columns. **Note that you can never have less than one row and one column.**

Once you feel a little familiar with how the Rows & Columns option works, close the file.

Wrapping Type Around Objects

Mixing text and graphics in an artistic way is the aim of the majority of designers. One of the ways in which we have traditionally mixed the two is by wrapping the text around graphics, so that both become an integral part of the design. Illustrator has the ability to achieve this, although I'll be very frank when I discuss the limitations of the feature. Those of you who have used the specialist page-layout applications such as Adobe InDesign,

Adobe PageMaker, or Quark XPress, will be a little disappointed with the level of complexity, but let's check out what it can do.

Creating a basic text wrap is very easy. Select both the text and the graphic, ensuring that the graphic is on top of the text, and then choose Type>Wrap>Make. We'll do a simple wrap and then learn some of those tips for making the wrap more interesting.

1.   Open the file called Wrap.ai. You'll see the trusty starfish once more! But this time it's surrounded by text. Our aim is to make that text flow around the starfish in an attractive manner, whilst at the same time paying attention to readability.

2.   Select the text block and the starfish in the upper region of the page, and choose Type>Wrap>Make.

Grenada is a rolling, mountainous island, covered with perfumed spice trees and extraordinary tropical flowers. Bordered by spectacular beaches, and dotted with picturesque towns, this lush island has long been a major source of nutmeg, cloves, ginger, cinnamon, and cocoa. In the interior of this volcanic island are cascading rivers and waterfalls, lush rainforests, and one of the most breathtakingly beautiful mountain lakes imaginable. The capital, St. George's, is widely held to be the loveliest city in the Caribbean. A pastel rainbow of dockside warehouses and the red-tiled roofs of traditional shops and homes has surround its horseshoe-shaped harbour. Grenada's physical beauty is complemented by its rich history and vibrant, living cultural heritage. Local festivals, fairs, and markets remain an integral part of life on Grenada. Its centuries old spice plantations and rum distilleries still use traditional methods, emphasizing quality rather than quantity. Although the tourist industry has become more substantial in recent years, the island's easy rhythms and the friendly openness of its residents evoke an atmosphere that long since vanished elsewhere in the Caribbean.

Admit it – the results are far from satisfactory! The text runs into the starfish graphic, and the words that have crept in under the starfish's legs are playing havoc with readability! Let's have another go.

3.   Have a look at the text and starfish in the lower region of the page. Switch to Outline View (CTRL/CMD+Y) and you'll notice something not visible before. You'll see there is an additional copy of the starfish, slightly larger and without a fill or stroke. This is the starfish we'll use for our text wrap, so solving one of our problems by pushing the text further away from the visible starfish.

4.   Carefully select the text and the 'invisible' outline, and choose Text>Wrap>Make. Immediately the result is more attractive, but we still have a problem with those pesky words creeping in under the starfish's legs.

5.	In Outline View, directly select a number of the anchor points on the larger starfish and drag them down so as to bump the words away. It's not ideal, but it is a workaround for those difficult situations.

Grenada is a rolling, mountainous island, covered with perfumed spice trees and extraordinary tropical flowers. Bordered by spectacular beaches, and dotted with picturesque towns, this lush island has long been a major source of nutmeg, cloves, ginger, cinnamon, and cocoa. In the interior of this volcanic island are cascading rivers and waterfalls, lush rainforests, and one of the most breathtakingly beautiful mountain lakes imaginable. The capital, St. George's, is widely held to be the loveliest city in the Caribbean. A pastel rainbow of dockside warehouses and the red-tiled roofs of traditional shops and homes surround its horseshoe-shaped harbour. Grenada's physical beauty is complemented by its rich history and vibrant, living cultural heritage. Local festivals, fairs, and markets remain an integral part of life on Grenada. Its centuries old spice plantations and rum distilleries still use traditional methods, emphasizing quality rather than quantity. Although the tourist industry has become more substantial in recent years, the island's easy rhythms and the friendly openness of its residents evoke an atmosphere that has long since vanished elsewhere in the Caribbean.

You could follow a similar procedure if you wanted to wrap text around the transparent areas of a photograph. You would need to draw an unfilled, unstroked shape which roughly followed the shape of those areas, but which was slightly bigger to force the text away. With that shape, not the photograph, and the text selected, you could then choose Type>Wrap>Make.

To release a text wrap, select the text wrap objects with the **Selection** tool. As they are automatically grouped, all components will be selected, and then choose Type>Wrap>Release.

Copying Type Attributes

There is, I must admit, a lack of support for what we have come to accept as standard in many page-layout and word-processing applications – the ability to format our text quickly and consistently with the use of **Type Styles**. At the moment, we can simulate this to a large extent with the use of the **Eyedropper** and **Paintbucket** tools.

As we can use these two tools to copy and then apply attributes to our text in a similar fashion to how we use them to copy and apply attributes to objects, this allows us to format our text quickly. Double-click on the **Eyedropper** or the **Paintbucket** tool to display the attributes we can use.

On the left-hand side of the dialog box are all the attributes that are sampled by the **Eyedropper** tool when we use it with type, whilst on the right are those attributes that can be applied using the **Paintbucket**. These features are in addition to aspects such as fill and stroke, which are included in the Appearance attributes.

The checked attributes are the ones that Illustrator would sample and apply to text when we use these two tools. If you want Illustrator to ignore certain attributes, you need to double-click the tool to display the options dialog box and make changes there before you attempted to sample the attributes. However, to be perfectly honest, it is seldom that you'll find the need to change the attributes being sampled.

There are two ways in which we can use these tools to sample and then apply attributes. The first step is to locate that perfectly formatted paragraph, and then to decide to where you wish to apply these formatting attributes. At this point, you can either:

1. Highlight the target paragraph and then switch to the **Eyedropper** tool and click on the source paragraph – the one from which you wish to sample attributes. As the target paragraph is already highlighted, as soon as you click on the source paragraph, the attributes will be applied to the target. Remember to stay away from those single letter tool shortcuts when you are working with text.

2. Or, click on the source paragraph with the **Eyedropper** tool, then switch to the **Paintbucket** tool, and click on the paragraphs to which you wish to apply the formatting. Remember you can swap between the two by holding down the ALT/OPTION key to toggle to the **Paintbucket**.

3. Open the file called Attributes.ai. Notice that the first paragraph has been formatted with various character and paragraph attributes. With the **Type** tool, create an insertion point in the first paragraph, avoiding the fancy formatting on the first word of the paragraph. Have a look at both the Character and Paragraph palettes, and see if you can predict what will happen when we apply these attributes to the remaining paragraphs.

4. Triple-click to select the second paragraph.

5. Switch to the **Eyedropper** tool. Click on the first paragraph – again avoiding that independently formatted first word. Notice how the attributes are automatically applied to the second paragraph.

6. Select the remaining paragraphs – note that because you are applying character formatting in addition to paragraph formatting, you must select all the characters in the paragraph. Switch back to the **Eyedropper** tool, sample the attributes from the first paragraph, and once again they are automatically applied to the highlighted text.

7. Now double-click on the first word 'In' at the beginning of the second paragraph, and with the **Eyedropper** tool, sample the attributes from the

independently formatted word at the beginning of the first paragraph. Repeat for the remaining paragraphs.

8. Close the file. There is no need to save this.

Finding and Replacing Fonts

The use of fonts across platforms, and even across machines can cause a problem if the original fonts used in the document are not available on the machine on which the document is being opened. In fact, you may well have seen the following dialog box a number of times as you have been opening the supplied sample files:

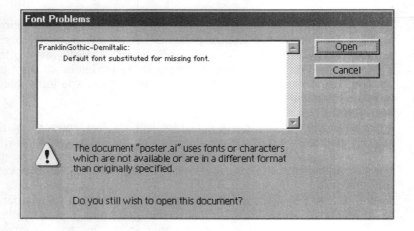

What this warning box is saying is that you do not have the specific font – in this case Franklin Gothic Demi-Italic – on your machine, and your default font will be substituted wherever the font has been used in the document. Now, if you are only opening a file to have a quick look at the layout, this does not pose a problem, but if the document has been handed over to you for finalizing, ignoring this warning could have dire consequences. You would be well advised to use the Find Font utility on the Type menu.

There is another instance in which this feature would become very useful. Imagine that at the last minute, George and Lucy have rushed into the office saying that they no longer like the font Arial or Helvetica that you have used throughout all their identity components, they now want you to use Verdana or Trebuchet! Instead of having to open each file and then manually highlight and reformat the text, the **Find Font** feature would allow you to replace each instance of the font automatically. Granted, you would have to open up each file in turn, but the process of re-formatting would be considerably shortened using this feature.

1. Open the file called Fonts.ai. I have used a serif font called Minion in this file, and of course, I'm dearly hoping that you do not have the font installed on your machine! You should see the warning dialog box saying that you do not have some of the fonts available. Open the file irrespective of this warning. We're going to replace all the usage of Minion with our standard Arial or Helvetica font. You should notice that the font is different.

2. With the file open, choose Type>Find Font to display the Find Font dialog box.

3. The first thing we'll need to do is locate the fonts we want to use, and then move on to specifying which of these substitute fonts will replace those used in the document. On the dialog box, notice the option Replace Font From. At the moment this is set to Document, but because we have not yet used our replacement fonts in this document, they will not be available to us. Choose System instead of Document, and the list of installed fonts on your system should appear.

4. Select the font you wish to replace – in this case Minion Regular – and then from the lower region of the dialog box, select the font you want to use as its replacement, Arial or Helvetica. You could click on the Change All button, but that's always a little foolhardy, especially when you are still getting used to the application. Notice the font change in your business card, and the fact that the next occurrence of the font has already been highlighted. Change that instance as well.

Pay attention to the fact that it is only the font that corresponds exactly to that chosen in the upper region of the dialog box that has been changed – all instances of the emboldened font still remain. The title Dive Instructor and the address and contact details have changed, but Sail & Scuba, George's name, Marine Quest Inc., and the text on the logo are still in Minion because we have not yet targeted that font.

5. Now we'll replace the Minion Bold font occurrences. In the Find Font dialog box, highlight Minion Bold in the upper region, and choose Arial Bold as the substitute font. Systematically work through all the occurrences, noticing that even the artistic text on the logo gets substituted.

Your business card should now look like the example below – with all the instances of Minion, both Regular and Bold, replaced with the comparable Arial font. Click the Done button to close the dialog box and close the file.

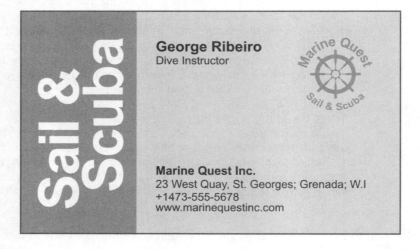

Creating Graphics from Text

In addition to using text as standard text, we can also create graphics from text, which we can manipulate in the same way as we would normal graphics by directly selecting their individual anchor points and direction handles. One thing to keep in mind though is that once you have converted the text to a graphic, you can no longer use any of the text formatting features we have been exploring in this chapter because in essence, the text is no longer text. Illustrator now views it as a graphic.

You might well be asking why we would want to change the text into a graphic if we are no longer able to manipulate it as text. Once converted, we can manipulate the shape as we want, use it as a clipping path to hold photos and textures, create our own 'font', or even pass it along with our publication without worrying about including the font for printing.

1. To create a graphic from text, type some text and then select it with the **Selection** tool.

2. With the text object selected, choose Convert to Outlines from the Type menu, and you'll notice immediately that the type is now made up of those all too familiar anchor points.

3. You can now manipulate the outline paths as you wish.

Case Study: Building a Brochure Page

Now it's time to put all that typographical knowledge to work so we'll only be building one page – the first introductory page, of the brochure. The grid has already been built for you, and a painting by one of the previous guests and a map of Grenada have already been placed on the page, but it's up to you to do the rest. I've already typed some of the copy, complete with a few typos. But I've left some for you to do as well.

Marine Quest

You're passionate about the sun, warm seas, islands, sailing and diving...

You want to relax in the ultimate style, comfort and elegance...

Our professional crew of three will create the perfect, tailor-made cruise according to your exact wishes, including your preferred menu, favourite watersports and desired diving sites.

Your chef, Henry, will prepare the finest cuisine in his large, gourmet galley area; and attend to every need, from preparing an exotic cocktail to ensuring that the accommodations are always perfect. Your Dive Instructor, George, will give you expert tuition in the necessary scuba skills, whilst showing you the most impressive and exciting dive locations in the area. Your skipper, Lucy, will coordinate the perfect itinerary, according to your desires, and act as hostess and guide along the way.

You'll live on board the magnicent catamaran, Mambo; a boat by which all other large multihulls are measured. You'll enjoy 1675 sqft of outdoor living space; and an enormous cockpit which is fully protected from sun, even when sailing. Soak up the sun or keep cool in the shade of the bimini - the perfect environment in which to enjoy that end of day sundowner cocktail.

Her large, stepped platforms will give you convenient access with to swimming, watersports and scuba activities, and your own personal rubber duck. The boat is fully equipped with a kayak, windsurfers, scuba equipment, wakeboards knreeboards, and floating mattresses - for those leaisurely days when you desire to do nothing but relax and enjoy.

Relax in the large, comfortable, air-conditioned saloon with a dedicated bar area from which George and Henry create magnificent cocktails and sundowners. There is also a library with a variety of board games, books,CDs and DVDs.

The saloon is fully equipped with state of the art communications devices including Radar, VHF radios, GPS, and autopilot. For your convenience, we also have satellite telephones, Internet access and email communications.

The 5 double cabins, provide a comfortable private retreat with detailed woodwork, generous space and elegant décor with the finest materials. Everything one could ever want is here, including air conditioning, 110 & 220 volts outlet, CD and DVD players. Each cabin has its own private ensuite head, lavatory and shower.

1. Open up the document called Brochure.ai. Notice the three layers that have already been created. On the Template layer is a guideline to help you with the creation of the design; then there is the carefully created grid

on the Grid layer; and also the graphics I've already placed on the upper layer.

2. The first text that we will create is the Marine Quest masthead on the top right-hand corner on the page. Create a text box by clicking and dragging with the **Type** tool, following the guides. Once you have created the text box, check the dimensions and positioning on the Transform palette:

> X-axis: 7.609 in
> Y-axis: 7.849 in
> Width: 3.036 in
> Height: 1.378 in

3. If you need to resize the text box, use the Bounding Box, which you can display by choosing View>Show Bounding Box.

4. Click in the text box at the upper left-hand corner, lining the cross-beam with the top of the text box. This will inform Illustrator that you want to type inside that particular text box. Type the text Marine Quest, and then format it as Arial or Helvetica, style Bold, size 43 pt, leading 40, using either the Type menu or the Character palette. There is no need to force the text onto two lines, it will naturally wrap. We are using such a tight leading value because there are no descenders in the word Marine, and we want to tighten up the space between the two lines.

5. On the Paragraph palette, right-align the text.

6. Fill the text using the darker blue in the Swatches palette.

7. Create a second text box for the full quote text. Again, check the dimensions and positioning on the Transform palette:

> X-axis: 7.609 in
> Y-axis: 6.765 in
> Width: 2.877 in
> Height: 2.181 in

8. Click in the text box at the upper left-hand corner, lining the cross-beam with the top of the text box. As Illustrator will remember the last size used, you may want to change the attributes on the Character palette before you begin to type. Use Times New Roman or Times, style Italic, size 18, 21.5 leading. On the Paragraph palette, ensure that the copy will still be right-aligned and set the Space before Paragraph to 25 pt.

9. Type the following text: "You're passionate about the sun, warm seas, islands, sailing and diving...". Press ENTER/RETURN to force the text to a new

line, and type: "You want to relax in the ultimate style, comfort and elegance...". If the font you are using is slightly different, adjust the leading or the Space before to ensure that all the type is visible.

10. Fill the text using the darker blue in the Swatches palette.

   I have already typed the remaining text for you in Microsoft Word, so you'll just have to import it...

11. Create the third and final text box in the lower region of the page, following the arrows. Click and drag from the left, down and to the right, creating a text box, which overlaps the map graphic. Your text box should have the following dimensions:

   X-axis: 1.521 in
   Y-axis: 4.417 in
   Width: 8.962 in
   Height: 3.275 in

12. Click inside the text box with the **Type** tool to create the insertion point. From the File menu, choose Place and then from the dialog box that appears, ensure that the Files as Type field is set to Microsoft Word. Locate the Text.doc file, and click Place. The text should flow into the text box from left to right. If the text does not flow into the box, it means that you did not create the insertion point inside the text box correctly. Delete the text, and try once again to create the insertion point. Notice the little square with a plus sign at the lower right of the text box – it indicates that you have more text, which is not yet visible.

13. These lines are too long for our reader to follow with ease, so we need to switch the text into two columns. With the **Selection** tool active, select the text box and choose Type>Rows & Columns. Change the number of columns to two.

14. The copy still does not fit but we've still a fair amount of formatting to do. With the **Type** tool, click inside the text box and then Select>All (CTRL/CMD+A) to highlight all the copy. Format the text as Arial Regular, size 9.5, with a leading value of 13 pt. On the Paragraph palette, set the First Line Indent to 13 pt as well.

15. Switch to Outline View (CTRL/CMD+Y). I've already created a shape, which is slightly bigger than the map, and it's that shape that we will use for the wrap around, in order to give us that standoff buffer essential for a cleaner design.

16. One of the first rules about creating a text wrap is that the graphic object, around which we wish to wrap the text, must be on top of the stacking order. Select the map outline, and choose Object>Arrange>Bring to Front, or access the context menu by CTRL+clicking (Mac) or right clicking (PC) on the selected map outline.

17. Select both the Text object and the larger map outline, and then choose Type>Wrap>Make. The text should now fit perfectly, unless I made that old mistake of pressing ENTER/RETURN when I was typing in Microsoft Word. This makes it look as if there is additional text even if there isn't. The last word in your text should be shower.

18. Now here's a logical one for you – let's see how well you can deal with those word processor-like issues. From the Type menu, choose Check Spelling. The Check Spelling dialog box will appear with a list of words, which Illustrator presumes have been misspelled.

19. Click on the Language button and choose US English as your dictionary. Some of the words listed are definite spelling mistakes, but you'll also notice that the dictionary does not cater for some of the sailing words – bimini and GPS – which we'll tell it to skip. Other words, such as multi-hulls, could do with hyphens to separate the words, and others are new jargon – Internet, e-mail, and DVD. As we're likely to meet these words more frequently, we'll add them to our dictionary list by choosing Add to List. Once you have completed the spell check, close the dialog box.

20. On the Layer palette, hide the Grid and Template layers and have a look at your brochure page! Save and close the document, and take a break!

Summary

So you can see the Illustrator application has now started to reveal more and more of its powerful capabilities – the ability to handle graphics, text, and imported photographs with ease. The more you examine its capabilities, the more astonishing it is that a graphical program can carry so much word processing power along with it as a secondary feature!

14 Preparing for Print

What We'll Cover in this Chapter:

- *Cleaning up your artwork with the Clean Up command*

- *Controlling how Complex Files will print*

- *Printing Simple Composites*

- *Printing Oversized Artwork*

- *Working with Crop Marks and Trim Marks*

- *Tips for Preparing for Commercial Printing*

▶

You've learned fantastic skills for creating graphics, manipulating text, and importing and managing images, and learned how to think like Illustrator. Yet now, at this late stage, I'm telling you that this is possibly the most important chapter of the whole book! There is no use being able to create the graphics for print if you do not pay close attention to getting that illustration printed properly!

Too often this aspect is overlooked. We concentrate on the creative aspect and leave the printing to look after itself and then we are so disappointed when the printed results do not live up to our expectations!

In this chapter our focus is two-fold. Initially we will be looking at how we can tidy up our artwork so that it prints efficiently and with predictable results. In the later part of the chapter we'll look at that printing process itself and how we can print the document ourselves, or deliver it in a suitable format to our commercial printer.

We'll be opening many of those documents we have created throughout the case study and looking carefully at the individual components, trying to discover those potential pitfalls in printing that we may have ignored thus far.

Cleaning Up your Artwork

You're in that creative stage and the last thing on your mind is whether or not the artwork is printable, or the points that you should be considering as you use various tools. As long as you realize that creating the art is only half of the process – and that second, all-important aspect of getting the art ready for print must be given equal, if not more consideration before you can consider your work is finished.

Granted, I would suggest that you always proceed with caution as you work, and pay attention to how you are creating it, and whether or not it is printable, but I admit that sometimes these concerns are swamped by our eagerness to create. Thus, always build in that time at the end of the project to do the 'housekeeping'.

Using the Clean Up Command

All too often as we create our computer artwork and make little mistakes – not those big glaring hiccups – we tend to ignore them! A case of what the eye doesn't see, the heart doesn't grieve over? But believe me, that printer attached to your computer sees it, as does the commercial imagesetter!

There's no need to panic. Once again we'll be putting Illustrator to work, this time as the housekeeper, looking for our little slip-ups and eliminating them before we go to print with the Clean Up command.

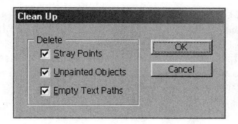

The Clean Up command looks for three problems in your file – Stray Points, Unpainted Objects, and Empty Text Paths. Each aspect can accrue additional information in your file, increasing the size of the file and possibly causing printing problems. We want lean, clean files, so we'll look at each of these in turn.

Eliminating Stray Points

What are these stray points and why should we eliminate them? Remember, when you were trying to come to terms with the Bezier Pen tool, and possibly inadvertently depositing extraneous anchor points on the page, you didn't worry about them because you really could not see them.

Open the file called Stray_points.ai, and I'll show you what I mean. At first glance there seems to be nothing wrong with it. Switch to Outline View (CTRL/CMD+Y), and you're in for a big surprise – notice all those little x marks scattered across the Artboard and in the scratch area – those are stray individual points. Now imagine that you wanted to use the Align feature to align the text and the graphic, or you wanted to print this, or export it in a format suitable for placement in a page-layout application. All those additional anchor points could cause you problems.

Remain in Outline View so you can visibly see Illustrator clean up the file. Choose Object>Path>Clean Up, and the Clean Up dialog box appears.

As we're specifically looking to eliminate Stray Points, uncheck all the other options on the Clean Up dialog box. The majority of the time it does not matter whether all three remain checked when you do a clean up, there is no need to run the function three times, once for each option.

Click OK or press ENTER/RETURN and all those stray points have disappeared. Close the file.

Eliminating Unpainted Objects

In essence, an unpainted object is an object or path, which has neither a fill nor a stroke. Sometimes we create them, but more often than not it is Illustrator that creates them for us when we use the **Pathfinder** commands. You may remember when we looked at the Pathfinder palette options that you could decide whether or not to have Illustrator remove unpainted artwork created as a result of using Divide and Outline. Yet there was no option to remove any unpainted artwork created by the other Pathfinder functions.

Open the sample file `Invisible.ai`. On the left is a sunrise, which extends beyond the background sky, so we'll use the Pathfinder Crop command to clean it up, and then we'll discover what Illustrator has left behind.

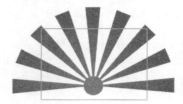 

With the **Selection** tool, select both the sun and the stroked rectangle in front of the sun. From the Pathfinder palette, choose the **Crop** option, fourth in from the left on the bottom row, to trim the protruding rays to the rectangular shape.

You may remember that whenever we use the Pathfinder commands the resulting shapes are grouped. Use the Object>Ungroup command (CTRL/CMD+SHIFT+G) to ungroup the shapes, and then deselect them. Select the sun shape and move it elsewhere on the artboard. Switch to Outline View (CTRL/CMD+Y) and you'll notice that there still seems to exist a reversed shape of the sun – those unpainted shapes.

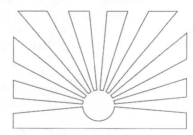

Remain in Outline View so that once again you can see Illustrator clean up your file. Choose Object>Path>Clean Up. This time we want to sort out Unpainted Objects, so deselect the other options, and then click OK, and all those unpainted objects have now gone.

There will be times that you deliberately create unpainted objects, objects that exist, but which are invisible to the reader. One such instance would be if you wanted to wrap text around an object or photograph and so created that slightly bigger invisible object to create the standoff. Let's open the `Brochure.ai` file and see what happens when we ask Illustrator to do a clean up for us!

With `Brochure.ai` open, switch to Outline View (CTRL/CMD+Y) and have a look at that slightly larger unpainted object surrounding the map, forcing the text away from the visible map.

I bet you're wondering what will happen if we run the Clean Up command on this file – what will happen to that shape we created, and then what will happen to the text wrap that we have? Well, it is possible to run Clean Up and preserve the text wrap intact, but we must be careful.

Whenever we create a text wrap, Illustrator groups the objects together. Switch to Outline View, and with the **Group Selection** tool, select the unpainted object. From the Object menu, choose Lock>Selection (CTRL/CMD+2). With the unpainted object locked, run the Clean Up command, and you'll notice that both the object and the text wrap remain untouched – a thought to bear in mind as you are creating, and cleaning your files. Close the file.

If you don't make sure to do this, although the change will not be apparent at the time, next time you open the file your perfect text wrapping will sadly be altered.

Eliminating Empty Text Paths

As with the previous two options on the Clean Up options dialog box, eliminating Empty Text Paths, even though they may be invisible in Preview mode, is something that we should do to ensure that these files remain lean and clean.

Open Text.ai, and you'll see the text that we used in the brochure exercise in the previous chapter and once again, all looks fine when we see the page in Preview. Switch to Outline View. Now you see all those little x marks, indicating where we may have clicked with the Type tool and then not typed any text. Also, you'll see rectangular shapes where we may have clicked and dragged with the Type tool to create a text box without entering any text into the box. This is extraneous material, increasing the size of our file and possibly creating complications when we export the file.

Following the same procedure that you used for removing stray points and unpainted objects, choose Object>Path>Clean Up and then select only Empty Text Paths in the Clean Up Options dialog box to remove the superfluous text paths.

In the previous three exercises we have focused separately on each of the aspects of your file that are affected when you use the Clean Up command, but this is not to say that you must always tackle each function separately. We did it this way to illustrate clearly what aspect of the file would be affected by using the various functions, but the majority of the time you can check all three options.

Cleaning up your Files with the Pathfinder Commands

We've only just started getting ready to print! Do you remember looking at the Pathfinder palette in a previous chapter? While I'm not going to go into much detail on the functions here – we did that in that chapter on Creating Complex Shapes – all I'll be doing here is drawing your attention to those functions to explain how they can be used to clean up your artwork for print.

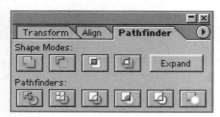

*Remember that whenever you use these Pathfinder commands, the resultant shapes are grouped. You'll either have to ungroup them if you want to use the **Selection** tool (V) to select individual components, or safer still, use that **Group Selection** tool with the object still grouped to preserve its relationship with other components within the group.*

So how can using these Pathfinder functions help get our artwork print ready? Essentially there are two aspects – one is the design aspect of neatening up the shapes in our designs so that edges are perfect. You may recall that as we were building up that brochure cover illustration, I said that you should not be concerned about how well the edges of the individual components shaped up, and this is because we can use functions such as the Crop command to neaten those edges.

Secondly, we often have shapes upon shapes upon shapes. It seems silly to have all this excess detail, which is hidden, but which still needs to be processed. Using options like Trim and Merge allow us to clean up and remove these excess areas. However, remember that production hint that I gave in the chapter on Complex Shapes – the suggestion of keeping a 'trimmed' and an 'untrimmed' file, in case the client calls for some groundbreaking changes. Using that untrimmed file would be so much easier.

A Word About Linked and Embedded Images

One aspect of Illustrator you will have to be aware of when preparing for print is that of **Placed** images. If you are looking to place an image from a separate file into your Illustrator document, the chances are you will have placed it by browsing through the File>Place command.

Within the **Place** dialog there is a **Link** check box. Linked files remain independent of the Illustrator file, which results in a smaller Illustrator file. Imagine your Illustrator file is 1mb and the image you place is 50mb. By linking the image to the Illustrator file you have avoided creating a file that weighs in at 51mb. Instead the 1mb Illustrator file shows a relatively small increase in file size to account for the linked file.

What happens if you don't have the Link check box enabled? In this instance, the image you place will be **Embedded**. Embedding an image physically imports the image into the Illustrator file, making it a part of the file in the same way as if you had created an object in Illustrator. To use the above example of the 1mb Illustrator file and the 50mb image, in the case of the Embedded image, you would end up with a 51mb file. The down side of this is you have a large file to manipulate and use up more system resources.

The process of linking and embedding images is not a complex one in itself. But like so many computerized processes, the simpler they are the greater scope they offer for problems further down the publishing line.

Here is a typical scenario. You create a poster that includes a number of linked images. Strictly speaking, the images are not there – all you are seeing on screen is a preview of an image that resides somewhere outside of the Illustrator document. You finish working on the file and in the frenzy that often accompanies the delivery of the file to the printer, you only send the Illustrator file and not the images, as they are still independent images.

Be aware of this, as you are going to add a red hue to your face when the puzzled printer picks you up on it.

Case Study: Cleaning Up the Brochure Cover Illustration (I)

One of the pieces of corporate identity materials that requires much cleaning and preparation for print is that complex cover illustration. We've used some very high-end tools in the illustration and it will need a couple of visits using skills that you'll learn in this chapter to get it to print reliably. What we'll be doing in this encounter is just cleaning up those edges which have been worrying George and Lucy as they've watched it developing. We'll start cleaning up the file now, although it will not be our last visit to the file in this chapter.

1. Open your brochure cover illustration, or open the file called Brochure_cover.ai. The components that we'll look at in this part of the case study are those overlapping regions on the layers highlighted in the screen shot below – the textured water, waves, and water layers. They protrude from the edge of the sky, and we want to remove that excess. Although we could perform this function only once, we want to maintain the components on their own separate layers, and give you a little practice, so we'll do it separately to each individual layer.

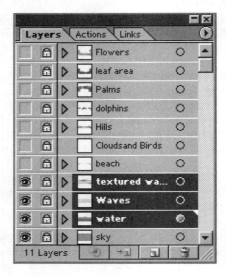

2. Unlock the sky layer because we'll be using that shape to trim the excess from our waves and water. Select the sky by clicking on the circle to the right of the layer. Copy the shape by choosing Edit>Copy (CTRL/CMD+C). Lock the sky layer, because we'll be pasting this shape in a moment, and we don't want to paste it onto its original layer.

3. Unlock the textured Waves layer and select the objects on that layer by clicking on the circle to the right as you did for the sky layer. Instead of pasting the sky, which would paste it in a slightly offset position, choose Edit>Paste in Front (CTRL/CMD+F) to paste a copy of the sky in exactly the same position on the X- and Y-axis as it was on the sky layer.

4. Ensure that all the layers excepting the textured waves are locked. Make all the other layers invisible as well just so you can see the results of your actions. Choose Select>All (CTRL/CMD+A) to select both the pasted sky and the textured waves, and select **Crop** from the Pathfinder palette. Notice that the excess has been trimmed from the edges, but also that an unpainted object has been created in the top area. Run the Clean Up command to remove that object.

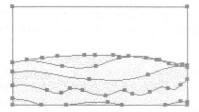

5. Lock the textured waves layer, and unlock the Waves layer. You still have a copy of the sky object in memory, so there is no need to copy it again. With the waves selected, choose Edit>Paste in Front (CTRL/CMD+F) to paste a copy of the sky in position. Select all of the objects on the layer and crop as before. Once again, you are left with that unpainted object. You can choose to remove it now, or wait till later, remembering that layers need to be unlocked for the function to work.

6. Lock the Waves layer and unlock the water layer. Repeat the process for the last time. Display the sky, water, waves, and textured waves layers. The layers should now be perfectly trimmed to that background sky layer. It's looking tidier already.

7. We'll do a little more tidying, before we close the file and move on to learning more about getting the file print ready. Hide the flowers and leaves layers. Unlock the Palms layer with all other layers still locked, and paste a copy of the sky object in front – Edit>Paste in Front (CTRL/CMD+F). This time we'll use the Clipping Mask command to trim the overlapping palms, and then we'll use that clipping mask to clip both the hills and beach.

8. On the palms layer, choose Select>All (CTRL/CMD+A) and then choose Object>Clipping Mask>Make. The palms should be trimmed inside the shape.

All we need to trim now are the beach and hills. As they are gradient meshes, we cannot use the Crop command, so our solution is to place these objects within the same clipping mask as the palms.

9. Unlock the Hills layer and the beach layer, and expand the group on the Palms layer. Notice the dotted lines between the paths on the palm layer. This indicates that they are part of that clipping group that you have just created.

10. Drag the two hill meshes from the hill layer to the bottom of the palm layer – we want them to fall behind the palm leaves – and place them below the palm leaves in the layer stacking order. Then drag the mesh from the beach layer to the palm layer, but place the beach mesh above the hills meshes in the stacking order to ensure that the beach is in front of the hills.

11. Your file should be almost ready for printing from a design point of view. You may wish to fine-tune the placement of some of your flower and leaf instances or even add a few more if you find you now have some gaps that you don't like.

12. Save and close the file, we'll return to it at the very end of the chapter.

Controlling How the File will Print

Our illustration is a pretty difficult file. Not only do we have a large number of intricate objects in the illustration, but we've also used all types of complex features like gradients, transparency, and meshes. These features can cause complications if we do not prepare for print properly, which is exactly what we are going to consider now. Several of the difficulties involved have been mentioned, but not explained as we progressed through the chapters – we were concentrating on the design process, now we are focusing on the technical aspects.

Many of the aspects that control how we set up our document for printing are located on the same dialog box. This seems a very good place to start our exploration of these features.

To display the relevant dialog box, choose File>Document Setup, and then choose Printing & Export from the drop-down menu at the top of the dialog box. There are five options that control how your file will be printed or exported, and we'll have a look at these options and discover how they can affect the way in which your document prints.

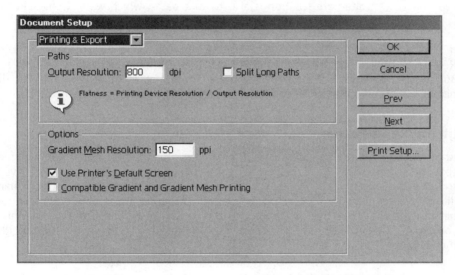

Changing the Output Resolution

You're familiar with those curved paths that you have been creating as you draw in Illustrator, but we've not yet told you how these curves are defined by the Postscript interpreter and how this can affect the printed appearance of your document.

The illustration above is a simulation of what happens when we print our curves. I have made it a little more blatant than it would print, but can you see the straight lines on the circle on the right? This is how our curves print – they are defined as very small straight-line segments. Obviously, the smaller those lines are, the more accurately our curve will be printed, but the smaller the lines, the more of those little segments we'll need. This means that the complexity of the file will increase, and if it becomes too complex, the curve can't print, and we may be greeted by a Postscript limit-check error.

The flatness of the curve is controlled by the output resolution. The lower that value is, the flatter the curve will be, with longer and fewer line segments. This means it will print faster, but it will be less accurate. Although Illustrator prints best using the default output resolution setting of 800dpi, in some cases, you might need to decrease this resolution. An example of such an instance would be if you were trying to print a very long curved path and you kept getting limit-check errors or the file was taking ages to print. But remember this is a trade-off in that the file might print and print quicker, but it will be less accurately reproduced. An alternate solution is also to split paths, which we will cover in the next section.

If you are experiencing difficulties printing, try changing the value in the Output Resolution field. If you are printing at 300 dpi, the recommended values are between 100-300dpi, and between 800-2400dpi if you are printing at 2400dpi. Bear in mind, that the higher the number, the more complex the file, but the more accurate it will be.

Splitting Long Paths

Another way in which we can assist Illustrator when it tries to print our complex files is to split these long paths. By using the Split Long Paths command, Illustrator will have a look to see if the length of the closed path exceeds what the printer's memory can handle. If Illustrator sees that the path is too long, it will split the path into two or more separate paths. Paths that have been split are indicated onscreen by lines through the path when you are in Outline View, but these cross lines will not print in the final output, neither are they visible in Preview mode.

> As you would save an unflattened file in Photoshop, it is a good idea to have a duplicate file in which the paths have not been split should you have to go back and do some major edits. Rejoining paths after they've been split is very time-consuming and fiddly.

Printing Gradients

You may find that some of the older Level 2 Postscript printers are unable to print your gradients without banding – visible bands of color. If you experience this, converting the gradient object to a JPEG can ease this problem, but do not switch this option on unless you are having problems printing the gradients as it will slow down printing.

Printing gradients on low-resolution printers can also result in banding, because many printers with a resolution of 600ppi or less are unable to output the necessary 256 shades of gray needed for those smooth gradients. If you switch off the Use Printer's Default Screen option, Illustrator will use the built-in Adobe screens to improve how the gradients are printed, but remember that this is only for printing to low resolution printers, if you are experiencing difficulties.

Printing Gradient Meshes

Although the majority of gradient mesh objects will print correctly if you are printing to a Level 3 Postscript printer, some Level 3 printers do have problems with gradient meshes, and with Level 2 printers, the meshes are written as both vector objects and JPEG images. As a result, you need to control the output of these objects to ensure that they print reliably. The Gradient Mesh Resolution setting in the Document Setup dialog box controls the resolution of the JPEG image. The default setting is 150ppi, which is not high enough if you want to output a high-resolution image, and I would suggest that you might wish to up the resolution to 300ppi.

Printing Transparent Artwork

Although Illustrator has provided support for transparent artwork since version 9, most print devices and Adobe PDF format prior to 1.4 (Acrobat 5) do not understand transparency. For this reason, we need to flatten our transparent artwork, creating a format that the printer will understand.

When we flatten artwork ourselves, or when we print or export transparent artwork to a format that does not understand transparency, the overlapping artwork is broken into individual pieces and converted into vectors or rasters or a combination of the two, depending on the complexity of the artwork, and on the settings we choose. Complex artwork may result in thousands of components, some of which are smaller than a pixel, and as such, the number of components may take considerable time and resources to compute.

There are a number of factors that we need to look at when we are concerned with how transparent areas in our document will print, and the first place to look will be in our Document Setup dialog box. Choose File>Document Setup, and from the drop-down menu at the top left of the dialog box, choose Transparency to display the following dialog box.

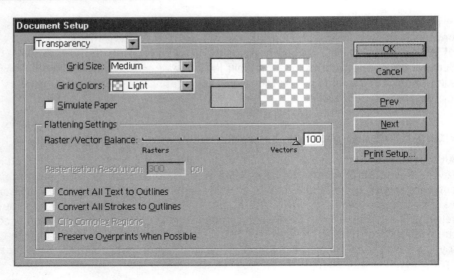

Although the default settings will consistently produce excellent results, there will be times when, with complex files or a need for high-resolution output, we need to manipulate the Flattening Settings ourselves to attain optimum results.

- Raster/Vector balance – the slider controls the amount of rasterization that will occur in complex areas of the illustration. With the slider all the way to the right, as much artwork as possible will be retained as a vector shape, whilst if we move the slider to the left all the artwork will be rasterized – converted to pixels – irrespective of whether it was transparent or not. In complex artwork with intricate areas of transparency, allowing regions to be converted to raster images may simplify the printing requirements.

- Rasterization Resolution – controls the resolution for those complex areas of the image that are rasterized. In most cases a value between 300-400ppi will be sufficient, but if you need a really high quality print, or if you have very small objects or fine text, you might need to take the value up to 600ppi. This will have the result of giving a higher quality, but a much larger file. Consider file size and speed of printing against the need for very high quality. Also remember that the value inputted here does not affect how gradient meshes are rasterized, this is set on the Printing and Export dialog box previously discussed.

- Convert All Text to Outlines – converts text to graphics and the width of the text will remain consistent during the flattening but can cause smaller text to look thicker.

- Convert All Strokes to Outlines – as with converting text to outlines, the width of the stroke will remain consistent but thin strokes may appear to be slightly thicker.

- Clip Complex Regions – ensures the boundary between vector and rasterized artwork falls along object paths, reducing the possibility of artifacts occuring when one part of an object is rasterized whilst the remaining part is still a vector. In a complex file with many clipped raster areas, the file may become too complex to print, so use this option with care.

- Preserve Overprints When Possible – if you are printing separations and the document contains overprinted objects, using this option will generally preserve overprint for objects not involved in transparency.

In addition to setting the Transparency settings for the entire document, we can also target individual objects and control how they are flattened. This is useful if you wish to maintain the majority of elements as vector shapes, but wish to specifically change how the transparency of a certain object is handled.

With the object selected, choose Object>Flatten Transparency. A dialog box similar to the one we have looked at under the Document Setup will appear, and you can make the same choices here, taking into consideration the warnings given about file size and complexity, and the effect on strokes and text.

However, there are more factors you may wish to consider at this point. When you set the Transparency options for the entire document under the File>Document Setup options, the file was viewed as a whole, and therefore background areas for objects converted to raster images would have been considered in relation to the entire file. This is not the case here, and you may be in for a few surprises if you flatten some individual objects using the raster options.

To illustrate how this can affect your files, open the file called Flatten1.ai. You'll notice our dolphins and our transparent waves from the cover illustration. What we'll do is select different parts of the illustration and use different settings to see how Illustrator implements these Flatten Transparency commands.

1. With the **Selection** tool, marquee drag around the first instance of the waves and dolphins.

2. Choose Object>Flatten Transparency, and leave the settings as indicated below. When the action is finished, have a look at how many vector objects have been created.

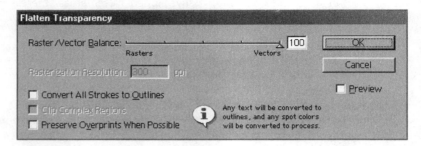

3. Marquee drag around the second instance of the illustrations, and this time, set the Raster/Vector Balance to 50, thus allowing Illustrator to convert more of the complex transparent aspects of the illustration to raster images. Leave all other options unchanged. You should notice that not only was the process a lot quicker, but greater regions of the illustration have been converted to raster areas.

4. Now select just the textured waves. They will be the topmost grouped objects in the sea stacking order, so clicking on the waves with the **Selection** tool will select the correct object. Choose Object>Flatten Transparency, and reset the Raster/Vector Balance to 100 – retaining as much as the image in vector format as possible. Zoom in and notice how each of the speckles in the waves has been converted into an independent vector object, within a number of stitched groups. You may also notice that the speckles have become a little more obvious.

5. Finally, select the textured waves in the bottom instance and once again set the Raster/Vector Balance to 50. That wasn't the result that you expected! Because you have flattened transparency on this one object and allowed the conversion of the transparent objects to rasters, you can no longer see through to the waves beneath.

Do not think that I'm advocating that you use only the Vector option when you are flattening transparency – this can result in very complex, large files. What I am saying is be aware of how certain objects will interact, and that sometimes you may get a result that is not quite what you expected. Because of this, when flattening transparent objects and allowing a greater degree of raserization to occur, you may well want to select the object and its background.

Printing an In-House Proof – The Composite Proof

There's no way that you would send your artwork off to a commercial printer without having first test printed it. In this section it is difficult for me to exactly describe the dialog boxes and additional options that you might meet in your situation as there are so many printers available out there. However, I will try and give you as many general pointers as possible for getting that print out of your machine.

In the first instance, we'll look at a simple graphic print on a piece of paper, which is identical to the size of our Artboard. In the second example, we'll consider how we would manage to output a composite copy from that oversized illustration we may well have created. To clarify, there are two kinds of printouts that we might wish to create, **Composite** and **Separations**.

A composite print is a printout with which I am sure you are already familiar, where the complete image comes out of our printer in black and white or color on one piece of paper – a representation of what the illustration should look like when it is commercially printed. Unfortunately the majority of our in-house printers do not reproduce colors exactly as they will be commercially printed, but that's not the focus of this chapter.

Separations are what your printer will create so that each individual CMYK color and any additional colors can be printed on their own plate, ready for that run through the printing press. This is not to say that you should not create a set of separations prints from your in-house printer as well. They can be a very useful checkpoint to see if colors are separating as you expected, and can also help you ascertain whether there are any unexpected additional plates that might print. We will be discussing what separations are in more detail, and how to make a separations print out a little later in this chapter, but for the moment, let's get back to discussing that simple composite print.

Creating a Simple Composite Print

Essentially there are three steps that you should consider when you are getting ready to print and although you may have seen some of these steps before, we'll go through them from the beginning one more time. Mistakes at the printing press can be extremely costly, and approaching the process with due care and attention is something worth doing.

Starting right back at the beginning, let's check that Artboard size by choosing File>Document Setup. Although in a simple print out, where we know that the size of our artwork is going to be smaller than the size of the paper in our printer, working through the procedure systematically every time is still a good idea.

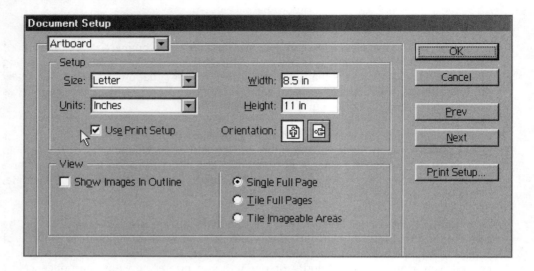

1. To make sure that the size of the Artboard and the paper are the same, check the Use Print Setup option. This will automatically reset the size of the Artboard to match the size and orientation of the paper in the printer. As this is a simple composite, which will print on one piece of paper, choose Single Full Page.

2. To ensure that the artwork is falling within the imageable area of the paper, choose View>Show Page Tiling. This will display that dotted rectangle with which you are now familiar.

3. If parts of the artwork fall outside the imageable area (it is doubtful that this would be the case in a simple file which did not cover the entire page), select the **Page** tool and reposition the imageable area as needed so that the artwork is bounded by the dotted rectangle.

4. From the drop-down menu, switch to the Printing and Export options, and ensure that the settings are as you would like them. Check the Transparency options by moving to that dialog box from the drop-down menu as well. Remember we discussed how these options will impact on your printout earlier on in this chapter.

Having ascertained that the document has been set up correctly, the next step is to ensure that the printing options have been selected correctly.

5. From the File menu choose Print Setup if you are on a PC, or choose Page Setup if you are on a Mac. If you have more than one printer attached to your machine or network, choose the target printer from the drop-down menu at the top of the dialog box.

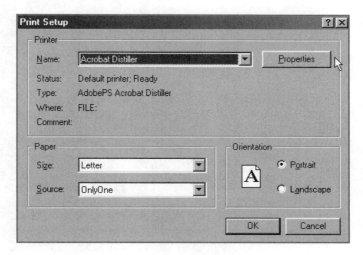

6. In Windows, click Properties and select the options you want. In Mac OS, select Page Attributes or PostScript Options from the pop-up menu and then select the options you want.

7. Click OK.

   Our final step now as we print this composite print, is to actually tell Illustrator that we want to print the document. We have everything in place correctly, we have checked both the document and print setup, and so we can safely proceed with that Print command.

8. From the File menu, choose Print (CTRL/CMD+P) to display the Print dialog box.

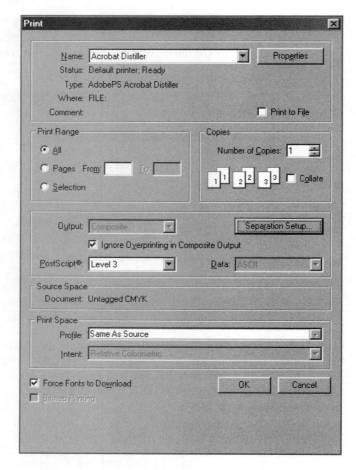

Choose the following options in the print dialog box to set the advanced printing options – note, on a Mac you'll have to choose Adobe Illustrator 10 from the drop-down menu first.

- In our simple composite, we have already selected the Single Full Page option in the Document Setup dialog box, so for Print Range check All and a single page will print. When we look at printing over-sized documents a little later, we'll re-visit this option where we can select which pages to print. Notice that if you had part of the image selected, you could also instruct Illustrator only to print that selection.

- If you need to print more than one copy of the artwork, enter the Number of Copies you require. And if you are printing multiple copies of multiple pages, you can instruct that a complete copy of each page is printed as a set, before the next copy is printed, by checking Collate.

- If you have not yet set the Separation parameters, then you have no choice here, a Composite print is the only option. As we wish to print a composite, this does not present a problem to us. We will be looking at the Separation Setup a little later when we prepare for commercial printing and in-house separations proofing.

- If your printer is Postscript compatible, choose the correct postscript language level. If your printer is a Level 3 printer, you should choose that option to ensure that the features, which enable you to optimize the output of complex artwork and gradient meshes, are used.

- The Data option for bitmap printing is available only to Mac users. By selecting Binary, you would decrease the amount of data being processed and therefore to speed up the printing of bitmap images, but choosing ASCII will make the data usable on a wider variety of printers and PC networks.

- Although having the fonts in use installed on your printer is the ideal situation, we can force the fonts we have used to be downloaded to our printer by checking the Force Fonts to Download option. This will allow us to print with the fonts, even though we may suffer a slight loss in print quality.

- Windows users with non-Postscript printers can select the Bitmap Printing option if they are experiencing problems printing some of those complex graphics. The image is sent to the printer as a bitmap or raster image. This does mean that the print speed may suffer, but you're less likely to see printing errors. Switch this option on only if you have tried to print an illustration and have failed, as it may help.

Case Study: Printing the Business Card

George and Lucy are back in the office, wanting hard copy printouts of your design projects. Seeing something onscreen somehow does not compare to holding the real thing. Let's quickly provide a printout of that business card.

You may remember that when you originally created that business card, we built in a bleed so that the color ran right to the edge of the card with no possibility of white gaps when the card was trimmed. We'll be looking at trim and crop marks in this chapter, but for the moment, let's just get a copy out of the printer.

1. Open the Biz_card.ai file. Unlock all the layers and use the Object>Path>Clean Up command to ensure there are no unnecessary elements in the file. What you're hoping to see is a dialog box saying No cleanup was necessary.

2. On the Layer palette ensure that the art layer is not visible. We'll be printing two copies of this file for George and Lucy – one with the alternate logo and one with the original. With hard copies, they might be in a better position to make a final decision about the design.

As we know that our business card is far smaller than our Artboard, there is no need for us to check the Artboard options in the Document Set Up dialog box, and the same is true for Transparency and the Printing and Export options.

3. To ensure that we have the correct printer selected, choose File>Print Setup and check that your desired target printer is selected, and the paper size and orientation are set correctly. In this instance, I would choose the Paper Size as Letter and the Orientation as Portrait.

4. Choose File>Print (CTRL/CMD+P). As both George and Lucy want their own copy, set the number of copies to two, and if you are using a Postscript printer, choose either Level 2 or Level 3 dependent on the capabilities of your printer.

5. Click OK (PC) or Print (Mac). Notice that by default, Illustrator prints only the visible layers.

6. In the file, hide the logo alternative layer and display the art layer.

7. Repeat the printing steps above, once again ensuring that you have two copies of the file. Save and close the file.

Printing Over-Sized Artwork

As you have already discovered, you will often find yourself creating documents or illustrations that are larger than the largest size of paper your in-house printer can hold, and yet you need to present the client with a full size print out of the document. It's not impossible to do this, despite the size restrictions of your printer. All you need is a little bit of planning, a pair of scissors and some glue or tape to put the final printouts together! We call this tiled artwork, and you were introduced to this concept in Chapter 12, Organizing your Artwork.

In the previous section on printing a simple composite, I took you step by step through the process of ensuring that the document and printer were set up correctly for printing. I said that checking the size of the Artboard was not that critical if we knew that our artwork was smaller than the artboard and paper in the printer. With over-sized artwork, those steps now become very important.

1. The first step in the process will be checking how we are going to view the Artboard in the Document Setup dialog box. From the File menu, choose Document Setup and check that Artboard is the option displayed in the drop-down menu at the top of the dialog box. In the View area, set the option to Tile Imageable Areas.

2. If you are unable to see where the individual tiles are on the artboard, choose View>Show Page Tiling. Notice the page numbers that appear at the bottom left-hand corner of every tile. You can use these page numbers to tell Illustrator the pages you wished to print to create the tiled artwork. If necessary, you can reposition the page tiles using the **Page** tool.

3. To specify which of the pages you wish to print, choose File>Print (CTRL/CMD+P) and in the Print Range options enter the number of the pages you want in the From: and To: fields. Unfortunately, if you wish to print non-consecutive pages, you will have to access this dialog box a number of times. Of course you could just print all the pages and discard those you did not need – not an eco-friendly approach!

Once you have set the pages to be printed, choose the remaining printing options as previously discussed, and print the pages. With the hard copies in your hand, all that remains is to get those real word tools – glue, scissors, and ruler – and cut and paste the pages together to create the full size composite.

Trimming our Artwork

Whenever you create artwork with bleed areas that need to be trimmed away, or artwork which will be printed onto a paper bigger than the final product, you need to include instructions to the printer, telling him where the product needs to be cut to size. These marks are commonly known as **Crop Marks**.

Crop Marks

Imaginary dashed lines showing effects of the crop marks

Final trimmed artwork

Creating Crop Marks

To create your crop marks, you need to draw a rectangle that will define the boundaries of your final printed object. It does not matter whether the rectangle has a fill or a stroke, or both, as it will disappear when you create the crop marks.

With the rectangle selected, choose Object>Crop Marks>Make, and the crop marks will replace the selected rectangle. If you do not create a rectangle before you use the command, the crop marks will be placed at the corners of the Artboard. Note that once you have created these crop marks you cannot edit them directly. If you needed to edit them, choose Object>Crop Marks>Release, but don't forget to remake them later.

If you plan to separate a color Illustrator file, you should first set crop marks in the artwork by creating the rectangles as explained above. If you do not, Illustrator will set them around the bounding box of all objects in the artwork, irrespective of whether they are on the Artboard or not.

Creating Trim Marks

So how can you use crop marks to indicate to your printer where he should trim multiple objects that you have on a page in an attempt to save paper and therefore costs? (Remember you should always ask your printer if this is how he wants the work delivered!) To achieve this, we do not use Crop marks, but rather we use **Trim Marks** to indicate where the individual objects on the page should be trimmed.

If you look carefully at the illustration below, you may notice that for this procedure to work effectively, we've had to re-design the business card slightly. This is because of the bleed at the left-hand edge of the business card, which could cause problems if the cards are not correctly trimmed on the right – small darker blue strips might appear. What we've done to overcome this problem is to create an additional blue strip on the right hand side of the business card. Consequently if the cards are not cut absolutely accurately, nobody will be any the wiser!

If you have no need for a bleed in your business card, creating the **Trim Marks** would simply entail selecting the bounding shape and choosing Filter>Create>Trim Marks.

However in our particular card design, we have had to create bleed areas, and this means that the shape we use to create the trim marks should be an additional smaller shape which is the exact size of our proposed final card. If you do create an additional shape, don't forget to delete it once you have created the Trim marks.

When Illustrator creates the trim marks, it will create internal trim marks which overlap the artwork and which are unnecessary. As the trim marks are grouped by default, select those you don't need with the **Group Selection** tool and delete them.

Creating Trim Marks

In this exercise, you have a chance to practice creating those trim marks on a number of business cards that have been grouped together on a page.

1. Open the file called `Trim.ai`. Notice that there are two layers – the locked artwork layer, and an additional layer for the trim rectangles. This

is not essential, it just makes it easier for us to select the rectangles without selecting parts of the business card.

2. With the **Selection** tool, select one of the rectangles and choose Filter>Create Trim Marks. Repeat the process for each of the rectangles, and then delete the rectangles from the file.

3. Illustrator has created the trim marks for us, but we have more than we need – the marks that fall inside the body of the business cards are unnecessary and could cause complications for us if the cards are not perfectly trimmed at the guillotine. Switch to the **Group Selection** tool and select those trim marks that are not needed. Delete them, and save and close the file.

Case Study: Providing Final Proofs

Instead of trying to explain the concept of printing to the edge and the need for bleeds to George and Lucy and the fact that this extra material will be trimmed away by the printer in the finishing department, you've decided to present them with a new print out of the business card complete with crop marks. Then they can take it away, cut it down to size using the crop marks as guides.

1. Open the `Bizcard.ai` file.

2. Draw a rectangle without being concerned about the stroke or the fill, as the rectangle will be removed automatically when we make the crop marks.

3. Using the Transform palette with the Reference Point at the top left of the icon, position and size the rectangle as follow:

   ```
   X: 0 in
   Y: 0 in
   W: 3.75 in
   H: 2.25 in
   ```

4. With the rectangular shape selected, choose Object>Crop Marks>Make. The rectangle will be removed, and in its place perfectly placed crop marks will appear.

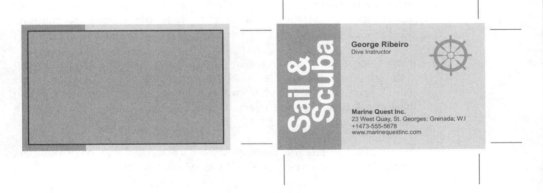

5. Print the file, give it to George and Lucy.

They have asked you whether you have any other components that are nearly print ready and whether they could have a look at them as well. You know that, to all intents and purposes, the design of the poster is pretty much finalized. Yes, there may be some considerations about process and spot color a little later on, but you're not going to get into that with them now.

6. Open the file called `Poster.ai` or if you have your own version to hand, use that instead. The poster is an oversized document, with a bleed as well. Consequently, not only are you going to have to print separate pages to tile together, but you'll also have to set some crop marks to indicate the final trim.

7. If you are greeted with a Font Problems dialog box, open the file and then replace the missing font with Arial Bold Italic using the Find Font feature on the Type.

8. The first thing we'll do is create those Crop marks. Draw a rectangle exactly on the guides already in place. If you wish to check the accuracy of your rectangle, use the positioning and measurements reflected in the Transform palette screenshot below.

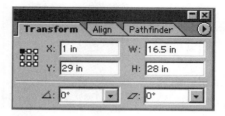

9. With the rectangle selected, choose Object>Crop Marks>Make. In order to see the Crop marks more clearly, hide the Guides by choosing View>Guides>Hide Guides (CTRL/CMD+;).

10. Now that the crop marks are in place, let's check our document setup and ask Illustrator to tile all those imageable areas for us. Choose File>Document Setup, and from the drop-down menu ensure that you have the Artboard option selected. Check Tile Imageable Areas and close the dialog box.

11. If you do not see the multiple dotted rectangles and page numbers displaying on the screen, choose View>Show Page Tiling.

12. Switch the guides back on by choosing View>Guides>Show Guides (CTRL/CMD+;). With the **Page** tool, reposition the imageable areas at the lower left hand base of the page, where the guides intersect. We're only being this fussy, because placing them exactly at this position will coincide with our crop marks, and that means less cutting and pasting for us!

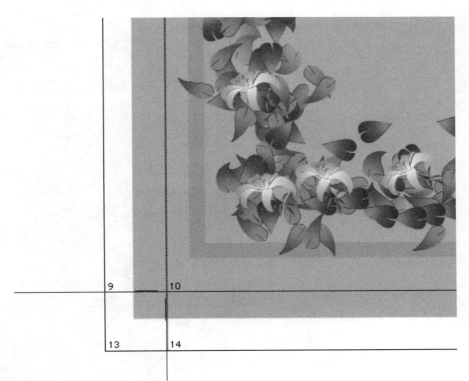

13. Now it's time to print those pages. Resize the view of the poster so that you can see the entire illustration, and look carefully at how the page tiles have fallen. Although Illustrator sees 16 imageable areas, with our careful placement of the page tiles, we should get away with printing only four pages, 6, 7, 10, and 11.

14. Choose File>Print (CTRL/CMD+P) and in addition to setting all the options as previously discussed, set the Print Range as pages 6-7 and print these two pages. Repeat for pages 10-11.

Preparing for Commercial Printing

An in-depth examination of the concepts involved behind the high-end preparation of files for commercial printing is beyond the scope of this book, however a few pieces of advice ought to point you in the right direction. First off, make friends with your bureau and printer – and in time, the rest of the knowledge will come.

The relationship you develop with your commercial service bureau and printer are the key to a successful print. The more advice you seek from your bureau and printer, before, during, and after the job is printed, the more confident you'll be that your designs will print correctly, especially as you venture into the realms of setting up the color separations.

Initially I would suggest that you hand over your native Illustrator files to the bureau or printer, and request that they handle the separations, and the final print preparation, including the setting and checking of overprints and bleeds. However, do not assume that the bureau or printer will automatically provide this service when you hand over files – you must make it clear that you are requesting this service from them.

Questions to Ask your Bureau or Printer

Below is a little checklist that should help you through this process. Have it handy whenever you are getting ready to prepare your separations and need to confer with either your bureau or printer.

- What PPD (postscript Printer Description) should be selected?

- Will the bureau or the printer supply the PPD?

- Ask for advice on the page size giving them details about the size of your illustration.

- Must the emulsion be set to Up or Down?

- What screen ruling value should you use? Remember you should have made a decision as to the type of paper you will be using by this stage as that will influence the line screen value which is best suited for your job.

- Should the image be set as a positive or negative?

- Inform the printer if you will be using spot colors – especially if you are using more than one – and ask for specific screen angles for each spot color.

- What bleed value suits the printer and this particular design?

- Should you set Black to overprint in the Separation dialog box?

- Should you include Printer's Marks?

These are the main questions that you should be asking your printer as you prepare those color separations. Of course this does depend on how much you have developed that relationship, but if for each answer to each question, you ask 'why?' you'll be accumulating loads of useful knowledge and understanding about the print process which will only stand you in good stead.

Summary

Congratulations, you've come through a major session on the intricacies of print preparation. We have only just scratched the surface regarding concerns for commercial printing, but if you keep developing that relationship with your printer and service bureau, you'll accumulate masses of knowledge, which will enable you to prepare your files for commercial printing with confidence. In the next chapter, we take a break from printing and concentrate on developing those materials for the Marine Quest website.

15 Preparing for Web Delivery

What We'll Cover in this Chapter:

- *The fundamentals of Web Graphics*

- *Slicing Artwork including Creating Slices, Choosing Slice Types, and Modifying Slices*

- *Optimizing Images for Web Output*

- *Generating an HTML table*

Illustrator has been around for a long while – since long before the Web became a truly viable medium for quality graphics. But in its most recent versions it has had to make lightyear leaps in Web compatibility. If you are a Web guru, you will learn in this chapter how many of the things you know are done the Illustrator way. If you are just graduating the Web kindergarten, then you are in for an exciting introduction to the diverse world of the Web, which may just change your life.

Let's begin by introducing you to one of Illustrator's new tools and commands and the reason for its existence.

Slicing Artwork

Slicing does what you might expect it to do. It slices your artwork in the same way you would slice a cake – into a number of square or rectangular sections. Why would you want to slice artwork? Well, take a look at the example. This is the Dive page of the Marine Quest web site as it was designed and produced in Illustrator.

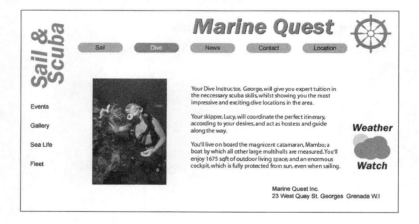

Currently this entire page is an Illustrator file, which means we need to convert it to a bitmap and save it in a format that is supported by the popular Web browsers such as Netscape Navigator or Microsoft Internet Explorer. We will come on to the file format and bitmap elements later in the chapter, but for the moment we are going to concentrate on the slicing part of the job.

There are three main reasons to slice artwork for the Web:

Reducing the Overall File Size of the Web Page

The easiest way to convert the above Illustrator file into a web page would be to simply rasterize and save the file in a web bitmap format. This would also be the worst thing you could do. The whole page measures 760 x 420 pixels and large areas of the page are blank. In its current vector format, all the visible artwork elements are independent objects. Any blank area of the page is just that, a blank part of a page. There is literally nothing there.

If we were to convert the whole page to a bitmap, we would have a bitmap that measures 760 x 420 pixels, making a total of 319,200 pixels and every pixel must be paid for as part of the total file size. A blank white area ceases to be blank and becomes a white pixel with an accompanying amount of bytes that contributes to the overall file size.

So clearly the first thing to do to reduce the file size is to discard any pixel based blank areas. However, we still want the user to see a white background and that's where slicing comes in. We can slice up sections that define the actual visible artwork, such as photographs, logos, buttons, and so on. What we are doing is making small independent images.

Thereafter, defining the color white in the HTML code can generate the original white background color using a fraction of the processing power. If the term HTML code or how the page will be constructed leaves you guessing, don't worry, we will look at these points by practical example shortly.

Isolating Elements Such as Buttons and Animated Images

Elements such as buttons that change color or display some other animated effect would not work if the button image was an integral part of the whole web page image. Slicing in this case is a necessary requirement in order to use the image as a separate entity.

Aiding the Download Speed of a Large Graphic

One simple way to reduce the time it takes to download an unwieldy image is to slice it into a number of segments. The browser will download several bite-sized chunks of an image faster than the whole image as one block.

Now that you know the reasons for slicing, let's see how it works. We are going to use the web page in the previous picture at the beginning of this section. Open the file now from the download folder called `Slicing.ai`.

Viewing Slices

To get some experience of this process we are going to create slices of a few of the artwork elements. First we need to make sure slices will be visible when you create them.

Go to the View menu. Make sure Hide Slices is showing in the menu. This means the slices will be visible when you create them. You can toggle between Show Slices and Hide Slices in the same way as you do with guides. Slices are only visible within Illustrator and not when you view the page in a browser.

Creating Slices

1. Select the photograph of the diver.

2. Go to Object>Slice>Make.

A slice is created based on the photograph as in the image below. But slices have also been created that encompass all the artwork on the page.

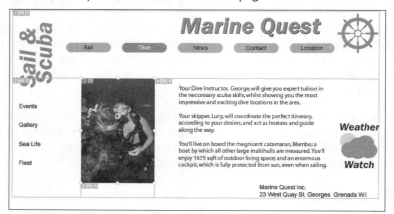

In total there are five slices. Illustrator attempts to create the most efficient use of slices, creating just enough to comfortably house all the elements of the design. You can see each of the slices numbered 1 to 5 in the picture above. The only slice you personally created (the **User Defined Slice**) was the one around the photo, whereas Illustrator created the others automatically. The color of the outline of your slice is dark red to signify that fact you created it intentionally, while all the other slices outlines are pale red.

The idea behind automatically creating slices that encompass all the elements of the page is so that the total page can be converted to a web page that appears in a browser with little further effort from you. We will look at this process towards the end of the chapter.

When you create a User Defined Slice, you have the ability to reposition the object and the slice at the same time, allowing you to fine tune your design.

3. Using the **Selection** tool, select the photo and drag it so it is a little higher than its current position. You will find the slices that surround the photo also move to accommodate the new position of the photo.

4. Drag the photo a little lower than its current position and then to the left and right to see the surrounding slices recreate themselves in a new layout. The image below is the result of dragging the photo towards the bottom left of the page. This resulting layout has only four slices in total, this being the optimum number as far as Illustrator is concerned to achieve the desired design.

Let's make another slice based on an object.

5. Select the Weather Watch logo on the right of the page. This is a group consisting of the text and cloud and sun artwork.

6. Go to Object>Slice>Make. My page now has seven slices. Two of the slices are now User Defined Slices, number 3 and number 6.

Now we are going to resize the Weather Watch logo.

7. Select the Weather Watch logo.

8. Double-click the **Scale** tool in the toolbox and type 75 in the Uniform Scale box, then click OK. The Logo will reduce in size to 75% of its original size, but so will the slice that surrounds it. Any other slices that surround it will also change to accommodate the new size and position of the logo if they need to. It is important to note the Weather Watch logo is a vector and as such can be scaled without any resultant loss in quality. Although you can also scale the diving photo, as it is a bitmap it will lose quality. This basic fact is not affected by the use of slices.

The only movable and resizable slices on this page are the ones you created around the photo and the Weather Watch logo. These are the User Defined Slices. None of the automatically generated slices can be moved or resized. As with many automatic functions we have looked at in Illustrator, this does not offer us the greatest flexibility. Take a look at the picture below. This is my page after the editing carried out so far.

Your page should look the same or similar if you have followed the same steps.

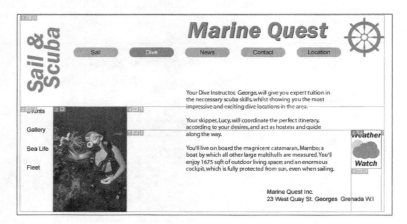

Look at how slices 4 and 5 run through the block of text. In many cases, and certainly in Marine Quest's case, the text will change on a fairly regular basis. This current slice configuration doesn't provide us with a very updateable design. Ideally we want to create a slice that just holds the text so we can update it as necessary.

We could do this easily enough as you have seen, just by selecting the text block and creating a slice from it. We could then create a graphic image of this text just as you would with the photo or the weather logo. There are benefits to doing this with text. Often text that has been saved as a graphic will look better than plain old Web regular HTML text.

The negative aspects of saving your text as a graphic are file size and editing ability. The file size will be larger because we are dealing with pixels again as a bitmap. Text editing is hindered because any time you wish to change the text, you will have to open the original graphics application, make the changes and then resave the file again. This can be irritating especially if you need to update text regularly – or if you make a simple typing error.

Because we are going to change this text regularly, we will create a slice that is designed to hold HTML text.

Defining a Slice Type

1. Select the block of text that begins with the words 'Your dive instructor'.

2. Go to Object>Slice>Make. As before, slices surrounding the one you have just created will readjust themselves in order to make the optimum amount of slices necessary for the design. The slice you have created is already selected.

3. With the slice still selected, go to Object>Slice>Slice Options.

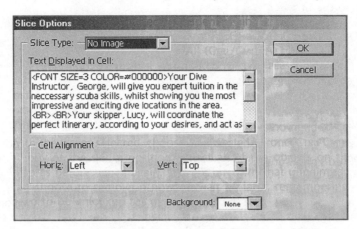

In the Slice Options dialog box that opens, you have the following three choices of Slice Type:

- Image – will result in the artwork within the slice being used as a graphic image on the web page.

- HTML Text – will result in HTML text being created within the slice, based on the text and characteristics on the page, but there are no options to change the text or HTML codes in this dialog box.

- No Image – allows you to type freely in the dialog box and enter your own HTML formatting codes if you can write HTML. This option also allows you to create a blank slice that only contains a color as defined using HTML code

We are going to use the last option, No Image. The text on the page already appears in the dialog box so no further action is required as far as the text is concerned.

Cell Alignment allows you to set the alignment of the text within the slice area. The settings in the screenshot above will result in the text being aligned to the left of the slice or cell in the horizontal plane (Horiz) and to the top of the cell in the vertical plane (Vert).

The drop-down box labeled Background allows you to specify a color for the background of the cell. Keep None as the option. This will create a cell with a transparent background so whichever color is defined for the web page background will show through.

It is important to remember that any text you type in the dialog box when you select the No Image option will not appear on the Illustrator page, but only in a browser. The same applies to the color you select from the Background drop-down box. For this reason you need to be careful in terms of how much text you type as if it is larger than the available space in the cell it will impact on the other slices and your layout will look different when viewed in the browser.

Click OK to close the dialog box.

We will be looking at the other options and settings later in the chapter when we prepare the page for final publishing.

Deleting Slices

The method you use for deleting slices depends on how you created the slice. We have only looked at one method of creating slices so far, so let's delete the slice that surrounds the diver photo.

The simplest way to delete this slice is to select the photo, which automatically selects its slice and then press the DELETE key. However, we created this slice by selecting the photo and then using the Make command. Because the object was used as the basis for this slice, we cannot simply delete the slice without deleting the photo also. So another method is required.

Select the photo, then go to Object>Slice>Release. The slice is now deleted, leaving the photo on the page.

Close the file without saving changes.

Creating Manual Slices

As well as creating slices automatically based on objects, as you were doing in the last exercise, you also have the option of creating slices manually. Why would you want to create a slice manually? Well let's take a look an example where manual slicing is required.

Open the file called Manual_slicing.ai from the download folder.

This gallery section of the web site displays a picture that comes close to filling our target screen size. For a general picture, this would be too big and cause an unnecessary delay in downloading the page, but this is a picture gallery and so one would expect to see pictures a little larger than average. That is not to say we should forget everything about keeping file sizes to a minimum. Even a gallery section needs to be aware that the viewer's patience is not infinite. So slicing will help to speed up the download wait.

We are going to slice the photo into eighths. The simple and quick way to do this is to make one large slice from the photo and then divide the slice up into eighths. However, it is not possible to divide a slice that has been created using the Make command.

So, we will use the **Slice** tool.

1. Select the **Slice** tool from the toolbox. Beware, there are two similar looking tools in this toolbox. The other tool is called the **Slice Select** tool and displays a small black arrow on its icon. We will look at this later.

2. With the **Slice** tool selected, hover the cursor over the top left corner of the photo. Place the tip of the **Slice** tool on the corner of the image. Drag diagonally towards the bottom right corner of the picture, releasing the mouse button when the point of the slice tool is near the corner. An outline will define the slice you are about to make. Try to ensure the outline fits snugly around the photo before you release the mouse.

Once the mouse is released you will see the familiar dark red line defining the User Defined Slice and the paler red lines defining the automatically created slices. On the face of it, there appears no difference in this method to the method you used earlier. The difference will become clear in a moment.

It is possible that your slice does not fit the picture perfectly. Not to worry – the **Slice Select** tool will save the day!

Using the Slice Select Tool

The Slice Select tool is used to move and resize slices. We will use it now to resize the slice so it fits the photo perfectly. As you can see, I got mine a bit wonky on the screenshot.

You will find it easier from this point if you zoom in to the top right corner of the photo by about 400%. At this zoom rate you can clearly see how far adrift the slice edge is from the edge of the photo.

1. Click on the **Slice Select** tool. You will need to keep the mouse pressed on the **Slice** tool in the toolbox and select the **Slice Selection** tool from the fly-out that appears.

2. Click inside the slice you are going to resize, in order to select it.

3. Place the cursor over the edge of the slice until the cursor changes to a double-headed arrow as in the picture below.

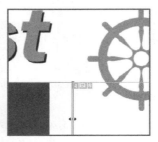

4. Drag the slice outline to the left until it lines up with the edge of the photo.

5. Adjust the other edges of the slice outline if you need to. Don't forget you must select the slice before you can drag the edges.

Your screen should now show four slices, with slice 3 perfectly encompassing the photo.

Dividing a Slice

Now that we have a slice that was created manually with the Slice tool, we are free to divide it up.

1. Select the slice containing the photo using the **Slice Select** tool.

2. Go to Object>Slice>Divide Slices to open the Divide Slices dialog box.

3. The slice can be divided horizontally and vertically by a set number of evenly spaced slices. The range is from 1 to 5 slices, down and across, evenly spaced. As we want to create evenly spaced slices based on sixteenths, enter a value of 4 in the upper field of each section. The other available option, Pixels per Slice, enables you to define slices by a fixed value. You can ignore this for now, as we are not going to select these options, and the numerical values showing in the fields will not have any effect.

4. Click OK.

The picture below is what you should be looking at.

The slices are now ready to be used to create the final graphics.

Optimizing Images for Web Output

You've been hearing a lot about keeping file sizes small in this chapter and others along the way. This is the section where we get down to the nuts and bolts of file size crunching. It is arguably the most important element of preparing images for the Web because it doesn't matter how beautiful your artwork is, no one is going to see it if it takes an age to download. It's worth remembering that the next website is just a click away.

The key to getting your images small in file size is **compression**. As the name suggests, big files are compressed into small files using a variety of compression methods. Which compression method (or **algorithm**) to use is an important. Use the wrong one and you will end up with a file that is still large and also looks lousy. So let's have a look at the two main file formats that use compression and are supported by the popular browsers. Both of these formats are bitmap formats.

Compressed File Formats

JPG (Joint Photographic Experts Group)

This is currently the format of choice for photographic images or any image with intricate textures or tones. The reason for this is that the JPG is capable of displaying millions of colors, making it ideal for photographs. It uses a powerful compression algorithm to drastically reduce the size of the file. However all this comes at a price. The JPG format is known as a **Lossy** format. The greater compression you apply, the greater the degradation of the photo. This degradation normally manifests as blurriness, pixelation, or small blobs appearing on the image.

GIF (Graphic Interchange Format)

The GIF file is an excellent format if your image is made up of a small number of solid colors – very handy when you're dealing with vector artwork. Its method of compression is **Lossless**, and it can save at some beautifully small file sizes. The negative aspect of the GIF is that it is only capable of displaying 256 colors – not brilliant for photographic images. Anyone who has saved a many-colored image as a GIF will know that it is quite capable of producing enormous files.

OK, enough theory, let's put these two formats through their paces. First we are going to see how the JPG option works.

Using the Save for Web Command for JPG Compression

This function has been inherited from Photoshop and works in exactly the same way, so your skills will easily be transferable between the two applications.

Open the file called `Girl.psd` from the download folder.

This is a Photoshop image. We are going to convert it to a JPG.

1. Go to File>Save For Web, which opens the Save for Web dialog box.

At the top of the dialog box you will see four tabs labeled as follows:

- Original – displays only the original image.

- Optimized – displays only the image with the compression applied.

- 2–Up – displays the original image on the left and the image with the compression applied on the right. This is the option currently showing.

- 4–Up – displays the original image in the top left corner and three other images with different levels of compression for reference.

If yours is not already displaying the 2-Up option, select it now.

For easy reference, the options we are going to be working with have been labeled A to I. The first thing to do is to select the correct file format.

2. From the File Format drop-down box [A] select **JPEG**. You will now see the other settings as above.

3. Drop-down boxes [B] and [D] do the same thing and work in parallel with each other. These are the compression quality settings. [B] provides a word to describe the amount of compression you will apply. [D] provides a numbered scale from 0 to 100. As you change a setting in one box, the other box changes to reflect the change. It doesn't matter which box you apply the setting to, although [D] gives you a greater range of settings.

The setting you apply here has the greatest impact on the look and size of the file. We are going to use [D] to specify the amount of compression. Setting 100 renders the largest amount of quality – and therefore the minimum amount of compression, and the largest file size. Setting 0 produces maximum compression, greatest loss of quality and smallest file.

4. Type 100 in drop-down box [D]. Look at the area labeled [I]. The number 521k is the file size of the image before any compression is applied. Now look at the area labeled [H]. It reads 97.91k. This is the new size of the file with the compression applied. This is known as the **optimized** file size. That is a pretty impressive reduction. You will see a slight loss of quality in the optimized image on the right. It looks a little less crisp than the original. But let's get a sense of perspective – for that kind of reduction in file size it would certainly be acceptable for a web graphic.

Let's try the other extreme.

5. Type 0 in the quality drop-down box [D]. Remember to click the gray part of the dialog box to update the setting. This produces a massive reduction in the quality of the optimized image. This is why the JPG format is known as a **Lossy** compression. We have lost the original quality as data is discarded. The result is the appearance of artifacts and square pixilated edges along with blurriness. Although the image looks very poor in quality, take a look at the new optimized file size in area [H]. 6.391k is tiny as image files go, but what's the point of a very small file size if it looks terrible?

The fact is, neither of the settings you have applied, quality 100 or quality 0 are suitable for images for the Web in most cases. One looks good but is still too large at 97k, and the other is too swampy to be of any use. The answer is to find a happy medium, which is what we will do now.

6. Type 40 in box [D]. The image quality improves immediately. Look at the new optimized file size. Just over 16k. The file size hasn't actually grown that much from the previous setting, only another 10k, but the image quality is far superior. In fact there is not a world of difference in the visual image quality between quality level 40 and quality level 100, but there is a big difference in the file size.

7. The Optimized check box [C] creates an enhanced JPG with a slightly smaller file size. Checking the box switches the function on. Some older browsers do not support this feature.

8. The Blur drop-down box [E] allows greater compression to be applied. The less contrast there is between pixels in an image, the smaller the file will be. Blurring serves the purpose of reducing contrast. Of course the flip side of this is that you now have a blurry image, which in most cases is what you are trying to avoid.

9. Selecting the Progressive option [G] causes the image to appear in the user's browser in a series of overlays. First a low-resolution version appears, and then progressively clearer images overlay the previous version until the final image is downloaded. This option is useful if you have to use large images that would take a long time to download or if your target audience averages a slow Internet connection. It is really a case of user perception. If users see something happening, even if it is a blurry picture, they are more likely to wait until the full image downloads than if they can see nothing at all.

10. Take at look at the area labeled [H] again. The picture states 36 sec @ 28.8 kbps. This is designed to give you an idea of how long it will take this image to download over a 28.8 kbps modem connection. Use this only as a rough guide. It is only using simple arithmetic. As stated earlier, there are many other factors that dictate how long an image will take to download such as how busy the connection is, quality of connection, and so on.

11. Use all the settings as above and click the Save button.

12. The Save As dialog box opens. Save the file as Girl, Images Only (*.jpg) with All Slices showing from the drop-down menu at the bottom.

That's it. We're done. You now have an optimized JPG image ready to use within a web page. The JPG image can be opened and used by many applications including bitmap applications like PhotoShop, Corel Photopaint, and Paintshop Pro, and web site creation tools such as Dreamweaver, Go Live, and Front Page.

Close down the Illustrator file without saving and we will look at the other popular compression format.

Using the Save for Web Command for GIF Compression

Open the file called Weather_watch.ai from the download folder.

This is one of the logos from the Marine Quest web site home page. We are going to convert this to a format suitable for the web. It is not photographic and there are no continuous tones of color so **GIF** is the perfect format. There are apparently only three colors – though we'll expand on this in a moment.

Let's start in the same way as you did when saving a JPG image.

1. Go to File>Save For Web.

The Save for Web dialog box opens. Once again labels have been used for identification of the elements we are gong to use.

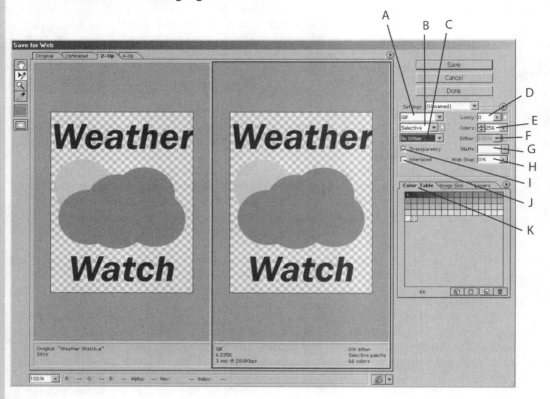

2.　　The first thing to do is set the required format from drop-down box [A]. Select GIF. Different options now appear as in the picture above. [K] defines the Color Table. This is the range of colors being used in the artwork up to a maximum of 256. Look at the area labeled [L]. It states 66 colors. Illustrator has already worked out the optimum amount of colors required in this image to provide good quality against low file size.

But wait, I hear you ask. This logo seems to consist of three colors, black, blue and yellow, so where have the other 63 colors suddenly appeared from? The answer is rasterization. The preview we are looking at is no longer a vector with smooth edges. It is now a bitmap and, as you know, bitmaps require anti-aliasing to simulate smooth edges. The anti-aliasing pixels are a variety of different colors and this accounts for the 66 colors.

Because Illustrator applies 66 colors to the image it doesn't mean you have to use 66 colors. The fewer colors you have the smaller the file will be. But of course fewer colors means there will be some loss of definition, so a balance is required again. Let's see how you can override the automatic amount of colors set by Illustrator.

Drop-down box [E] allows you to set a number of colors up a maximum of 256. Select 2 from the drop-down box. The optimized image on the right of the screen updates to reflect your new artwork using only two colors. If all your settings match those in the picture, you will be looking at completely blue artwork. The other color is transparent. This is the defined by the gray and white background in the image window. I know it sounds odd, but transparency is considered a color. Now take a look at the size of the file in area [M]. The optimized image with two colors is just over 2.6k, as opposed to the original that shows 391k.

Let's increase the amount of colors and see how it affects file size and visual quality.

3. Select 4 from the Colors drop-down box [E]. Check the optimized file size and you will see it has grown slightly, but the image also looks better as now we can see all of its colors. The quality isn't great though. If you look at where the yellow and blue meet you will note a jagged edge. This is because there are not enough colors to create the required anti-aliased pixels to simulate a smooth edge. Type 66 in box [E] to return to the Illustrator automatic setting. Remember to click on a blank gray part of the dialog box to update the change.

Ok, we've decided to use 66 colors as specified by Illustrator, because the file size is acceptable and the quality looks fine. Next we need to decide on the **Color Reduction Method**.

4. The Color Reduction Method drop-down box [B] applies different preset methods to make its selection of colors based on a maximum number that you set. In this case, you have selected 66 colors. In fact you won't see any difference as we go through the methods because we have simple, flat color artwork. These methods come into their own if you had complex vector artwork with gradients and blends or were attempting to save a photograph as a GIF format.

You already know that it would not be a good idea to do this, but there are situations where it would be necessary. One such situation would be if you wanted to make a series of photographs into GIF animation. (This is a simple sequence of bitmap images that displays in a numbered order. It is similar in concept to a child's flipbook, where the pages are flipped revealing a sequence of simple drawings that appear to move.) The GIF animation only works with GIFs so there would be no choice but to save the photographs as GIFs.

The following summarizes how each of the methods work:

- Perceptual – gives priority to colors that are more sensitive to the human eye.

- Selective – similar to Perceptual, but has a bias to broad areas of color and also preserves web safe colors. Using this method normally produces images with the greatest color integrity. Selective is the option of choice in Illustrator.

- Adaptive – this option only samples colors from the visible spectrum that are concentrated in the image, so if an image contains predominantly reds and yellows, only reds and yellows will be sampled.

- Web – only uses the standard 216 web safe color palette. You will remember from Chapter 2 on color that the web safe palette consists of colors that will not dither on monitors capable of displaying only 256 colors.

- The Lossy drop-down box [D] allows you to define a degree of further compression. As you discovered earlier, the GIF format is a lossless compression format by nature. If you need to shrink the file further, this option will introduce a lossy function. The higher the setting, the smaller the file size, but quality will suffer. Try changing the setting to see the effect it has on the visual quality and file size. Use with caution, if at all.

- The Diffusion drop-down box [C] creates dithering, the thing we are always trying to avoid on 256 display monitors and the reason for the creation of the web safe color palette. So why would we want to intentionally create it? For this logo we are working on we wouldn't. Simple flat artwork works best without dithering. If we had a gradient or a continuous tone image such as a photograph that could not be reproduced because there are not enough colors within the range of 256, then dithering would help to create the illusion. The options available in this drop-down box are summarized below:

- Diffusion – works by applying a random pattern of pixels of different shades across adjacent pixels.

- Pattern – similar to diffusion but this setting applies a halftone-like square pattern in an attempt to interpret colors that cannot be created.

- Noise – works in a very similar way to diffusion but this option does not apply its effect across adjacent pixels. This can result in a less blocky effect compared to the Diffusion method.

Whichever option you choose, depending on your image, the effect may be so subtle that it hardly makes any difference.

5. Working in tandem with Diffusion is the Dither box [F]. If you have applied any of the settings other than No Dither, this box will become enabled and allow you to set the amount up to 100%. Higher settings result in a more pronounced effect.

6. Web Snap [H] relates to web safe colors. Set the box to 100 to use only colors from the web safe palette. The lower the setting, the lower the tolerance will be in shifting colors to the nearest web safe equivalent. If you do not intend to use the web safe palette, make sure this box is set to 0.

7. Checking the Transparency [I] box preserves any transparent areas in the image. The gray and white chequerboard you see in the image background currently denotes the transparent areas. We are gong to use this transparency with the next option, Matte.

8. Matte [G] enables you to substitute the transparent areas in the image with a color of your choice. In practical terms, this usually means matching the color of the web page background. If the web page background was red and we wanted our logo to sit seamlessly on the red background, we can select a red from this box and the anti-aliased pixels around the edges of the artwork would have the correct shades of red to match the background perfectly. We will do this now so you can see how it works. Click the Matte [G] drop-down box and select Other.

9. In the color picker that opens select bright red as in the picture. The value is:

$$R = 255, G = 0, B = 0.$$

10. Click OK.

I chose bright red to make it really obvious. You will now be able to see the red anti-aliased pixels surrounding all the artwork elements. Look at the Color Table [K] and you will still see that we have 66 colors but the colors have changed to reflect the addition of the red anti-aliased pixels. The Matte box also displays the red color. We don't actually want red, so the next step will change the red to white.

11. Click the Matte [G] drop-down box and select White. This returns your image to its previous state.

Interlaced [J] is to GIF what Progressive was to JPG. A low-resolution version of the image appears in the browser while the full image file is downloading. This option does increase file size and is best kept for very large images or a target audience with slow connections.

12. Apply all the settings as at the start of the section and click the Save button.

13. In the Save As dialog box that opens, name the file Weather Watch selecting Images only as the Save as type. Save the image in the same folder as the original Illustrator file.

Just as with the JPG, the saved GIF image can be used in the same way, being utilized by the other applications mentioned earlier.

Using the methods you have just learned, you would be able to save all the GIF and JPG images required for your web pages.

Applications I mentioned earlier, such as Macromedia Dreamweaver, generate HTML code without the developer or designer actually writing any code by hand. Illustrator too is capable of writing HTML code without you having to know anything about the code. This means as a designer you are free to design within Illustrator and let the program generate the code when you are happy with the final result.

One of the most commonplace techniques for laying out web pages in HTML is through the use of an HTML table. You may have used a table in a word processing application such as Microsoft Word or even in a spreadsheet program. The concept is the same. The table is divided into rows and columns and text and pictures are placed inside each of the cells. The borders of the cells can be invisible so all the user sees is the content. This is what we are going to do, or rather what Illustrator is going to do for us as we put the final elements into place prior to publishing a working web page.

Optimizing and Saving Slices within an HTML Table

Open the File called Final_output.ai from the download folder.

You have already seen and worked on this file when you looked at dividing slices into smaller slices to aid download speeds. I have finished off this file by creating slices for the buttons on the left as well as the text elements and ships wheel logo. The slices will form the basis for the HTML table that Illustrator will generate automatically.

We are going to use the Save For Web command again.

1. Go to File>Save For Web to open the Save for Web dialog box

2. Click the Optimized tab at the top of the screen. You are doing this because it is easier to work when you can see the full page. The Optimized tab will show you the effect of the compression as you apply the settings.

3. Click the Zoom drop-down box in the bottom left corner of the screen and select Fit on Screen. This setting fits the whole page into the available space on your screen.

The slices should be visible on the screen. Visibility can be toggled on and off by clicking the button in the top left of the dialog box as in the picture below. When the button is depressed the slices are visible. Make sure they are visible now.

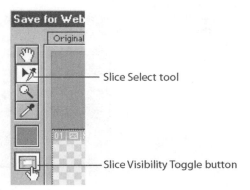

4. We are going to select all the slices by using the **Slice Select** tool as labeled above. With the **Slice Select** tool selected click inside slice 1 and drag towards the bottom right corner of the page as described in the picture below. This is the same principle as when you select multiple objects on the page by dragging a marquee selection. The black rectangle you can see in the picture below is the marquee created by dragging with the Slice Select tool. It is only necessary to make contact with a slice to select it.

When you release the mouse you will have selected all the slices. You know a slice is selected when it has a yellow outline. All the slices will now display this yellow outline.

Our page is a mixture of a photograph, flat color artwork, and blank areas, so different compression formats will be necessary for each slice. The first thing we are going to do is apply the GIF format to all the slices that are now selected and then we will change the format for other slices as necessary.

5. Make sure all the slices are still selected and then enter the settings from the right of the dialog box as below.

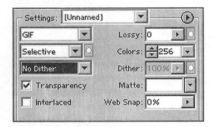

Linking Slices

All the slices have now been setup so when we save the page these are the values that will be applied. We can now adjust each slice independently and apply the relevant amount of colors for that slice. All the green navigation buttons on the left of the page share a similar color palette so we are going to **Link** these slices which will have the effect of forcing them to use one common set of colors. This is a time-saver, as we will not have to apply a setting to each button slice separately.

1. Using the **Slice Select** tool again, select the Sail button (slice 12). Only this slice now has a yellow outline. Now press and hold down the SHIFT key and select each of the other green buttons. Pressing the SHIFT key allows you to select multiple slices. All five slices should have yellow outlines signifying they are selected.

2. Click the **Optimize Menu** button (the arrow button to the left of the settings field) and select Link Slices.

The numbered label of each of the navigation buttons now changes to a different color from all the other slices to signify they have been linked. Look at the Color Table on the right of the screen and you will see the optimum set of colors that Illustrator has chosen for you automatically. This color set will be used for all five slices containing the green buttons.

The photograph is split into 16 slices. As this is a photograph, it needs to be a JPG format. Once again it would be tedious to apply the setting to each slice independently, so we will link all 16 slices that make up the photograph and then set the format to JPG. The process is exactly the same as you just performed for the green buttons, except this time we can select all the slices of the photograph by dragging a marquee from slice 6 to slice 34 with the **Slice Select** tool.

3.   Link the slices as before by selecting Link Slices from the **Optimize** menu button.

These slices now take on a different label color to signify they are linked. Now they are linked and selected we can apply the JPG compression format to all of them in one go.

4.   Apply the settings as in the picture below. I used a quality setting of 40. You can use your own judgment if you wish.

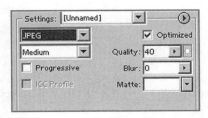

Slice 2 is the word Gallery, Slice 4 is the Marine Quest text, and slice 5 is the ship's wheel. One of the first things you did was apply the GIF format to all of the slices, so these three slices have already been set up. Click each of these slices and you will see the Color Table change to reflect the optimum colors in each slice.

We have now completed the optimization process and all that remains is to generate the HTML table and save the images.

Setting HTML Output Options

1. Click the Save button so the Save As dialog box opens.

2. Apply the settings as follows:

   - Call the file Gallery.

   - Save as type – Save as HTML and Images (*.html) to save the HTML page and the image files, in this case GIFs and JPGs.

   - All Slices means all the slices will be saved. The other option is to save only selected slices.

   - Use the same folder that contains this Illustrator file as the location to save the new files we are about to create.

3. Click the Output Settings button to open the dialog box:

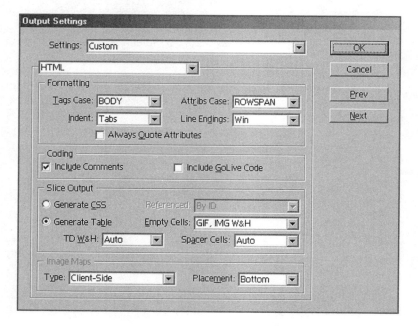

4. Select HTML from the second drop-down box as shown above. This enables you to specify how the HTML code will be written.

- Formatting – These drop-down boxes allow you to specify whether upper, lower, or mixed case should be used when writing code for the Tags and Attributes. If you do not know HTML code, don't let this worry you. The settings you apply, or don't apply for that matter, will not have any impact on the success of your finished web page. These options serve to assist a coder when editing pages. Some coders prefer reading upper case, some lower. The other options in this section allow you to specify whether tabs should be used to indent lines of code and how lines should end with regard to compatibility on windows, macs, or unix systems.

- Coding – Here you can choose to have comments added to the code. These are simple descriptive lines that provide information about the line of code. Include Go Live Code reformats code in the style used by GoLive. This is an HTML generating application made by Adobe. Select this option if you intend to re-optimize slices in GoLive.

- Slice Output – Generate Table is the option we want. This will create the required code as an HTML table as described earlier. This is the best option for cross browser compatibility. Use the default settings as shown above to create the optimum code with the widest possible support.

5. Leave all the default settings as they appear and click OK.

You will be returned to the Illustrator page. All the files you saved will be in the Exercises folder, unless you chose another location. Let's go and take a look at these now. Go into My Computer or Windows Explorer (not the browser) on a PC or the Finder on a Mac. Navigate to the folder you nominated to save the files. Here you will see a file called Gallery. This is an HTML file. There is also a new folder called images. The new folder is created by default and stores all the GIF and JPG images that make up the page. We can now view the completed web page in a browser. Double-click Gallery to launch the browser and display the page within it.

The picture below shows the finished web page viewed using Microsoft Internet Explorer.

This completed page can now be used in your favorite web page authoring program or even edited using manual HTML code and developed and linked to the rest of the web site.

This introduction to the fundamentals of the Web, and Illustrator's implementation of many web technologies, breaks new ground for vector applications. If you are new to the Web, you may be inspired by this chapter to learn more about Internet technologies and the other software that makes it tick. If you do progress further down the Web road you can be sure that Illustrator is now firmly accepted as a valuable addition to the web designers toolkit.

Summary

In this chapter you have learned the essential differences between preparing graphics for the Web as opposed to for print. There are many limitations that bind web designers from working as freely as they might in a print environment. These limitations, borne out of an Internet technology whose progress and popularity have far exceeded its original objectives, must be accepted and countered.

The nuts and bolts of the Web come down to graphic optimization. You have looked extensively at the different compression file formats and how and where each of these should be used. Using the Save for Web command, you now know how to achieve acceptable quality graphics with realistic file sizes. What's more, you have created a complete web page by combining what you learned about slicing artwork with your new knowledge of image compression formats.

16 Saving and Exporting

What We'll Cover in this Chapter:

- *The difference between Saving and Exporting files*

- *Saving files in the native Illustrator (AI) format*

- *Saving files in Illustrator EPS format*

- *Saving files in Adobe Acrobat PDF*

- *Using Acrobat files to soft-proof documents*

- *An overview of alternate export file formats*

▶

Throughout the book, I've concentrated on explaining how Illustrator is a wonderful application, a workhorse that toils solidly in the background helping you create awe-inspiring graphics and documents for both the web and print. However, I do realize that Illustrator has its limitations in certain areas. There are times when because of these limitations, or because our particular needs are different, we may choose to export our graphics from Illustrator in a format that can be imported into other applications – be they for print, web, motion, or other destinations.

In this final chapter, I'll be concentrating on how you can save and also export from Illustrator in various file formats. I'll also be pointing out all the finer details for many of the save and export functions so that you get the most from each file format, and I'll be giving you explanations as to why and when you should use the formats. Although Illustrator exports equally to web and print suitable formats, I'll concentrate more on the options for print in this chapter as you had an in-depth look at the web formats in the previous chapter. Of course, this does not mean I'll not be dropping hints and tips about options suitable for the web as we look at the various formats.

> *Before you start this chapter, check that you have Adobe Acrobat Reader installed on your machine, as we'll be using Adobe Acrobat PDF files. If you don't have it installed, there is a copy of the application supplied on your original Adobe Illustrator CD. Insert the CD into your CD-ROM drive and follow the installation instructions. It can also be downloaded from* www.adobe.com

Saving Versus Exporting

The first factor we'll consider is when we should save a file, and when we should export a file. I would recommend that you always save your files in progress the native Illustrator format, the AI file, until you have completed your design and are ready to finalize the piece of work for which it was designed.

Saving in the native Illustrator format means that you'll always be able to open the file in Illustrator and retain all of the information within that file in a format that can be edited as you wish.The same is true of the other formats available from the drop-down menu on the Save As dialog box. My personal workflow tells me that any file saved in an `Illustrator.ai` format is a work in progress, whereas any of the other formats, irrespective of whether they are in an alternate Illustrator editable format or in an exported format, are works that have been completed.

I'd only export a file into another format at the very end of my design process if I needed to have it in an alternate format so that I could manipulate it further in another application. If you export a file and then at a later stage decide that you need to re-edit the file in Illustrator, you'll find that some of the native data that would have been retained had the file been saved in an Illustrator format has been discarded and you will be unable to edit it fully. For Photoshop users, I can draw the following comparison – you always save an unflattened version of your Photoshop files so that you can edit them easily at a later stage, and the same logic follows here – always save a copy of your final artwork in an Illustrator format before you export it. You never know what changes the client may wish to introduce at that last minute!

Saving Illustrator Files

As you have already seen, there are five native Illustrator formats in which we can save our files, each with their own particular options. You looked at the SVG formats in the previous chapter, thus we'll concentrate on the Illustrator (AI), Illustrator EPS (EPS), and Adobe Acrobat (PDF) formats.

Adobe Illustrator (*.AI) File Format

The default format when you save a file is the standard Illustrator (AI) file format, and this is the one that you'll use most often as you develop your artwork. The very first time you save the file as an Illustrator file, you will be greeted with the following dialog box, which you've seen constantly as you've developed the case study, but now we'll look at those options in detail.

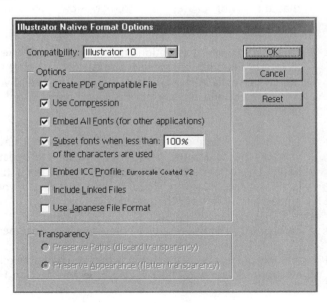

- Compatibility – determines with which Illustrator version you want the file to be compatible. From the drop-down menu to the right of the field, you can choose from a number of previous versions.

Why would you want to save back to an earlier version of Illustrator, especially as saving back can mean that you will lose support for features introduced in recent versions? It may be that you want to use the file in another application that does not yet support Illustrator 10 file formats, for example a slightly older version of a page layout application, or that you want to ship a file to someone with an older version of Illustrator.

I mentioned that certain features are not supported in earlier versions of Illustrator; and an example of this is the transparency feature we have used extensively in our case study. If you chose to save the file as an Illustrator 8 or earlier version, the Transparency area at the bottom of the Save As dialog box will become active because transparency is not supported in these versions.

- Create PDF Compatible File – saves a PDF representation of the document in the Illustrator file. This is useful if you want your file to be compatible with other Adobe applications.

- Use Compression – compresses the PDF data that you have chosen to include in the file. There is a trade-off between speed and file size here, as using compression will mean that saving the files will be a slower process, but it does mean that the file will be smaller. If you are finding that the saving process is extremely slow, you may wish to uncheck this option.

- Embed All Fonts – this option ensures that if someone else looks at your Illustrator file on their machine, and they do not have the font, it will still display correctly. Although, it will increase the size of your file, thus if size is a problem and the correct display of fonts is not, you may wish to uncheck it.

- Subset Fonts – embeds only those characters that have been used. The value in the field is the percentage of characters that have to be used before Illustrator decides that it should embed the entire font rather than just a subset. Subsetting fonts is only available if you have chosen to embed all the fonts in the previous option.

- Embed ICC Profile – creates a color-managed document.

- Include Linked Files – embeds any files you had previously linked with the Illustrator document. This will also have an effect on file size.

- Use Japanese File Format – saves the artwork as a Japanese language file when you save a file in a format compatible with Illustrator versions 3, 4, or 5.

- Transparency – transparency is not supported with Illustrator 8 or earlier and consequently you have to tell Illustrator how it should handle any transparent objects.

  - Preserve Paths discards any transparency effects and resets those transparent areas to 100 percent opacity.

  - Preserve Appearance flattens transparent areas in the artwork and thus maintains the appearance of transparency. If your artwork contains intricate, overlapping areas and you require high-resolution output, you should cancel this Save command and set your rasterization settings before returning to this dialog box and saving the file.

Adobe Illustrator EPS (*.EPS) File Format

An EPS file is the format recognized by the majority of page-layout, word-processing, and graphics applications, yet this format also preserves many of the graphic elements created in Illustrator. This means that you can prepare your graphic for inclusion in your other application, and yet still be able to open and edit it in Illustrator. (Of course, ideally you should also save a backup.)

Imagine we have decided to create the entire brochure for the Marine Quest project would be easier in a page-layout application which does not recognize Illustrator AI files, such as QuarkXPress, so we can take advantage of features like automatic page numbering, master pages, and more. Does this mean that we have to finalize our artwork and then export it, and that we are unable to make further edits to the original? It depends very much on the format you choose. If you exported the file as a TIFF or other format, the scenario would be that you would have to open it in the original Illustrator format, make the edits, re-export it as a TIFF, and then update the link. However, if you save the file in an EPS format, your page-layout application will recognize the file, and you can still open and edit that same file in Illustrator, and then update the link. This means you need only one file – no duplicate files in different formats, a workflow that often causes confusion.

Now that you have been convinced of the versatility of the EPS format, let's look at those saving options. From the File menu, choose Save As (CTRL/CMD+SHIFT+S) to display the Save As dialog box. From the drop-down menu at the base of the dialog box, choose Illustrator EPS, and click Save.

Illustrator now presents you with another dialog box, enabling you to fine-tune the way in which the file was saved. Notice that a number of these options are similar to those already discussed in the Illustrator AI format so we will only look at those that are different.

- Preview options – Many applications into which you may place your EPS file are unable to display the EPS artwork on the screen, and instead what we see is a low-resolution preview of what the artwork looks like. With the Preview options, you decide whether or not to create a preview image, and if you have a preview, whether it will be in black-and-white or color. If you choose to have a TIFF (8-bit Color) format, you can then select to have either a transparent or opaque (solid) background for the preview image. Note that if you intend to place your EPS file in a Microsoft Office application, you must choose the opaque option.

- Include Document Thumbnails – creates a thumbnail image of the artwork, which is displayed in the Illustrator Open and Place dialog boxes.

- CMYK PostScript – Some applications into which you might wish to import your EPS file do not support RGB output. If you select this option, it allows RGB color documents to be printed from those applications, but preserves the RGB colors within the document if the file is re-opened in Illustrator.

- PostScript – determines what level of Postscript is used to save the artwork. You must keep in mind the capability of that final output device – and also the contents of your file.

There are two warnings that you might encounter when you save a file in an EPS format, so we'll look at those now.

Transparency and Illustrator EPS Files

At the base of the EPS Format Options dialog box, you may have noticed a small warning icon and the comment that the file contains transparent artwork that requires flattening. If you are going to use the EPS file in an application that does not support transparency, this needs careful thought and consideration in your workflow. Factors that you must bear in mind are:

- At what stage do you flatten the artwork?
- What objects are selected when you flatten the artwork?
- How is the artwork to be flattened?

If you decide to flatten the artwork on your first save of the file as an EPS, you will be removing that transparency editability, and if this is a work in progress, flattening so early in the design process would be silly.

If you follow my suggested workflow approach, this would mean that you would only save as an EPS right at the end when you are ready to place the file in another application. Doing so would mean that you got this warning right at the very end of the process, and besides retaining all aspects of editability until the final moment, it would also decrease the possibility of your forgetting to flatten the artwork.

If see the warning when you're trying to save, your best bet is to cancel the save and go back and flatten the image. You may wish to take a quick glance at the concerns addressed in the section on printing transparent artwork in the chapter on printing to help decide which objects are selected when you flatten the artwork and the settings which will be used.

RGB Images and Illustrator EPS Files

The other warning dialog box that you may encounter is when you have placed a Tiff file in an Illustrator document. You know that in order for photographs to separate correctly when they are printed, they must be in a CMYK format. Often when we are working with our images in Photoshop we may forget to convert from RGB to CMYK, and thus place an RGB file in our Illustrator document designed for print.

If we do this, as we attempt to save the file as an EPS, Illustrator gives us the following warning about the RGB image. I would suggest that you always cancel the operation, open the offending image in your application of choice, convert the file to a CMYK mode, save the file, update your link and then, and only then, save the files as an Illustrator EPS.

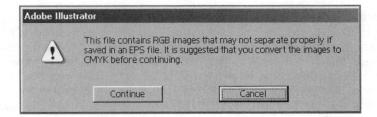

Creating Adobe PDF Files from your Illustrator Artwork

There are a number of reasons why you would save your Illustrator artwork as a PDF file because this is an extremely useful format for your file, irrespective of its final destination.

One of the most common reasons for creating an Adobe Acrobat PDF file is for soft-proofing. What do we mean by soft-proofing a file? Let's go back to our Marine Quest scenario to make this explanation a little clearer. Imagine that George and Lucy have returned to Grenada to finalize some aspects of the business. You have completed the design of one of the components and need them to have a look at it and give their approval. Of course, it would be easy with today's modern communications and email, for you to simply attach the Illustrator artwork to an email and send it off to them, as they'd have it in a couple of minutes, but there is a problem.

They don't have Adobe Illustrator on their little office machine, and even if they could find someone in the marina with Illustrator, they also don't have the fonts you have used. This is where creating an Acrobat PDF for soft-proofing comes into it's own.

Adobe Acrobat PDF files are relatively small – therefore they are ideal for attaching to emails. They contain all the information including the fonts, so your client does not need to have Illustrator or the relevant fonts installed on their machine. Best of all, the Adobe Acrobat Reader, the application they would use to view the PDF, is free.

This means that you could attach the PDF to the email, send it to them in their lovely sunny environment, they could open it with Acrobat Reader, seeing it as you had intended, and approve and sign-off the design all in a couple of minutes. What's more, if they had the complete copy of Adobe Acrobat, they could attach comments, digital signatures and more to the PDF and return it to you. A discussion of the strengths of Adobe Acrobat as a full-fledged proofing tool is beyond the scope of the book.

Furthermore, if you save the file in a PDF format, many of the word-processing, page-layout, and graphics applications will allow you to import a PDF. So, if you save as a PDF and check the Preserve Illustrator Editing Capabilities, you can create a file which other applications can recognize, but you can still edit in Illustrator.

We can also save PDF files with a quality sufficiently high that these files can be used as our source files for digital or direct to plate printing.

Convinced it's a useful format for print work, but still wondering about its use on the web? Viewing HTML pages on the web have inherent problems. You can never be sure that the viewer has the same fonts as you, so you stick to the standard fonts or convert the text to GIF files so that they display as you desired. Resizing browser windows and different browsers can also introduce an element of uncertainty. If we save the file as a PDF, the person interested in our pages can choose to view the PDF online or download it to read offline, and we can rest assured that they will see it exactly as we had designed it, complete with all the fonts and graphics.

Once again when you save in any format from Illustrator, Illustrator presents you with a dialog box full of options so that you can create the best possible file. Let's look at those options now From the drop-down menu at the base of the Save As dialog box, choose Adobe PDF, and click Save.

As I've already mentioned the final purpose of your PDF file can vary greatly, and with this in mind, there are a number of choices to be made when you save a file in a PDF format.

- Options Set – you can select one of two preset settings; or if you choose to change some of your settings, the Options set will automatically change to Custom.

  - Default – settings designed for artwork that will be printed.

- Screen Optimized – designed for artwork that will be displayed on screen and not necessarily printed. As a result all the artwork in the file will be converted to RGB mode, which as you know is how our screens show colors.

The options for saving PDF files are divided into two categories – General and Compression. Make sure that General is showing in your Adobe Acrobat Format Options dialog box. Again, we will only look at the settings which are different than for the above file formats.

- File Compatibility – determines in which version of Adobe Acrobat the PDF file is saved. Acrobat 5.0 format preserves transparency, text, and spot colors in the artwork, but because this is a relatively new version of the format, not all applications support this data. Notice how if you change the Option Set to Screen Optimized, the File Compatibility setting is automatically changed to Acrobat 4. This is because at time of development, many people would not yet have converted to the latest version of Acrobat Reader – and if you are designing for the file to be viewed by the biggest possible audience, you want to make sure that they can all open it.

- Preserve Illustrator Editing Capabilities – to reopen and edit the PDF file in Adobe Illustrator, but this will result in a larger file size.

- Generate Thumbnails – creates a thumbnail image of artwork that is displayed in the Illustrator Open or Place dialog box, and also when you display Thumbnails in Adobe Acrobat. Once again, this additional feature will add to the file size.

Saving in PDF format also enables you to determine how the graphics should be compressed, this is directly related to where you will be showing this file. If it is intended as a soft-proof, you'll be more concerned about quality than file size, whereas if the PDF is going to be available online, you might pay more attention to the file size than the quality of images, knowing that the document was going to be previewed on screen and not necessarily printed. To view the **Compression** settings, choose Compression from the drop-down menu below the Options Set menu.

Notice how if the Options Set is set to Default, there is no compression of the images – this is because our concern is more with a quality representation than with file size.

The Compressions dialog box is divided into three areas, each concerned with the compression and resampling values that will be applied to different types of bitmap images. As the options for compression have certain features in common, what we'll do is look at the different types of images being referred to, and then discuss the compression options as they relate to these bitmap image types.

The three types of images that we are discussing here are:

- **Color Bitmap Images** – full color photographs that you have placed in your Illustrator files.

- **Grayscale Bitmap Images** – what you would have called a black-and-white photograph before you learned that they are really composed of 256 shades of gray.

- **Monochrome Bitmap Images** – true black and white images, composed either of black pixels or white pixels – there's no gray area here.

When it comes to deciding on the compression values we will apply to our images in the Illustrator document, we have the following options:

- Average Downsampling – reduces the resolution of our image to a specified pixels per inch value. If you were intending to print the PDF, then it is doubtful whether you would want to downsample the file, but if you wanted to place this on the web where file size was a concern, you would switch this option on. The lowest value you would use for compression on color and grayscale images if you were designing for the web is 72ppi, but if there is any possibility that the reader may zoom in on an image you might want to up that resolution to 144ppi, which allows them to zoom to 200% without any visible loss in image quality. But remember that increasing the resolution will increase the size of the file. For those monochrome bitmaps, keep the resolution up at 300ppi, to avoid horrible jagged edges on the image.

- Compression – you have a number of different options, and dependent on which option you choose, then the options available for quality will also change. Let's look first at the different types of Compression and then at how this affects the Quality options:

  - JPEG compression is suitable for continuous tone grayscale or color images – your standard photographic type image. As JPEG compression is lossy, there may be a minimal loss in image quality as it reduces file size. This is dependent on the setting set under the Quality drop-down menu. The higher the value, the smaller the loss of quality, but the greater the file size, with the converse also being true. Do not avoid the use of JPEG compression because you are worried about data loss, handled with care, you'll get far better results for your continuous tone images and smaller file sizes.

- ZIP compression works well on images with large areas of single colors or repeating patterns and for black-and-white images that contain repeating patterns. It is not suitable for use on those continuous tone photographs we have just been discussing.

- Automatic – use if your document contains a mix of images, some with continuous tones and others with large areas of solid color. Automatic sets the best possible compression and quality for the artwork contained in the file. For most files, this option produces acceptable results.

- CCITT Group 4 produces good compression for most monochromatic (black-and-white) images.

- CCITT Group 3, which is used by most fax machines, compresses monochromatic bitmaps one row at a time.

- Run Length – use for images that contain large areas of solid black or white.

- Quality – dependent on which compression options you have chosen, different Quality options will be available.

  - If you choose either Automatic or JPEG, the quality drop-down menu will range from Minimum to Maximum. Here you need to find the best balance between quality and file size. If you choose Minimum, the file size will be small, but the image will be considerably degraded, whilst Maximum will create a larger file with a better quality image.

  - If you have chosen Zip as your Compression format, Illustrator provides 4-bit and 8-bit ZIP compression options. I'd suggest you used 8-bit to avoid inadvertently causing data loss in your images.

Remember all the compression options discussed refer to bitmap images included in your Illustrator document and not to the vector graphics that you have created.

- Compress Text and Line Art – applies lossless ZIP compression to all text and line art (vector graphics) in the file.

Case Study: Providing a Soft-Proof PDF File

As we expected, George and Lucy have headed back off to Grenada, to sunshine and open skies before you had time to provide them with hard copies of all the alternate business card designs for them to make a final decision. But you're not worried – they're connected to the Internet, you've checked that they have Adobe Acrobat Reader installed on their machine, and so the way is open for you to send them an Acrobat PDF file with all four variations.

1. Open the file called `Biz_cards.ai`. This is the page you need to get to them to have proofed before you can select the final design and send it off to the printer.

2. Choose File > Save As (CTRL/CMD+S), name the file `Cardsmall`, and choose Adobe PDF from the drop-down menu.

3. We're using this as a soft-proof, so we'll opt for the Default Options Set and then make any changes that we need. Ensure that Default is chosen at the top of the dialog box.

4. We're not too sure whether they have Acrobat Reader 4 or Acrobat Reader 5, so to be on the safe side, we'll save the file back into Acrobat 4 format.

5. As we're sending this PDF by email, our concern is as much with file size as it is with any other factor. They will not need to open the file in Illustrator, so in order to reduce the size we can uncheck the Preserve Illustrator Editing Capabilities. Illustrator will warn us that we may have a possible data loss, but we're okay with this. We'll be using our original business card AI files for print after they have made their final decision.

6. To ensure that all the fonts display and print correctly, check Embed All Fonts, and because we've not used the entire font, we'll also save file size by subsetting the fonts.

7. Our last little size saver is to not generate the thumbnails, as every little byte that we can save will make the transmission of this file smaller.

8. On the Compression options, you don't need to be concerned about compression values for images as we've not included any images in this file, but leave the Compress Text and Line Art option checked.

9. Save and close the file.

Now we'll repeat the process, but this time setting different options.

10. Open the file called Bizcards.ai. Choose File > Save As (CTRL/CMD+S), call the file Cardbig, and choose Adobe PDF from the drop-down menu.

As you've already been through the process once, I'll not lead you through all the options again. Set the Options Set back to Default, and use all the default settings, making sure that Preserve Illustrator Editing Capabilities and Generate Thumbnails are checked. In the Compression dialog box, check Compress Text and Line Art. Save and close the file.

Now let's compare our results. The first thing we'll look at is file size, do not be concerned if the size of your files is slightly different from mine, when you see the figures, you'll be convinced.

Locate the three files on your hard drive. My files were the following sizes:

- BizCards.ai – 251 KB
- Cardsmall.pdf – 46 KB
- Cardbig.pdf – 251 KB

You can see that in this instance our Cardsmall.pdf file is less than 20% of the size of the other two files. When our concern is getting this attached to an email, and sending it quickly across the Internet, it's clear which route we would take. Before we make our decision, we had better check the quality, as it's no use sending a small file if the quality is just not there.

1. Launch Adobe Acrobat Reader. Choose File>Open and navigate through the hard drive to locate and open your Cardsmall.pdf file. Repeat the process and open the Cardbig.pdf file. From the Window menu choose Tile > Vertically to arrange the two files side by side.

2. Look carefully at each image. At this view level you'll definitely not see any difference in quality. Choose the Zoom tool, and click and drag around a small area on the Cardbig.pdf file. Zoom in on roughly the same area on the Cardsmall.pdf file, and you'll notice you still see no difference in quality.

Guess that pretty much proves the point about file size and quality. But if you're still not convinced, try printing a copy of each of the files, and comparing the quality.

We have just one more comparison to do – comparing how the two different files react in Illustrator. Remember we saved the Cardsmall.pdf file with the Preserve Illustrator Editing Capabilities unchecked. Close Adobe Acrobat Reader, and switch back to Adobe Illustrator.

3. Open both the Cardsmall.pdf file and the Cardbig.pdf file.

4. With the **Selection** Tool, select components in each file. Try changing colors, editing text, and generally making changes to each of the files – it's doubtful that with such a simple file, you'll see much difference. You've lost the grouping of objects in the Cardsmall.pdf file – have a look at the Layer palette for each file and compare that.

This is the sort of thing you'd notice, especially as your files got more complex and you had created gradient meshes, transparent areas, and used different blending modes. For our purpose in this exercise, getting that file across to George and Lucy quickly so that they could proof it and sign it off without editability and thumbnails has certainly paid off.

There are two other formats that we can use with the Save command in Illustrator – the SVG and SVG Compressed format, but you studied them in the previous chapter on Preparing for Web Delivery, so I'll not go into any detail here.

Exporting Files from Illustrator

There are times when we need to export files in different formats, and Illustrator provides us with an extensive list of export formats from which we can choose. You have already covered some of these formats in previous chapters, especially those that are related to formats expressly designed for web usage.

Let's take a brief look at some of the other formats in which you can export your Illustrator files. We'll not go into much detail concerning the options for each of the different types of formats as many of them are rare, and if you are using applications that require them then chances are you already have some knowledge of their options.

AutoCAD Drawing (*.DWG) and AutoCAD Interchange File (*.DXF) Formats

These formats are used if you need to export your artwork from Illustrator in a format that is supported by the AutoCAD drawing applications. The options available allow you to stipulate to which version you wish to export the file, the number of colors you require, and how it should handle any bitmap images and text in the file.

Bitmap Format (*.BMP)

BMP is the standard Windows bitmap image format on Windows compatible computers. When you export in this format, you can stipulate the color mode, resolution, and whether anti-aliasing will be used. The BMP format is similar to other bitmap formats, so you might be better off using one of the more widely used formats such as the TIFF format.

Computer Graphics Metafile Format (*.CGM)

CGM is a vector based format, which can be useful if you are trying to export your vector graphics to an application which does not support any of the other vector based formats. CGM is not a good option for exporting text files as it converts paragraph text into single separate lines. One of the little known uses for a CGM file is that it can be used as a short cut for quickly adding all used colour swatches to your Swatches palette.

1. Open the file called CGM.ai. It's our picture of our yacht. Have a look at the Swatches palette and you'll notice that other than the most basic of colour swatches, we have none of the colours used in the illustration listed in the palette. Of course, we could manually select all the individual components and add the swatches to the palette, but that would take an absolute age, and with all those deadlines looming, we just don't have time for that.

2. Export the file as a CGM file by choosing File > Export, and opting for the Computer Graphics Metafile format from the drop-down menu at the base of the dialog box, and close the file.

3. Open the exported CGM file – you may have to wait a couple of minutes, but have a look at that Swatches palette. You may think that there are far too many colors and that some of them have not been used.

4. Clear the palette by choosing Select all Unused from the Swatches palette context menu, and notice that none of those colours that were imported when you placed the CGM file have been selected. This little workaround can save you so much time!

Notice that the opened CGM file is automatically in an RGB format.

Enhanced Meta File Format (*.EMF)

The Enhanced Meta File format is extensively used by Windows applications as an intermediate format for exchanging vector graphics data, when no other common format is recognized by the source and target application. However, some of your vector information may be rasterized by Illustrator when it exports the artwork.

PCX Format (*.PCX)

PCX format is a bitmap format common on the Windows platform. When you export in this format, you can stipulate the color mode, resolution, and whether anti-aliasing will be used. Like the BMP format, PCX is similar to other bitmap formats, but I would still suggest that you opted for one of the more widely used cross-platform formats such as the TIFF format.

Macintosh PICT Format (*.PIC)

The PICT format is widely used on the Macintosh platform as an intermediary file format for transferring files between applications. The PICT format is especially effective at compressing images that contain large areas of solid color. On the Windows platform, exporting a file as a PICT file can result in a very complex file with numerous anchor points being used to describe the shape of the object.

PIXAR Format (*.PXR)

The PIXAR format is designed specifically for high-end graphics applications, such as those used for rendering three-dimensional images and animation. It is a bitmap format and when you export, you can specify the color mode, resolution, and whether anti-aliasing should be used.

Targa Format (*.TGA)

The TGA format is a bitmap format designed for use on systems that use the Truevision® video board. As with other bitmap export formats, options exist to stipulate the color mode, resolution, and use of anti-aliasing.

Tagged-Image File Format (*.TIFF)

TIFF is one of the most widely used bitmap formats. It is recognized on all major computer platforms, and by the majority of page-layout, word-processing, graphics, and image applications. It is used to exchange files between applications. When you export Illustrator artwork in TIFF, you can choose an RGB, CMYK, or grayscale color model, and specify the image resolution. The LZW compression option is a lossless format that results in a smaller file size.

Text Format (*.TXT)

It doesn't happen often – but there is definitely going to be that odd time when you need to export all the text from your Illustrator file for use in another application. It really is easy to achieve just by choosing the TXT format as your export option. If you highlight text before you export the file, only that text will be exported. If no text is highlighted, then all the text in the file will be exported.

Windows Meta File Format (*.WMF)

Similar in format to the EMF file format, which should be used in preference to the WMF wherever possible, the WMF is used as an exchange format between Windows based applications when the source and target applications have no other format in common.

Summary

This sadly is the end of your voyage of discovery through this wonderful application. By this stage you have mastered a wealth of design skills, learned useful design and production tips for both the web and print media, and are well on your way to becoming an accomplished Illustrator.

You have also taken a project from brief to completion. You should be confident that you are capable of completing pretty much any real world project that a client might throw at you.

Congratulations! This book has given you a firm grounding in this versatile application, and I hope it has inspired you to experiment for yourself, and to bring your artistic inspirations into reality through the wonderful medium of Illustrator.

Index

The index is arranged hierarchically, in alphabetical order, with symbols preceding the letter A. Many second-level entries also occur as first-level entries. This is to ensure that users will find the information they require however they choose to search for it.

DESIGNER TO DESIGNER™

friends of ED writes books for you. Any suggestions, or ideas about how you want information given in your ideal book will be studied by our team.

Your comments are valued by friends of ED.

For technical support please contact support@friendsofed.com.

Freephone in USA	800.873.9769
Fax	312.893.8001
UK contact: Tel:	0121.258.8858
Fax:	0121.258.8868

Registration Code : ☐

Foundation Illustrator 10 - Registration Card

Name ....

Address ....

City ....State/Region ....

Country ....Postcode/Zip ....

E-mail ....

Profession: design student ☐ freelance designer ☐
part of an agency ☐ inhouse designer ☐
other (please specify) ....

Age: Under 20 ☐ 20-25 ☐ 25-30 ☐ 30-40 ☐ over 40 ☐

Do you use: mac ☐ pc ☐ both ☐

How did you hear about this book?..

Book review (name)..

Advertisement (name) ....

Recommendation ....

Catalog ....

Other ....

Where did you buy this book? ....

Bookstore (name) ....City..........................

Computer Store (name)..

Mail Order..

Other..

How did you rate the overall content of this book?
Excellent ☐ Good ☐
Average ☐ Poor ☐

What applications/technologies do you intend to learn in the near future?..
....

What did you find most useful about this book? ....
....

What did you find the least useful about this book? ....
....

Please add any additional comments ....
....

What other subjects will you buy a computer book on soon?
....

What is the best computer book you have used this year?
....
....

Note: This information will only be used to keep you upd about new friends of ED titles and will not be used for any o purpose or passed to any other third party.

friendsof

D E S I G N E R   T O   D E S I G N E R™

NB. If you post the bounce back card below in the UK, please send it to:

friends of ED Ltd.,
30 Lincoln Road,
Olton,
Birmingham.
B27 6PA

BUSINESS REPLY MAIL

FIRST CLASS   PERMIT #64   *CHICAGO, IL*

POSTAGE WILL BE PAID BY ADDRESSEE

friends of ED,
29 S. La Salle St.
Suite 520
Chicago Il 60603–USA